"Finding time for family devotions is a high hurdle. But finding something enjoyable to do as a family that also illuminates God's Word can be an even higher impediment. In this wonderfully helpful book, you've found the answer to the second challenge. And Marty's clear writing and creativity will help you make the time (even if you don't think you have it) to clear the first hurdle. It's my pleasure to recommend this book—and the devotional experience it provides—to you and your family."

Dr. Robert Wolgemuth, Author of *The Most Important Place on Earth: What a Christian Home Looks Like and How to Build One*

"The church wants parents to lead their homes spiritually; the parents don't know how. Marty Machowski's *Old Story New* is the answer for both church and parents. Marty has invested his time in the best way possible—helping parents shepherd their children with more than stories and morals, but with the central theme of Jesus illuminated clearly in every story."

Scott Thomas, Pastor, The Journey Church, St. Louis, MO; author of *Gospel Coach: Shepherding Leaders to Glorify God*

"Marty Machowski 'gets' families. Even more importantly, he knows how to connect them to the Bible with simple, relatable New Testament studies that make much of Jesus in every lesson. If you want your kids to see the Savior through his Word, spend some time in this exciting new devotional."

Dave Harvey, Church Planting and Church Care, Sovereign Grace Ministries; author of *When Sinners Say I Do: Discovering the Power of the Gospel for Marriage*

"So much of the family devotional material available today does little more than use the Bible to teach half-truths and full-out moralism. The reason my wife and I love Marty Machowski's books and the reason they have become important resources as we seek to raise our children in 'the discipline and instruction of the Lord,' is their consistent focus on the big picture of the Bible's big story. *Old Story New* is yet another wonderful resource that we gladly commend and look forward to reading with our children."

Tim Challies, Author; pastor; blogger

"Marty Machowski's *Old Story New*, like Marty's children's ministry curriculum and Old Testament devotional, *Long Story Short*, is a great asset to parents, pastors, and children's ministry teachers. I am particularly excited about the way Marty connects each New Testament story to the gospel of Christ. Marty's book will help your kids learn to see Jesus as the center of every part of the Bible. And what might God do with such a generation raised to rightly handle the word of truth, the gospel of our salvation?"

Josh Blount, Pastor, Living Faith Church

"Nurturing our children requires us to gain the attention of their hearts as soon as possible. So, what should we use to seize their interest? Thinly veiled morality tales that leave our children wandering in a desert of demands? In *Old Story New*, Christ is the beacon that captures the imagination of our children. Let this beautiful book lead your children out of the desert and into the oasis of Jesus, so he can quench their thirsty hearts."

David E. Tate, Pastor, Manor Presbyterian Church

Old Story New

Ten-Minute Devotions
to Draw Your Family to God

New Testament

Marty Machowski

WWW.NEWGROWTHPRESS.COM

New Growth Press, Greensboro, NC 27404
www.newgrowthpress.com
Copyright © 2012 by Covenant Fellowship Church.

Unless otherwise indicated, all Scripture quotations are taken from *The Holy Bible, English Standard Version®*. (ESV®), copyright © 2001 by Crossway, a publishing ministry of Good News Publishers. Used by permission. All rights reserved.

Scriptures designated (NIV) are from the *Holy Bible: New International Version®*. *NIV®*. Copyright © 1973, 1978, 1984 by Biblica. Quoted by permission. All rights reserved worldwide.

Cover Art: A. E. Macha
Cover Design: Tandem Creative, Tom Temple, tandemcreative.net
Interior Design: Faceout Books, faceoutstudio.com
Typesetting: Lisa Parnell, lparnell.com

ISBN-13: 978-1-936768-66-0
ISBN-10: 1-936768-66-6

Library of Congress Cataloging-in-Publication Data
Machowski, Martin, 1963–
    Old story new : ten-minute devotions to draw your family to God (New Testament) / Martin Machowski.
        p.   cm.
    Includes bibliographical references and index.
    ISBN-13: 978-1-936768-66-0 (alk. paper)
    ISBN-10: 1-936768-66-6 (alk. paper)
    1. Bible. N. T.—Devotional literature. 2. Families—Prayers and devotions. I. Title.
BS2341.55.M33 2012
249—dc23
                                                                    2012016595
Printed in the United States of America

22 21 20 19 18 17 16   5 6 7 8

I would like to dedicate this volume
to my loving wife, LOIS,
and my six children—
EMMA, NATHAN, MARTHA, NOAH, ANNA, and AMELIA.
They graciously supported me and provided regular
encouragement through the many hours
that I spent writing this devotional.

Contents

Foreword   *viii*

Acknowledgments   *x*

Introduction   *1*

Week 1: The Birth of Jesus
Foretold   *8*

Week 2: The Birth of Jesus   *15*

Week 3: Jesus Presented
in the Temple   *22*

Week 4: The Ministry of John
the Baptist   *29*

Week 5: The Baptism of Jesus   *36*

Week 6: The Temptation of Jesus   *43*

Week 7: The Wedding Feast   *50*

Week 8: Jesus Cleanses the Temple
                                            57

Week 9: Nicodemus   *64*

Week 10: Good News   *71*

Week 11: The Miraculous Catch   *78*

Week 12: Jesus Heals the Paralyzed
Man   *85*

Week 13: The Sermon on the
Mount—The Beatitudes   *92*

Week 14: The Sermon on the
Mount—Love Your Enemies   *99*

Week 15: The Lord's Prayer   *107*

Week 16: Treasure in Heaven   *114*

Week 17: The Wise & Foolish
Builders   *121*

Week 18: The Four Soils   *128*

Week 19: The Hidden Treasure   *135*

Week 20: Jesus Calms the Storm   *142*

Week 21: Jesus Feeds the Multitude
                                            149

Week 22: Jesus Walks on Water   *156*

Week 23: Take Up Your Cross   *162*

Week 24: The Transfiguration   *169*

Week 25: Jesus Cleanses Ten Lepers
                                            176

Week 26: Jesus Claims to Be God
                                            183

Week 27: The Pharisee & the Tax
Collector   *190*

Week 28: Lazarus   *196*

Week 29: Jesus & Zacchaeus   *203*

Week 30: The Triumphal Entry   *211*

Week 31: The Widow's Offering   *218*

Week 32: Jesus Washes the Disciples'
Feet   *225*

Week 33: The Last Supper   *232*

Week 34: Jesus Promises to Send
the Holy Spirit   *239*

Week 35: Jesus Is Arrested   *246*

Week 36: Peter Denies Jesus   253

Week 37: The Crucifixion & the
Criminals   259

Week 38: The Death of Christ   266

Week 39: The Resurrection   273

Week 40: Doubting Thomas   279

Week 41: Another Miraculous
Catch   286

Week 42: The Great Commission
293

Week 43: The Ascension   300

Week 44: Pentecost   307

Week 45: Peter & the Prophet Joel
314

Week 46: New Believers   321

Week 47: The Lame Beggar Walks
328

Week 48: Ananias & Sapphira   335

Week 49: The Death of Stephen 342

Week 50: Saul Is Knocked to the
Ground   349

Week 51: The Gentiles Are
Converted   357

Week 52: The Fruit of the Spirit 364

Week 53: The Body of Christ   371

Week 54: Love   378

Week 55: Paul's Work in Ephesus
384

Week 56: A New Creation   391

Week 57: God Loves a Cheerful
Giver   398

Week 58: A Gift of Righteousness
405

Week 59: Abraham: Father to All
by Faith   412

Week 60: Believe and Confess   420

Week 61: Paul in Chains   427

Week 62: The Supremacy of Christ
434

Week 63: Chosen before the World
Began   441

Week 64: From Death to Life   447

Week 65: The Gift of Men   453

Week 66: Putting Off the Old Self
460

Week 67: The Armor of God   467

Week 68: The Humility of Christ
474

Week 69: Keep Your Eyes on the
Prize   481

Week 70: Character Counts   488

Week 71: God Breathed the
Scriptures   495

Week 72: The Heart's Desires   502

Week 73: Born Again!   509

Week 74: God's Word Is Living   516

Week 75: By Faith   523

Week 76: Loving One Another   530

Week 77: Worthy Is the Lamb   537

Week 78: At the Throne Worshiping
544

Foreword
By Dr. Tedd Tripp

Marty Machowski has done it again! This book, along with the earlier Old Testament devotional book, *Long Story Short*, is another masterful devotional book for families. It is simple without being shallow. It is theologically robust without being pedantic. It is comprehensive without being overwhelming. Best of all, it is doable for busy parents with children.

In an age filled with intrusive voices that speak to your children, the need for families to provide a biblical narrative for their children is profound. Remember the culture is always providing a narrative that tells your children how to interpret life. The iPod, iPad, Facebook, Little League, dance studio, and video games are all giving your kids a narrative for life. Entertainment, the arts and music, literature, manners, sports, work, leisure, and recreation all provide a false narrative for interpreting life. The culture's narrative tells your children how to think about authority, justice, honor, amusement, responsibility, service, gender, and image. Tragically, the narrative of the majority culture is a lie from the father of lies.

Marty Machowski provides us with a different narrative—the Bible broken down into doable, ten-minute family devotions. Family worship is essential for your children. In ten-minute blocks day after day, you can provide your children with a truthful narrative about themselves, God, and the world.

It was my privilege to be raised in a home in which we always had family worship. My dad would have benefitted from having a tool like *Old Story New*, but the value of daily family worship still shaped life for me and my brothers and sister. The primary place for your children to be taught the ways of God is not the church, it is not Christian school, not VBS or summer camp; it is the home. Psalm 78 captures this truth, "... *things that we have heard and known, that our fathers have told us. We will not hide them from their children, but tell to the coming generation the glorious deeds of the LORD, and his might, and the wonders that he has done.*

He established a testimony in Jacob and appointed a law in Israel, which he commanded our fathers to teach to their children, that the next generation might know them, the children yet unborn, and arise and tell them to their children, so that they should set their hope in God and not forget the works of God, but keep his commandments" (Psalm 78:3–7).

The benefit of daily family worship is impossible to overstate. I recently read the story of Philip Henry, a British pastor, who faithfully led his family in daily worship. At the end of the week he would ask questions to remind them all of the daily lessons. He called it "Sweeping up the crumbs so nothing would be lost." You might be wondering, who was Philip Henry? He was the father of Matthew Henry, whose commentaries on the Bible are perhaps the most widely read Bible commentaries of the last couple of hundred years. What kind of home produces a man with the biblical insight and understanding of Matthew Henry? It is a home where children hear the rich narrative of Scripture.

In this volume Marty Machowski has thoughtfully broken down the story of the biblical narrative into doable pieces. He has done the heavy lifting that makes family worship seem so scary to dads. Daily readings are followed by thoughtful questions—questions that do not merely rehearse the reading, but actually cull out the content (meaning) of the passage.

Take the time to read with care Machowski's introduction to the book and how to use it with children of various ages. His observations will enhance your ability to use this book effectively with your children.

One thing more, something I always look for: the gospel is here. Machowski's focus is not just the story, but THE story in the story. Christ and the gospel are present in each devotional. Our profound need of grace and the glorious gospel of grace meet our needs and our children's needs at every point.

Dr. Tedd Tripp
August 2012

Acknowledgments

I would like to thank Dave Harvey for his encouragement to develop and publish this material for a broader audience beyond our own church. Thank you to the pastors of Covenant Fellowship Church for their example, which taught me how to live out the gospel in my ministry and life.

My labors in writing this book rest on the shoulders of greater men whose books have influenced my thinking. Of particular note are *Living the Cross Centered Life* by C. J. Mahaney, *The Unfolding Mystery* by Edmund Clowney, *Promise and Deliverance* by S. G. De Graff, *Systematic Theology* by Wayne Grudem, and the *ESV Study Bible* by the folks at Crossway.

As I finished the manuscript for this book I grew increasingly grateful for the scores of people who worked with me in writing it. The project began ten years ago when I started to put together the *God's Story* curriculum for the children and parents of Covenant Fellowship. Through the years I sent the manuscript through a gauntlet of editors and proofreaders. This published devotional would never have made it this far if it were not for their efforts.

So, thanks to Bill Patton, Michelle Janes, Sarajane Orlando, and Janel Feldman, along with Dwayne and Toni Bennett who have served by my side in Promise Kingdom, our Sunday morning children's ministry program. More recently, I would like to thank my wife, Lois, and Jared Mellinger, who read through my draft manuscript, and Jeff Gerke for his skillful editing to help transform deep biblical truth into easy-to-understand weekly devotions. I would also like to thank Charity Imfeld for her administration and helpful skills behind the scenes.

I am very grateful for the folks at New Growth for their investment and commitment to provide solid biblical resources for families and churches. Finally, I would also like to thank the families of Covenant Fellowship Church for their example, support, and prayers through the completion of this project.

Introduction

The greatest hope of all Christian parents is to see their children come to a personal faith in Jesus Christ. Most parents would climb the highest mountain or slay the fiercest dragon should it guarantee their children's salvation. But just as our conversion was a work of grace, so the conversion of each of our children depends upon the transforming work of the Holy Spirit, not our labors. And yet we are not powerless to act, for in God's kindness he chose to partner with us in his saving work by giving us something to do.

We get to tell God's story to our children—the mighty life-transforming message of the gospel. The gospel, the Bible tells us, is the power of God for the salvation of everyone who believes (Romans 1:16). We are sowers who plant the seeds of faith each time we speak the truth of God's story to our children. Like a farmer sprinkling the newly planted seed with his watering can, we send our prayers to God while we keep our eyes fixed upon the soil of their lives, waiting to rejoice with the first sprouting leaves. Even then, though we've sown the seeds of the gospel, we still marvel and wonder about how they sprouted (Mark 4:26–29).

The gospel story, filled with adventure, suspense, drama, and mystery, easily captures the attention of our children. A good book is said to come alive when you read it if it captures the imagination. The gospel story in the Bible goes a long step further: It *is* alive and able to cut through the hardest sinful heart, giving life to the deadest, unbelieving soul.

Like a double-edged sword cuts an apple in two, the Word of God cuts through our pride to show us our sin. Then it points us to Jesus, the only hope for our forgiveness before a holy God. As John said toward the end of his Gospel, it was written "so that you may believe that Jesus is the Christ, the Son of God, and that by believing you may have life in his name" (John 20:31). We are saved, and our children are saved by the Holy Spirit as we review the story of Christ in the gospel.

Why is it, then, that, for so many Christian families, the Bible sits on a table unopened or remains hidden on a shelf, sandwiched between storybooks and a dictionary? One common explanation that some good Christian parents offer is that they don't know where to begin. The Bible seems long and sometimes complicated. They are not sure how much to read at one time or what to say to their children about what they just read. They are not sure where to begin or how much to share and, if they give it a try only to be met at the end by their children's blank stares, they get discouraged.

Many parents have burst out of the gate running like a racehorse with all the excitement of how the Bible was going to transform their children, only to tire after the first bend in the track. Somehow their Bible ends up back on the shelf with the other books. Discouraged, they say to themselves, I guess I must not be one of the super-parents who can explain the Bible with commentaries and teach their children words from the original Greek.

There are no super-parents. We all struggle, and we all need help to stay on course. That is where I hope *Old Story New* can help make sharing the Bible with your children a whole lot easier. By dividing the Bible story into shorter parts and giving you everything you need to lead a ten-minute family devotion, *Old Story New* does the hard work for you. Simple discussion questions (and answers!) for each day's devotion help you interact with your children over what you read to them. You'll get fewer blank stares, and you will be surprised at how much they understand and remember from day to day.

As you read and discuss God's Word, you can be sure the Holy Spirit is also at work drawing your children closer to God and opening their minds to understand the life-giving message of the gospel. Remember, our job is to plant the seeds and water—God is the one who makes the seeds grow.

All You Need Is Ten Minutes a Day!

If you can find ten minutes a day, you can use this tool to pass on the most valuable treasure the world has ever known. Contrary to what many believe, daily family Bible study need not take a lot of time. God can use a short, simple family devotion consistently practiced over time to yield more fruit in the lives of our children than we realize—a quick daily devotion not as easily derailed by our busy schedules. Each day as the gospel is presented, God is at work.

Our hope in God is to see our children reading their Bibles and having devotions on their own, not because they have to, but because they want to. The truth of God's Word brings us to Christ and is effective to sustain us and help us to grow all of our days. There is simply no greater delight for Christian parents than watching the Spirit of God guiding their children through faith-filled study of God's Word. No earthly treasure compares.

God's Word, when hidden in our hearts as children, is used again and again in our lives later on. The Spirit of God will bring it back to our minds to help us in our walk with God and to enable us to encourage others we meet along the way.

Every family can find a few minutes in the daily routine. Some families gather for their devotional at the start of their day; others try the dinnertime approach. Lay the devotional book and your Bible(s) beside your plate at the dinner table. As soon as everyone is finished eating, take ten minutes for family Bible study. *Old Story New* does the work for you! All you need to do is read the passage of Scripture for the day, follow that with the short commentary, and then ask the listed questions. Finish it all up by inviting one of your children to pray.

It's Simple to Use

Old Story New when used with *Long Story Short* is a family devotional program designed to explain God's plan of salvation from Genesis through Revelation. *Long Story Short* covers the Old Testament, and this volume, *Old Story New*, covers the New Testament. Together, they provide three years of family Bible study! For every Old Testament lesson your family will learn the answer to the question, "How does this passage point forward to Jesus?" For every New Testament lesson the question is, "Where is the gospel?" Since the Bible is the story of God's unfolding plan of redemption, every passage of Scripture points forward or back to Calvary.

Each week starts off with a creative activity, exercise, or bit of trivia to introduce the passage. On days one through four you review a portion of the week's Scripture passage. Special attention is given on day three to connect the current passage to the gospel. On day four we've added a question for your older children to ask *you*, and on day five you and your family will investigate a Bible passage from the book of Psalms or an excerpt from one of the prophets to discover how the passage points forward to Christ.

This devotional book can be used differently depending on the ages of your children. Since this book is rich in gospel truth, it works for families with children of all ages. Take a look at the following categories to find the one that best describes your family.

If Your Children Are Preschoolers

The best time to start consistent daily Bible study is with children in the four- through six-year-old age group. *Long Story Short* and *Old Story New* work wonderfully with children in this age group. Don't be fooled by your five-year-old's inability to answer the listed questions. Children at this age can often understand much more than they can express. Consider some of the following techniques:

:: Feel free to skip the discussion questions and just read the answers, most of which are in complete sentences. The first time through, use the study to familiarize children with the Bible. If your child starts the program at age four, he or she will finish three years later at age seven with a tremendous foundation of gospel truth that has accumulated day by day and week by week.

:: You can also skip over the creative introductions and save them for a second time through when your children reach grade school.

:: Try rephrasing the questions to make them very simple or by making them multiple choice.

:: Another parent can be the helper, actually whispering the answers to your children. This might sound dishonest but in reality it is the repetition that helps them remember the material.

:: You can make up simple questions for your toddlers yourself. Basic questions about the characters such as, "How did Jesus heal the man?" are great for younger children.

If Your Children Are in Grade School

Elementary school is the time to call for your children to participate with you in family Bible study. Don't be afraid to call them to that participation. Some children might be reluctant at first, but persistence soon pays off. Even the most challenging child is able to handle ten minutes a day. Remember, day by day they are being exposed to the gospel truth God uses to transform lives. The creative introductions at the beginning of each week will pique the interest of your children. Read them yourself a day or so ahead to give you time to gather any objects needed for the lesson.

Start by making sure all your children have a Bible. You might have toddlers mixed in with your grade school students. That's okay. Just have them open up their toddler Bibles to the right page (that means anywhere close). Read through the passage for the day. On days when the passage is shorter, try having your older children read. (Remember, labored reading won't encourage them or the others, so wait until your children can read well before passing that responsibility to them.) If you have toddlers in the mix, let them come along for the ride but don't cater to their lower learning level. All day long they are learning by watching the older children in their daily routines. They learn about God the same way.

Read the passage, the short paragraph summary, and then move to the questions. Here are a few ideas to consider to make your discussion time work well:

:: After asking a question of your family, look back in the passage and tell them which verse to look for to find the answer.

:: Encourage all attempts to answer the question even if they miss the answer.

:: Consider inviting children to add to their brothers' and sisters' answers. Sometimes children who are reluctant to start an answer can add to an answer to expand it.

:: Don't be afraid to call on your older children. If they seem stumped even after you tell them which verse they can find the answer in, give them clues.

Finish by asking your children to pray. Help your youngest children by having them repeat after you. As your children grow older, encourage them to pray on their own. Always help them along if they get stuck. Soon, they will be praying on their own without your help.

If Your Children Are Moving Out of Grade School

Long Story Short and *Old Story New* work well with older grade school children and young teens too! They set a wonderful example for their younger brothers and sisters in answering the questions and even leading the devotions themselves.

If you have a teen who thinks the Bible studies are too easy or boring, try this exercise. Open up randomly to one of the Bible studies and start asking her a few questions. She is sure to find out like we all have in our lives that everybody needs to review.

Try some of the following ideas with your older children:

:: Use your older children to lead the creative introductions at the beginning of each week with their younger brothers and sisters.

:: Try holding your older children in reserve, allowing the younger children to answer first. Then, have the older children amplify the answers their younger siblings gave.

:: Pair up a younger child with an older child and allow the older child to help give the answer to his younger brother or sister. This might sound like cheating but the value is in hearing and remembering the details of the gospel over and over.

:: Consider where your children are in their lives on a given day. Feel the freedom to add a more subjective question to draw them out about how the passage relates to their lives personally. Questions like, "What does God want to teach you from reading this passage?" can be used for any lesson.

:: If your mix of children includes a teen, assign her to lead the Bible study once a week. Encourage her to read the passage and the devotion a day in advance to become familiar with what is being asked. If you pull her aside later and offer some encouragement, she will be all the more eager to lead Bible study again.

Remember, the devotional is designed to work through simple repetition over time. If you skip a day, that's okay, just pick up where you left off.

Reaping the Harvest

So, there is no need to climb a tall mountain or go toe-to-toe with a dragon to battle for your children's salvation—God will do that work. Remember, we plant the seed, do a little watering, and then God makes it grow—that is his promise! Consider these words from Isaiah:

> For as the heavens are higher than the earth, so are my ways higher than your ways and my thoughts than your thoughts. For as the rain and the snow come down from heaven and do not return there but water the earth, making it bring forth and sprout, giving seed to the sower and bread to the eater, so shall my word be that goes out from my mouth; it shall not return to me empty, but it shall accomplish that which I purpose, and shall succeed in the thing for which I sent it. For you shall go out in joy and be led forth in peace; the mountains and the hills before you shall break forth into singing, and all the trees of the field shall clap their hands. (Isaiah 55:9–12)

God's Word will accomplish his purpose and will not return empty. So, as you faithfully lead your children through the devotions in this book, don't just read it as history. It is history, but it is so much more! Lead with expectation that the God of history will visit with your family. Wait and watch to see what God will do. Cling with faith to this hope: that through the gospel proclamation in your home, the Holy Spirit will regenerate the hearts of your children and lead them to faith alone, in Christ alone, by grace alone!

Week 1

The Birth of Jesus Foretold

Story 79 – *The Gospel Story Bible*

Prior to Bible study, find a photograph of some people (in a magazine or online) that has a lot of detail. Make a list of questions to ask your children that will test their skills of observation. The children will look closely at the photo and then answer questions to see how well they remember the details. Questions like, "What color shirt was the man wearing?" or "What was sitting on the table?" will work well to test the skill of your eyewitnesses. During Bible study, give everyone one minute to study the photograph taking in as much detail as they can. Then ask the questions from your list to see how observant they are. Explain to your children that this week you will be reading from Luke's Gospel, which was written from eyewitness accounts.

DAY ONE

Picture It

Can you remember a time when you were startled? Perhaps someone walked up behind you in a quiet room, and you didn't know anyone was there until you felt a hand on your shoulder. If something like that can scare us, imagine what it would be like to be alone in your room and suddenly see an angel appear out of nowhere. Probably you would either scream in fright or be scared into silence. Let's see what happened to Zechariah and Mary in our story today when angels suddenly appeared to them.

 Read Luke 1:1–38.

Think about It Some More

When we read the story it can seem like seeing angels was a normal part of life, but it wasn't. Zechariah had been a priest all his life but he'd never seen an angel before. Serving in the temple was scary enough, for God's presence lived inside the temple. Even before he saw the angel, Zechariah would have walked very cautiously into the temple's inner room. He knew God was holy and that he was a sinner. If he made a mistake, he could die—like Uzzah, who had touched the holy ark with his hand and been killed (2 Samuel 6:6–7). So when the angel suddenly appeared, fear must've shot through him like a lightning bolt. Similarly, when the angel appeared to Mary, she also was afraid. Angels had to calm people's fears before speaking their messages.

Talk about It

- Why did Zechariah lose his voice? *(Zechariah lost his voice because he didn't believe the angel's words to him.)*

- How was Mary's answer to the angel different from Zechariah's answer? *(Mary trusted that what the angel said to her was true. She had faith and did not doubt.)*

- Whose throne was Jesus going to sit on? *(Verse 32 tells us that Jesus would sit upon David's throne. If you have smaller children, you can read verse 32 and ask them to raise their hands when they hear whose throne Jesus would be sitting upon.)*

Pray about It

Thank God for sending his Son, Jesus, to the earth to die on the cross for our sins.

DAY TWO _____

Remember It

What do you remember about yesterday's story? What do you think is going to happen today?

Read Luke 1:39–45.

Think about It Some More

After the angel told Mary about God's plan, Mary went to see Elizabeth, a relative of hers. When Mary arrived and walked through Elizabeth's front door, the little baby growing in Elizabeth's tummy jumped, and Elizabeth was filled with the Holy Spirit. Even before Mary could tell Elizabeth that she was pregnant, Elizabeth already knew. The Holy Spirit told her that Mary was going to have a baby, a very special baby. She said that Mary's baby would be her Lord! That means that she knew Mary's baby was God and would rule over her life.

Talk about It

- :: What was amazing about Elizabeth's greeting? *(She knew what happened to Mary even though Mary didn't tell her.)*

- :: What did Elizabeth's baby do when Mary arrived? *(Elizabeth's baby, who was later to be known as John the Baptist, jumped inside of her.)*

- :: Why did Elizabeth's baby jump inside her? What was so special about Mary's baby? *(Jesus was no ordinary baby; he was the Son of God. Jesus came to earth so that he could die on the cross for our sins. He is only a little baby in our story, but he is still the Savior of the world.)*

 Pray about It

Thank God for the way he used Mary and Elizabeth to work out his plan to send us Jesus.

DAY THREE _____

Connect It to the Gospel

Today is the day we connect this week's Bible story to the gospel. The gospel is the life, death, and resurrection of Jesus for our salvation. Can anyone guess how our story this week looks forward to or back at the gospel?

 Read Luke 1:46–56.

Think about It Some More

When Mary saw that Elizabeth was also going to have a baby, she realized that all that the angel Gabriel had told her was true, and she began to praise God. Mary understood that the baby inside of her was no ordinary baby. He was going to grow up to become her Savior—the one who would save her from her sins. Although Mary was very special to be chosen to give birth to Jesus, she was a sinner like you and me. She needed to be forgiven and saved from her sins too.

Her prayer tells us that she understood that God's promise to Abraham was connected to the baby growing inside of her. When God told Abraham that all the nations of the earth would be blessed through him (Genesis 12:3), he was pointing to Jesus. Jesus was born into the family of Abraham and died on the cross so that people from every nation could be saved.

Talk about It

:: What does the word *savior* mean? *(A savior is someone who rescues. Jesus is our Savior because he rescues us from our sins.)*

:: Why did Mary call God her Savior? *(Mary called God her Savior because she knew that she was a sinner and that only God could save her from her sin.)*

:: Do *we* also need a Savior? Why? *(Yes, we also need a Savior. Our sin separates us from God. As sinners, we can never save ourselves. It is only by God's mercy in sending Jesus that we can be saved.)*

 Pray about It

Thank Jesus for coming to earth to save us from our sin.

DAY FOUR

Remember It

What has God been teaching you this week through our Bible story?

 Read Luke 1:57–80.

Think about It Some More

Can you imagine losing your voice for almost a year? That is what happened to Zechariah. From the day the angel appeared to him until the day his newborn son was named John, he could not speak. It all happened just as the angel of the Lord said it would. Elizabeth gave birth to a son, and as soon as Zechariah wrote on a tablet that the child's name was John, he was able to talk again. And when he spoke, God used Zechariah as a prophet to announce that the time had come for God's people to be saved.

He said that God was raising up a "horn of salvation" from the house of David to save them (v. 69). The people listening didn't know it yet, but Zechariah was talking about the baby Jesus, who was soon to be born as the Savior of the world. Zechariah's son John grew up to be the man God used to announce the start of Jesus' ministry.

Talk about It

> ● ● KIDS, ask your parents if they can remember why
> ● ● they picked your name for you when you were
> born.

(Parents, let your children know why you picked the names you did for them.)

:: Do you remember why Zechariah and Elizabeth named their baby John? *(The angel told them to call him John [Luke 1:13].)*

:: After Zechariah could talk again, he spoke a prophecy about Jesus. What do we learn about Jesus from what he said? *(Parents, if you have younger children, reread verses 68–79, and instruct them to raise their hands when they hear something about Jesus. Jesus is the "horn of salvation" [v. 69] from the house of David. Jesus will bring "holiness and righteousness" [v. 75] to God's people, and will save us from our enemies [v. 71]. "Holiness and righteousness" speaks of Jesus' perfect, sinless life that he would give all of us in exchange for our sins when he died for us on the cross.)*

:: What did Zechariah say about his own son? *(Zechariah said his son, John, would become a prophet and go before the Lord to prepare a way for him [v. 76].)*

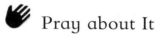 Pray about It

Praise God for his wonderful plan of salvation. God had a plan to save us through Jesus long before Jesus was even born.

DAY FIVE _____

Discover It

Today is the day we look at a different Bible passage—from the book of Psalms or one of the prophets—to see what we can learn from it about Jesus or our salvation.

 Read Isaiah 4:2–3.

Think about It Some More

After God gave Zechariah his voice back, Zechariah was filled with the Holy Spirit and began to speak words that God gave him—he began to prophesy—about what was going to happen in the future. He said that God was bringing salvation out of King David's family line, just as the prophets of old had foretold. Isaiah was one of the prophets who talked about Jesus long before Jesus was ever born, and he wrote the Scripture we read today.

In his prophecy, Isaiah talked about a "branch" that will be "beautiful and glorious." The word *branch* is something like a code word the prophets used in their prophecies to describe the Savior. Jeremiah and Zechariah also called the coming Messiah the branch. We know that Jesus is the branch Isaiah is talking about. This branch, Isaiah said, was going to grow out of the family tree of King David and Jesse, David's father (see Isaiah 11:1, 10), and become a king who would rule forever.

Talk about It

:: What words did Isaiah use to describe the branch? *(Isaiah said the branch was beautiful and glorious.)*

:: What are all the people left in Jerusalem going to be called? *(The people left in Jerusalem—all of God's people—will be called holy.)*

:: How do you think sinners—who are not holy because they sin against God—will become holy? *(Jesus, the branch, is*

*going to die on the cross to take their sins away and then give them,
as their own, his perfect, obedient life to make them holy.)*

 Pray about It

Thank God for sending the branch—his Son, Jesus—to die on the cross
so we could be forgiven and have our sins taken away.

Week 2

The Birth of Jesus

Story 80 – *The Gospel Story Bible*

Whatever month it is, when you begin this week's Bible study take some time to celebrate Christmas. Pull out the Christmas decorations and place a few ornaments around the room. Get a small gift for each child: a candy bar or snack bar wrapped up in leftover Christmas wrapping paper works well. Give your children the presents on Day One and announce, "Merry Christmas! This week we will be reviewing the Christmas story."

DAY ONE

Picture It

When a leader wants to know how many people are living in his kingdom or nation, he can call for a *census,* which is just a fancy word for counting up the people. In our Bible story today, Caesar Augustus, the ruler of Rome, wanted to count all the people in the whole Roman Empire. To make counting them easier, he told everyone to go back to the town their family came from. That is why Mary and Joseph had to return to Bethlehem, since both their families were from that town.

Imagine if our president commanded that kind of census today. How far would your family have to travel to get back to your dad's hometown? Then imagine you had to walk there! Remember, back in Mary and Joseph's day, there were no cars. The best they had were donkeys and camels or chariots, but most people had to walk—some for hundreds of miles!

 Read Luke 2:1–7 and Matthew 2:1–6.

Think about It Some More

In Matthew's version of the Christmas story, at the spot where the wise men came to find baby Jesus, Matthew included a very special prophecy, which had been given by the prophet Micah. Long before Jesus was born, even before Mary and Joseph were born, God told Micah that a Savior would be born in Bethlehem. That tells us that Jesus was not born in Bethlehem by accident. All of it—even Caesar's census—was all a part of God's plan. God picked the town of Bethlehem, and God picked the perfect time. Later in the Bible, the apostle Paul said that Jesus was born at just the perfect moment in time according to God's plan (Galatians 4:4).

Talk about It

:: How did the chief priests know that Jesus would be born in Bethlehem? *(The prophet Micah had written about it in his book in the Bible.)*

:: How did Micah know which city Jesus was going to be born in long before it happened? *(God told Micah where Jesus was going to be born.)*

:: Read Galatians 4:4. What do we learn about how Jesus was born from what Paul said in this verse? *(We learn that Jesus was born in the "fullness of time." That simply means that he was born at the exact right time—the time God planned it. From Paul's writing we learn that Jesus was born according to God's plan at just the right time.)*

:: How should God's ability to plan all things encourage us? *(Not only was Jesus born at the perfect time, so were we! Read Acts 17:26. We are all a part of God's perfect plan!)*

 ## Pray about It

Praise God for the way he is in control of all things.

DAY TWO _____

Remember It

What do you remember about yesterday's story? What do you think is going to happen in today's story?

 Read Luke 2:8–21.

Think about It Some More

Each year when families set out their Christmas decorations, a manger scene is often among them. It usually consists of a shepherd or two, a few animals, the wise men, Mary and Joseph, and the baby Jesus lying in a manger (a food box that animals eat from). Many children first learn the story of Christmas from their family's manger scene.

Did you know that what those manger scenes depict is the story we read from Luke's gospel today? Imagine what it would have been like to be one of the shepherds who saw the heavens opened with thousands of angels announcing Jesus' birth. Or imagine Mary when the shepherds told her all they had seen. Or picture the wise men arriving sometime later to see the Savior. Next Christmas, when you set up your manger scene, remember that it tells a true story—a story that really happened!

Talk about It

:: Can you think of a Christmas song that tells part of the story from our Bible passage today? *(Parents, see if your children can think of a Christmas song like "Silent Night" or "O Little Town of Bethlehem." Take time to sing a verse or two. It is good not to limit your celebration of the Christmas story to December.)*

:: What did the angel of the Lord tell the shepherds? *(The angel said he had good news of great joy for all people, and that the shepherds would find the Christ child lying in a manger.)*

:: What did Mary do with the story the shepherds told her? *(She treasured it up in her heart.)*

:: Why was the angels' message—that Jesus was born—considered good news? *(The announcement of Jesus' birth was good news because Jesus would grow up and one day die on the cross for our sins to open a way for us to live in heaven forever.)*

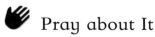 Pray about It

Sing your favorite Christmas hymn and then thank God for the good news—that Jesus Christ was born!

DAY THREE _____

Connect It to the Gospel

Today is the day we connect this week's Bible story to the gospel. The gospel is the life, death, and resurrection of Jesus for our salvation. Can anyone guess how our story this week looks forward to or back at the gospel?

 Read Luke 2:10–11.

Think about It Some More

Even though these are the same verses we read yesterday, rereading them today encourages us to take a closer look at the angel's words to the shepherds.

Did you notice the angel of the Lord called Jesus a Savior? Savior is a word we use to describe someone who rescues someone else. A lifeguard who saves a drowning person could be called a savior—with a lowercase "s." But when we call Jesus a Savior we use an uppercase "S" because Jesus was God who came as the Savior of the world. Jesus came to die on the cross and save everyone who believes in him from the punishment we deserve for our sins.

Talk about It

:: What does the title savior mean? *(The title savior simply means someone who rescues someone else.)*

:: Can you think of people who live around us that we could give that title to because they save people from danger? *(A lifeguard could be called a savior, as could a doctor who prescribes medicine to save us from disease, or a fireman who rescues people from a fire.)*

:: How is Jesus a savior? *(Jesus came to die on the cross to save us from the punishment we deserve for our sins.)*

:: Why do we use an uppercase "S" when we are calling Jesus Savior? *(We use an uppercase "S" because Jesus is God.)*

Pray about It

Thank Jesus for coming to earth as our Savior to die on the cross for our sins.

DAY FOUR

Remember It

What has God been teaching you this week through our Bible story?

 Read Matthew 2:7–21.

Think about It Some More

God's plan is unstoppable. That means that no one can stop what God wants to do. But not long after Jesus was born, King Herod attempted to stop God's plan by trying to kill Jesus. Herod did not want someone else to be king. Nevertheless God's plan to bring a Savior to his people could not be stopped, even by a powerful king. When Herod found out he had been fooled by the wise men, he again tried to stop God's plan by having all the baby boys younger than two years old killed. But once again, God was a step ahead of the evil ruler and sent Jesus to Egypt until Herod was dead. Not only did God win the battle against Herod, God knew what would happen even before Herod was born.

Hundreds of years beforehand, the prophet Hosea foretold the day when Jesus would be sent to Egypt and then brought back out again. In Hosea 11:1, the prophet foretold this: "Out of Egypt I called my son." God was not surprised by Herod's threats; even those threats were a part of God's unstoppable plan.

Talk about It

> KIDS, ask your parents to tell you what their favorite part of the Christmas story is.

(Parents, think of the shepherds, wise men, or another part of the Christmas story and share what part you like best and why. Then ask your children to tell you what their favorite part of the story is.)

:: Why did Herod want to kill the baby Jesus? *(Herod heard that Jesus was going to become a king. Herod wanted to be the only king in Israel.)*

:: Why did God make sure to stop King Herod's evil plan? *(Parents, this is an interesting question. At first you might think that God would not allow anyone to kill his only Son, but then God did not stop the Jews from killing him on the cross. God did not allow Jesus to die as a baby because it was not God's plan. God sent his Son, Jesus, to die, but not as a baby. God's plan was for Jesus to die on the cross for our sins.)*

 Pray about It

Thank God the Father for protecting the baby Jesus from Herod's evil plans.

DAY FIVE _____

Discover It

Today is the day we look at a different Bible passage—from the book of Psalms or one of the prophets—to see what we can learn from it about Jesus or our salvation.

 Read Hosea 11:1–2.

Think about It Some More

Sometimes Bible passages have two meanings. In today's passage, Hosea was writing about Israel coming out of Egypt. Do you remember how God's people were slaves in Egypt and God sent Moses to deliver them? While the Holy Spirit moved Hosea to write about Israel, Matthew tells us that God was also using him to talk about Jesus.

It is amazing to think that long ago in Hosea's day God was already planning to send his Son, Jesus. God's plan to save his people from Egypt points us to Jesus. God gave hidden clues through the prophets of how he was going to do it. This passage in Hosea is one of God's hidden clues that Matthew reveals to us. If it were not for Matthew, we probably never would have guessed it. Looking back we can see that all history is directed by God.

Talk about It

:: Parents, have your children recount as much of the exodus story (when God delivered Israel from Egypt) as they can remember.

:: What other parts of the exodus story point to Jesus? *(The most important part that points to Jesus is when the blood of the lamb is placed on the doorframes of the Israelites so that the angel of* death will pass over them. *That points forward to when Jesus would die for our sins so that God's judgment would pass over us. See Exodus 12:6–12.)*

:: How was God able to know that Jesus was going to go to Egypt and come back out again? *(God controls the future. God knows all things and makes all things happen. He is not a human like you and me; he is God over all.)*

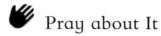 Pray about It

Praise God for the way he knows and controls all things.

Week 3

Jesus Presented in the Temple

Story 81 – *The Gospel Story Bible*

Play a game of "Simon Says" with your children, but change the name of the game to "The Law Says." Go through a series of commands explaining to your children that they should obey only if "the law says" precedes the command. So if you say, "The law says lift your right hand," they should lift their right hands; but if you just say, "Lift your right hand," they should not obey. See how quickly you can catch your children in a mistake. Then explain that in order to live a perfect life Jesus had to obey all of God's law each and every day of his life.

Say, "James tells us that even if we disobey one of God's commands we break the whole law (James 2:10). It is hard enough to obey the commands of a game. No one except Jesus was able to obey the law perfectly. This week, we will see that, even as a baby, God had Mary and Joseph follow the law in the way they presented their son Jesus in the temple."

DAY ONE

Picture It

Perfect is a word we use to describe someone who doesn't make a mistake. To make a perfect score on a test that has one hundred questions, you have to get all one hundred questions correct. If an Olympic gymnast falls during a tumbling routine, she can't get a perfect score because she made a mistake. A perfect diamond must be crystal clear with no little bubbles or black spots inside it. If a person sins even once, he can't be perfect; and since we were all born sinners, none of us can ever have a perfect record.

But Jesus was born sinless, and in order to die on the cross to pay for our sins, Jesus had to live a perfect life, obeying God's laws perfectly, not making even one mistake, his whole life!

 Read Luke 2:21–24.

Think about It Some More

From the very beginning of his life, and even as a baby, Jesus had to follow God's law perfectly. God made sure to give Jesus parents who obeyed the law when Jesus was still a baby. For example, God told Moses that every baby boy should be circumcised when he is eight days old. Joseph and Mary obeyed this law and took Jesus to be circumcised. The law also said that every firstborn son belonged to the Lord and the parents must sacrifice an animal for him. Once again, Mary and Joseph obeyed God's law and sacrificed two young pigeons to the Lord for Jesus so that even as a small baby Jesus obeyed God's law perfectly. By living a perfect life and not sinning even once, Jesus could die on the cross to take our sins away.

Talk about It

:: What does the word *perfect* mean? *(The word* perfect *means without mistake or any flaw.)*

:: Why was it important for us that Jesus live a perfect life? *(If Jesus were going to trade his perfect life for our sinful life, he had to first live a perfect life here on earth. Also, since Jesus was God, and since God is perfect, he could live a perfect life.)*

:: Who helped Jesus live a perfect life of obedience to the law while he was a baby? *(Mary and Joseph helped Jesus by following God's laws for Jesus while he was a baby.)*

 Pray about It

Thank God for the way he used Mary and Joseph to help Jesus obey God's law even while he was a baby.

DAY TWO

Remember It

What do you remember about yesterday's story? What do you think is going to happen today?

 Read Luke 2:36–40.

Think about It Some More

God the Father made sure that Jesus had a welcome party when he was born. First, God opened the heavens with a host of angels; then he saw to it that shepherds would travel to greet baby Jesus in a manger. Though most people didn't know that the Savior of the world had been born, God did tell a few people about his Son. In our story today, Anna, a very old widow, was at the temple worshiping when God showed her that Jesus was the one who came to save his people. That is why she told everyone about Jesus.

Talk about It

:: The Bible calls Anna a prophetess. What is a prophetess? *(A prophetess is a woman who has the gift of prophecy. A prophet receives messages from God and then conveys them to the people. In this case, Anna tells everyone about Jesus.)*

:: Anna told all the people who were waiting for the redemption of Jerusalem—Israel—about Jesus. What does the word *redemption* mean? (Redemption *means "to purchase or buy back." So when we read that Jesus came for our redemption, it means that Jesus came to buy us back or save us. He did that by dying on the cross to take our punishment.)*

:: Who showed Anna that Jesus was the one who would redeem or save God's people from their sin? *(God showed Anna.)*

:: How can we be like Anna? *(We can pray and worship God and tell everyone that Jesus is the Savior.)*

 Pray about It

Ask God to help you be like Anna who prayed and worshiped God every day.

DAY THREE

Connect It to the Gospel

Today is the day we connect this week's Bible story to the gospel. The gospel is the life, death, and resurrection of Jesus for our salvation. Can anyone guess how our story this week looks forward to or back at the gospel?

 Read Luke 2:25–35.

Think about It Some More

Like Anna, Simeon was also part of Jesus' welcoming party. God promised him that he would not die until he saw the Savior. Simeon came to the temple the same day Mary and Joseph brought Jesus. Mary and Joseph did not shout, "Our baby is going to grow up and save the world. Attention everyone, come see the Messiah." But the Spirit of God was upon Simeon and showed him that Jesus was the Savior, the one God had promised to show Simeon before he died.

When Simeon took Jesus into his arms he began to prophesy that salvation had come to God's people and that Jesus was going to bring salvation not only to the Jewish people but to the Gentiles too. Simeon also knew that some people wouldn't like Jesus and would oppose him. Simeon's words proved to be true when men sent Jesus to the cross.

Talk about It

:: Who promised Simeon that he would get to see the Christ—the Messiah—who would save God's people? *(God promised Simeon.)*

:: How did Simeon know that Jesus was the Savior? *(The Holy Spirit was upon Simeon as he came to the temple that morning. It was the Holy Spirit who showed him.)*

:: As Simeon looked at baby Jesus he said that his eyes had seen God's salvation. What was Jesus going to do to bring God's salvation? *(When Jesus grew up to be a man he was going to die on the cross for the sins of God's people. That is how he would bring salvation.)*

Pray about It

Thank God for bringing Simeon to welcome Jesus into the temple.

DAY FOUR _____

Remember It

What has God been teaching you this week through our Bible story?

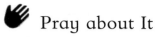 Read Luke 2:41–52.

Think about It Some More

When Jesus was a boy, families came to Jerusalem to celebrate the Passover every year. They often traveled in groups for protection. On one of those annual trips, Jesus went missing. Jesus was twelve years old. He probably had younger brothers and sisters by this time. Now that Jesus was older and could take care of himself, Mary and Joseph likely gave their attention to the younger children and didn't notice at first that Jesus wasn't with them on their return trip. When they realized Jesus was missing they had to go back to the city to find him. That is likely why it took them three days to find him.

Talk about It

> ● ● KIDS, ask your parents if they can remember a
> ● ● time when they lost one of you, even for a short
> time. Ask them how they felt.

(Parents, try to remember a time when you lost your son or daughter in a store or at the beach, and share what it felt like. Talk about how Mary and Joseph must have felt during their three-day search for Jesus.)

:: Where did Mary and Joseph find Jesus? *(They found him in the temple sitting with the teachers, listening to them and asking them questions.)*

:: When his parents found him, what did Jesus call the temple? *(Jesus called the temple his Father's house.)*

:: Why did Jesus call the temple his Father's house? *(The temple was built as a house for God the Father. Since Jesus was his Son, he called God his Father and the temple his Father's house.)*

 Pray about It

Thank God the Father for sending his Son, Jesus, so that whoever believes in him can be saved from their sins.

DAY FIVE

Discover It

Today is the day we look at a different Bible passage—from the book of Psalms or one of the prophets—to see what we can learn from it about Jesus or our salvation.

 Read Psalm 9:7–14.

Think about It Some More

This is a psalm that David wrote about how God saved him from his enemies. But it also seems to talk about the future day when God will judge the whole earth, and it points to a day when God would save David from his sins. David said, "Be gracious to me, O LORD! . . . that I may rejoice in your salvation" (vv. 13–14). That line is similar to what Simeon said when he saw Jesus. Simeon said, "For my eyes have seen your salvation."

Salvation is the word that describes the way God protected his people from their enemies, but it often also points to God's future plan to save his people from their sins. So when the psalms talk about salvation, they are often giving us a hint about God's salvation through Jesus, whom God sent to earth to save us by dying on the cross.

Talk about It

:: Who was David, the author of many of the psalms? *(David was one of the kings of Israel. He was the one who killed the giant Goliath.)*

:: How did God plan to bring his salvation to save sinners? *(God planned to send Jesus, his only Son, to die on the cross for sinners so they could be saved.)*

:: How are Simeon and David's words the same? *(They both
speak about God's salvation.)*

 Pray about It

Thank God for sending Jesus to die on the cross for our sins so that we
could be saved.

Week 4

The Ministry of John the Baptist

Story 82 – *The Gospel Story Bible*

Ahead of time prepare for each child a spoon with a dab of honey, a piece of cracker, and a raisin. (Keep them out of sight.) To start Bible study, explain to the children that you are going to give them a clue to what this week's lesson is about.

Have them close their eyes and open their mouths, and one by one, give each child a prepared spoon. As they are chewing up the raisin and cracker, tell them there is one more part of the clue. Say, "And his food was locusts and wild honey." If you announce that soon after you give them the honey, you'll likely get a fun reaction. Say, "This week you will learn about John the Baptist, who ate locusts and wild honey."

DAY ONE

Picture It

There are a lot of different jobs you could do when you grow up. You could have a job that is all about helping people, like a police officer, firefighter, or doctor. Or you could work in a store. Or maybe create things like an engineer, architect, or designer. You could become a performer such as a singer, musician, comedian, or dancer.

But imagine what your parents would say if you came home dressed in an outfit made of camel hair and announced, "I'm not going to go to college. Instead, I'm leaving home to live in the desert, eat bugs and honey, and become a prophet for the Lord." At some point, that is what John told his parents. But they were probably not too surprised, since the angel, who had first come to John's father, had said John was going to walk in the spirit and power of the Old Testament prophet Elijah (Luke 1:17).

 Read Matthew 3:1–3.

Think about It Some More

Long before John was even born, the prophet Isaiah wrote about him and how God would use him to prepare a way for Jesus (Isaiah 40). To do that, John told the people of Israel that they were sinners who needed to repent of—turn away from—their sins. That took a lot of courage, for not everyone wanted to hear that they were sinners. But John was faithful to speak that message to everyone, including the leaders who could have him thrown in prison. Later, when Jesus began to teach, Jesus said that of all the men that were ever born there was no one greater than John (see Matthew 11:7–12).

Talk about It

:: What was the name of the prophet who wrote about John before John was even born? *(The prophet Isaiah wrote about John.)*

:: What did the angel who first visited John's father, Zechariah, tell him about the son God would give him? *(If your children don't remember, read Luke 1:13–17 then ask them to answer the question. The angel said God was going to use John in the spirit and power of Elijah to turn the hearts of the fathers to the children and to make ready a way for Jesus.)*

:: John told the people to repent. What does the word *repent* mean? *(The word* repent *means to turn away from something. John wanted the people to repent of—turn away from—their sin.)*

:: Why is John's call to repent of, or turn away from, sin, a good thing for us to do too? *(We are sinners just like the people in John's day, and we need Jesus to save us from our sin just as they did.)*

 Pray about It

Ask God to help you repent of, or turn away from, your sins.

DAY TWO

Remember It

What do you remember about yesterday's story? What do you think is going to happen today?

 Read Matthew 3:4–11.

Think about It Some More

John was called John the Baptist because he found people who wanted to turn away from their sins, and he baptized them in the river. The word *baptize* means to dip or dunk under water. Baptism was a picture or symbol to show that when the people confessed their sins and were baptized, their sins were washed away. But not all people were willing to turn away from their sins.

The Pharisees and Sadducees, who were the religious leaders in John's day, didn't want any part of it. They did their best to seem good on the outside, but inside they were sinners just like everyone else. John called them a bunch of snakes and warned them to turn away from their sins to escape God's anger.

Talk about It

:: What were the people who were getting baptized doing? *(The people getting baptized were confessing their sins.)*

:: What does it mean to confess your sins? *(Confessing sin is when we admit it and agree that what we did was wrong.)*

:: Can you think of a sin you should confess? *(Parents, help your children practice confession. You can do this by leading the way yourself. If you have spoken harsh words or been impatient with them over the last few days, take time now to confess your sins. Then help them think of ways they have sinned over the last week or so.)*

 Pray about It

Pray and ask God to forgive your sins.

DAY THREE

Connect It to the Gospel

Today is the day we connect this week's Bible story to the gospel. The gospel is the life, death, and resurrection of Jesus for our salvation. Can anyone guess how our story this week looks forward to or back at the gospel?

 Read Luke 3:1–9.

Think about It Some More

In Luke's Gospel he tells us a little more of what the prophet Isaiah said about John the Baptist. Not only did Isaiah say that John was going to prepare a way for the Lord, but he also said that in John's day all people ("all flesh") would see the salvation of God. When Isaiah talked about the salvation of God, he was talking about Jesus.

Jesus' death on the cross was the way God kept his promise to Abraham to bless all the nations of the world through his offspring, for Jesus was born into Abraham's family, and salvation is now offered to all people. Isaiah saw that God's salvation was not only for the people of Israel, but also for people from every nation and language.

Talk about It

:: What was the name of the river in which John was baptizing people? *(John was baptizing in the Jordan River.)*

:: What did the prophet Isaiah say that "all flesh"—all people—would see? *(Parents, if necessary reread verse 6 and have the children raise their hands if they know the answer. Isaiah said that all people would see the salvation of God.)*

:: What does Luke 3:6 mean when it says that all flesh—all people—shall see the salvation of God? *(This means that God was going to save people from every nation, not just from Israel.)*

Pray about It

Thank God for bringing his salvation to people of every nation—for opening the way for anyone to be saved.

DAY FOUR

Remember It

What has God been teaching you this week through our Bible story?

 Read Luke 3:10–18.

Think about It Some More

It had been a long time since God had sent a prophet to Israel. That is why some of the people listening to John thought that *he* was the Messiah (the one God promised to send to save Israel). But John was quick to correct them, saying that he was unfit to even untie the sandals of the Messiah. John said that he baptized with water, but that the Messiah to come would baptize with the Holy Spirit.

John's baptism couldn't really take away the people's sins, nor could it change their sinful hearts. Only believing in Jesus can do that. Jesus died in our place on the cross to take the punishment we deserved. When anyone believes and trusts in Jesus, the Lord forgives his sins and pours out his Holy Spirit on him.

Talk about It

> KIDS, ask your parents if God has poured out his Holy Spirit on them.

(Parents, this is a great opportunity to share with your children the story of how God saved you.)

:: What is the difference between John's baptism and Jesus' baptism? *(If your children can't remember the answer, reread verse 16 to see if they can tell you the difference. John baptized with water, but Jesus baptized with the Holy Spirit.)*

:: John said that Jesus was going to gather the wheat (the part of the plant you eat) into his barn, but burn the chaff (the husks you throw away) with fire. What kind of people do you think the wheat and the chaff represent? *(The wheat is a picture of everyone that God is going to bring into heaven, and the chaff is a picture of everyone who refuses to believe and will be thrown into the fires of hell.)*

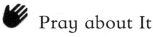 Pray about It

Ask God to help you to believe so that you can be like the wheat gathered into the barn and go to heaven to live with God.

DAY FIVE

Discover It

Today is the day we look at a different Bible passage—from the book of Psalms or one of the prophets—to see what we can learn from it about Jesus or our salvation.

 Read Isaiah 40:1–5.

Think about It Some More

Although the prophet Isaiah lived hundreds of years before John the Baptist was born, God told him what was going to happen in the future. Notice Isaiah said that it was the Lord who was speaking through what he wrote down. Back in Isaiah's day, if God wanted to speak to his people, he used a prophet like Isaiah to speak for him. God told his prophet what to say, and then the prophet would go and tell the people. Since God knows all things, even what is going to happen in the future, he could tell Isaiah about John the Baptist long before John was even born. Matthew and Luke both record Isaiah's words and tell us that he was talking about how John the Baptist would announce the ministry of Jesus.

Talk about It

:: Who did Isaiah say his message came from? *(Parents, if necessary reread verses 1 and 5. Isaiah said it was the Lord who spoke; the message he gave the people actually came from God.)*

:: How could Isaiah know about John the Baptist hundreds of years before John the Baptist was even born? *(Isaiah was a prophet to whom God spoke. So Isaiah repeated what he learned from the Holy Spirit.)*

:: Isaiah said "and the glory of the LORD shall be revealed." Who did John introduce to the people to whom he was preaching? *(John introduced the people to Jesus. When Isaiah says that the glory of the Lord shall be revealed, he is talking about John the Baptist letting people know who the Messiah or Deliverer was. He told them it was Jesus.)*

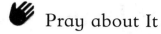 ## Pray about It

Thank God for speaking through the prophets to tell his people about Jesus.

The Baptism of Jesus

Story 83 – *The Gospel Story Bible*

There is simply no way to illustrate the Trinity (that God is three in one) without running into problems. Some like to use the example of water, ice, and steam but for that to be an accurate representation of God, all three would need to exist at the same time from the same measure of water, and that is impossible.

The Trinity is incomprehensible, that is, we cannot fully comprehend its mystery. We can know that there is one God in three persons, but how exactly they can be three and one at the same time is something we cannot completely understand.

So, let your children have a try. Talk about how God is three in one and see if they can come up with something that is both three separate things and yet only one at the same time. Say, "This week we will read about Jesus' baptism, where we see all three persons in the Godhead: God the Father speaks, the Spirit descends as a dove, and Jesus is baptized.

DAY ONE _____

Picture It

Imagine that our church held a car wash to bless the people in the neighborhood, and many of the families from church came out with their kids for a fun day of washing cars. First, an old pickup truck full of scratches pulled up and the parents let their kids scrub away. But the next car was a brand new, shiny white Cadillac. The children were ready to wash the car with the same excitement as they did the pickup. But the parents, seeing the brand new, white car, held the children back for it was brand new and waxed with a perfect shine.

It was only after the owner stepped out and invited the children to wash his car that the parents cautiously allowed them to move forward. Carefully, they helped their children wash the car. Even though the car didn't need to be washed, the owner wanted to join in the community car wash.

Today in our story, Jesus came up to John to be baptized. But like the brand new car that didn't have any dirt on it, Jesus didn't have any sin to repent of and didn't need to be baptized. That is why John didn't want to baptize him.

 Read Matthew 3:13–15.

Think about It Some More

John the Baptist told the crowd at the Jordan River to turn away from their sins, for he knew the people were sinful and needed God's forgiveness. We learned last week that he called the religious rulers a bunch of snakes who needed to stop sinning and follow God, and he told them to turn away from their sins. So you can imagine how surprised John was when Jesus stepped forward and asked John to baptize *him*.

Jesus, who never sinned even once, was the last person John expected to come forward to be baptized. But Jesus didn't step forward to get baptized because of his own sin; Jesus stood in our place and was baptized because of *our* sin. Even at the start of his ministry Jesus knew his mission was to take our sin upon himself. Paul tells us that though Jesus had no sin, God made him to be sin for us (2 Corinthians 5:21).

Talk about It

:: What would you have said to Jesus if he had asked you to baptize him? *(Parents, help your children step into John's sandals. Remember, John was calling for sinners to repent. Let the children identify with John's problem and say things like, "No way, Jesus, you can't be baptized. You are not a sinner.")*

:: Jesus said he needed to be baptized "to fulfill all righteousness." What does the word *righteousness* mean? *(Righteousness means goodness before God, a good record or standing before God. If righteousness were a piece of cloth, it would be brand new and perfectly clean. But our sins make our cloth look like a dirty rag. We can't go to heaven with our filthy rag—we need a perfectly clean cloth. Jesus didn't have any sins of his own sins to repent of, but even at his baptism, he stood in our place, that our sins might be washed away.")*

:: Why did John say to Jesus, "I need to be baptized by you"? *(John knew that he was a sinner and needed his sins washed away. Jesus, however, did not have any sin. That is why John said that Jesus should be the one to baptize him.)*

:: What are some of the sins that you need to have washed away? *(Parents, help your children identify with John as a sinner in need of cleansing.)*

 Pray about It

Confess your sins to God, and ask him to forgive you and wash away your sins.

DAY TWO

Remember It

What do you remember about yesterday's story? What do you think is going to happen today?

 Read Matthew 3:16–17.

Think about It Some More

Did you notice that all three persons of God were present at Jesus' baptism? Jesus, who was God the Son, was the one who was baptized. God the Holy Spirit came as a dove and rested upon Jesus, while God the Father spoke out from the heavens. Even though they are three different persons, the Father, Son, and Holy Spirit make up one God. That is why we use the word *Trinity* to describe God. The word *Trinity* means three in one. God is three persons, but only one God—the Trinity.

Talk about It

:: What do you think the people watching thought when God spoke out of the heavens? *(Parents, there are no wrong answers here. Draw out your children to see if they can put themselves into the story.)*

:: What does the word *trinity* mean? *(Trinity means three in one.)*

:: Who are the three persons who make up one God in the Trinity? *(The three persons of the Trinity are God the Father, God the Son, and God the Holy Spirit.)*

 Pray about It

If you know the melody and words to "Praise God from Whom All Blessings Flow," then sing it with your family and talk about the words of the song. If not, then praise God for the amazing way he is three in one.

DAY THREE

Connect It to the Gospel

Today is the day we connect this week's Bible story to the gospel. The gospel is the life, death, and resurrection of Jesus for our salvation. Can anyone guess how our story this week looks forward to or back at the gospel?

 Read John 1:29–34.

Think about It Some More

Did you know that John the Baptist was related to Jesus? Most Bible teachers believe they were cousins! So it is possible that John and Jesus knew each other as young boys. But John probably didn't know that his cousin Jesus was the Messiah. Even when he was older, God had to give John a clue to recognize his chosen One. When the Spirit of God came down on Jesus as a dove, John knew his cousin was the One and called Jesus, "the Lamb of God who takes away the sin of the world!" (John 1:29).

The name *Lamb* came from the Old Testament when Israel would kill lambs to cover their sins. Remember the story of Moses and the Passover when God told all of Israel to sacrifice a lamb and put the blood on the doorframes of their houses? The blood of the lamb was a sign that a lamb had been killed in place of the firstborn son. When God saw the blood, he passed over that house and didn't bring death to the firstborn son. Jesus is our lamb who was sacrificed for us. When we trust in Jesus, God's punishment passes over us. That is why John called Jesus the Lamb of God who takes away our sins.

Talk about It

:: What name did John call Jesus at his baptism? *(John called Jesus the Lamb of God who takes away the sin of the world. John also called Jesus the Son of God.)*

:: What was the sign God gave John so that he knew for sure who the Messiah was? *(God told him that the Spirit would fall upon his Chosen One and that is how John would know [v. 33].)*

:: Why is Jesus called the Lamb of God? *(Jesus is called the Lamb of God because like the lambs in the Old Testament he was going to be killed—sacrificed—in our place and take our punishment so we could be forgiven.)*

 Pray about It

Praise God for sending his Son, Jesus, to be the Lamb who takes away our sins.

DAY FOUR _____

Remember It

What has God been teaching you this week through our Bible story?

 Read Mark 6:17–29.

Think about It Some More

John the Baptist was a bold man who called all people to repent of—turn away from—their sins. He even corrected King Herod for stealing his brother's wife, Herodias, and making her his own wife. Herod knew John was a good man, sent by God. However, to please his wife he sent John to prison and eventually had him killed. John paid the price of his own life for obeying God and speaking the truth. John had completed his mission, to prepare a way for Jesus. A few years later, Jesus was arrested and died on the cross. By his death, Jesus made a way for John and all of us who believe in him to go to heaven. Today, John the Baptist is rejoicing with Jesus in heaven.

Talk about It

> :: :: KIDS, ask your parents if they know a story of
> :: :: another person who was killed because they were
> serving God.

*(Parents, you can tell a story of a modern-day martyr like Jim Elliot
or you can tell a story from the New Testament, such as the story of
Stephen [Acts 6—7]. Afterward, point your children to Jesus, who
gave up his glorious place of honor in heaven to come to earth as a
servant and die in our place so that we could be forgiven.)*

:: Why did Herod have John the Baptist thrown into prison?
*(John the Baptist told Herod it was wrong for him to steal his
brother's wife and marry her. That made Herodias [the wife] mad.
To make his new wife happy, Herod had John arrested and thrown
into prison.)*

:: Who was Herod trying to please more than God? *(Herod
wanted to please Herodias, his wife, and the people at the banquet
more than he wanted to please God.)*

 Pray about It

Thank God for sending Jesus to die on the cross so that John the Baptist, and all of us who believe, can go to heaven.

DAY FIVE _____

Discover It

Today is the day we look at a different Bible passage—from the book
of Psalms or one of the prophets—to see what we can learn from it
about Jesus or our salvation.

 Read Isaiah 11:1–5.

Think about It Some More

Did you know that the Bible is filled with clues that pointed to Jesus
even before he was born? For example, long before the day of Jesus'
baptism, Isaiah foretold that the Spirit of God would rest upon him.

God gave Isaiah other hints about Jesus too. Isaiah called Jesus a shoot from the stump of Jesse. That meant that Jesse, King David's father, would one day have a great far-off grandson (pictured by the shoot coming off the stump). This future grandson would be blessed by God whose Spirit would rest on him. He would be a righteous judge; he would be powerful and punish wickedness; and he would be good and faithful.

Looking back, it is easy for us to see that Isaiah's description perfectly fits Jesus. Long before Jesus was even born, God was giving his people clues about Jesus.

Talk about It

:: Point out some of the things Isaiah said in this Bible passage that refer to Jesus. *(Parents, if you have younger children, reread the passage and have them raise their hands when they hear something they think describes Jesus. You can even change the inflection of your voice to help them.)*

:: What are some of the names Isaiah used to describe the Spirit of the Lord? *(Isaiah said the Spirit of the Lord is the Spirit of wisdom, understanding, counsel, might, knowledge, and the fear of the Lord. Again, parents, you can reread the passage and have your younger children raise their hands when they hear the correct answer.)*

:: How could Isaiah know all these things about Jesus before Jesus was even born? *(Isaiah and the others who wrote parts of the Bible had the help of the Holy Spirit, who told them what they should write down. So even though the words were written by humans, God directed them to know what to write.)*

 Pray about It

Praise God for the wonderful way he used the prophets of old to tell us about Jesus even before he was born.

Week 6

The Temptation of Jesus
Story 84 – *The Gospel Story Bible*

Use this exercise to help your children understand the concept of temptation. You will need a shiny new quarter and penny for this exercise. Take the shiny new quarter, place it in your palm, and show it to your children. After they take a look, put in your pocket. Then take out the shiny new penny and place it in your palm. This time tempt them to take it, by saying, "I'll bet you're not fast enough to take this penny out of my hand." Then move your hand closer and taunt them. They should take the challenge and try to grab the penny.

After they make a few unsuccessful attempts, put the penny back in your pocket and ask them why they didn't try to grab the quarter out of your hand earlier. Talk about how your comments tempted them to go after the penny. Then explain what temptation is. Say, "This week we will hear how Satan tempted Jesus."

DAY ONE

Picture It

If someone told you to hit another child what would you say? Hopefully, you would say no because it is wrong to hit others. But what if that same person began to tempt you by promising to give you something? What if she said, "If you hit your little brother I will give you twenty dollars"? What would you say then? It is still just as wrong as before, but you might be more tempted to do it.

Perhaps you are very obedient and would still refuse. What if she increased her offer? What if she said, "I tell you what, if you hit your little brother I will give you five hundred dollars," and she held up five brand new one-hundred-dollar bills? Perhaps that might get you thinking, *I don't have to hit him hard. I could just hit him lightly so I can get the money.*

In today's Scripture you will see how the devil tempted Jesus to sin by offering Jesus what he thought Jesus wanted.

 Read Luke 4:1–4.

Think about It Some More

The devil knew that Jesus was fasting and would be hungry. (Fasting is not eating for a time to show that God the Father is more important than food.) That is why he told Jesus to turn stones into bread. He wanted to tempt Jesus to obey *his* command instead of the commands of God the Father in heaven. But Jesus fought the devil's temptation by quoting a Bible verse: "Man does not live by bread alone" (Deuteronomy 8:3). Jesus quoted this verse to show that obeying God the Father is more important than food.

Moses first spoke these words to Israel to teach them the very same thing—that they needed God more than food. Moses reminded them of the forty years they had spent wandering in the wilderness and how God had provided manna for them to eat each morning. But sadly they still complained and rejected God.

By saying no to the devil's temptations, Jesus showed that he was not going to make the same mistake that Israel had made. They complained and rejected God, but Jesus did not reject God his Father to give in to the devil's temptations. Jesus obeyed God perfectly and did not fail as Israel had.

Talk about It

:: Why did the devil say Jesus should turn the stones into bread? *(The devil knew Jesus was hungry, and he was trying to tempt Jesus to obey his command by suggesting he turn the stones into bread.)*

:: How did Jesus fight the devil? *(Jesus used the Word of God to fight the devil.)*

:: Why was it important for Jesus to win the battle against Satan's temptations? *(Jesus had to live a perfect life without any sins so that he would be qualified to take away our sins. If Jesus had sinned even once, he could not have been our perfect sacrifice. The good news is that Jesus was tempted but he did not sin! See Hebrews 4:15.)*

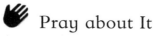 Pray about It

Praise Jesus for standing against the devil and living a perfect life in our place.

DAY TWO

Remember It

What do you remember about yesterday's story? What do you think is going to happen today?

 Read Luke 4:5–8.

Think about It Some More

When the devil saw that getting Jesus to turn the stones into bread didn't work, he tried something else. He offered to give the whole world to Jesus. All Jesus had to do to get the whole world was worship the devil.

That of course would be a terrible sin. But Jesus didn't fall for the devil's trick. Jesus knew that one day all the evil of the world would be destroyed, and he would be king. But Jesus' victory would come through his death on the cross not through a bargain with the devil. So Jesus quoted another Bible verse from the Old Testament book of Deuteronomy. By resisting the devil's trick, Jesus did what Israel failed to do: worship God alone. Remember how Israel failed when they worshiped the golden calf? Where Israel failed, Jesus succeeded.

Talk about It

:: Why was Satan's temptation so powerful? (*Satan was trying to offer Jesus the most valuable thing he thought he had to offer: the kingdom of the whole earth. His temptation offered Jesus a shortcut to a kingdom. Satan was saying that Jesus could have an earthly kingdom by not paying the price on the cross.*)

:: The devil thought he had the power to give all the kingdoms of the earth to Jesus, but who really rules over the earth? (*God is the ruler over the earth, and the Bible tells us that Jesus is the ruler over all things [Colossians 1:15–18]. The only kingdom the devil had to offer was the kingdom of sin and darkness.*

If Jesus had taken Satan's offer—and we know he never would—he would've become evil just like the devil.)

:: Can you think of a time when you were tempted to sin and then gave in and sinned? *(Parents, help your children to see that each time they sin they give in to a temptation to do so.)*

 Pray about It

Confess the ways you fall into temptation and sin and ask God to forgive you and save you from your sins.

DAY THREE

Connect It to the Gospel

Today is the day we connect this week's Bible story to the gospel. The gospel is the life, death, and resurrection of Jesus for our salvation. Can anyone guess how our story this week looks forward to or back at the gospel?

 Read Hebrews 4:14–16.

Think about It Some More

If you have ever broken a bone and had to wear a cast, you know how difficult it can be to keep it clean and dry for six weeks, and how itchy a cast can get during the last two weeks you have to wear it. But if you've never broken a bone, it's not as easy to understand how uncomfortable a cast is. It's easier to encourage people going through challenges similar to the ones we've experienced because we know what it's like.

In our Bible passage today, the writer of the book of Hebrews tells us that Jesus can sympathize (feel how hard it is) when we are tempted, because he was tempted just like we are. But there is a big difference between us and Jesus. When we are tempted we often give in to sin, but even though Jesus was tempted like us, he never sinned. Jesus understands how hard it is to fight temptation. So when our temptation to sin gets really hard, we can pray to Jesus for help, knowing that he died on the cross to set us free from sin and that he knows how hard it is for us to fight sin.

Talk about It

:: Why is it easy for Jesus to understand how hard it can be to fight temptation? *(When Jesus was on the earth he was tempted just like we are, so he knows from his own experience how hard it is to fight temptation.)*

:: Jesus was tempted like we are, but how was his reaction to temptation different from our reaction? *(Even though Jesus was tempted like we are, he never ever gave in to the temptation. Every time Jesus was tempted, he said no to sin.)*

:: Can you think of a time when you were tempted and you said *no* to sin? *(Parents, help your children think of a time when, perhaps, they wanted to hit their brother or sister because they were angry, but they did not hit them. Or, maybe there was a time when they were tempted to lie, but, instead, told the truth.)*

 Pray about It

Praise Jesus for never giving in to temptation, and praise him for the times when he helped you overcome temptation too.

DAY FOUR _____

Remember It

What has God been teaching you this week through our Bible story?

 Read Luke 4:9–13.

Think about It Some More

Another way a person can tempt us is to "dare" us to do something. For instance, a friend could say to you, "I'll bet you're afraid to throw a snowball at a car." Now you might know that it is foolish to throw a snowball at a car, especially one that is moving, but because he dared you, you may be more tempted to do it.

In our story today, the devil was basically saying to Jesus, "Let's see if your angels are really as powerful as you say they are. I'll bet you're afraid to throw yourself down from way up here because your angels really won't be able to save you from falling."

The devil quoted the Bible and basically said, "If your word is true, prove it to me." But the devil is not God, and he can't command Jesus.

Instead of obeying the devil, Jesus refused. Once the devil realized that Jesus was not going to give in to his temptations, he left until a better opportunity arose.

Talk about It

> KIDS, ask your parents if they have ever fallen into temptation and sinned.

(Parents, try to remember a time when you were tempted and gave in to the temptation. We want to help our children see that Jesus is very different from us. He is the only one who could stand against temptation and never sin.)

:: Parents, now ask your kids the very same question: Have any of you ever been tempted and failed, giving into sin? *(Parents, you may have a better memory than they do. Try to help them remember a time when they were tempted and gave in to sin.)*

:: How was Jesus different from us? *(Jesus never gave in to temptation even once. We sin every day.)*

 ## Pray about It

Share a prayer of confession as a family admitting that you all have given in to temptation and sinned. Then ask God to save each person in your family from their sins.

DAY FIVE

Discover It

Today is the day we look at a different Bible passage—from the book of Psalms or one of the prophets—to see what we can learn from it about Jesus or our salvation.

Read Isaiah 61:1–3.

Think about It Some More

After the devil left him, Jesus returned from the wilderness and went to Nazareth, his hometown. Going into the place of worship, the synagogue, Jesus read from the book of Isaiah (see Luke 4:17–19). He opened the scroll to the verses we read today and told the people that Isaiah was talking about him.

Jesus is the person Isaiah said was going to preach good news to the poor. Jesus was going to preach the good news so that people would no longer be captives to sin. Jesus would free them by dying on the cross for their sins. Everyone who trusts in his work on the cross is forgiven and free to go to heaven. That is good news for sure!

Talk about It

:: Isaiah said, "The Spirit of the Lord GOD is upon me." How is this about Jesus? *(Before going into the wilderness, the Holy Spirit came upon Jesus at his baptism. Reread Luke 4:1 and 4:14 to show your children how Jesus matched the Isaiah's description.)*

:: Do you know what Isaiah meant when he said that Jesus was going to "bring good news to the poor"? What is the "good news" Isaiah was talking about? *(The "good news" is the message of the gospel, that Jesus was going to die on the cross for our sins and then rise again so that everyone who believes in him can be forgiven and go to heaven to be with God when they die.)*

:: Was the good news that Jesus brought just for the people in his day or is it still good news for us today? *(It is still good news for us today because if we believe in Jesus we too can be forgiven and go to be with Jesus in heaven when we die.)*

 Pray about It

Thank Jesus for coming to bring us the good news of the gospel.

Week 7

The Wedding Feast

Story 85 – *The Gospel Story Bible*

Bring a pitcher of water, a wooden spoon, and a few wine glasses to your kitchen table. After you have called your family in to watch, start stirring the water and say, "Fill the jars with water," and "Draw some out and take it to the master of the feast." Pour some of the water into a glass and then take it to one of your children and ask them to taste it and let you know what it tastes like. They will be perplexed, taste it, and say it doesn't taste like anything or that it tastes like water. Take the glass from them and taste it yourself. Tell them they are right: it is only water and you will need to try it again.

Repeat the whole process. Then explain that you can't understand why you, doing the same things Jesus did at the wedding banquet, can't turn water into wine. See if they can tell you what you're missing—that you are not all-powerful like God. Say, "This week we will be learning about Jesus' first miracle where he did turn water into wine."

DAY ONE

Picture It

Imagine that you are having a birthday party, and it is time for the cake and ice cream. But soon after scooping out the vanilla ice cream, Mom realizes there is not enough for everyone. *We just can't run out of ice cream!* she thinks. So quickly and quietly she asks one of the adults present to make a quick trip to the store. Within minutes he returns with four large containers of premium chocolate chip cookie dough ice cream. He arrives just as the vanilla runs out so the last five people get the chocolate chip cookie dough flavor. Soon everyone is asking for the new ice cream, wondering why your mom saved the best for last.

 Read John 2:1–5.

Think about It Some More

Back in Jesus' day, running out of wine at a wedding was kind of like running out of ice cream at a birthday party. When Mary, Jesus' mother, found out that they were running out of wine at the wedding, she went to Jesus. She didn't ask him to do a miracle, but she seemed to know that he might be able to help. Jesus told his mother that his hour had not yet come. That meant that it wasn't time for him to show that he was God. But Mary had a sense that her son could help out, so she told the servants to obey Jesus' instructions.

Talk about It

:: Why did Mary ask Jesus for help? *(The wine supply at the wedding banquet was running low. Running out of wine would have been embarrassing to the hosts.)*

:: What did Jesus mean when he said, "My hour has not yet come"? *(Even though Jesus was God, he was living a normal life. He had not done any miracles yet. He meant it wasn't time to show people he was God, be rejected by them, and die on the cross.)*

:: What do you think is going to happen in the next part of the story? *(Parents, your children probably know that Jesus is going to turn the water into wine. You can have a little fun by changing the story around a bit. After they answer, try challenging them by saying, "Oh, I think you are wrong. I think Jesus is going to run to the store to buy some wine. After all, he said his time had not yet come.")*

:: How can we follow the example of Mary, who came to Jesus with her problem? *(Both Psalm 55:22 and 1 Peter 5:7 tell us that we can cast our cares upon the Lord. In Philippians 4:6, Paul tells us not to be anxious but to present our requests to God in prayer.)*

 Pray about It

Think of some of the needs your family has and present them to the Lord and ask him to help you. *(Parents, guide your children to present requests more serious than just the things they want.)*

DAY TWO

Remember It

What do you remember about yesterday's story? What do you think is going to happen today?

 Read John 2:6–10.

Think about It Some More

Even though Jesus said his hour had not come, which means he wasn't ready to reveal to everyone that he was God, Jesus decided to provide wine for the wedding anyway. One thing was certain, when Jesus was finished making wine, the wedding would not run out of wine again. The jars in the story held about one hundred gallons of water, that is, over twenty-five hundred glasses of wine! Although Jesus performed this miracle quietly so that most people didn't know where the wine came from, Mary, the disciples, and the servants saw what happened. They knew that no ordinary man could turn water into wine.

Jesus, of course, was no ordinary man. Colossians 1:16 tells us that Jesus is the creator of the world, and that by him, through him, and for him all things were made. When the master of the feast tasted the wine, he was impressed. He didn't realize that it was made by the best wine maker in the world, God. Wine normally takes months or even years to be aged to perfection—that is, unless it is perfectly made!

Talk about It

:: How many people knew that Jesus was the one who turned the water into wine? *(Since it was not yet time for Jesus to show that he was God, Jesus turned the water into wine very quietly so that only the servants and his mother would know.)*

:: How did Jesus turn the water into wine? *(Parents, see if your children can explain it. If they run into difficulty help them understand that Jesus simply willed that the water turn into wine, which means that he didn't even have to say, "Water, I command you to become wine." All he had to do was want the water to become wine, and it did. That is because Jesus is the creator of the world and can create things out of nothing at all.)*

:: Why can't we turn water into wine by pouring it into large jars? *(Parents, help your children see that God is so much different*

from us. You might even introduce the word holy *in describing God.*
Holy *means that God is completely different from us, and that he is all good.)*

Pray about It

Praise God that he is all-powerful and can create anything he wants.

DAY THREE

Connect It to the Gospel

Today is the day we connect this week's Bible story to the gospel. The gospel is the life, death, and resurrection of Jesus for our salvation. Can anyone guess how our story this week looks forward to or back at the gospel?

Read John 12:23–32.

Think about It Some More

When Jesus answered his mother at the wedding he said, "My hour has not yet come." That might seem like a strange answer, but God had planned down to the exact time of every detail how and when our salvation would unfold (Galatians 4:4). It wasn't yet time for Jesus to reveal his miraculous power. Jesus knew that at first the people would follow him with joy, and even try to make him king, but that soon they would reject and crucify him.

In contrast to what Jesus said at the wedding, in the Bible verses we read today, Jesus told his disciples that the hour *had* come. But the hour he was talking about here was the time of his suffering. Even at the wedding Jesus knew the cross was not far away.

Talk about It

:: When Jesus said that he was going to be "lifted up" (v. 32), what was he going to be lifted up on? *(Jesus was going to be lifted up onto a cross to die for our sins.)*

:: Jesus said that the reason he came was for "this hour." What does "this hour" mean? *(Jesus came to die on the cross for our sins. When Jesus uses the words, "this hour" he means the time around when he would be crucified and take our sins upon himself.)*

:: At the wedding, when Jesus told his mother, "My hour has not yet come," what did Jesus know was going to soon happen? *(Jesus knew that he was soon going to die on the cross.)*

 ## Pray about It

Thank Jesus for coming to earth to die on the cross for our sins.

DAY FOUR   _____

Remember It

What has God been teaching you this week through our Bible story?

 Read John 2:11–12.

Think about It Some More

In our Bible passage today, John said that when Jesus turned the water into wine it "manifested his glory." *Glory* is not a word we use to describe our ordinary lives, but it is a word that we use to describe God. It is a word that points to all that is amazing and wonderful about God. Turning water into wine showed his mother, the disciples, and the servants that Jesus was no ordinary man.

When the disciples saw what happened, they believed. Although they did not yet know Jesus was God, they at least believed he was sent by God. It wouldn't be long until Jesus would die on the cross and rise again from the dead. Then the disciples would know he wasn't just sent by God—they would know that Jesus *was* God.

Talk about It

> ● ● KIDS, ask your parents which of the miracles of
> ● ● Jesus best manifested (or showed) his glory.

(Parents, Jesus' raising of the dead, e.g., Lazarus, is a good choice.)

:: What do you think it would have been like to be one of Jesus' brothers or sisters? *(Parents, draw out your children here. Remember, Jesus never sinned. Imagine having a brother who never did anything wrong.)*

:: What did the disciples do after seeing Jesus turn the water into wine? *(They believed in Jesus after he turned the water into wine.)*

:: How can reading the stories about what Jesus did help us believe? *(By reading the stories, we can see that Jesus was no ordinary man. Then as the Holy Spirit changes our hearts we can believe like the disciples did.)*

 Pray about It

Ask Jesus to help you believe that he is the Son of God who died on the cross for your sins and trust him with your whole life.

DAY FIVE

Discover It

Today is the day we look at a different Bible passage—from the book of Psalms or one of the prophets—to see what we can learn from it about Jesus or our salvation.

 Read Isaiah 62:11–12.

Think about It Some More

When the disciples left the wedding, they could have shouted the words Isaiah wrote long ago: "Behold your salvation comes." The miracle of turning the water into wine was the first of many miracles that Jesus performed. Jesus saved the wedding hosts from the embarrassment of running out of wine, but soon Jesus would go on to save people from their diseases and even save them from death. But the greatest salvation Jesus brought is saving from their sins those people who believe in him.

Isaiah saw ahead to that day. That is why Isaiah said that God's people would be called the "Holy People." Even though we are sinners, we can be called God's holy people because Jesus died to take away the sins of everyone who believes. There is only one person to whom Isaiah could be referring in this Bible passage, because there is only one person who saved us from our sins. That person is Jesus.

Talk about It

:: When Isaiah talks about our salvation coming, what is he talking about? What are we saved from? *(Parents, this is a difficult but important concept. Help your children to realize that they are sinners who deserve God's punishment. Understanding this will help them to see that what God saved us from is the punishment we deserve for our sins.)*

:: Who stood in our place and took the punishment we deserved so that we could be saved? *(Jesus stood in our place taking our punishment.)*

:: Isaiah said that God's people would be called "The Holy People," which means a people who, like God, are holy and without sin. How could people who are sinners be called holy? *(Jesus died on the cross to take away our sins. Once you believe in Jesus and he takes away your sins, you become one of his holy people because your sins have been taken away.)*

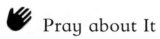 Pray about It

Thank God for making it possible for your sins to be taken away.

Week 8

Jesus Cleanses the Temple

Story 86 – *The Gospel Story Bible*

One day early this week, when you set out the dishes for dinner, set a dirty plate out for one of your children. When she objects to the dirty plate, ask her why the dirty plate is a problem. She will likely say that she needs to have a clean plate to eat from or she might get sick. Ask her if the old food belongs on the plate. Ask her what needs to happen to the plate. She will say the plate needs to be washed. Congratulate her on her correct response and give her a clean plate.

Explain that just as the old food doesn't belong on the plate and must be cleaned, so the money-changers didn't belong in the temple and Jesus needed to clean them out. Conclude by saying, "That is what our Bible story this week is about."

DAY ONE

Picture It

Imagine that you are a farmer with a flock of sheep. One day you notice that the gate to the sheep pen is open and the sheep have escaped. What would you do if you saw the sheep going into your house through an open door? Wouldn't you want to run to your house to chase the sheep out and back into the pen where they belong?

That is what Jesus had to do with the money-changers and animal sellers who set up shop in the temple. They had a marketplace outside the temple where they could sell things. That was where they should have been exchanging money and selling the animals. The temple in Jerusalem wasn't built as a place to sell sheep. It had another purpose:

It was God's house where people came to worship him. Let's see what Jesus did when he found the money-changers in the temple.

 Read John 2:13–17.

Think about It Some More

The temple was God's house; it was never a market. It was the place where God lived with his people. They came there to pray and to worship the Lord by offering animals as sacrifices for their sins. But instead of praying and worshiping God, the shopkeepers were more interested in making money. Not only that, but Matthew tells us that Jesus called the money-changers thieves because they were cheating the people (Matthew 21:13).

When Jesus arrived at the temple, he drove the shopkeepers out and he overturned the tables of the money-changers. Though Jesus was clearing them out, he had respect for their property. Their coins could be gathered again and a whip of cords would not hurt the sheep and oxen. Jesus didn't smash or open the cages of the pigeons to let them out. He was only trying to send them a message that God's house was neither a marketplace nor a place for thieves. Since Jesus was God, he did not sin when he was correcting them. We usually get sinfully angry when we correct someone, but Jesus did not.

Talk about It

:: Whose house did Jesus say the temple was? *(The temple was his Father's house.)*

:: What was wrong with what was going on in the temple? *(There were those who were selling animals and cheating the people.)*

:: Jesus chased the animal sellers and the money-changers out of the temple, but who didn't Jesus chase out of the temple? *(Jesus did not chase out those who came to worship. In John 6:37 Jesus says, "All that the Father gives me will come to me, and whoever comes to me I will never cast out." God does not cast out those who come to worship!)*

 Pray about It

Thank God for never chasing away anyone who comes to worship him.

DAY TWO

Remember It

What do you remember about yesterday's story? What do you think is going to happen today?

 Read John 2:18–22.

Think about It Some More

The Jews were upset when they saw Jesus overturn the tables of the money-changers and chase away the people selling animals. They knew Jesus was right about the temple, but they demanded that Jesus give them a sign to prove he was allowed to do what he did. Jesus gave them an interesting answer. He said that if they tore down the temple he could rebuild it in three days. But he wasn't talking about the temple building made of stones. Jesus was talking about his own body.

You see, the temple was the place where God lived with his people. Once Jesus came, God was with the people wherever he went. That is why it is true to say that Jesus' body was God's temple, a place where God lived among his people. Not long after Jesus cleared out the temple, the Jews had Jesus killed. On the third day when Jesus rose again, the disciples remembered what Jesus had said about rebuilding the temple in three days and realized that Jesus had been talking about his resurrection from the dead the whole time.

Talk about It

:: What did the Jews demand that Jesus give them? *(The Jews demanded that Jesus give them a sign to show he was allowed to chase out the money-changers.)*

:: Why do you think the Jews demanded a sign? *(The Jews didn't believe Jesus had been sent by God, so they demanded proof by asking for a miraculous sign. People who do not believe by faith want proof they can see or touch. When the Pharisees demanded a sign, as recorded in Mark 8:11, Jesus told them that no sign would be given.)*

:: How was Jesus himself God's temple? *(God's temple is the place where his presence lives among the people. Wherever he went God was among the people because Jesus was God. In heaven there*

*won't be a temple building. The Lord God Almighty and the Lamb
are its temple. See Revelation 21:22.)*

 Pray about It

Ask Jesus to help you believe and not be like the Jews who demanded
a sign before they would believe.

DAY THREE _____

Connect It to the Gospel

Today is the day we connect this week's Bible story to the gospel. The
gospel is the life, death, and resurrection of Jesus for our salvation. Can
anyone guess how our story this week looks forward to or back at the
gospel?

 Read Matthew 27:39–43.

Think about It Some More

The disciples didn't know what Jesus was talking about when he told
the Jews that he could rebuild the temple in three days. But we now
know that Jesus was referring to his resurrection. After Jesus rose from
the dead, the disciples remembered (see John 2:22). Even while Jesus
hung on the cross, people hurled insults at him, mocking what he'd said
about rebuilding the temple (see Matthew 27:39–40). By rising from
the dead Jesus proved what he said and gave us the greatest sign of all
to help us believe. By rising from the dead Jesus proved that he is Lord
over all; Lord not only of the money-changers at the temple but also
Lord of life and death.

Talk about It

:: What did the chief priests challenge Jesus to do? *(Just as they
had before, they refused to believe and demanded a sign. They said
if Jesus came down from the cross they would believe him, but they
were really mocking Jesus.)*

:: Why did the people mock Jesus while he was on the cross
with what he said about rebuilding the temple in three
days? *(The people mocked Jesus thinking him a liar. They didn't
believe he was the Son of God.)*

:: What did Jesus do to prove that he could rebuild the temple in three days? *(Jesus rose again from the dead on the third day. That is what Jesus meant all along when he said he could rebuild the temple in three days.)*

 Pray about It

Have everyone in your family take a turn praising Jesus for rising from the dead. Although the religious rulers mocked him, we have the privilege of praising him!

DAY FOUR

Remember It

What has God been teaching you this week through our Bible story?

 Read John 2:23–25.

Think about It Some More

After Jesus chased the dishonest money-changers out of the temple, he performed many miracles and many people said they believed in him. But it's easy to say you believe on the outside and not trust God on the inside. That is why John said that Jesus did not entrust himself to the people. Jesus knew that although the people said they believed, they were not ready to follow him. In fact, among these so-called believers were likely those who yelled, "Crucify him!" when Jesus was on trial.

Talk about It

> ● ● KIDS, ask your parents if they ever said they
> ● ● believed in Jesus before they really trusted in him.

(Parents, many people say they are Christians but really don't believe. If this was true of you before you gave your life to Christ, tell your children about it and help them to see that what we say is not as important as what we believe in our heart.)

:: What kinds of things did Jesus do that are called "signs" in this Bible passage? *(Jesus healed people and cast out demons as signs to show he was really the Messiah.)*

:: Did the people really believe Jesus in their heart, or were they only saying they believed? *(We know from Jesus' response that they didn't really believe.)*

:: How could Jesus know a person's thoughts and beliefs? *(Jesus is God, and God knows everything about us, even what we think and believe.)*

 Pray about It

Ask Jesus to help you believe in your heart that he is the Savior, and ask God to help every person in your family trust in him.

DAY FIVE _____

Discover It

Today is the day we look at a different Bible passage—from the book of Psalms or one of the prophets—to see what we can learn from it about Jesus or our salvation.

 Read Psalm 69:7–13.

Think about It Some More

When the disciples saw Jesus chase the money-changers out of the temple, it reminded them of a psalm that King David wrote—Psalm 69. In this psalm, David talks about a person who had a zeal (strong love) for God's house. It also says that he would bear the reproaches or sins of others upon himself (v. 9). Although David was probably thinking about something that happened in his own life when he wrote this, the disciples used this psalm to describe Jesus. Not only did Jesus have a zeal for God's house, but also the other part of verse fits Jesus, who took our sins upon himself when he died on the cross.

Talk about It

:: What did Jesus do that showed his zeal for God's house? *(Jesus chased the money-changers out of God's house.)*

:: In this psalm, the person David described bore the reproaches or sins of others. What did Jesus do to bear our sins? *(Jesus took our sins on himself when he died on the cross.)*

:: Can we still have zeal for God's house today? *(Yes, we don't have the temple anymore, but God's Spirit lives in the lives of his people. All together, everyone who believes in Jesus make up the new temple of God. We call that new temple the Church, and Jesus is the head of the Church. So, to have zeal for God's house means that we show a strong love for God's church and a strong love for Jesus. By keeping sin out of our lives, we keep the temple clean. Saying no to sin is a great way to show zeal for God's house.)*

 Pray about It

Ask God to help you to believe in Jesus so you can become a part of God's temple too and have God live inside your heart!

Week 9

Nicodemus

Story 87 – *The Gospel Story Bible*

You will need a working flashlight and a dark place like a basement, a very large closet, or a room with all the blinds closed. Bring your children in and say that you have discovered something: the darkness hates the light. To show them what you mean, ask them to find the darkest place in the room. When they point it out to you, ask them to stand back and watch. Point the flashlight at the darkness and then turn it on. "Look," tell your children, "the darkness is gone. It hates the light."

Try this again giving the kids an opportunity to operate the flashlight. Explain to them that God's holiness—God's perfect, awesome goodness—is like the light, and our sin is like the darkness. Unless God changes our hearts to take away the darkness in them, our dark sinfulness could never stay in the light of his holiness.

Say, "This week, we will be learning that God has a name for how he changes our hearts, he calls it being born again. Because God is holy—that is, perfectly good without any sin at all—only those people who have been born again can go to heaven to be with him."

DAY ONE

Picture It

If you were going to play hide and seek, would you rather play in the daytime in a brightly lit room or at night in the dark? Most older kids would rather play at night when it is harder for people to find them. If you were playing hide and seek in the daytime, you could never hide by lying down on the living room sofa, for example. Your friends would see you in a second. But in the blackness of night, when it is hard to see, your friends could mistake your body on the couch for a line of pillows and pass right by. It is easier to hide at night in the darkness, and that is just what Nicodemus, the main character in our story, did. He could have gone to talk to Jesus in the daytime, but he didn't want anyone to see him talking to Jesus. That's why he went to him at night.

 Read John 3:1–8.

Think about It Some More

Like the other Pharisees and religious rulers in Jerusalem, Nicodemus was watching Jesus. Nicodemus, who probably saw or at least heard about Jesus' miracles, believed that Jesus was sent by God. Some of the other religious rulers thought Jesus was from the devil, but not Nicodemus. He knew that only someone sent by God could heal the sick and give sight to the blind. Yet Nicodemus wanted to know more, so he went to talk with Jesus face-to-face.

As a Pharisee, Nicodemus believed that to be accepted by God you had to be a good Israelite and avoid sinning. But Jesus told Nicodemus something very different. Jesus said that finding the way to God is like being born. It is not something you can do for yourself; it is something that happens to you. In this case, it is something God does by his Spirit. This was a new teaching for Nicodemus, one he wasn't so sure about. He realized that no one could make himself be born a second time, and that if Jesus' words were true, no one could work his way to heaven. Everyone would have to be born again by God.

Talk about It

:: Why did Nicodemus come to Jesus at night? *(Nicodemus did not want the other Pharisees to see that he was talking to Jesus, so he came at night when it was easier to hide and all the other Pharisees might be sleeping.)*

:: Jesus told Nicodemus that something had to happen before he could get into the kingdom of God. What was it that had to happen? *(Jesus said Nicodemus had to be born again.)*

:: Is being born again something we can do for ourselves, or does God need to do it for us? *(Only God can make a person born again.)*

:: What does God change about a person when he makes him born again? *(When God makes a person born again, he changes a sinful heart that wants to reject God into a worshiping heart that is forgiven and wants to please God.)*

 Pray about It

Think of someone you know who doesn't know God. Ask God to cause that person to be born again and be a part of God's kingdom.

DAY TWO

Remember It

What do you remember about yesterday's story? What do you think is going to happen today?

 Read John 3:9–15.

Think about It Some More

After hearing Jesus talk about being born again, Nicodemus was confused. All his life he'd been taught that a person had to be a Jew and keep the law to be saved and go to heaven. Now Jesus was saying that even if you did all that, you still could not get to heaven unless the Spirit of God made you born again.

To Nicodemus, the idea of being born again was a riddle. Surely Jesus couldn't be saying that it was up to God to save us—that we couldn't save ourselves. What Nicodemus didn't understand was that he was a sinner who needed to be saved from his sins, and that no matter how hard he tried he could not do that himself. Only God could save him.

To help Nicodemus understand, Jesus recalled the Old Testament story when God's people disobeyed and were bitten by snakes. The people could only be healed if they trusted God and looked at the bronze snake lifted high on a pole. Jesus continued by telling Nicodemus that the Son of Man would also be lifted up. He was giving Nicodemus a clue, pointing to the cross and how it is only by looking to Jesus that we can be saved. One day, Nicodemus would see Jesus lifted up on a cross and then he would better understand.

Talk about It

:: What story did Jesus tell Nicodemus from the Old Testament? *(Jesus told Nicodemus the story of the bronze serpent that Moses lifted up in the desert. See Numbers 21:4–9.)*

:: Jesus said that the Son of Man was going to be lifted up like the bronze snake was lifted up. Who is the Son of Man? *(The Son of Man is one of the names Jesus gave himself. So when Jesus said that the Son of Man must be lifted up, he meant that he was going to be lifted up.)*

:: How are we healed by looking to Jesus lifted up on the cross? *(Just as people in Moses' day were healed when they looked with faith up at the bronze snake on the pole, so we also are healed of our sin when we look with faith to Jesus on the cross and place our hope and trust in him.)*

 Pray about It

Pray and ask God to help each person in your family look to Jesus on the cross so they can be forgiven.

DAY THREE _____

Connect It to the Gospel

Today is the day we connect this week's Bible story to the gospel. The gospel is the life, death, and resurrection of Jesus for our salvation. Can anyone guess how our story this week looks forward to or back at the gospel?

 Read John 3:16–18.

Think about It Some More

John 3:16 is probably the most well-known verse in the whole Bible. Children in churches all over the world memorize this verse because it describes God's great love for us. God the Father gave us the greatest gift he could give: his only Son. But the Father didn't send Jesus just to visit or to be a good teacher: he sent his Son to die a terrible death in our place. We all deserve to be punished for our sin. But God loved us so much he gave his only Son to take that punishment for us, so that anyone who believes in Jesus and places his or her trust in him can be forgiven.

The verses that follow John 3:16 are important ones too. They give us a warning: those who refuse to believe and trust in Jesus will not be saved but will be punished for their sins. We all must choose. Either we believe and trust in Jesus and his work on the cross or we reject him and go our own way.

Talk about It

:: Why did God send his only Son to earth for us? *(God sent Jesus because he loved us. He sent Jesus to die in our place on the cross.)*

:: What do you have to do to be saved? *(You must believe in Jesus and trust that when he died on the cross he died to take away your sins.)*

:: What happens to the people who refuse to believe in Jesus? *(They will not be saved. They will be punished for their sins and for refusing God's wonderful gift.)*

 Pray about It

Pray for the folks you know who still are not trusting in Jesus and ask God to open their eyes to believe.

DAY FOUR _____

Remember It

What has God been teaching you this week through our Bible story?

 Read John 3:19–21.

Think about It Some More

Thieves love to do their stealing at night when it is easy to hide. They also like to wear black clothes so they blend into the darkness. Sin is like that: sin loves the darkness because that is where it can hide. When we are caught in a sin we will often try to keep it hidden by lying. Perhaps you can remember a time when you got caught in a sin and said, "No, Mom, I didn't do it." The reason we want to keep our sins hidden is so we don't get punished. But if we keep our sins secret, they grow bigger and bigger. It is only by exposing them and telling the truth that our sin shrivels up and dies.

John tells us that Jesus came into the world as light to expose our sin. God wants us to live in the light, not the darkness. God wants us to be free from sin. When we bring our sin out into the light and admit we did something wrong, we can be forgiven.

Talk about It

> KIDS, ask your parents if they can remember something sinful they kept hidden. Ask them why they wanted to keep it hidden.

(Parents, take the opportunity here to use an illustration from your own childhood that your children can connect to their lives. We want to make sure we help them understand that we are not perfect, we still at times walk in darkness, and we still need Jesus to help us walk in the light, just like they do.)

:: Why does our sin like the darkness? *(Sin can hide in the darkness. In the same way that a robber wants to do his stealing at night, we try to keep our sins hidden.)*

:: What does God want us to do with our secret, hidden sins? *(God wants us to bring them out into the light. That means to confess them. When we confess our sins and ask Jesus to forgive us and save us, he will. But if we keep our sins hidden and pretend that we don't have them, we are not trusting in Jesus, we are trusting in ourselves.)*

 Pray about It

Ask God to help you bring all your sins out into the light by confessing them and asking Jesus to forgive you and change you.

DAY FIVE _____

Discover It

Today is the day we look at a different Bible passage—from the book of Psalms or one of the prophets—to see what we can learn from it about Jesus or our salvation.

Read Isaiah 60:1–5.

Think about It Some More

Long before Jesus had his talk with Nicodemus, God spoke through the prophet Isaiah and foretold a day when God would send his people a great light. The light would come to shine in the darkness of sin and call people from every nation into the light. In that day, when God revealed his wonderful light, people would be very excited.

Nicodemus was a Pharisee and would have read the book of Isaiah and known that Isaiah talked about this. You can imagine how curious Nicodemus would have been when Jesus said to him that the light had now come into the world.

Later, Jesus told the scribes and Pharisees, "I am the light of the world. Whoever follows me will not walk in darkness, but will have the light of life" (John 8:12). It could be that Nicodemus was there that day to hear Jesus too. In the end, Nicodemus trusted his life to Jesus. John tells us that after Jesus died it was Nicodemus who came to help take care of his body (John 19:39), giving us a clue that he believed and became a follower of Jesus.

Talk about It

:: Who is the light of the world Isaiah said was going to come one day? *(Jesus is the light of the world.)*

:: What does the darkness stand for? *(The darkness stands for sin and evil.)*

:: Who did God say was going to come into the light? *(Parents, if your children are nonreaders, read the Isaiah passage again and have them raise their hands when they hear you say the correct answer. If you have really young children, you can change the inflection of your voice to give them a clue. Verse 3 tells us that all nations will come into God's light, which is a repeat of God's promise to bless all nations through the children of Abraham.)*

Pray about It

Thank God for sending Jesus to be the light of the world.

Week 10

Good News

Story 88 – *The Gospel Story Bible*

Purchase a container of ice cream, a can of whipped cream, and several toppings to make ice cream sundaes for your family for dessert, but keep it a secret from your children. Sometime before dinner on the day you want to serve the ice cream, tell your youngest child (if he is capable of delivering a message) to pass on some good news to the rest of the family. Tell him to run to the others and say, "I have good news for you." Then he is to tell them about the ice cream and all the toppings. If you have one child, have him or her announce it to your spouse.

After dinner, have this child make another announcement. Have him say, "Attention everyone, I have good news. It is time for ice cream." Once you have served the ice cream, tell your children the purpose behind the ice cream announcement. Say, "This week we will be learning about the 'good news' that Jesus brought." As you enjoy your ice cream ask, "Can anyone guess what Jesus' good news was?"

DAY ONE

Picture It

Imagine that Dad was in the army reserves and was sent to fight in a very large battle. What would it be like to wait for news of the battle? Picture how carefully you would listen when an update on the war was broadcast on the news. Imagine the reporter saying, "One hour ago our army attacked the enemy and won a great victory. The enemy is fleeing; no one from our army was killed." Don't you think everyone in your family would be jumping up and down over the good news you'd heard?

Listen carefully to our Scripture passage today to hear the good news Jesus announced to those listening to his teaching in the synagogue.

 Read Luke 4:14–21.

Think about It Some More

If you could not find the words *good news* in today's Bible passage, don't be concerned. Some Bibles say *good news* while other Bibles use the word *gospel* instead. But they both mean the same thing. The word *gospel* means "good news." So, whether your Bible says, "the Spirit…has anointed me to proclaim good news" or "the Spirit has anointed me to proclaim the gospel," it is saying the same thing.

Isaiah saw a day in the future when God would send a messenger to bring the good news of the gospel. Jesus told everyone listening that he was that messenger sent by God. Soon Jesus would heal the blind so that they could see and set others free who were oppressed by demons. When Isaiah wrote his prophecy, he was writing about Jesus.

Talk about It

:: From which book of the Bible did Jesus read on the Sabbath? *(Jesus read from the book of Isaiah.)*

:: What does the word *gospel* mean? *(The word* gospel *means "good news.")*

:: Can you remember any of the things Isaiah said the servant sent by God would do? *(Parents, if your children cannot remember, reread Luke 4:18–19 and then have them answer the question, for the answer is a simple repeat of those verses.)*

:: What did Jesus do every Sabbath? *(Jesus went to the synagogue, which is a lot like us going to church.)*

 Pray about It

Thank God for sending Jesus to bring us the good news of the gospel.

DAY TWO

Remember It

What do you remember about yesterday's story? What do you think is going to happen today?

 Read Luke 4:22–30.

Think about It Some More

As long as Jesus taught them what they wanted to hear, the people of Nazareth loved listening to him. But Jesus knew they were not ready to believe and follow him. Jesus knew the Jews were going to reject him and send him to die on a cross. That is why Jesus reminded them about the past and how Israel had rejected God's prophets. And when Israel rejected God's prophets, God blessed people outside of Israel. When Israel rejected Elijah, God sent him to a Sidonian widow. When Israel rejected Elisha, God healed a Syrian man. But instead of hearing Jesus' warning, the people became so angry that they tried to kill Jesus. In the end, they rejected Jesus just as the people of Israel had rejected God's prophets long ago.

Talk about It

:: When the people got angry, what did they try to do to Jesus? *(They tried to kill him by throwing him off a cliff.)*

:: How did Jesus escape? *(It wasn't time for Jesus to die, so he just slipped away.)*

:: Why did Jesus allow himself to be crucified when clearly he could have escaped like he did in today's story? *(The Bible tells us that Jesus could have called angels down to rescue him, but didn't so that he could die in our place taking the punishment we deserve for our sin. That is why the Bible tells us that Jesus gave up his life for us.)*

 Pray about It

Pray and ask God to help you to believe and trust in Jesus and not reject him as they did in Nazareth.

DAY THREE _____

Connect It to the Gospel

Today is the day we connect this week's Bible story to the gospel. The gospel is the life, death, and resurrection of Jesus for our salvation. Can anyone guess how our story this week looks forward to or back at the gospel?

 Read Luke 4:31–37.

Think about It Some More

The people of Nazareth who tried to throw Jesus off a cliff didn't realize that he was the one God had sent to save them. But the demon who possessed the man in the next town knew exactly who Jesus was. He called Jesus the Holy One of God. He knew that Jesus was more than a man—he knew that Jesus was God. When Jesus read from the scroll of Isaiah, he said that he had come to set free those who were oppressed and held prisoner. That is exactly what he did for the man with the demon.

Even though we are not all possessed by demons, Jesus came to set us free too. For we are all held prisoner by the power of sin. Because Jesus is a man, Jesus could die in our place and take the punishment we deserve for our sin. Because he is God and never did anything wrong, Jesus won a victory over death and rose again on the third day. Now, if we believe in Jesus and what he did for us, we can be set free from sin and live with God forever in heaven.

Talk about It

:: What did the demon call Jesus? *(The demon called Jesus the Holy One of God.)*

:: What did Jesus do to the demon? *(Jesus told him to be quiet and then commanded the demon to come out of the man.)*

:: *(The people of Capernaum were amazed by Jesus' teaching and that he had the authority to drive out demons. Ask your children to tell you what most amazes them about Jesus.)*

:: What did Jesus do to set us free? *(Jesus died on the cross to set us free from the power of sin and to take the punishment we deserve for our sin.)*

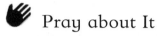 Pray about It

Praise God for sending Jesus to set captives free from demons and to set us free from the power of sin.

DAY FOUR _____

Remember It

What has God been teaching you this week through our Bible story?

 Read Luke 4:38–44.

Think about It Some More

Once word spread that Jesus had healed a man with a demon, people who were sick came from all around to find Jesus. They tracked him to Simon's house, where Jesus was visiting. Once again the demons shouted out. This time they called him the Son of God. They knew that Jesus was the Christ, the one God the Father had sent to rescue his people.

The name *Christ* means "Messiah" or "God's anointed one." The word *anointed* comes from Old Testament. Back in the early days of Israel, God sent the prophet Samuel to anoint one of Jesse's sons as king. After looking at all the sons, Samuel chose David and anointed him with oil, pouring it on his head to show he was the one God had chosen. Jesus is called the "Christ" (the anointed one) because he is God and because he is the one whom God chose to be king and save his people.

Talk about It

> 🌑 🌑 KIDS, ask your parents if they have ever preached
> 🌑 🌑 the good news.

(Parents, recount a time when you shared the gospel with someone, e.g., a coworker, a friend, or a neighbor.)

:: What did Jesus do for Simon's mother-in-law? *(She was sick and Jesus healed her.)*

:: What did the demon call Jesus? *(The demon called Jesus the Son of God.)*

:: Jesus is also called "Christ" in the Bible. What does the name *Christ* mean? *(The name* Christ *means anointed one or God's chosen one. Jesus was God the Father's chosen one to save his people from their sin.)*

 Pray about It

Thank God for sending his Son, Jesus, as the anointed one to save us from our sins.

DAY FIVE

Discover It

Today is the day we look at a different Bible passage—from the book of Psalms or one of the prophets—to see what we can learn from it about Jesus or our salvation.

 Read Ezekiel 37:24–28.

Think about It Some More

The first line of this prophecy of Ezekiel seems to be talking about King David, but when you read on, you discover that Ezekiel isn't talking about King David after all; he is talking about Jesus. Ezekiel said in verse 25 that David would be the prince of Israel forever. David died a long time before Ezekiel wrote this prophecy, so we know Ezekiel was not talking about him. But Jesus, one of David's far-off great-grandchildren, is still alive today and is King of Israel in heaven and will be king forever and ever. Jesus is whom Ezekiel was talking about.

And there is more about Jesus in this passage. If you keep the story of Jesus in mind when you read what the prophets wrote, you will see that they gave all kinds of clues about Jesus to the people of Israel. Jesus is the one who made a covenant or a promise of peace. He did that when he died on the cross for our sins. Before that, we didn't have peace with God because we deserved to be punished for our sins. But when Jesus died in our place and took our punishment upon himself, he made a way for us to have peace with God.

Talk about It

:: Why can't Ezekiel's prophecy be about King David? *(King David had already died, so he couldn't be the prince Ezekiel was writing about.)*

:: Who is Ezekiel writing about when he says, "David my servant shall be their prince forever"? *(Ezekiel is writing about Jesus, one of King David's far-off great-grandsons. King David's life pointed forward to Jesus.)*

:: This prophecy tells us that God will dwell or live with his people. How did Jesus' coming to earth make this prophecy come true? *(Since Jesus was God, when he came to earth to live with us he kept the promise of this prophecy. But that is not all. When we believe in Jesus he puts his Spirit into our hearts to live with us, and when we go to heaven we will be living with him there too. So you see, Jesus made a way for God to live with his people.)*

:: What did Jesus do to make a way for us to have peace with God? *(Parents, the answer to this question is, "Jesus died on the cross," but your children may not understand the real answer. Explain to them that God is angry with sin because it is wrong. Since we are sinners, God's anger is against us, so he must punish us. When Jesus died on the cross, God poured out his holy anger for our sin against Jesus. Jesus took all of God's anger until there was no more left. Now, even though we are still sinners, we can have peace with God.)*

 Pray about It

Thank Jesus for taking our punishment so that we could have peace with God the Father and live forever with him in heaven.

Week 11

The Miraculous Catch

Story 89 – *The Gospel Story Bible*

Purchase a large bag of goldfish snack crackers or pretzels. Gather your children and tell them to pretend their hand is a net and you are going to drop a fish in it. Then take the box of goldfish or pretzels and dump so many into their hands that they cannot hold them all. They will be shocked and surprised. Give them a plate or cup to collect their "catch," and then sit down to go over the story of the miraculous catch of fish while they snack on their crackers.

DAY ONE _____

Picture It

Imagine for a moment that Jesus came to earth in your lifetime, met you, and said, "Come follow me." What would you need to leave behind to follow Jesus? Make a list of your five most precious possessions and decide which one would be the most difficult to leave. Even though Jesus is not physically walking on earth, he still calls us through the Bible to leave the riches of the world to follow and serve him.

God will call some of us to make big sacrifices to follow and serve Jesus. Many pastors, for instance, make far less money serving the church than they could earn running a business. Others leave jobs to travel to foreign lands to preach the gospel or to translate the Bible into other languages. So whether we are called to love God more than the treasures of this world or if God calls us to travel far away from the comforts of home, we are all called to give something up to follow Jesus.

 Read John 1:40–51.

Think about It Some More

After his baptism, Jesus began to teach and call men to follow him. Some of the men whom Jesus called were so excited they had to go and tell their family and friends. When Andrew met Jesus, he went to get his brother Simon Peter. When Philip met Jesus, he went to get his friend Nathaniel. This still happens today. When God opens our eyes to see that Jesus is more than a teacher—that Jesus is the Son of God—we want to tell everyone we know all about him. Most of the people who join the church today come in because a friend told them about Jesus.

Talk about It

:: What did Andrew and Philip both do once they realized that Jesus was the Messiah, the one God sent to deliver his people? *(Both Andrew and Philip told someone about Jesus.)*

:: What two words did Jesus speak to Philip when he invited him to become one of his followers—one of his disciples? *(Jesus simply said, "Follow me.")*

:: What do you think Philip's and Andrew's other friends and family members must have thought when they said they were leaving their jobs to follow Jesus? Remember, Jesus didn't agree to pay them. *(Parents, draw out your children here and help them understand that their family may have thought it a little hard to believe. After all, where would they get money to live?)*

:: When was the last time you told somebody about Jesus? *(Parents, answer this question first for yourself, then create a family plan to reach out to a friend or neighbor and invite them to church or over for dinner so you can talk about Jesus.)*

 Pray about It

Ask God to help you follow Jesus and tell everyone about him.

DAY TWO _____

Remember It

What do you remember about yesterday's story? What do you think is going to happen today?

 Read Luke 5:1–9.

Think about It Some More

Even though Peter (called by his other name, Simon, in Luke) had already met Jesus (John 1:35–42), he didn't yet realize that Jesus was God. He probably thought Jesus was like any other man. That is why, when Jesus told him to throw out his nets again, he wasn't very excited. He must have thought, *What does a rabbi know about fishing?* But when the net came in bursting full of fish, Peter saw that Jesus was not just any other man—he was sent from God. That made Peter think of all his sins and all the ways he had not followed God. That is why he asked Jesus to leave. He thought he didn't deserve to be around Jesus because Jesus demonstrated God's power, and Peter knew that he was a sinful man.

Talk about It

:: How many fish do you think Simon Peter caught? *(The Bible doesn't tell us, but it will be fun for your children to guess. Likely it was in the hundreds. In a similar account in John 21:11, they caught 153 fish. So it is likely that they caught a similar amount this time.)*

:: Peter had fished all night and caught nothing. How was it that he caught so many fish when he obeyed Jesus? *(Either Jesus knew the fish were there or he commanded them to swim into their nets. Either way, Peter's nets were filled by the power of God.)*

:: Why did Peter fall to his knees and tell Jesus to go away? *(Peter knew that he was a sinner, and he saw that Jesus had come from God. He was so convicted of his sin that he felt he didn't deserve to be with Jesus.)*

:: What if you were Peter? What sins from your own life would you be thinking about? *(Parents, help your children to realize that we are all like Peter: we are all sinners. When we read this story we might assume from his reaction that Peter had done something more terrible than we have. That would be a mistake. Peter was ashamed of his sin as we would be if we stood face-to-face with Jesus in all his holiness and power.)*

 ## Pray about It

Confess one of your sins and ask God to forgive you and help you to follow him. *(Parents, be sure to lead in this time of confession and help your younger children remember something they can confess too.)*

DAY THREE

Connect It to the Gospel

Today is the day we connect this week's Bible story to the gospel. The gospel is the life, death, and resurrection of Jesus for our salvation. Can anyone guess how our story this week looks forward to or back at the gospel?

 Read Luke 5:10.

Think about It Some More

When Peter saw the incredible amount of fish in the nets, he knew Jesus was no ordinary man, and he fell to his knees confessing that he was a sinner. But instead of bringing judgment upon Peter and punishing him for his sins, Jesus told Peter not to be afraid, for he would be catching men from now on. Jesus knew that soon he was going to die on the cross for Peter's sins and, after his resurrection, return to heaven. After all of that had happened, Peter preached to a large crowd. After he spoke, about three thousand people turned away from their sins and believed in Jesus. That catch of people would match this catch of fish (see Acts 2:41).

Talk about It

:: Why was Peter afraid? *(Peter saw the power of God at work in Jesus' life in the catching of the fish. Because he was a sinner, he became afraid.)*

:: What two things did Jesus say to Peter? *(This is a simple repeat of the verse, but it will help your children remember what Jesus said. If your children can't read, go ahead and repeat the verse and have them raise their hands when they hear something that Jesus said.)*

:: What did Jesus mean when he said that Peter would catch men instead of fish? *(Jesus meant that Peter would be telling people about Jesus and bringing them into the church.)*

 ## Pray about It

Thank God for the way he is reaching out to sinners like you and me much as he did to Peter two thousand years ago. God calls us and gives us the grace to believe. He forgives us of our sins. Then he makes all of us fishers of men as we tell others about Jesus.

DAY FOUR _____

Remember It
What has God been teaching you this week through our Bible story?

 Read Luke 5:11.

Think about It Some More
Although the verse we read is a short one, it is incredible to think that Peter, James, and John left everything to follow Jesus. Imagine leaving your fishing business and the biggest catch of fish you have ever seen in your life to follow a wandering teacher with no job and no place to live. Of course, Jesus was more than a wandering teacher—he was the Messiah sent by God! One day he would be king and sit on David's throne. So the disciples may have thought following Jesus wasn't such a bad idea. But what they didn't know was that Jesus was not going to become an earthly king with treasures of silver and gold for them to share. Jesus *would* be king, but Jesus' throne is in heaven. On earth he would be rejected by his own people, arrested, found guilty, and crucified.

Talk about It

> KIDS, ask your parents if they can think of something they gave up to follow Jesus.

(Parents, think of some of the attractions of the world that you gave up when you decided to follow Jesus.)

:: What did Peter, James, and John leave when Jesus called them to follow him? *(They left everything to follow Jesus.)*

:: Why would men leave their fishing business to follow Jesus? *(They believed that Jesus was the Messiah, the one sent by God to deliver Israel.)*

:: The early disciples called Jesus the King of Israel. If Jesus really did become an earthly king over Israel, what do you think they would get out of it? *(Parents, help your children here with some clues. Our text today does not give the answer. But earlier in the week, on Monday, we learned that Nathaniel called Jesus the King of Israel. Jesus' followers might have thought that if Jesus became the earthly king of Israel, they might get rich along with him. But what they didn't know was that Jesus came to be a different kind of king: a heavenly King. The disciples did get rich, but not with earthly gold and silver.)*

 Pray about It

Ask Jesus to help you leave anything you love more than him—your toys, your friends, or even your family so that you can follow and obey him.

DAY FIVE _____

Discover It

Today is the day we look at a different Bible passage—from the book of Psalms or one of the prophets—to see what we can learn from it about Jesus or our salvation.

 Read Isaiah 43:8–13.

Think about It Some More

Long before Jesus started his ministry on earth and called the disciples to follow him, Isaiah spoke about his coming. Isaiah, inspired by the Holy Spirit, foretold a day when the blind would see and the deaf would hear. Isaiah told of a day when the Lord would choose witnesses who would believe in the only Savior. Well, Jesus is the only Savior, and he chose a dozen men to follow him and become witnesses of all that he did and taught. They watched as Jesus made the blind to see and the deaf to hear. Even more, Jesus came to open the eyes and ears of our hearts so that we would believe in him.

Talk about It

:: What is a witness? *(A witness is someone who sees something happen and then can tell others about it.)*

:: Why did Jesus call disciples to be his witnesses? *(After Jesus returns to heaven God uses these witnesses to tell everyone about Jesus.)*

:: What do verses 10 and 11 say about God? *(Parents, if your children are not strong readers yet, you can read these verses and have them raise their hands when they hear the correct answer. These verses tell us that no other gods came before the one true God and that there is no Savior other than our Lord.)*

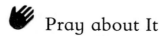 Pray about It

Praise God that he alone is God, and that Jesus alone is our Savior.

Week 12

Jesus Heals the Paralyzed Man

Story 90 – *The Gospel Story Bible*

For this exercise you will need two boxes, one large and one small. Fill the larger one with packing foam so that it is very light, and fill the smaller one with books, bricks, or other heavy items. Tell your children that you want to know which box looks easier to lift, the large one or the smaller one. They should say the smaller box looks easier to lift. Then have them try to lift both boxes. They should be surprised at how heavy the small one is. Explain that this week in our story Jesus forgave a crippled man of his sin and healed him.

The Pharisees probably thought it was easier to say, "Your sins are forgiven" than to say "You are healed," because everyone would be able to see whether or not the man was actually healed; no one would be able to see whether or not his sins were forgiven. Jesus saying that the crippled man's sins were forgiven may have looked easy— like the smaller box looked light—but that forgiveness cost Jesus his life. Say, "This week we will learn how Jesus both healed the paralyzed man and forgave his sins."

DAY ONE

Picture It

A father was visiting Disney World with his children who wanted to see some of the Disney characters. But when they went to the place where Goofy and Donald Duck were supposed to be, there was such a large crowd that they couldn't see them. The same thing happened with Snow White. So the dad came up with a plan. Instead of trying to fight the crowd at the place where Winnie the Pooh was scheduled to be, he looked for the secret path that Pooh would have to walk on to get to the greeting place. Once he found the path, he took his children there and waited. In a little while, right on schedule, Winnie the Pooh came walking down the path right toward them. All the children got to meet Pooh, in spite of the large crowd.

In our story today, there was such a large crowd around Jesus that a crippled man couldn't get near him. Let's see how his friends found a way to get around the crowd so he could meet Jesus.

 Read Luke 5:17–20.

Think about It Some More

Did you notice who was gathered to hear Jesus in the story you just read? It wasn't the local town folk or even the disciples. In this story the religious rulers came to check Jesus out. They must have organized themselves after hearing all about the healing and teaching Jesus was doing, for so many of them came that the crippled man could not get close to Jesus. His friends carried him up on the roof of the house.

How would you have liked to have been the crippled man up on the roof? I'll bet he was pretty nervous. Then, after they'd ripped a hole in the roof and lowered their friend, Jesus said something they didn't expect. Instead of saying "Rise up and walk," Jesus said something even more powerful: "Your sins are forgiven."

Talk about It

:: Who was crowded in the house to see Jesus? *(Religious rulers were gathered to see Jesus.)*

:: Why do you think the religious rulers came to see Jesus? *(It was their job to check out new teachers to be sure no one was spreading false teaching. They all came to listen to Jesus to see just what kind of a teacher he was.)*

:: Why did the men have to lower the crippled man through the roof? *(The house was too crowded for the crippled man to get in any other way, so he had to be lowered through the roof.)*

:: Jesus first said to the crippled man, "Your sins are forgiven." Why is that even better than Jesus saying, "Get up and walk"? *(Having legs that work improved his life on earth, but having his sins forgiven meant that he could look forward to living in heaven with God forever and ever.)*

 Pray about It

Praise God for forgiving the crippled man's sins.

DAY TWO

Remember It

What do you remember about yesterday's story? What do you think is going to happen today?

 Read Luke 5:21–23.

Think about It Some More

One of the things this story teaches us is that you can't hide your sins from God. When the crippled man was lowered through the roof, Jesus told him his sins were forgiven. That means Jesus knew what his sins were. Then, when Jesus forgave the sins of the crippled man, the Pharisees questioned him in their minds. They didn't think Jesus had the power to forgive sins. But Jesus knew what they were thinking; he knew they didn't believe in him.

If Jesus knew the sins of the crippled man and the thoughts of the Pharisees, he knows our sins and thoughts too. We might be able to hide our sins from other people, but we can't hide them from God.

Talk about It

:: How did Jesus know what the religious rulers were thinking? Did someone tell him? *(No one told Jesus. He knew what they were thinking because he is God and knows our thoughts.)*

:: Jesus asked the religious rulers whether it was harder to forgive the man's sins or to heal his legs and enable him to walk. Which one do you think the religious rulers thought was harder? *(Anyone can say your sins are forgiven. Even a fake can say that, because you can't see if a person's sins are forgiven. But if you say to a crippled man, rise up and walk, everyone can see if he is healed or not. If you are a fake, everyone will know because the man will not be able to walk.)*

:: Why can't we hide our sins from God? *(Just as Jesus knew the religious rulers' thoughts, God sees and knows all we do and all we think.)*

 Pray about It

Ask God to help you live for him and not try to hide your sin.

DAY THREE _____

Connect It to the Gospel

Today is the day we connect this week's Bible story to the gospel. The gospel is the life, death, and resurrection of Jesus for our salvation. Can anyone guess how our story this week looks forward to or back at the gospel?

 Read Luke 5:24–26.

Think about It Some More

It is interesting to see what happened after Jesus healed the crippled man. The paralytic left that place praising God, and everyone, including the religious rulers, gave praise to God. Perhaps they thought that Jesus was a prophet, for prophets like Elijah had sometimes healed people. If they did think that, they would be correct. Jesus was a prophet, for he came to speak the word of God.

But Jesus was more than a prophet. Jesus did something the prophets of old never did: he forgave sins. What the religious rulers didn't realize was that Jesus was God. Jesus could forgive the sins of the crippled man because he was going to take the man's sins upon himself when he died on the cross. By taking the punishment for the crippled man, Jesus had the power to say, "Your sins are forgiven."

Talk about It

:: Why did the religious rulers glorify (praise) God? *(They were amazed by the crippled man's healing. Even though they didn't realize Jesus was God, they knew that only God could heal a crippled man.)*

:: What did the paralyzed man do after Jesus healed him? *(He went home praising God.)*

:: Pretend you are the healed man when he got home and act out what he told his family. *(Parents, this is a great exercise to prompt your children to retell the story.)*

:: What can you do this week to draw near to God? *(Parents, help your children think of ways to draw near to God, like reading their Bible and spending time in prayer.)*

 Pray about It

Praise Jesus for dying on the cross for the crippled man's sins and for your sins too. Ask him to help you draw near to him.

DAY FOUR _____

Remember It

What has God been teaching you this week through our Bible story?

 Read Matthew 9:1–8.

Think about It Some More

This story is very similar to the story about the crippled man who was lowered through the roof. Once again there were religious leaders, called *scribes*, present. And like our last story, Jesus knew what was in their hearts. That is why he told the man, "Your sins are forgiven." He knew the scribes would not like that. They thought Jesus was *blaspheming*. That is a big word that means they thought he was showing God disrespect by pretending he could do something that only God could do—in this case, forgiving a person's sins.

But what the scribes didn't know was that Jesus *was* God. They also didn't know that Jesus was going to die on the cross for the paralyzed man and all those who place their trust in Christ so that their sins could be forgiven.

Talk about It

> KIDS, ask your parents what it felt like for them when they first realized that Jesus forgave them for their sins.

(Parents, this is an opportunity to talk to your children about your testimony. Even if you have shared it before, tell it again.)

∷ Why did the religious rulers think Jesus was blaspheming—showing disrespect to—God? *(They knew that only God could forgive sins and that it was wrong for any man to claim to do the things that only God could do. What they didn't know was that Jesus was God.)*

∷ Besides healing the man in our story, what did Jesus do to prove that he was God? *(Jesus fulfilled prophecy by healing—by making the blind to see and the lame to walk. He even raised some from the dead. Also, he controlled the forces of nature.)*

Pray about It

Ask God to help you believe that Jesus is more than a teacher—he is God.

DAY FIVE _____

Discover It

Today is the day we look at a different Bible passage—from the book of Psalms or one of the prophets—to see what we can learn from it about Jesus or our salvation.

Read Psalm 119:97–104.

Think about It Some More

If you were to read all of Psalm 119 you would see that this psalm is one long praise about God's Word. To follow what it says, you would have to love God's Word perfectly all the time. Now we know that we are supposed to love God's Word perfectly all the time, but because of sin we fail. There is only one person who ever loved God's Word perfectly all the time, and his name was Jesus. Jesus is the only one who always obeyed God's law and never sinned. Jesus is the only one who meditated on (thought about) God's Word all day long, and Jesus is the only one who kept all of God's rules. The exciting part is that Jesus lived a perfect life in our place. We should all try to love God's Word perfectly, but where we fall short we should look to Jesus.

Talk about It

:: Who is the only person who was able to follow perfectly the verses we read today from Psalm 119? *(Jesus followed these verses perfectly.)*

:: Can you remember how Jesus demonstrated his love for God's Word? *(Jesus never sinned, but kept the law perfectly. He was often in the temple reading and preaching from God's law. Jesus answered Satan's temptations by quoting Scripture.)*

:: Why do you think God gave us this psalm? *(Parents, draw out your children here. By reading about the perfect way to love God's Word we can learn ways that we can grow in our love for God's Word.)*

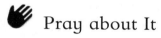 Pray about It

Ask God to help you be like Jesus who loved God's Word perfectly.

Week 13

The Sermon on the Mount—The Beatitudes

Story 91 – *The Gospel Story Bible*

Purchase two bags of pretzels, one with salt and another without salt. (You may substitute another food whose flavor benefits from saltiness, e.g., eggs, popcorn, French fries, etc.) Give each of your children a pretzel without salt and ask them to tell you how they like it. Then give them a pretzel with salt and ask them to describe the difference. Now let them try it again. Then explain that salt enhances the flavor of food; it makes it taste better. God calls Christians the salt of the earth. Say, "This week we will learn about the Beatitudes and how living for Jesus can touch the lives of people all around us."

DAY ONE

Picture It

Imagine that your mom's boss gave her four free club box tickets to a professional baseball game. Normally when you go to the game you can afford only the cheapest tickets, for seats that are far away in the outfield, and you have to bring your own snacks. But these tickets give you the best of the best—and everything is free.

When you arrive you get free parking close to the stadium. All the ushers greet you with a smile, give you free hats, and wipe the dust off your seats. You also can have all the free food and drinks you want. The best part of all is watching a perfect no-hitter baseball game with your team getting a home run in every inning! From the first pitch to the last pitch all you do is cheer and celebrate.

In some ways, that experience is a little like heaven. Our Bible passage today talks about heaven. In heaven, the last will be first, the poor will be rich, and the weak will be strong!

 Read Matthew 5:1–12.

Think about It Some More

Each beatitude has two parts. The first part describes life here on earth, and the second part describes life in God's kingdom. If you put all the second parts of the verses together, you get a wonderful description of what it will be like to be with Jesus in heaven and enjoy his kingdom. In the kingdom of heaven, we will be comforted, inherit the earth, be satisfied, receive mercy, and see God. We will be called the children of God and receive a great reward. Now that is something to look forward to.

You might think that to get to heaven a person must be strong and confident and a hard worker. But that is not what Jesus taught. You see, we are weak and poor in spirit, and none of us can make it to heaven on our own strength or by our good works. It is only by trusting in Jesus and what he did on the cross that we can get there.

Talk about It

:: Can you tell me one of the Beatitudes? *(Parents, see if your children can repeat one of the Beatitudes. If they can't, give them the first half and see if they can supply the second half.)*

:: What is the kingdom of God (heaven) going to be like? *(Parents, see if your children can remember some of what Jesus said the kingdom of heaven is going to be like from the second half of these verses.)*

:: Jesus said that some would be persecuted. What does *persecuted* mean? (Persecuted *is a word that describes when people are treated badly for something they believe. Christians can be persecuted for believing in Jesus. They can be beaten or even killed for their faith. Jesus says that if you are persecuted here on earth because of your faith, he will reward you in heaven.)*

 Pray about It

Ask God to help you trust in Jesus and not yourself to get to heaven.

DAY TWO

Remember It

What do you remember about yesterday's story? What do you think is going to happen today?

 Read Matthew 5:13–16.

Think about It Some More

It is difficult to tell one soldier from the next when they are all wearing the same uniform because they all look alike. But what if one soldier were wearing a white uniform while the others were dressed in green? That soldier would stand out. In our Bible passage today, Jesus taught that Christians are supposed to stand out and be different because of the way they live. When everyone is unkind, Christians should be kind. When everyone lives for themselves, Christians should live to serve others. By living like Jesus lived, we shine the light of Jesus on others.

When people notice our lives and ask us why we are different, we get to tell them all about Jesus. Jesus said it's like being salt. We know that salt makes food taste better. If you set out five bowls of potato chips at a party, but only one of them is salty, people will soon discover that the salted chips taste better. They would want to keep coming back to the bowl with the salted potato chips. In the same way, when we treat others with the love of Jesus, they will want to be around us and find out why we live godly lives. Again, that is when we get to tell them about Jesus.

Talk about It

:: Who is the light in our hearts that we are supposed to shine forth so others can see? *(Jesus is the light in our hearts.)*

:: What kinds of things can we do to shine that light? *(If you go back to the Beatitudes you can see some of the things we can do. We can be humble or meek, merciful, peacemaking, and thirsty for righteousness. When we live like that in a sinful world, people will notice. Then we can tell them about Jesus.)*

:: Can you think of a good work you could do for others this week so that they might see your light and glorify God? *(Parents, help your children to see that they can be a light right in their own family. When they treat one another kindly or when they respect their parents they are being lights. When others see your family loving one another they will want to know why your family is different from everyone else. Then you can tell them about Jesus.)*

 Pray about It

Pray and ask God to help you be a light right in your own home.

DAY THREE _____

Connect It to the Gospel

Today is the day we connect this week's Bible story to the gospel. The gospel is the life, death, and resurrection of Jesus for our salvation. Can anyone guess how our story this week looks forward to or back at the gospel?

 Read Matthew 5:17–20.

Think about It Some More

How good do you think you are? If you were grading yourself on a scale of 1–10, with 10 being perfect, what score would you give yourself? Very few people would say they were a perfect 10, but many of us would say we are pretty high on the scale, maybe a 7 or 8.

The religious rulers of Jesus' day, the scribes and Pharisees, were like that. They thought they were pretty good because they did a lot of good things. But Jesus warned that they were not good enough to get to heaven. Jesus said that if we want to get to heaven we would have to be more righteous than the scribes and Pharisees were. Even though the Pharisees were good at keeping the law on the outside, they were still sinners on the inside and needed Jesus to rescue them from their sins. Sadly, many of them thought they were good enough on their own and didn't need Jesus.

Talk about It

:: How well did the Pharisees keep the law? *(The Pharisees were very good at keeping the law on the outside, but they still struggled with sin on the inside.)*

:: Why couldn't the Pharisees go to heaven? *(The Pharisees kept the law, but they still had sin in their hearts. They needed to be perfect both on the outside and on the inside to get to heaven.)*

:: Who is the only one who kept all of God's law perfectly, all of the time? *(Jesus)*

:: How can we go to heaven? *(Jesus lived a perfect life in our place. When we believe in Jesus and place our faith in him, Jesus makes a wonderful trade: he takes our sins away and gives us his perfect obedience, his righteousness. We go to heaven based on what Jesus did, not based on what we did.)*

 Pray about It

Thank Jesus for living a perfectly righteous life for us so we could have a righteousness greater than the good works of the Pharisees.

DAY FOUR

Remember It

What has God been teaching you this week through our Bible story?

 Read Matthew 5:21–26.

Think about It Some More

Jesus knew he was going to have to help the scribes and Pharisees understand that they were sinners, for they thought that as long as they kept the commandments on the outside they were perfect, like God. But Jesus knew that even if you didn't murder someone you could still be sinning by being angry at them in your thoughts. That is why Jesus told the crowd that if they had anger in their hearts against someone they were committing murder in their hearts, breaking God's commandment.

Jesus wanted to teach the religious rulers that no one can obey God's commandments perfectly. Once you realize that keeping the law means you can't sin in your thoughts at all, you realize that it is impossible for any of us to keep the law. A true disciple of Jesus is one who realizes he can't be righteous (perfectly good) by his own good works and trusts in the good work of Jesus, who lived a perfect life in our place and gives us his righteousness when we believe.

Talk about It

> ● ● KIDS, ask your parents if they ever sinned by
> ● ● being angry in their hearts.

(Parents, this is a great opportunity to help your children understand that you are a sinner and need Jesus just as they do. By confessing your own sin and need for Jesus, you will make it easier for them to confess theirs and understand that they need Jesus too.)

:: *(All of us are guilty of sinful anger.)*

:: *(We have no hope of keeping God's rules ourselves. Our only hope is in Jesus, who kept all of God's law in our place and gives us his perfect obedience when we believe and trust in him.)*

:: Can you think of a time when you were angry and sinned? *(Parents, help your children here. It is important for all of us to realize we are guilty of breaking God's commands.)*

 Pray about It

Confess your anger to God and ask him to forgive you and help you to trust in Jesus, who obeyed all of God's laws all of the time.

DAY FIVE _____

Discover It

Today is the day we look at a different Bible passage—from the book of Psalms or one of the prophets—to see what we can learn from it about Jesus or our salvation.

 Read Isaiah 55:1–13.

Think about It Some More

Do you remember what the demons called Jesus before he cast them out? (If not, go back and read Luke 4:34.) That's right, the demons called Jesus the Holy One of God. Here in this prophecy, Isaiah talks about the Holy One of Israel (v. 5)—he is talking about Jesus. Isaiah said that there would come a day when people who were hungry and thirsty would be satisfied by the Holy One of Israel. Jesus said, "I am the bread of life; whoever comes to me shall not hunger, and whoever believes in me shall never thirst" (John 6:35).

Talk about It

:: Isaiah promised that God was going to give us food and drink for free. Is he talking about soda and hamburgers or a different kind of food? *(Isaiah is not talking about the kind of food we eat every day. He is talking about food that satisfies a hunger and thirst for God.)*

:: Who did God the Father send to satisfy all those who are hungry and thirsty for God? *(God sent Jesus so that everyone who believes in him would be filled with the Holy Spirit all the time and never be dying of hunger or thirst for God again.)*

:: "Seek the LORD while he may be found; call upon him while he is near." What do you think Isaiah meant by these words in verse 6? *(Any time we are learning about God or hearing God's Word, the Lord is near and gives us a chance to believe. Instead of rejecting or turning away from God, we should believe and give God our lives. We can never be sure that we will get another chance.)*

 Pray about It

Ask God to help you believe and trust in him today instead of waiting until tomorrow.

Week 14

The Sermon on the Mount—Love Your Enemies

Story 92 – *The Gospel Story Bible*

Write the words anger, hate, mad, hurt, hit, cheat, lie, steal, disrespect, mock, betray, *and* rob *on twelve sheets of paper with a marker. Then crumple them up into balls. Call your children into the room and tell them you are going to have a paper ball war. Divide them into two teams and explain that you are going to give each side six balls. The object of the game is to get the paper balls on the other team's side of the room when time is up. Use a stopwatch. Tell your children that when you say Go, each team should throw their balls at the other team. They can also pick up the other team's balls and throw them back at them.*

Shout Go and start the timer. After one minute shout Stop to end the round. The team with the least number of balls is the winner. Play the best two out of three rounds. The adults can participate if you need more players. At the end of the game uncrumple the paper balls to show what you have been throwing at each other. Explain that just as you threw a paper marked anger, hit, or rob, we can also sin against one another the very same way, and when we do, we are treating one another like enemies. Say, "This week we will see how we should respond to people who treat us like enemies."

DAY ONE

Picture It

When you hear the word *enemy*, what do you think of? *Enemy* is a strong word that brings to mind enemy soldiers, thieves, or those who would attack you with a knife or gun. But we can act like enemies toward one another too when we are unkind; call each other names; or pinch, push, pull, or hit one another, because we become their enemy in that moment. Can you think of a time when you acted like an enemy toward someone? In our Bible passage today, Jesus teaches a surprising way for us to act toward those who treat us like enemies.

 Read Matthew 5:38–42.

Think about It Some More

"An eye for an eye and a tooth for a tooth" was a law that God gave Moses to help him gauge the punishment a misdeed deserved. It was a great way to keep revenge from escalating. But in Jesus' day people were using that rule as a way to get back at those who sinned against them. So, if a person hit them, they thought God allowed them to hit the person back. If a person stole their goat, they could steal one back to get even.

In our Bible passage today, Jesus taught a different way. He said that if someone slaps you as an insult, we should not strike back. If someone takes you to court and wins your coat as payment, rather than responding with revenge you should give him even more than he asks for. Jesus lived this way. When the Jews arrested and then crucified him on a cross, Jesus did not do anything to get back at them; instead, he asked his Father to forgive them (Luke 23:34).

Loving our enemies, is really hard to do. But Jesus sent his Holy Spirit to help us. Jesus called the Holy Spirit our "Helper" (John 14:16). God sends his Holy Spirit to live in the hearts of everyone who turns away from their sin and believes in Jesus. The Holy Spirit helps us to know when something is wrong, reminds us of Bible passages we've read that speak to us, and helps us to obey. You can be sure if you are trusting in Jesus the Holy Spirit is there to help you follow him and love your enemies too.

Talk about It

:: What does the word *revenge* mean? *(We take revenge when we try to get even with someone who hurt us by doing something back to him. For example, if someone hits you, you might try to take revenge by hitting him back.)*

:: If someone hits you, what should you do? *(The Bible tells us we should forgive them as Jesus Christ forgives us. Hitting them back would be wrong.)*

:: Whom did Jesus send to help us love our enemies? *(Jesus sent the Holy Spirit into the heart of everyone who believes. The Holy Spirit helps us to remember Jesus' example and follow Jesus' teaching to love our enemies.)*

 Pray about It

Ask God to help you forgive those who sin against you and not take revenge on them.

DAY TWO

Remember It

What do you remember about yesterday's story? What do you think is going to happen today?

 Read Matthew 5:43–47.

Think about It Some More

If your friend had a pack of gum and shared a piece with you, the next time you had a pack of gum you would want to share a piece with him, remembering that he first gave a piece to you. But what if your friend gave a piece to all his other friends but said you could not have one? Wouldn't that make it much harder to share with him? In today's passage, Jesus said that it is easy to love someone who loves you, but that we should also love those who are against us. In the Old Testament, God told Israel that they should love their neighbors as themselves (Leviticus 19:18). But in our Bible verse today, Jesus said we should love even our enemies.

Talk about It

:: Whom did Jesus say we should love? *(Jesus said we should love our neighbors and those who love us, but he also said we should love our enemies and those who treat us badly.)*

:: The Bible says that we are all sinners and enemies of God because of our sin (Romans 5:10). What did Jesus do to show love to us while we were his enemies? *(Jesus died on the cross for us while we were his enemies.)*

:: What kinds of things can you do to follow Jesus' teaching about loving your enemies this week? *(You might not think you have any enemies, but even your brothers and sisters and friends can become your enemies when they treat you badly. In these situations God wants us to practice loving those who have hurt us. Instead of getting angry back, we should love and forgive them. We need the Holy Spirit to help us live this way.)*

 Pray about It

Ask God to help you treat your brothers and sisters and friends with love even when they sin against you.

DAY THREE _____

Connect It to the Gospel

Today is the day we connect this week's Bible story to the gospel. The gospel is the life, death, and resurrection of Jesus for our salvation. Can anyone guess how our story this week looks forward to or back at the gospel?

 Read Romans 5:9–10.

Think about It Some More

Our Bible verse today says that before Jesus died on the cross we were his enemies. We were his enemies because we sinned and disobeyed God. Sin is evil and stands against God, who is perfectly good. That is why God must destroy all sin. When we sin, we become God's enemies. Because God is all good, he must pour out his wrath (holy anger) against all sin and everyone who sins, including us. But instead of punishing us for our sin, God loved us and punished his only Son, Jesus, in our place. Once all of God's wrath against sin was poured out on Jesus, there was no more left for us.

If we place our faith in what Jesus did and turn away from our sins, God will forgive us our sins and place his Holy Spirit in our lives to help us live for him. When that happens, we go from being an enemy of God to becoming a son or daughter of God, a part of his family. Then, remembering how God so loved us that he would die for us, we can love those around us, even if they are treating us poorly.

Talk about It

:: Why does God get angry at sin? *(Sin is evil and stands against God who is good. Because God is good he must destroy all evil.)*

:: Why are we all God's enemies? *(Each of us who sins is an enemy of God because God must destroy all sin and evil.)*

:: If we are God's enemy, how can we be saved? *(The only way we can get right or be reconciled to God once we sin is to trust in Jesus, who died on the cross to take our sin upon himself. Once we trust in Jesus and he takes our sins away, we are not God's enemies anymore.)*

 Pray about It

Praise God for sending Jesus to make a way for his enemies to be forgiven and become God's friends again.

DAY FOUR

Remember It

What has God been teaching you this week through our Bible story?

 Read Matthew 5:48.

Think about It Some More

If you want to see how hard it is to be perfect, take a piece of paper and a pencil and try to draw a perfect circle. No matter how hard you try you won't be able to draw a perfect circle. Our lives are like that. No matter how hard we try, we cannot be perfect. One lie, one angry word, one disrespectful answer to our mom or dad, and we are not perfect.

So if we have to be perfect to get to heaven, how does anyone ever get to heaven? The answer is found in Jesus. Jesus lived a perfect life in our place. It is like Jesus drawing the perfect circle for you. When we place our faith and trust in Jesus, we gain *his* perfect obedience as if we were perfect too. If we make a mistake, we don't have to worry, because Jesus took the punishment for our sins and gave us his perfect life instead. We obey out of love for what Jesus did, not to try to earn our way to heaven. What is really amazing is that Jesus, by his death, can forgive all our sins—all the sins of your past, those you commit today, and even the sins you will commit tomorrow.

Talk about It

> KIDS, ask your parents how the Holy Spirit has helped them obey God.

(Parents, every time you are convicted by God's Word, the Holy Spirit is at work in your life, and every time you choose to obey God out of love for Jesus, the Holy Spirit is helping you. Share an example from your life where the Holy Spirit helped you.)

:: If we can't be perfect, why shouldn't we just give up trying to be good? *(If we had to be perfect on our own, we might as well all give up. But if we trust in Jesus he gives us his perfect life of obedience and gives us his Holy Spirit to help us obey too.)*

:: What do we need to do to get the perfect life Jesus offers us? *(We need to believe that Jesus died on the cross for us and rose from the dead. When we place our trust in Jesus, he changes us, takes our sins away, and gives us his perfect life so that we can go to heaven.)*

 Pray about It

Ask God to help you trust in Jesus who lived a perfect life, and ask him to fill you with his Holy Spirit to help you obey and follow his example.

DAY FIVE

Discover It

Today is the day we look at a different Bible passage—from the book of Psalms or one of the prophets—to see what we can learn from it about Jesus or our salvation.

 Read Isaiah 50:5–6.

Think about It Some More

This part of the Bible talks about a man who did not fight back but allowed men to strike his back with a whip and pull his beard and who did not hide his face from people saying bad things about him or spitting on him. Doesn't that sound like the way Jesus responded after his arrest? Jesus could have called down angels to stop the men who were beating him, but he did not. Jesus followed the teaching he gave us in the Sermon on the Mount: He did not fight back. The reason Jesus did not fight back is he knew that God his Father wanted him to take the punishment on the cross to save even his enemies from their sins. Long before Jesus was born, God gave the prophet Isaiah this picture of Jesus' life.

Talk about It

:: What did Isaiah say that Jesus would allow others to do to him? *(Although Isaiah does not mention Jesus by name, it is clear that he is talking about the suffering of our Lord. He said Jesus would allow people to strike his back, pull his beard, spit in his face, insult him, and disgrace him. If you have smaller children and they cannot read or remember what has been read, read through the passage again and have them raise their hands when they hear something bad that was going to happen to Jesus.)*

:: Why didn't Jesus fight back? *(Jesus allowed himself to be beaten and mocked because he knew that by dying on the cross he would be able to rescue all of God's children from their sins.)*

:: How could the Holy Spirit use Jesus' example to show us how we should treat those who come against us? *(If Jesus loved us while we were his enemies, we should be willing to love those who are our enemies. If Jesus forgave those who sinned against him, we should be willing to forgive those who sin against us. If*

Jesus didn't seek revenge to get back at those who hurt him, we should not seek revenge to get back at those who hurt us.)

:: Can you think of a time when someone treated you badly, and you needed to forgive him? *(Parents, help your children remember a time when a sibling hurt them and they needed to forgive the offender. This week, look for opportunities to help your children treat each other like Jesus treated us when they sin against each other.)*

 Pray about It

Ask God to help you trust in him and to fill you with his Spirit to help you to be like Jesus who did not fight back against his enemies but forgave them instead.

Week 15

The Lord's Prayer

Story 93 – *The Gospel Story Bible*

When your family gathers, make this announcement: "Did you know that I was adopted?" If they don't know what adopted means, explain that it is when parents agree to invite a child who is born outside the family to become a part of their family. Go on to explain that your adoption was into the family of God.

Say, "At one time we were not sons and daughters of God, but were instead slaves to sin. The apostle Paul tells us that we become children of God through faith in Jesus Christ. That means that not everyone can call God Father. In fact, Jesus told the Jews (in John 8) that their father was the devil. When we have faith in Christ, God adopts us into his family. It is then that we can call God Father. This week, we will learn the prayer Jesus taught his disciples to pray to God the Father."

DAY ONE

Picture It

Moms and dads all across the country work quietly and humbly every day to prepare dinners for their families. But imagine what it would be like if these parents wanted to draw attention to themselves. Think of how different it would be in your house if, before starting dinner preparations, your parent pulled out a trumpet, started blowing on it, and announced to the whole family, "Attention everyone, I am about to start cooking dinner. The first thing I will do is turn on the oven." After the oven is turned on, the trumpet is blown three more times and you hear the announcement, "I am putting the chicken in the oven." What if mom or dad continued sounding the trumpet with each step of the meal? And if they went around to each person after the meal was finished looking for high fives, you might think they were a bit proud. Now of course we know our parents don't act like that, but in our story today Jesus tells us that this is how the Pharisees lived. They wanted to impress everyone by announcing all the good things they did.

 Read Matthew 6:1–6.

Think about It Some More

In Matthew 5:16, Jesus said we should let our light shine before men so that they could see our good works and give glory to God. In today's Bible passage, it seems that Jesus is teaching something different—that we should not do our good works in front of men at all. Jesus isn't trying to confuse us; he is teaching about the motives of our hearts, the reasons why we do what we do. God wants us to do good works for him and not for our own glory.

The hypocrites, like the Pharisees, didn't do their good works to honor God; they did their good works so they could look good in front of others. If the people saw them give to the poor and spend time praying, the Pharisees thought the people would look up to them and think they were special. The Pharisees wanted the people to think they loved God. That is why Jesus said they used trumpets to announce their good works. But we can't fool God because he always knows what is going on in our hearts. God is more interested in why we do things than what we do. This week, look for some secret nice thing you can do for someone.

Talk about It

:: What is a hypocrite? *(A hypocrite is a pretender who, inside, is a sinner like everybody else, but who on the outside does good things for everyone to see so he can try to fool them into thinking he is really something he's not.)*

:: What did the hypocrites do to make sure everyone knew they were giving to the poor? *(They blew trumpets to announce their good works.)*

:: Do we have to hide all the good things that we do so no one knows we are doing them? *(No, we don't have to hide our good works. But we should not draw attention to ourselves when we do them. Sometimes it is better to do them in secret so that only God knows.)*

Pray about It

Ask God to help you do good works for his glory and not for your own.

DAY TWO

Remember It

What do you remember about yesterday's story? What do you think is going to happen today?

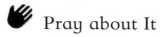 Read Matthew 6:7–13.

Think about It Some More

Wouldn't you be surprised if, when ordering a meal at a fast-food restaurant, the person behind the counter already knew what you wanted to order? What if she got your order perfectly correct before you told her anything? That would be amazing. We all know that the order takers at fast-food restaurants can't read our minds: we have to tell them what we want.

But God is different. In our Bible passage today, Jesus said that even before we pray, God knows what we need! But that doesn't mean we shouldn't ask. God loves it when we depend on him and ask him for what we need. Even though God already knew what the disciples needed, Jesus encouraged his disciples to pray, and he taught them how by giving them a very special prayer that we call the Lord's Prayer. This is a great part of the Bible to memorize.

Talk about It

:: Who knows what we need even before we ask? *(God)*

:: Can you remember any part of the Lord's Prayer? *(Parents, see if your children can remember a portion of the prayer. If they can't, try saying a few words of each line to see if they can say the rest. A good way to memorize this passage of Scripture for young readers is to write it on a whiteboard, and, each time you say it, erase a word so that your children have to fill in the blank.)*

:: When you ask God for your daily bread, what are you asking for? *(When you ask for your daily bread you are asking God to provide the food you need for today. But more than our food, we should ask God for everything we need, like our food, clothes, water to drink, a warm house in winter, etc.)*

 Pray about It

Pray the Lord's Prayer. *(Parents, help your children ask for the specific things they need and for help with some of the temptations they struggle with.)*

DAY THREE

Connect It to the Gospel

Today is the day we connect this week's Bible story to the gospel. The gospel is the life, death, and resurrection of Jesus for our salvation. Can anyone guess how our story this week looks forward to or back at the gospel?

 Read Matthew 6:14–15.

Think about It Some More

If God could give up his only Son so that we could be forgiven, we should be willing to forgive others when they hurt us. Jesus gave up a lot for us to be forgiven. He left his place in heaven to be born here on earth as a man. Our forgiveness cost Jesus a lot. He was arrested, beaten, and nailed to a cross for our forgiveness. Now when people sin against us, God asks us to do the same and forgive others as Jesus freely forgave us.

A good way to help children understand forgiveness is to use the illustration of a loan that you can't repay. If I lend you fifty dollars, but you can't pay me back, I could forgive or cancel your debt. Even though you owe me the money, I choose to forget about it and bear the loss of the fifty dollars. When we forgive others for sinning against us, we are saying that we will not hold their sin against them and not make them pay by punishing them for what they did. Remembering all that God did to forgive us makes it easier for us to forgive others.

Talk about It

:: What does God want us to do when people sin against us? *(God wants us to forgive them.)*

:: What does it mean to forgive someone who sins against you? *(When we forgive others for sinning against us, we are saying that we will not hold their sin against them and not make them pay by punishing them for what they did.)*

:: How did Jesus make a way for us to be forgiven for our sins? *(Jesus left his place as God the Son in heaven, became a man, and suffered and died on the cross so we could be forgiven and brought into God's family.)*

 Pray about It

Thank God for forgiving you and ask for his help in forgiving others.

DAY FOUR

Remember It

What has God been teaching you this week through our Bible story?

 Read Matthew 6:16–18.

Think about It Some More

The Pharisees wanted to do good works to impress people. But Jesus taught that we should want to impress God, not men. That is why Jesus said to keep our good works hidden where only God can see them. If you show off and people praise you for your good works on earth, their praise becomes your reward. But if you do your good works in secret, Jesus promised that one day you would get a heavenly reward.

Talk about It

> ● ● KIDS, ask your parents if they can remember a
> ● ● time when they wanted people to see their good
> works like the Pharisees did.

(Parents, this is a great opportunity to help your children see that we are all tempted to do things that will earn the praise of others.

Consider a time when you may have had an argument in the car on your way to church. You may have been arguing all the way up to the front door. But as soon as you had contact with others, you changed your tone, hid your anger, and pretended to be filled with joy so that people would think you were joyful, not angry. We all struggle at some point in seeking the praise of other people instead of the praise of God.)

:: Can you remember something the Pharisees did in public to earn praise from people? *(They gave money, fasted, and prayed in a way so that people would see what they were doing.)*

:: What did Jesus say the Father would give us if we do our good works in secret? *(We will get a reward.)*

:: In today's example, Jesus talks about fasting, which is giving up food for a time to pray and read God's Word. Why would we want to fast? *(It is easy to forget how much we need God's Word, which is our spiritual food. But if we give up food, we will soon see how weak we really are. Fasting helps us to remember how much we need God and his Word.)*

 Pray about It

Have each of your children find a quiet place to pray in secret.

DAY FIVE _____

Discover It

Today is the day we look at a different Bible passage—from the book of Psalms or one of the prophets—to see what we can learn from it about Jesus or our salvation.

 Read Isaiah 53:8.

Think about It Some More

Although Isaiah didn't know Jesus' name, when he wrote these words, he was describing Jesus. He wrote of a servant of God who would be punished for our sins. Jesus was the only person who could take our punishment. That's why we know that Isaiah was talking about Jesus. All of Isaiah 53 describes how Jesus would suffer, and in today's verse we learn that Jesus was taken away (arrested) to be judged. When it says that "Jesus was stricken for the transgressions of" God's people, it means that he was given the punishment *we* deserved, which was all planned by God as a way to save us from our sins. Later, in the New Testament, the apostle Paul wrote that Jesus died just the way the Bible said he would—"in accordance with the Scriptures" (1 Corinthians 15:3).

Talk about It

:: What does the word *transgression* mean? *(Transgression is another name for sin.)*

:: What part of Jesus' life is Isaiah talking about when he tells us that Jesus was "stricken" for our transgressions? *(Isaiah is talking about Jesus' death on the cross, when God struck his Son with the punishment we deserved for our sins. Jesus was punished in our place.)*

:: How did Isaiah know that Jesus was going to die for our sins even though Jesus wasn't even born yet? *(God told Isaiah about his plan to send a Savior.)*

 ## Pray about It

Thank God for planning the death of his Son, Jesus, as a way to pay for our sins.

Week 16

Treasure in Heaven

Story 94 – *The Gospel Story Bible*

Make out a check to your church or a ministry for a particular need you are aware of. Write a letter along with the check thanking them for their work. Place the letter and the check in an addressed envelope but do not seal the envelope. When you begin Bible study, ask your family if you can take money with you to heaven when you die.

Tell them that although you can't take any money or treasure with you, you can send it on ahead of you. Show them the envelope and tell them that you decided to send some money ahead to heaven. After their initial shock, tell them that the way we send money ahead is by giving it away now. The Bible tells us that God rewards us for the good things we do, so when we give our money away, we store up for ourselves treasure in heaven! Say, "This week, we will learn about treasure in heaven."

DAY ONE _____

Picture It

There once was a man who tried to save all his money. During the day, he worked at a restaurant as a cook, and at night he worked as a janitor in a large apartment building. As a part of the pay for his job during the day, he got to eat for free. As a part of his pay for his job at night, he got to live in a small apartment for free. Since he didn't have to buy much food, and he didn't have to pay for rent, he could save most of his money. Day by day, he saved more and more until he became very rich. At first, he was saving his money to buy a car and then a house, but somewhere along the way the man fell in love with his money instead, and never spent it on a car or a house.

One day a thief followed him home from the bank where the man had gone to cash a paycheck. Peeking through his window, the thief saw the man put a stack of one hundred dollar bills into a hidden hole in the wall. That very night, while the man was sleeping, the robber came and quietly stole every last penny. When the man told the police that a robber had stolen over a million dollars from him, they didn't believe him, and they chided him for storing his money in the wall. They told him he should have stored his money in a bank where it would've been safe. Today in our Bible story, you will hear about a place where we can store our treasure so no thief can ever take it away.

 Read Matthew 6:19–24.

Think about It Some More

Jesus said that our hearts can hold love for only one treasure. We will either live for the things of this world or we will live for God, who created all things. Our love for the Lord helps us let go of our earthly treasures. When we have the greatest treasure of all, a relationship with Jesus, it is easier to give away our money and things to those in need. And when we give away our money or things, God rewards us with treasure in heaven. That is kind of like a bank account in heaven.

Since there are no robbers in heaven, our treasure there will always remain safe. Unfortunately, the opposite is also true: If our hearts are filled with a love of money or the things money can buy, there is no room left for the Lord. And when we die, we can't take any of our treasure with us.

Talk about It

:: Why do people love money and want to store it up? *(People love money because it can buy them nice things.)*

:: Besides money, what other things can we love more than we love God? *(You name it. Just about anything people like to collect can become a treasure they love more than God. We can make our toys, cars, baseball cards, clothes, video games, and many other things our treasures here on earth.)*

:: What kinds of earthly treasures do you love the most? What would you most hate to lose if a robber stole something of yours? *(Parents, help your children here. You probably know what they would most hate to lose if a robber came into your house.)*

:: What kinds of things could you do to store up treasure in heaven this week? *(Parents, help your children think of something they could do to earn treasure in heaven.)*

 Pray about It

Ask God to help you love him more than all the treasures of this world.

DAY TWO _____

Remember It

What do you remember about yesterday's story? What do you think is going to happen today?

 Read Matthew 6:25–32.

Think about It Some More

Most people don't think of thanking God for the clothes they put on each morning. When we have plenty to eat, it is easy to forget to thank God for what he's given to us. When we enter a season when we don't have enough money, it is easy to worry instead of trusting God.

But Jesus taught that if God can provide food for millions and millions of birds, not to mention fish and other animals too, we should believe that he can provide food for us too. If God can clothe the flowers of the field with beautiful colors, he can provide us with the clothes we need. So, if you have plenty of food and clothes to wear, remember that God is the one who provided the money for those things. Or if you are living through a season when you don't have a lot of money, remember that God is still the one who can provide what you need.

Talk about It

:: What did Jesus say God does for the birds? *(Jesus said God feeds the birds, and he used that as an example to say that if God can feed the birds, surely he will provide food for us.)*

:: What did Jesus say God does for the flowers of the field? *(Jesus said that God provides their clothes—their wonderful colors. If God can give the flowers such beautiful colors, we should trust that God will give us the clothes we need.)*

:: Today, did you thank God for your clothes or your food? *(Parents, draw out your children here and help them to see how easy it is for us to take God's provision for granted. Have your children take turns giving thanks for the food at meals this week.)*

:: What do you think we should do when we need food or clothing? *(We should pray and ask God to provide for our needs. Worry will not get us any food or clothing. It only makes us fearful and sad. But when we pray to God and trust him, we become hopeful, and our worry goes away.)*

 ## Pray about It

Thank God for providing you with food and clothing, and ask him to give you what you need. *(Parents, if you have a specific need, pray for that with your children. Then see how God provides for you over time.)*

DAY THREE _____

Connect It to the Gospel

Today is the day we connect this week's Bible story to the gospel. The gospel is the life, death, and resurrection of Jesus for our salvation. Can anyone guess how our story this week looks forward to or back at the gospel?

 Read Matthew 6:33.

Think about It Some More

Most kings rule over a country. To *seek a king's kingdom* means you are looking for the land where he rules as king. God is a king too, but God is much different. He doesn't rule over one country, he rules over everything and everyone. That is why the Bible tells us that he is "King of kings" (Revelation 17:14).

When Jesus said we should seek God's kingdom, he meant that we should allow God to rule over our hearts and lives. But our sin wants to kick God off the throne and not let him rule over us. That is why we have to fight against our sin and ask God to help us turn away from sin and run after righteousness—all that is good. When God causes us to be born again, he fills us with his Holy Spirit. Then the Spirit of God starts working in our hearts to help us live for God.

Talk about It

:: What did Jesus say we needed to do instead of worrying? *(Parents, if you have young children you may want to say the words "seek first" as a clue to see if they can come up with "seek first the kingdom of God and his righteousness.")*

:: What does it mean to seek God's kingdom? *(Seeking God's kingdom means we want God to rule over our lives.)*

:: Where is the one place we don't want God to rule because of our sin? *(We don't want God to rule over our hearts and lives.)*

:: Who helps us to keep living for God so we don't ever give up seeking after God? *(The Holy Spirit helps us. In John 14:16 he is called our Helper.)*

 ## Pray about It

Ask Jesus to take away your sin and fill you with his Holy Spirit so that you will want to seek the kingdom of God and his righteousness.

DAY FOUR _____

Remember It

What has God been teaching you this week through our Bible story?

 Read Matthew 6:34.

Think about It Some More

If we trust in Jesus and live for him, God takes away our sin and adopts us into his family as his sons and daughters. If God did that for us, it seems silly to worry about clothes or food, doesn't it? Our job is to do the work he gives us to do and trust God to provide what we need. That is why God tells us not to worry about those kinds of things. If we seek his kingdom and trust in him, our God, who is king over all, will provide for us.

If you were home with your mom and started to get hungry, you would ask her for something to eat. It would seem silly to remain quiet and worry about your hunger instead of asking for some food. Since you are her son or daughter, you can be sure that if you ask, your mom will give you something to eat. It is the same with God. But remember, we learned last week that God knows what we need even before we ask (Matthew 6:8). We don't need to be fearful that unless we ask God won't supply our needs, because our God is a generous God who is always looking out for us.

Talk about It

> KIDS, ask your parents to tell you what they are most tempted to worry about.

(Parents, confess one of the things you worry about, and then explain to your children that instead of worrying you should ask God for what you need and trust him to provide. That will set them up with the answer to the next question.)

:: Instead of worrying, what should we do? *(We should ask God for the things we need and trust him.)*

:: Parents, ask your children if they have ever worried about something, and have them share what it is. *(Many children worry about going to bed in the dark or staying away from home when you go away.)*

Pray about It

Ask God to help you not to worry but to trust him instead.

DAY FIVE _____

Discover It

Today is the day we look at a different Bible passage—from the book of Psalms or one of the prophets—to see what we can learn from it about Jesus or our salvation.

Read 2 Samuel 22:1–4.

Think about It Some More

When David sang this song he celebrated how God saved him from Saul and from all his enemies. Now as we look back at his song, we can know that God also saved David from his greatest enemies: sin and death. Even if David wasn't thinking about Jesus saving him from his sin, his song points forward to a truth that is bigger than he realized. God saved David by sending Jesus to die on the cross for his sin. If we think about all that Jesus did for us, we can sing the words to David's song too. When Jesus died on the cross for our sins, he saved us from our enemies and became our rock, our fortress, and our deliverer!

Talk about It

:: Who did God save David from? *(God saved David from Saul, and God saved David from sin and death when Jesus died on the cross for David's sins.)*

:: How is this a song we can sing about our lives? *(God saved us from our enemies too. That is why we can sing that God is our Savior, our fortress, and our deliverer.)*

:: What did God do to save us? *(God sent his only Son, Jesus, to die on the cross and take the punishment for our sins so we could be forgiven.)*

 Pray about It

Use David's song as a prayer, and thank God for being our rock, fortress, and deliverer.

Week 17

The Wise & Foolish Builders

Story 95 – *The Gospel Story Bible*

Most children don't understand the concept of a foundation. If you have a basement in your home, give them a tour of your foundation (the stone, cement, or block walls your house is built on). If your house is built on a concrete slab, go to a place where the cement is exposed, like your front porch or a garage, and have them tap on it with their hand to see how hard it is. Ask your children what would happen if your house's foundation were made of sand and it rained real hard. Ask them to imagine what would happen to the sand holding the house up. Say, "This week we will learn that building our lives on God is like building our house on a solid foundation."

DAY ONE

Picture It

Little Red Riding Hood is a fairy tale about a young girl with a red cape who goes to visit her grandmother at her home in the forest. Red Riding Hood doesn't know it, but a wolf has locked her grandmother in a closet and put on her nightgown and cap. When the girl arrives at the house, the wolf lies in the bed and pretends to be her grandmother. But Little Red Riding Hood is not fooled. Her grandmother's clothes can't hide the wolf's large ears, eyes, or big teeth. In the end, when the wolf springs to attack Red Riding Hood, a woodcutter saves the day and kills the wolf.

I'll bet you didn't know the Bible also tells a story about a wolf who dresses up in a disguise. In today's Bible passage, Jesus tells of a wolf dressed up like a sheep.

 Read Matthew 7:15–20.

Think about It Some More

A false prophet is someone who pretends to speak for God. False prophets are liars. Jesus called false prophets wolves pretending to be one of God's people, the sheep. To protect us from these wolves, Jesus gave us the way to see through their disguise. Jesus said that all you have to do is watch their lives. If they are sent by God, they will follow God's commands and live for God. But if they are pretending that God is speaking through them, their lives will be filled with sins that you can see. Jesus called those sins bad fruit. So if a person claims to speak for God but her life is filled with bad fruit, or sin, we should not follow her because she could be a wolf who will lead us astray.

Talk about It

:: Whom did Jesus compare to a wolf? *(Jesus compared a false prophet to a wolf.)*

:: How is a diseased or sick tree with bad fruit like the wolf Jesus talked about? *(If you have a diseased or sick tree, you can expect to get diseased or bad fruit. So if you are a wolf, lying to God's people, you are going to sin in other areas of your life too.)*

:: If a person tells you God gave him a message to teach to you, how can you know whether or not you should follow him? *(You should look at his life to see if he is living according to God's Word and obeying all that it says. You can also see if his message matches what the Bible teaches. For instance, if someone were to say that Jesus didn't really rise from the dead, we would know that he was a false prophet because the Bible tells us that Jesus rose from the dead and that over five hundred people saw him [1 Corinthians 15:6].)*

 Pray about It

Thank God for giving us the Bible to warn us against false prophets who might try to lead us away from God.

DAY TWO

Remember It

What do you remember about yesterday's story? What do you think is going to happen today?

 Read Matthew 7:21–23.

Think about It Some More

Have you ever told someone you would do something but then you never actually did it? Perhaps you told your dad that you would clean your room, but later that day looking into your room he found the same big mess as was there in the morning. You see, it is easier to say you will do something than it is to actually do it. Words, all by themselves, are cheap, but words backed up by our actions are valuable. Jesus knew that not everyone who called God Lord really believed and followed God in his heart. The demons, for instance, called Jesus the "Holy one of Israel," but they didn't follow God. It is easy to say you are a Christian or to say Christian things, but it is much harder to follow Jesus and live for him by obeying his Word.

Talk about It

:: Can you think of a time when you said you would do something but didn't do it? *(Parents, help your children here. Try to help them remember a time when they said they would do their homework, clean up a mess, put their clothes away, or do something else that they never ended up doing. Be on the lookout for fresh illustrations.)*

:: Why can't we just *say* we believe in Jesus—why do we have to *live* for Jesus too? *(Anyone can say she believes, but a person who really believes that Jesus is God and his Words are the words of life will want to obey and live according to God's Word.)*

:: Why is it easier to say something than to actually do it? *(Words don't cost you anything; they are cheap. It is easy to tell someone you will work all day for them, but it is much harder to work all day. In the same way, it is easier to say you believe in Jesus and will live for him than it is to actually obey God's Word and live for God in all you do.)*

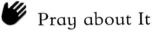 Pray about It

Ask God to help you to really live for God, not just say you will live for God.

DAY THREE _____

Connect It to the Gospel

Today is the day we connect this week's Bible story to the gospel. The gospel is the life, death, and resurrection of Jesus for our salvation. Can anyone guess how our story this week looks forward to or back at the gospel?

 Read Matthew 7:24–27.

Think about It Some More

It is easy to see that building your house on something strong and solid like a rock is a better idea than building on sand. But Jesus was not trying to teach about house construction. Jesus was talking about building our lives on the strong foundation of God's Word, which teaches us to follow Jesus.

Later in the Bible, the apostle Paul said that Jesus is the rock that we should build on. If you follow Jesus' teaching in the Bible and live for him, you are building upon the rock of Christ. But if you turn away from the Bible to follow your own way, you are building on sand. At first, you might think your life is as strong as the life of the person building upon Jesus, the rock. But when the storms of life crash against you, you will fall into fear and may even get angry with God and turn away from him. That would be as terrible for your life as it would be for a house built on sand to come crashing down in a storm.

Talk about It

:: What happens to a house built on a rock when strong winds and floodwaters crash against it? (*The rock stands firm and so does the house built upon it.*)

:: If you built a house on the sand and the wind and waves came in and washed the sand away, what would happen to the house? (*It would break apart and get washed away.*)

:: What was Jesus trying to teach us by talking about the two houses? *(Jesus was teaching that we should live for God and obey his word so that our lives don't fall apart like the house on the sand.)*

:: Can you think of a Bible verse that gives wisdom for how to live? *(Parents, help your children to think about the commandments.)*

 ## Pray about It

Ask God to help you obey God's Word so that you will be like the wise man in Jesus' story.

DAY FOUR _____

Remember It

What has God been teaching you this week through our Bible story?

 Read Matthew 7:28–29.

Think about It Some More

If you were walking down the street, and a stranger shouted, "Hey, you! Stop right where you are!" you might pause for a moment, but would then probably keep on walking. You might think he was talking to someone else or joking with you. But if a uniformed police officer shouted the very same thing, you would stop quickly and wait to find out what she wanted. Unlike the stranger, the police officer has the authority or power to command you to stop, and you have to listen. If you don't, you could get arrested.

In Jesus' day the crowds listened to him because, they said, he taught with authority. That means they felt Jesus' words came with the power to command. Those people were exactly right: Jesus had the power to command because he was God, not just an ordinary man like the scribes (the religious leaders).

Talk about It

> ● ● KIDS, ask your parents to tell you how Jesus'
> ● ● teaching has affected their lives.

(Parents, think back to how Jesus' teaching has affected you.)

:: Can you think of another person besides a police officer
who has authority? *(The president or ruler of a country has
authority over the country's citizens, and a general has authority
over the army. Parents have authority over their children too.)*

:: Who does Jesus have authority over? *(Jesus has authority over
everything and everyone. He created the world, and the whole earth
should obey his commands.)*

 ## Pray about It

Try to think of at least five words that describe Jesus' teaching. We
already have the word *authority* from today's Bible passage. Once you
have five words, use them in a prayer of praise to thank God for his
teaching.

DAY FIVE _____

Discover It

Today is the day we look at a different Bible passage—from the book
of Psalms or one of the prophets—to see what we can learn from it
about Jesus or our salvation.

 Read Isaiah 51:5–8.

Think about It Some More

This Bible passage talks about a salvation that lasts forever. The word
forever is used to describe something that never ends. Isaiah said that
the earth will wear out but that God's salvation will last forever (v. 6).
We know Isaiah couldn't be talking about one of the many times God
saved Israel, because each time he saved her she sinned and needed to
be saved again.

But there is another salvation, one that lasts forever. It comes
through Jesus. Jesus died on the cross so that those who believe in him

could be forgiven from all their sins forever. Our past sins, our present sins, and our future sins have all been paid for by Jesus' death on the cross.

Talk about It

:: What does the word *forever* mean? *(Forever is a word we use to describe something that never goes away and always lasts.)*

:: Can you think of something that lasts forever? *(Parents, young children may guess several things that do not last forever. If they do, use this to contrast the things of God and the things of the world.)*

:: What does God say in verse 7 that his people should have in their heart? *(Parents, reread the verse for your younger children and have them raise their hands when they hear the correct answer: the law.)*

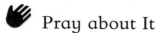 Pray about It

Thank God for a salvation that will last forever and ever.

The Four Soils

Story 96 – *The Gospel Story Bible*

To help your children understand how seeds sprout, try this fun activity. Purchase a packet of radish seeds. (If you don't have radish seeds, you can use dry lima beans.) Fill a shallow aluminum pan with soil and then have your children sow the seeds on the top of the soil. Water the seeds with a plant sprayer to dampen the soil. Then place your seeds in a warm sunny location and keep them damp by spraying or sprinkling a bit of water over them each day. They should sprout and start to grow by the end of your week.

This activity can help your children as they observe the tiny roots push down into the soil to provide nourishment for the young plants. You can refer back to this activity as you discuss the four soils in the parable you will learn this week.

DAY ONE

Picture It

A boy volunteered to bring to school a bag of dried lima beans for a science experiment. The next day, when he handed the bag of lima beans to his teacher, she asked, "Are the beans dead or alive?" "They are dead," he replied, for the beans were hard as a rock with no sign of life at all. The teacher smiled and said, "I asked you a trick question. Right now the beans look dead because they have no roots or shoots. But when we put them into soil and give them a drink of water and a bit of sunshine, they will spring to life again."

The young boy was excited to see if the beans really would grow. After pushing his bean into a soil-filled cup and giving it a drink of water, he placed it on the window ledge and waited. About a week later, just as the teacher said, his bean popped up out of the soil, and soon a green shoot appeared out of the pale white bean. Within three weeks, the boy transplanted a young lima bean plant into his garden at home. By the end of the summer his plant had produced a dozen bean pods, which the boy collected and dried. In the end, his one little bean had produced a hundred more. Today, we will read about another person who scattered seeds to grow. Let's see what happened to his seeds.

 Read Matthew 13:1–9.

Think about It Some More

After sharing the parable, Jesus said, "He who has ears, let him hear." That sounds like a strange thing to say. What Jesus meant was, "Pay attention, and think about what I am saying because it is important." Many of the people listening to Jesus did not have a clue that he was the Messiah giving them a message that could change their lives. They were not paying close attention to his words.

Some people read the Bible like that today. They read the stories, but they don't pay close attention to what they mean. The Bible holds life-changing truth that can rescue us from our sins. But if you only read it like a storybook and think of Jesus as merely a good teacher, you could come away missing the whole point of the Bible. The four soils represent our lives and our openness to the gospel message.

Talk about It

:: Why did Jesus say, "He who has ears, let him hear"? *(Jesus wanted everyone listening to pay close attention to what he was saying.)*

:: Why did Jesus want them to pay close attention? *(The message that Jesus was sharing would change their lives. It was more than a story about farming: the parable was a description of our hearts and whether or not we are open to hearing about Jesus.)*

:: Why would Jesus tell a story like this? *(Parents, if your children have never heard this parable before they may have no idea. Explain that the people and things in Jesus' parable are meant to represent other things and tell a hidden story to teach a lesson. Only the people Jesus explained them to, or those who understood why Jesus came to earth, could understand them.)*

:: What kind of soil is your heart most like? *(Parents, help your children think this through. Our children start out with hard, rocky, weed-infested hearts. It is only after God softens their hearts and breaks up the soil that they become fertile and open to the gospel.)*

 Pray about It

Ask God to soften your heart, to kill off the weeds that choke out his Word, and to help his roots grow deep so that you can understand the gospel message and grow strong in the Lord.

DAY TWO

Remember It

What do you remember about yesterday's story? What do you think is going to happen today?

 Read Matthew 13:10–16.

Think about It Some More

Did you ever notice that you are blind in the dark? Even though you have perfectly normal eyes, you can't see without light. You could be staring at a hundred-dollar bill someone lost along the road, but if it is pitch black outside, you would walk right by the money and never take notice. Learning about God is like that. Unless God opens our eyes to see and opens our ears to hear, we would not believe in him.

The reason we are blind is that our hearts and minds have become hard because of sin. But God can soften our hearts and open our eyes to understand. Imagine someone turning on a flashlight in the dark and lighting up your path. If the light shone on that hundred-dollar bill, you would pick it up at once. No one would pass by a hundred-dollar bill and leave it on the ground once he saw it. That is how it is with God. We would never turn away from God once he opens our eyes to see how awesome he is.

Talk about It

:: What did Isaiah say (in verses 14 and 15) has happened to people's hearts, eyes, and ears? *(Isaiah said their hearts have grown dull, their eyes were blind, and their ears were deaf. That doesn't mean they couldn't see anything, just that they could not see that Jesus was God and they could not understand his teaching.)*

:: What is different about the eyes and ears of those who follow Jesus? *(Their eyes can see and their ears can hear, so they believe in Jesus and understand his teaching.)*

:: Who opens our eyes and ears so we can understand and believe in Jesus and his teachings? *(God)*

 Pray about It

Ask God to open your eyes and ears so that you will believe and place your faith in Jesus.

DAY THREE

Connect It to the Gospel

Today is the day we connect this week's Bible story to the gospel. The gospel is the life, death, and resurrection of Jesus for our salvation. Can anyone guess how our story this week looks forward to or back at the gospel?

 Read Matthew 13:17.

Think about It Some More

Did you ever have to wait for a special day? Remember how you couldn't wait until it came, perhaps a vacation or your birthday? Now think about something you need to wait for that is farther off, like your high-school graduation. That is an exciting special day you need to wait years to see.

The prophets whom Jesus talked about in our Bible passage today waited their whole lives hoping to see the Messiah come, for they knew he was going to save God's people from their sin (1 Peter 1:10–11). But all the Old Testament prophets died before Jesus came. They waited and waited for that special day but never saw it. That is why we should be grateful and pay close attention to everything Jesus taught. Jesus told his disciples that they were blessed because they got to walk and talk with the one whom the prophets had longed to see.

Talk about It

:: Can you remember a time when it was hard to wait patiently for something you were excited about? *(Parents, remind your children of a time when they were very excited and found it hard to wait for a special day.)*

:: What were the prophets excited about and longing to see? *(The prophets longed to see how God was going to deliver his people. They longed to see Jesus, though they didn't know his name.)*

:: Why did Jesus tell the disciples about the prophets? What did he want them to do? *(Jesus wanted the disciples to realize how blessed they were to see Jesus. He wanted them to pay close attention to his words. We are blessed too because we can read all about Jesus in the Bible. We should pay close attention to everything it tells us about Jesus.)*

 ## Pray about It

Thank God for giving you the Bible so that you could know who Jesus is and all that he did. Then ask God to help you believe in Jesus and trust in him.

DAY FOUR _____

Remember It

What has God been teaching you this week through our Bible story?

 Read Matthew 13:18–23.

Think about It Some More

To help his disciples understand what he was talking about, Jesus explained the parable of the sower to them. The seed is the word of the kingdom—the gospel message about Jesus. The four different soils represent four different kinds of people. Only one kind heard the message and understood it. Jesus wants us all to be like the fertile soil. The fertile soil is a person who doesn't love the world more than he loves God and who can trust God even when times get tough. When the gospel comes to him, he keeps it in his heart and doesn't let the cares of the world steal it away or choke it out.

Talk about It

> KIDS, ask your parents if they ever had something try to choke out the message of Jesus from their lives.

(Parents, remember that Jesus said the thorns or the cares of the world and money could choke out the message of Jesus. Try to think if one of these things has ever affected your love for God.)

:: What did Jesus say could cause us to give up on him and fall away? *(Jesus said that the person who falls away does so because of the tribulations or troubles of life. It is easy for them to trust Jesus when all is going well, but when times get tough, they fall away.)*

:: What kind of soil do you want to be? *(Parents, see if your children can make the connection to the parable and say that they want to be the fertile soil. Then surprise them with this follow-up question: Why? Kids can often come up with the right answer without really thinking much about it. Asking a why question helps them think about their answer.)*

Pray about It

Ask God to help you love Jesus more than the things of the world, and ask God to help you trust him in good times and in bad.

DAY FIVE

Discover It

Today is the day we look at a different Bible passage—from the book of Psalms or one of the prophets—to see what we can learn from it about Jesus or our salvation.

Read Psalm 14:1–7.

Think about It Some More

In Romans 3:10–12, Paul quoted this Bible passage about Jesus. Even though David pointed out that we are all sinners (Psalm 14:3), he both prayed and predicted that God would send salvation from

Zion—Jerusalem. In Romans 3:21–24, Paul continued by saying that even though we are lost in our sin we can be right with God by trusting in Jesus, who is the salvation that David said would come. Paul taught that although we all have sinned against God, we can all be forgiven if we believe in what Jesus did on the cross. When David said our salvation would come out of Jerusalem, he was pointing us to Jesus.

Talk about It

:: Why is the message of verse three—that no one does good, not even one—bad news for you and me? *(It means we are all sinners who can't go to heaven and be with God unless we are saved.)*

:: Have you sinned in your life? *(Parents, help your children see that what David said is true about them. All we have to do is sin once and we cannot live with God in heaven unless our sin is taken away.)*

:: Read Romans 3:21–24. What does Paul say we need to do? *(Parents, if your children don't know the answer, reread the verse and emphasize the word* believe. *Then ask them what we are supposed to believe.)*

 ## Pray about It

Admit in prayer that each person in your family is a sinner who needs Jesus to rescue them from his or her sins.

Week 19

The Hidden Treasure

Story 97 – *The Gospel Story Bible*

While your kids are sleeping, hide little treasures all around your house. You can use gold foil-covered chocolate coins, United States President dollar coins, or, shiny gold costume jewelry. When your children come together for Bible study, tell them about the hidden treasure and have them begin the search. After they have collected the treasure, gather them for this week's devotion, where they will learn several more of Jesus' parables, including the parable about the treasure hidden in a field.

DAY ONE

Picture It

There once was a hardworking squirrel that collected all the acorns that fell from a large oak tree. One by one, the squirrel buried them all in the ground to save for the cold months of winter. When the spring rains came, three forgotten acorns sprouted into little oak trees behind the barn of a local farmer. The farmer decided to keep the tiny oak saplings, and he placed a wire fence around each of them.

As years passed, the trees grew taller and taller. When fully grown, the strong trees were over one hundred feet tall. By then it was hard to believe that such large trees had started from an acorn about the size of a quarter. In today's story, we will learn about a tree that grows from a very tiny seed about the size of the lower case letter "o" in this paragraph.

 Read Matthew 13:31–33.

Think about It Some More

In the parables of the mustard seed and the yeast, Jesus taught about things that start out very small but that quickly grow into something much larger. Jesus used these stories to describe how the kingdom of heaven was going to start small but grow really big. Jesus brought the kingdom of heaven to earth and expanded it when he chose his disciples. By the time Jesus left, the kingdom had expanded to about a hundred or so true believers. But after the Holy Spirit came upon them and they began to preach, God's kingdom really began to grow. Thousands of people believed and became Christians. Those people told others, and daily, God added people to the church.

Today, God's kingdom is still growing. There are now millions and millions of people who believe in Jesus. It all started with Jesus, the mustard seed, and then it grew into a giant tree, called the church, that we are all a part of.

Talk about It

:: What is the kingdom of heaven? *(A kingdom consists of the land and people ruled by a king or queen. When Jesus talks about the kingdom of heaven, he is talking about all the people who have been saved and made a part of his family.)*

:: What two things did Jesus talk about to show how the kingdom of heaven would grow? *(A mustard seed and yeast [leaven] both grow quickly and are good pictures of how God's kingdom grew.)*

:: Can you think of anything else that starts out small but gets big quickly? *(Parents, this is a great opportunity to get the children to think. A watermelon is a huge fruit that starts from a tiny seed. A balloon is small until you blow it up. Did you know that a hot air balloon as big as a house can, before being inflated, be stuffed into a large car trunk?)*

:: How can we become a part of God's kingdom? *(All we have to do to become a part of God's kingdom is place our trust in King Jesus who died on the cross and then rose again to defeat death and make a way for us to be forgiven.)*

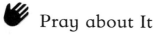 Pray about It

Ask God to help you trust in Jesus so that you can be a part of his growing kingdom.

DAY TWO _____

Remember It

What do you remember about yesterday's story? What do you think is going to happen today?

 Read Matthew 13:34–35.

Think about It Some More

In our Bible passage today, Matthew quoted one of Asaph's songs (from the book of Psalms) and said that it pointed to Jesus. In Psalm 78, Asaph said that one day the secrets of God would be revealed by a man who taught in parables. The Jews, who read what the prophets said about a coming Messiah, began to search to learn who the Messiah would be.

When Jesus came, the mystery was over and the secret was revealed. Jesus was the Messiah the prophets had spoken about years and years ago. God's angels announced Jesus' birth to the shepherds. John the Baptist said he was the Lamb of God who would take away the sins of the world. God the Father announced that Jesus was his Son at his baptism, and even the demons couldn't help but call him the Holy One of God.

Talk about It

:: Can you remember a time when you had to keep a secret? *(Parents, help your children remember a time when they were aware of a present that was coming for a birthday or other occasion and had to keep it a secret. If you can't think of a secret they kept, share a story of your own.)*

:: What was the secret that was kept hidden for a very long time? *(Jesus)*

:: How did Asaph, who lived way before Jesus was even born, know that Jesus would speak in parables? *(Even though Asaph didn't know the name Jesus, he and the other prophets looked forward to a day when God would send the Messiah to deliver his people. The Holy Spirit inspired Asaph to write what he did.)*

 ## Pray about It

Thank God that you know the best secret of all time: Jesus is the Savior of the world!

DAY THREE

Connect It to the Gospel

Today is the day we connect this week's Bible story to the gospel. The gospel is the life, death, and resurrection of Jesus for our salvation. Can anyone guess how our story this week looks forward to or back at the gospel?

 Read Matthew 13:44.

Think about It Some More

If you find a treasure in a field, the treasure belongs to the person who owns the field. But if you buy the field, the treasure becomes yours. That is why the man in Jesus' story hid the treasure he found and bought the field. The man who found the treasure may have walked through that same field a hundred times but had never thought of buying it. But once he knew it held a great treasure, he sold everything that he had to get it.

That is what it is like to first learn what a valuable treasure Jesus is. A lot of people have heard about Jesus, but they think of him as just a good teacher, like any other man. But once they realize that Jesus is the Son of God who came to die on the cross to take away their sins, they see him as a treasure. Like the man in the parable, they will give up anything they have to for Jesus.

Talk about It

:: What did the man in the story find in the field? *(He found a treasure.)*

:: Why did the man hide the treasure again after he found it? *(The man wanted the treasure for himself, but had to buy the field before the treasure could be his.)*

:: Why is Jesus our treasure? *(Jesus gave up his life for us so that we could be forgiven for our sins. You can't buy forgiveness no matter how much money you have. Even the richest person in the world can't buy forgiveness. But God gives it to us for free if we trust in Jesus, his Son.)*

 Pray about It

Ask God to help you love Jesus so much that you would give up anything that might draw your attention away from the Lord.

DAY FOUR

Remember It

What has God been teaching you this week through our Bible story?

 Read Matthew 13:45–46.

Think about It Some More

Natural pearls of any size are extremely rare. One of the biggest natural pearls ever found is the bright orange "Sunrise" pearl. The Sunrise pearl is almost as large as a ping-pong ball. Few oysters or snails live long enough to make such a large pearl. Because it was so rare and so big and so beautiful, one man offered to pay seven million dollars for the Sunrise pearl, but the owner refused to sell it.

Jesus compared heaven to a pearl. But the problem is that we can't buy our way into heaven. Even all the money in the world piled up together would not be enough to buy our way in. But there is a person who paid the price to get us into heaven. Jesus paid the price of his own life by taking our sins on the cross and giving up his life in our place. Now Jesus offers heaven and eternal life to anyone who believes in him. That makes Jesus himself the pearl of great price that we should be willing to follow no matter the cost.

Talk about It

> :: :: KIDS, ask your parents what is the most valuable
> :: :: thing they own.

(Parents, most of us have a diamond ring or a rare coin or something of high value. Passing it around to show your children and talking about its value can bring life to the verses we read today.)

:: Why would anyone sell everything they owned to buy one pearl? *(The only reason someone would sell everything they own to buy one pearl is because they wanted that pearl more than anything else in the world.)*

:: How is Jesus like the pearl in our story today? *(Jesus said the kingdom of heaven is like a pearl. Jesus meant that because he is the way to heaven he himself is the pearl of great value. Following Jesus is worth giving up everything. You can't buy your way into heaven, but you can give up anything you love more than Jesus to follow him.)*

 Pray about It

Ask God to help you leave the things of the world behind to follow Jesus.

DAY FIVE _____

Discover It

Today is the day we look at a different Bible passage—from the book of Psalms or one of the prophets—to see what we can learn from it about Jesus or our salvation.

 Read Amos 9:7–15.

Think about It Some More

Through the prophet Amos, God spoke of a day when he would tear down the great walls of Israel. Then, in verse 11, Amos said God would repair David's fallen booth (a booth is another name for a tent). The great walls and cities of Israel would fall, but David's house would rise up and be rebuilt. Amos didn't mean God was going to send someone to fix a tent. The booth or tent of David was a way to talk about

David's family and how God would bring the Messiah from his family. When that happened, all the nations would be blessed by God. In Acts 15 the apostle James quoted this passage to explain why the Gentiles were receiving the gospel (Acts 15:13–18).

Talk about It

:: What person is represented by David's tent or house rising up? *(Jesus is the person God raised up from David's family who would save his people from their sins.)*

:: How is Amos's prophecy like God's promise to Abraham? *(God promised to bless all nations through Abraham. Through Amos, God repeats that all nations will be "called by my name" [v. 12].)*

:: What nation are you from? *(Think for a minute about your own family. Do you have an Israelite background, or are you from one of the other nations this prophecy is speaking about? Whether you are Jewish or not, God welcomes all people into his family.)*

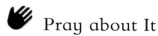 Pray about It

Thank God for blessing people from every nation and welcoming them into his family.

Week 20

Jesus Calms the Storm

Story 98 – *The Gospel Story Bible*

Here is an exercise you can do the day before you start this week's study or anytime in the middle of the week. Look for an opportunity when your family is together at home engaged in active conversation. Stand in the middle of everyone and shout, "Quiet!" Everyone should stop their conversation, startled by your sharp command, and look at you. Smile, and say, "It worked!" When they ask, "What worked?" explain that you were able to quiet your family, which is your sphere of authority, just like Jesus was able to quiet the wind and the waves in the Bible story for this week. Say, "Jesus can quiet the wind and the waves because he has supreme authority over all things."

DAY ONE

Picture It

Little children are sometimes afraid of the dark. At night, even the faintest sound, like that of the rain hitting the roof or the wind blowing in the trees can scare them. As children grow older they begin to trust the judgment of their parents. Even if there are real dangers outside, with mom and dad at home in a sturdy house with strong doors, they learn that they do not need to be afraid. Today in our story the disciples learned a similar lesson. They learned that even when there is danger, if they trust Jesus, there is no reason to be afraid. With Jesus to protect you, even the most dangerous things are as harmless as the sound of the rain on the roof.

 Read Luke 8:22–25.

Think about It Some More

The disciples already knew that Jesus was a remarkable man when they got into the boat with him that day before the storm. The disciples had never seen Jesus sin. They had watched him heal people of their sicknesses, and they had listened to the wonderful teachings Jesus had presented. Still in this story they discovered that Jesus had powers greater than they'd ever imagined. That is why when a fierce storm threatened to crash their boat and kill them, they all became afraid. They had no idea that, while Jesus was with them, the ferocious storm was as harmless as drops of rain on your roof. When Jesus calmed the storm, the disciples were amazed and wondered just who Jesus could really be.

Talk about It

:: What are you most afraid of? *(Parents, draw out your children here. If you remember a story of something they were afraid of, like the dark or perhaps the thought that something was under their bed or in their closet at night, remind them.)*

:: Why were the disciples afraid? *(The disciples were caught in a terrible storm that could have sunk their small boat. They didn't realize that Jesus had power over the wind and the waves, so they were afraid for their lives.)*

:: Why did Jesus say to the disciples that they shouldn't be afraid even though the storm was really dangerous? *(Jesus was in the boat with them, and he controlled the wind and the waves. Even though the storm was dangerous, the disciples were not in any danger with Jesus there.)*

 Pray about It

Ask God to help you trust him when you are in danger or are afraid.

DAY TWO _____

Remember It

What do you remember about yesterday's story? What do you think is going to happen today?

 Read Luke 8:26–33.

Think about It Some More

In yesterday's story, the disciples were amazed when they saw Jesus calm the storm, and wondered who he could be. The demons in our story today knew exactly who Jesus was—and he terrified them. They called him the Son of the Most High God. They knew who Jesus was because they had once been angels in heaven and had worshiped him. However, they had then followed Satan and turned away from God becoming his enemies. God had sent them out of heaven to roam the earth until their time of final judgment (see Isaiah 14:12–14 and Revelation 12:9).

Talk about It

:: Who did the demons say Jesus was? *(God's Son)*

:: How did the demons know who Jesus was? *(The demons had been angels in heaven who had worshiped God, so they knew who he was.)*

:: How do we know, from our story, that Jesus was more powerful than the demons? *(The demons didn't try to fight Jesus. They were afraid of him and even asked permission to go into the pigs. They knew Jesus could destroy them.)*

 Pray about It

Praise God that he is more powerful than anything in heaven or on earth. Nothing is stronger than our God. He is Lord over all.

DAY THREE

Connect It to the Gospel

Today is the day we connect this week's Bible story to the gospel. The gospel is the life, death, and resurrection of Jesus for our salvation. Can anyone guess how our story this week looks forward to or back at the gospel?

 Read Luke 8:34–39.

Think about It Some More

When the herdsmen saw what happened to their pigs, they ran away. When the people came to see the man who had been rescued from the demons, they were afraid. When the people from the surrounding country heard what had happened, they were seized with great fear as well. But the man whom Jesus saved was not afraid. He didn't run away; he wanted to go with Jesus because Jesus had delivered him. God's power and judgment should make us, as sinners, afraid. But if we trust in Jesus to take our sins away, we don't have to fear God's judgment anymore.

Talk about It

:: Why were the people in the story afraid? *(Parents, draw out your children. First, it is pretty scary to hear demons and then watch a herd of pigs run down and drown themselves. But the other people only heard about those things. They were more afraid of how powerful Jesus was. God is all-powerful, and when he uses his power, it can be a scary thing.)*

:: Why wasn't the man who was delivered from the demons afraid of Jesus? *(The man who was delivered was finally free. He, more than anyone there, understood that Jesus had the power to set us free from evil.)*

:: What did the man who was healed want to do? *(He wanted to go with Jesus.)*

:: What job did Jesus give him that he also gives us? *(Jesus told the man to let everyone in his hometown know what God had done for him. That is the same command Jesus gave the disciples to pass on to us, to go and tell everyone about him.)*

 Pray about It

Take time to pray for people you know who need Jesus to help them. *(Parents, this could be relatives or friends who do not believe in or love God or, if appropriate, people your children might already be aware of who are enslaved to alcohol or drugs. You can pray for God to set them free.)*

DAY FOUR

Remember It

What has God been teaching you this week through our Bible story?

 Read Luke 8:40–56.

Think about It Some More

All through the eighth chapter of Luke we have been learning how Jesus had power and authority over everything. On the first day, we learned that he had authority over nature, as he commanded the wind and the waves. On the second day, we learned that he had authority over demons. Today, we read that Jesus had authority over sickness and even death. When Jesus told those gathered over the dead girl that she was only sleeping, they laughed at him because they knew she was dead. But Jesus brought her back to life with two words, "Child, arise." Nothing is impossible for God, and since Jesus is God, nothing—even raising the dead—is impossible for him.

Talk about It

> ⚬ ⚬ KIDS, ask your parents how the stories you read
> ⚬ ⚬ about help them to trust in Jesus for the things they
> need.

(Parents, when we see that Jesus is all-powerful even over death, it makes our needs seem small. If God can raise the dead, then surely he can care for us. Knowing how powerful he has been in the past helps us to trust him now.)

:: How old was the man's daughter who died? *(She was twelve years old.)*

:: Why didn't Jesus want the parents to tell people that he raised their daughter from the dead? *(In other places, when Jesus did miracles, the people tried to force Jesus to be king before his time [see John 6:15]. It could be that Jesus didn't want that to happen.)*

 Pray about It

Pray for those who you know are sick, that God would heal them.

DAY FIVE

Discover It

Today is the day we look at a different Bible passage—from the book of Psalms or one of the prophets—to see what we can learn from it about Jesus or our salvation.

 Read Psalm 23.

Think about It Some More

There are many ways that this psalm points to Jesus. David called the Lord his shepherd, and we know that Jesus said he was the Good Shepherd (John 10:11). David was satisfied in the Lord because of how God provided him rest. Jesus said, "Come to me, all who labor and are heavy laden, and I will give you rest" (Matthew 11:28).

In Revelation 7:17 we read that one day the Lamb, who is Jesus, will lead us to springs of water and wipe every tear from our eyes and live with us forever. That matches the description David gives in his psalm. Although this passage does not claim to be a prophecy about Jesus, it certainly points to him. The only way David, who was a sinner, could walk on paths of righteousness is if God took his sin away. That is exactly what Jesus did on the cross. And it is only by believing in God's plan of salvation, which came through Jesus, that David could live in the house of the Lord forever.

Talk about It

:: Can you think of one way this psalm points forward to Jesus? *(Parents, if your children can't remember any of the ways this psalm points to Jesus, read it again slowly and have them raise their hands when they think they know a way. You can also give them clues by emphasizing the words* shepherd, rest, *and other words that point to Jesus as you read.)*

:: How can this psalm of David comfort us today? *(In the same way that David trusted the Lord in his time of trouble, we can too. The Lord is also our shepherd.)*

:: Why should this psalm be even more special to us than it was for David? *(When David wrote the psalm and trusted the Lord, he did not know Jesus. He didn't know how God was going to save him and bring him into the Lord's house forever. We know the whole glorious, wonderful story of Jesus. If David could trust the Lord with the little he knew, we should be able to trust the Lord even more since we know the whole gospel story.)*

 Pray about It

Ask God to help you trust in Jesus to both rescue you from your sins and provide the things you need each day.

Week 21

Jesus Feeds the Multitude

Story 99 – *The Gospel Story Bible*

You will need five small loaves of bread or dinner rolls, a large basket, and a can of sardines for this exercise. Prior to Bible study, show the objects to your children and see if they can guess which Bible story you are going to be reviewing this week. (They may not know what the sardines are, so if you want, open the can so they can see the fish.) Once they guess the story, ask them if they would like to try the same meal Jesus provided for the crowds. Then offer them a taste of the fish and some bread.

DAY ONE

Picture It

Once a person becomes famous, people want to be around him or her. That is why movie stars, professional sports players, and the president all draw big crowds wherever they go. To avoid the large crowds, famous people keep their travel plans a secret. Even so, as soon as someone recognizes them, word spreads quickly, and more and more people come, often wanting their autograph. That is what happened to Jesus. Whenever someone saw him, they spread the word, and soon crowds would form. But instead of autographs, they wanted him to heal their sick. Although Jesus didn't announce his schedule, the crowds always seemed to find him.

 Read John 6:1–4.

Think about It Some More

Back in Jesus' day, people didn't have as many kinds of good medicine or as much medical knowledge as we have, so there were a lot more sick people with no cures. Today, we can cure leprosy, treat epilepsy, and even give people artificial legs to help them walk if they are lame. But back then, the doctors could not do any of that. So you can imagine just how exciting it was to bring sick people to Jesus and watch him heal them instantly.

If Jesus walked the earth today, we could bring him people with diseases we have no cure for, like some kinds of cancer. So even though we can cure many diseases, the same kind of crowds would form. We would track Jesus via the TV news, and word would spread quickly on the Internet and by text messages. If Jesus thought it was difficult to get away from the crowds back in his day, it would be even harder today.

Talk about It

:: Do you remember what the Passover feast is all about? *(The Passover feast was celebrated by Israel to remember the last plague and their ancestors' deliverance from slavery in Egypt. If you remember, they put the blood of a lamb on their doorframes so that the angel of death would "pass over" their house and not kill their firstborn sons.)*

:: Why did Jesus go up a mountain or out on a boat when a large crowd was coming? *(Jesus liked to go up mountains or out on a boat when a large crowd was coming because that made it easier for the people to see and hear him.)*

:: Why do you think the people were so attracted to Jesus? *(They had never seen anything like what Jesus was doing. Blind people received sight, the lame walked, and the deaf were made to hear. The people hoped that Jesus' miracles were a sign that God was going to deliver them from the Romans, who ruled over them.)*

 Pray about It

Make a list of some of the miracles Jesus did and then praise him for each one and how it showed to everyone that he was the Son of God.

DAY TWO

Remember It

What do you remember about yesterday's story? What do you think is going to happen today?

 Read John 6:5–13.

Think about It Some More

John, the disciple who wrote this story, said there were five thousand men present the day Jesus multiplied the fishes and the loaves. But there were also women and children there. That means there could have been as many as ten or fifteen thousand people on the hillside. How did Jesus multiply such a small amount of food to satisfy the hunger of more than fifteen thousand people—and still have twelve baskets full of leftovers? Did the two fish and five barley loaves suddenly grow into two giant fish and five enormous loaves of bread? Or did the two fish suddenly turn into twenty thousand fish as Jesus lifted up his hands to pray?

The Bible doesn't describe exactly how Jesus did it, but it would have been fun to sit there and watch. Whatever way it happened, this miracle shows us that Jesus had the power to create—the same power he used when he created the world.

Talk about It

:: How do you think the fish and bread grew to feed all the people? *(Parents, this is just a fun question. We really don't know how it happened. Give each of your children a chance to talk about how they think it happened.)*

:: How could Jesus multiply the fish and the loaves to feed so many people? *(Parents, draw out your children to see if they remember that Jesus was actually the one who created the world [see Colossians 1:16]. If Jesus could create the world from nothing, then multiplying the fish and loaves would've been no big deal.)*

:: How can this story help build our faith? *(At times, we might find ourselves in what seem like impossible situations. Knowing that God is all-powerful and that he loves to help us in our time of need builds faith. In the past he has worked in power to help people. This can encourage us to pray and ask God for help.)*

:: How should God's provision for the five thousand men and their families encourage us as we trust God for the food we need? *(This story helps us to see that God can and will provide all of our needs.)*

 Pray about It

Praise Jesus for his mighty power, which could create the world and multiply the fishes and the loaves of bread.

DAY THREE

Connect It to the Gospel

Today is the day we connect this week's Bible story to the gospel. The gospel is the life, death, and resurrection of Jesus for our salvation. Can anyone guess how our story this week looks forward to or back at the gospel?

 Read John 6:14–27.

Think about It Some More

When the people saw Jesus multiply the fishes and the loaves, they thought he was the Messiah, the promised deliverer whom they thought would lead them to victory over their Roman overlords. That was why they wanted to make Jesus king. When they called Jesus the prophet who was to come into the world, they were remembering a prophecy Moses had given.

In Deuteronomy, Moses said, "The LORD your God will raise up for you a prophet like me from among you, from your brothers—it is to him you shall listen. . . . I will raise up for them a prophet like you from among their brothers. And I will put my words in his mouth, and he shall speak to them all that I command him" (Deuteronomy 18:15, 18). The people were correct: Jesus *was* the prophet Moses had talked about. But he didn't come to deliver the Jews from the rule of the Romans. Jesus came to save his people from greater enemies—sin and death. He came to give them peace in heaven forever, not just peace on earth from Rome.

Talk about It

:: When the people saw Jesus multiply the fishes and the loaves, what did they want to do with Jesus? *(When they saw Jesus multiply the fishes and the loaves they believed Jesus was a great prophet and wanted to make him king so he could deliver Israel from the Romans.)*

:: Why didn't Jesus want the people to make him king? *(Jesus didn't come to earth to rule as an earthly king to save them from an earthly enemy. Jesus came to be their heavenly king and to destroy sin and death so that everyone who believes in him can live forever.)*

:: If you were there to see Jesus multiply the fishes and the loaves, what do you think you would have done? *(We all would have joined the crowd and wanted to make Jesus our king. Making Jesus king was not a bad response; it was a good one. It was just that the people didn't understand that Jesus had come to give them so much more than earthly freedom and treasure. Jesus had come to give them heavenly treasure and freedom from sin.)*

 ## Pray about It

Ask God to help you love Jesus and heaven more than riches here on earth.

DAY FOUR _____

Remember It

What has God been teaching you this week through our Bible story?

 Read John 6:28–40.

Think about It Some More

It seems amazing that Jesus could feed upwards of fifteen thousand people with only two fish and five small barley loaves. But that is not as amazing as Jesus saving an uncountable multitude (Revelation 7:9) of lost people by dying on the cross for their sins. The feeding of the crowd is meant to be a picture for us of something more special. It is meant to show us that Jesus can provide all we need. Not just what we need to live here on earth, but all that we need to live forever in heaven. That is why Jesus called himself the bread of life. Jesus will rescue all of

God's children, not losing even one person whom God had planned to save. We have a great hope. If we believe in Jesus, he will save us. That is God's promise.

Talk about It

> ● ● KIDS, ask your parents to tell you how God has
> ● ● met their needs through the years.

(Parents, share a story in which God has provided for you when you really needed something.)

:: What answer did Jesus give to the people who asked, "What must we do?" *(Jesus told them that they should believe in the one whom God had sent.)*

:: Who is the one God sent? *(Jesus)*

:: Who did Jesus say will rise on the last day (v. 40)? *(Parents, if you have younger children who are not strong readers, reread verse 40 and have them raise their hands when they hear the answer: "everyone who looks on the Son and believes in him.")*

 Pray about It

Ask God to help you believe in Jesus so that you will be adopted into God's family and become a child of God, with all of your sins forgiven.

DAY FIVE _____

Discover It

Today is the day we look at a different Bible passage—from the book of Psalms or one of the prophets—to see what we can learn from it about Jesus or our salvation.

 Read Isaiah 29:18–20.

Think about It Some More

Some of the Old Testament prophecies that talk about Jesus are hard to figure out. But it is easy to see Jesus in this one. The "Holy One of Israel" is one of the names the prophets gave for the Messiah who would one day come. When Jesus was on earth, the demons called him the "Holy One of God" (Mark 1:24; John 6:69). And we know that Jesus healed the blind and the deaf. Jesus didn't go to the rich or the rulers; he went to the poor and needy. And when he taught them and healed their diseases, they were filled with joy and gave praise to God. One day, just as Isaiah 29:20 tells us, the Holy One of Israel will put an end to all evil. That will happen when Jesus comes again.

Talk about It

:: What name for Jesus does Isaiah use in his prophecy? *(Parents, if your children don't get the answer [the "Holy One of Israel"] correct, reread the passage and highlight the correct answer by changing the tone of your voice.)*

:: What other clues, besides the name Holy One of Israel, tell us that Isaiah was talking about Jesus? *(Isaiah said the deaf would hear and the blind would see.)*

:: When will Jesus put an end to all evil? *(When Jesus comes again he will throw into the fire all sinners who have not turned away from their sin to trust in him [see Revelation 21:8].)*

 Pray about It

Praise the Holy One of Israel for opening the ears of the deaf, giving sight to the blind, and one day, putting an end to all evil.

Week 22

Jesus Walks on Water

Story 100 – *The Gospel Story Bible*

Fill a glass with water and float a one-inch square piece of tissue on the surface of the water. Place a paperclip or needle on the tissue raft. Then carefully push down on and sink the tissue without touching the paper clip or needle. If you are careful, the paper clip or needle will remain afloat on the surface tension of the water. Now, if you add a drop of liquid soap, the surface tension will break and the clip or needle will sink. You can use this interesting exercise to introduce this week's story about Jesus walking on the water.

DAY ONE

Picture It

It's hard to concentrate and think clearly when there is a lot of noise going on around you. That is why you are not supposed to talk loudly at the library while people are trying to read. When you get to school and are taking a test, your teacher will also insist that you don't talk or make noise. That way, the students taking the test won't be interrupted.

Some people do their Bible study in the morning and call it their "quiet time." They like to do this in the morning before there is a lot of noise and activity in the house. In the quiet it's easier to concentrate on praying to God and reading the Bible. Today, we will see that even Jesus liked to have a quiet time.

 Read Matthew 14:22–23.

Think about It Some More

After sending away the crowd who wanted to make him king (John 6:14–15), Jesus found a quiet spot to pray, away from the crowds. The Bible doesn't say what Jesus prayed about, but we know from his other prayers that Jesus loved talking to his Father. It could be that Jesus talked to his Father about how all the people wanted to make him king. Remember that Jesus was tempted like us in every way, but he did not give in to sin (Hebrews 4:15).

Imagine how tempting it would be to have a crowd of over ten thousand people clamoring to make you king. Wouldn't you be tempted to just go along with them? But what if you knew that you had to be arrested and die instead? Rather than pleasing the people, Jesus turned away from the crowd to obey his Father and find his joy in completing the mission his Father had given him. Jesus knew that one day he would sit on the throne with all the people he saved worshiping around him, and that brought him great joy (Hebrews 12:2).

Talk about It

:: Why did Jesus send the people away? *(They wanted to make him king.)*

:: Why wouldn't Jesus want to be king? *(Jesus didn't come to earth to be king; he came to earth to die on the cross for our sins. He would be king, but only after completing his mission.)*

:: What could be some of the reasons Jesus wanted to be alone to pray? *(Jesus came to die on the cross, yet the crowd wanted to make him king. That may have provided a temptation for Jesus. Instead of turning to the people, Jesus turned to the Father.)*

:: How can prayer help us to fight temptation? *(God will help us fight temptation when we turn away from it and turn to him in prayer. Parents, you can help your children by suggesting a time they could pray each day, or, in the midst of the day when they are tempted.)*

 Pray about It

Ask God to help you spend time each day in prayer.

DAY TWO

Remember It

What do you remember about yesterday's story? What do you think is going to happen today?

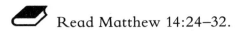 Read Matthew 14:24–32.

Think about It Some More

After the disciples started back across the lake in their boat, they ran into a storm with strong winds that kept them from moving very fast. So when a ghost came after them (at least that is what they thought Jesus was), they couldn't get away. Imagine their panic as they rowed faster but the ghost was catching up to them. If you were in a boat on stormy seas and you saw someone walking on the water toward your boat, you would be afraid too.

Jesus had healed the sick, raised the dead, and multiplied the fishes and the loaves, but walking on water was new to the disciples. Once Peter recognized Jesus, he asked permission to walk on water himself. At first he did okay, but as soon as he took his eyes off of Jesus and paid attention to the storm, he began to sink.

Peter's sinking is a good picture of what happens to us when we take our eyes off of Jesus. When we look away from Jesus and pay attention to our troubles, we sink into fear. So if ever we find ourselves in trouble and fall into fear, we should remember Peter's words, "Lord, save me." Those three words are perhaps the most powerful short prayer in the whole Bible.

Talk about It

:: What did Peter ask when he saw Jesus walking on the water? *(Peter asked Jesus if he could come out on the water with him.)*

:: Why did Peter sink? *(At first Peter walked on the water like Jesus did. But he began to sink when his gaze shifted from Jesus to the waves. As long as he trusted in Jesus, he didn't sink.)*

:: What did Peter cry out to Jesus when he began to sink? *("Lord, save me!")*

Pray about It

Make a list of things you need Jesus to save you from, and then offer them up in a prayer to God. We all need Jesus to rescue us from our sin, so you can start your prayer there. But you might also need God's healing for a sickness or provision for something that you need.

DAY THREE

Connect It to the Gospel

Today is the day we connect this week's Bible story to the gospel. The gospel is the life, death, and resurrection of Jesus for our salvation. Can anyone guess how our story this week looks forward to or back at the gospel?

 Read Matthew 14:33.

Think about It Some More

As Jesus climbed into the boat after walking on the sea, the disciples worshiped him. The Bible clearly states that we should worship God alone. Jesus himself told Satan, "You shall worship the Lord your God and him only shall you serve" (Matthew 4:10). So if Jesus were not really God, he should have rebuked the disciples for worshiping him. But Jesus did not correct them—because Jesus really is God. The disciples were starting to realize that although Jesus was a real man, he was also God.

It was very important that Jesus was both God and man at the same time. As a man, Jesus could die in our place. As God, Jesus was able to keep from sinning even once and defeat death by rising again. The disciples were correct to worship Jesus, and they also were correct when they called him God's Son.

Talk about It

:: What did the disciples do when Jesus got back in the boat? *(They worshiped Jesus as God.)*

:: What did the disciples call Jesus? *(The disciples called Jesus the Son of God.)*

:: Why was it important that Jesus be both a man and God? *(Jesus had to be a man to die for our sins, and he had to be God to live a perfect life and then rise from the dead.)*

 Pray about It

Come up with your own prayer of praise so that you can worship Jesus as God like the disciples did.

DAY FOUR

Remember It

What has God been teaching you this week through our Bible story?

 Read Matthew 14:34–36.

Think about It Some More

What would you think if your doctor said that there was a medicine so powerful that all you needed to do was touch the bottle the pills were stored in and your sickness would go away? You would probably not believe it. But if you touched the bottle and you were healed, you would believe that the medicine really was indeed very powerful. In our Bible passage today, we learn that the power of God in Jesus to heal the sick was so strong that to be healed all a sick person had to do was to have enough faith to touch the fringe of Jesus' robe.

Talk about It

> ●● KIDS, ask your parents what they think it would
> ●● be like if Jesus were alive today and healing people.

(Parents, think of what the news reporters would say and think of what kinds of people would come to Jesus for healing.)

:: Why did the men on the shore spread the word that Jesus was there? *(They knew that Jesus could heal the sick, so they spread word for people to bring the sick to Jesus so he could heal them.)*

:: What did the people who were sick need to do to be healed? *(All the sick people needed to do was get close enough to touch Jesus clothes, and they would be healed.)*

:: What should we do when people we know are sick, now that Jesus has gone back to heaven? *(Since God can hear our prayers, we can still pray and ask God to heal them.)*

 Pray about It

Pray for all those you know who are sick and ask God to heal them.

DAY FIVE

Discover It

Today is the day we look at a different Bible passage—from the book of Psalms or one of the prophets—to see what we can learn from it about Jesus or our salvation.

 Read Isaiah 53:4.

Think about It Some More

Did you ever notice that sin has a way of bringing sadness? If you disobey your parents, they are sad, and then you become sad when you see they are disappointed in what you did. If you then are punished, you suffer the loss of something. Or think of when people fight. If one man strikes another on the face, causing a bruise, the wound will be painful for days, and the injured man will have to suffer with everyone asking why he has a bruise on his face.

If you add up all the sins of everyone whom God planned to save and add up all the sadness from all that sin, that is the sorrow Jesus carried with him onto the cross. Jesus took the punishment we deserved for all that sin. But the saddest part of the cross was when God the Father turned his love away from his Son to pour out his wrathful anger on him for our sins. That is why when Jesus was on the cross he cried out, "My God, my God, why have you forsaken me?" (Matthew 27:46). That was Jesus' saddest moment.

Talk about It

:: What did Jesus do for us when he died on the cross? *(Jesus took our sins on himself when he died on the cross.)*

:: Why did God the Father punish Jesus if Jesus never did anything wrong? *(God the Father didn't punish Jesus for his own sin, he punished Jesus for our sin.)*

:: What do we need to do to have Jesus take our sins away? *(All we need to do is believe in Jesus and call out to him with the same words Peter used from our story this week when he was sinking into the sea, "Lord, save me.")*

Pray about It

Thank Jesus for taking our sins on himself and taking our punishment on the cross.

Week 23

Take Up Your Cross

Story 101 – *The Gospel Story Bible*

Look for the most worn-out dollar bill you can find. As you pass it around to your children, tell them that the average dollar bill lasts about eighteen months before it wears out and has to be replaced. The bill you are passing around is likely to be shredded the next time it moves through the banking system. Can you imagine living your life for money instead of God? One dollar bill lasts eighteen months, and a whole life's fortune is lost when we die, but God is our treasure forever. Say, "This week, you will learn that there is a cost for following Jesus, but the reward is everlasting."

DAY ONE

Picture It

If you asked your friends to describe you in three to five words, what do you think they would say? How do you think people who don't like you very much would describe you? Today in our story Jesus asks the disciples a similar question.

 Read Luke 9:18–20.

Think about It Some More

When Jesus asked his disciples who the crowds said that he was, he wasn't asking if they knew his name. Jesus wanted to know who they *believed* he was. His question was testing their faith. Remember, Jesus was performing miracles and teaching with authority. He was not your average carpenter from Nazareth. The people knew that Jesus was special, but their answers to the question of who he was were wrong. But the answer Peter gave was correct. Peter said Jesus was the Christ, which means the anointed one.

Back when God gave Israel its first kings, he sent a prophet to anoint them by pouring oil over their head. That was the way God showed everyone whom he had chosen to be king. So when Peter called Jesus the Christ—the anointed one—he was saying that Jesus was God's choice to be king and to deliver his people. When Matthew wrote about this same story, he said that Jesus commended Peter and told him that God the Father had given him the correct answer, and that apart from God showing him, Peter could not have known who Jesus really was (Matthew 16:17).

Talk about It

:: Who did the crowds think Jesus was? *(Parents, if your younger children can't remember, reread the passage and have them raise their hands when they hear the correct answer.)*

:: Who did Peter say Jesus was? *(The Christ)*

:: What does the name *Christ* mean? *(The name* Christ *means anointed one—the one whom God had chosen to be king.)*

:: Who gave Peter the correct answer? *(God the Father revealed to Peter that Jesus was the Messiah.)*

 Pray about It

Pray for all the people who still do not know that Jesus is the one who came into the world to save us from our sins. Some people think he was only a good teacher. They need our prayers so that God will show them that Jesus is the Messiah, God's chosen one, who came to save us from our sins.

DAY TWO

Remember It

What do you remember about yesterday's story? What do you think is going to happen today?

 Read Luke 9:22.

Think about It Some More

Did you ever guess ahead of time what your parents were planning to get your brother or sister for his or her birthday? Chances are that if you guessed correctly, your parents would tell you to keep it a secret. Well, as soon as the disciples figured out that Jesus was the Messiah, Jesus told them to keep it a secret. The people around him already wanted to force him to be king, and if the disciples started telling everyone that Jesus was the Messiah, it could stir up the people even more.

Jesus didn't come to be an earthly king over Israel and rescue them from Rome. Jesus came as King of every nation, and his plan was to bring salvation to people from every nation. But he knew there was only way to do that. He had to go to the cross and die for their sins and then rise again in victory on the third day. Even though Jesus told the disciples exactly what was going to take place, they didn't understand what he meant. But as we look back at his words, it is clear that Jesus knew all about the cross ahead of time and knew that suffering and death were waiting for him.

Talk about It

:: Even though we normally talk about the gospel connection on Day Three, today's verses contain the gospel message. Where do you see the gospel in these verses? *(Parents, help your children first remember what the gospel message is—Jesus' death on the cross and resurrection. Then have them look for the gospel in the verses. If you have young readers, reread the passage and have them raise their hands when they hear the gospel.)*

:: Why didn't Jesus want the disciples to tell everyone that he was the Messiah? *(The people were trying to force Jesus to be their king. It wasn't God's plan to make him king of only one nation, and it wasn't yet time for Jesus to die on the cross.)*

:: Jesus said that he would suffer. Can you remember any of the ways that Jesus suffered? *(Jesus was arrested, beaten, spit upon, slapped, insulted, lied about, made to wear a crown of thorns on his head, and crucified.)*

 Pray about It

Thank Jesus for coming to earth to suffer and die in our place to take our punishment so that we could be saved.

DAY THREE

Connect It to the Gospel

Today is the day we connect this week's Bible story to the gospel. The gospel is the life, death, and resurrection of Jesus for our salvation. Can anyone guess how our story this week looks forward to or back at the gospel?

 Read Luke 9:23–25.

Think about It Some More

Yesterday's Bible passage connected our story to the gospel. In those verses, Jesus said he had to die and then rise from the dead. In our passage today, Jesus told the disciples they also had a cross to take up. That didn't mean that all the disciples and anyone who wants to follow Jesus will also die on a cross. Jesus was trying to show that, in order to follow him, we have to die to the other desires or things we love more than him. We can't love the world or the things of the world and love Jesus too. We have to give up (or die to) loving the things of the world and love Jesus instead.

That means we can't love our toys more than we love God, we can't spend all our money on ourselves, and we shouldn't spend all of our time playing on our computer and not read our Bibles. Giving those things up can be hard, but that is what Jesus calls us to. He wants us to love him more than we love anything else in the world. The good news of the gospel helps us here too! Paul said it like this: "Work out your own salvation with fear and trembling, for it is God who works in you, both to will and to work for his good pleasure" (Philippians 2:12–13). It is a comfort to know that even though God calls us to work, he is doing the work himself within us!

Talk about It

:: What did Jesus say we needed to give up to follow him? (*Jesus said we needed to give up our lives—that is, anything we love more than God.*)

:: What did Jesus warn us about a person who gains the whole world but doesn't have love for God? (*Jesus said you could have all the money in the world or all the power or even both—all the money and all the power—and still not go to heaven, if you love those things more than you love God.)*

:: What are you tempted to love more than God? *(Parents, help your children remember the things of the world they love that can take their attention away from God. A good example is something they refuse to stop doing if you ask them to do something else. They become angry because they love it more than they love obeying God who said that children should obey their parents.)*

 Pray about It

Ask God to help you love him most of all, and ask God to help you love him more than you love anything you mentioned above.

DAY FOUR _____

Remember It

What has God been teaching you this week through our Bible story?

 Read Luke 9:26–27.

Think about It Some More

Jesus is the greatest treasure of all, and yet Christians can refuse to tell people about Jesus because they are afraid of what others will think of them. The apostle Paul told Timothy that we should never be ashamed to talk about Jesus (2 Timothy 1:8). Pretend for a moment that all the people of the earth are lost, wandering in a desert, dying of thirst, and you are with them. If you found a spring of water and drank your fill, wouldn't you want to tell others about the water so they wouldn't die of thirst?

In the same way, we are all lost living in the desert of our sin and need to believe and trust in Jesus so that we can be forgiven and receive the living water of eternal life. Having God forgive our sin is even better than finding a spring of water in the desert. So we should always be willing to tell people the good news about Jesus, even those who refuse to believe.

Talk about It

> KIDS, ask your parents to share a time when they told somebody about Jesus.

(Parents, think of a time when you were able to share your faith. It could have been a witnessing opportunity with unbelievers or even a teaching opportunity with your own children.)

:: Why should we want to tell others about Jesus? *(Jesus is the only way people can be rescued from their sins. He is the greatest treasure of all.)*

:: Why are some people ashamed to talk about Jesus? *(Some people are more concerned with what others think about them. They can be afraid that others will reject them for talking about Jesus.)*

Pray about It

Ask God to give you courage to tell others about Jesus.

DAY FIVE

Discover It

Today is the day we look at a different Bible passage—from the book of Psalms or one of the prophets—to see what we can learn from it about Jesus or our salvation.

Read Isaiah 53:1–3.

Think about It Some More

Jesus is the one whom Isaiah said would grow up like a young plant but then be rejected by men. Like Isaiah, Jesus also prophesied that he must suffer and be rejected and killed. We read about it earlier this week, in Luke 9:22. Isaiah said that Jesus would be despised and rejected, and that is exactly what happened to Jesus when his own people spat on him and made fun of him. Isaiah also said Jesus would be a man of sorrows.

We know that Jesus was filled with sorrow in the Garden of Gethsemane as he prayed before he was arrested. It was very hard for him to take our sins upon himself and suffer on the cross in our place. God revealed these things to Isaiah so he could write them down many years before they happened. That way, we would know that Jesus' suffering and death were all planned by God (Acts 2:23). It might sound terrible for God to plan for his Son, Jesus, to die, but that is the only way our sin could be paid for.

Talk about It

:: Where do you see Jesus in Isaiah's description of the suffering servant? *(Parents, you may need to reread the passage and have your children raise their hands when they hear something that describes what happened to Jesus.)*

:: Kings show their majesty or greatness by wearing gold jewelry and sitting on a gold throne and wearing beautiful clothing. Jesus was a king but Isaiah said there was no majesty about him. Why was that true? *(Jesus was born in a manger, lived as a carpenter, and wore common clothes. He even refused to be made king. When he was given a royal robe, it was only to make fun of him, and the only crown he was given here on earth was one made of thorns.)*

:: Isaiah said that men would hide their faces from Jesus and not look at him. Can you think of when that might have happened in Jesus' life? *(When Jesus was dying on the cross with all of his wounds, no one cared. While Jesus was suffering, people turned away and did not help him. The best Jesus got was a drink of sour wine.)*

 Pray about It

Thank Jesus for his willingness to suffer for us and die such a terrible death on the cross.

Week 24

The Transfiguration

Story 102 – *The Gospel Story Bible*

Bring a small, bright flashlight to Bible study. With the flashlight turned off, have your children look at the bulb and describe it to you. (Hold the flashlight in your hand as they describe it.) They might say the bulb is clear and round in shape. Then without warning, turn the light on, shining it into their faces. The brightness should startle them. Now have them describe the bulb again, this time with the light on. It will be difficult for them to even look at the lightbulb while it is on. Say, "This week we will be learning about the transfiguration of Jesus. If a lightbulb can startle us with its brightness, imagine the shock the disciples felt when the Lord revealed his glory."

DAY ONE

Picture It

There once was a young man who left home to go to college and had to wash his own clothes for the very first time in his life. Not sure how to even use a washer, he crammed all his clothes into one large load at the college laundry. On top of the washer were two plastic bins filled with white powder. Each bin had a scoop in it. The young man wasn't sure which powder to add to the wash load. Taking a guess, he added three scoops of the powder in the left bin to the washing machine. He then added two more scoops to make sure his clothes came out nice and clean. Then he started the washer and went for a cup of coffee.

When he returned and opened the washer, he was shocked. All of his blue jeans were white. That was when he realized that he had used powdered bleach instead of soap to wash his clothes. Bleach can turn dark clothes white and make white clothes even whiter. But it can't make them as white as Jesus' clothes became when he was transfigured on the mountain.

 Read Mark 9:2–4.

Think about It Some More

If you were driving in a car at night on a winding road and another car came around a bend in front of you with its high beams on, you would be blinded by the bright lights. But the brightness of a car's headlights is nothing when compared with the radiant light that came from Jesus at his transfiguration.

Matthew recorded it this way in his gospel: "His face shone like the sun, and his clothes became white as light" (Matthew 17:2). Imagine hiking with Jesus up a mountain when suddenly you see his face turn white as the sun! That would make you turn your face away. And if that didn't shock the disciples enough, Moses and Elijah, who had been dead for hundreds of years, showed up on the scene. There was a reason for this. Jesus wanted to give a few of his disciples a glimpse of his glory. And by talking with Moses, the giver of the law, and with Elijah, the great and powerful prophet, Jesus was showing that he was not against the law and the prophets but that he came to complete the work they had foretold (Matthew 5:17).

Talk about It

:: Think of this story. What does the word *transfigured* mean? *(Your kids may not know the word* transfigured, *but they may know the word* transformed. *Both words mean a dramatic change in appearance.)*

:: What does the transfiguration tell us about Jesus? *(The transfiguration shows us that Jesus was God and was all-powerful. It also shows us that, although Jesus set aside the full measure of his glory to become a man, he never lost his glory.)*

:: Will we get to see Jesus in all his glory like the disciples did that day? *(We will see Jesus' glory when we go to heaven to be with him. We won't need sunshine or electric lights in heaven because the glory of Jesus will shine there [see Revelation 21:23].)*

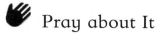 Pray about It

Thank Jesus for giving up the fullness of his glory to become a man so that he could die for us.

DAY TWO

Remember It

What do you remember about yesterday's story? What do you think is going to happen today?

 Read Mark 9:5–8.

Think about It Some More

You can find instructions on the Internet for doing just about anything. You can find out how to fix the brakes on your car, what is the proper way to set the table, and even what you should do if you are attacked by a grizzly bear. But you won't find directions anywhere to tell you what to do when Moses and Elijah show up during a transfiguration. The disciples had no clue what to do. The best they could come up with was to suggest that they pitch three tents, one for each of the three men present.

Then, as if the whole experience were not scary enough already, clouds came down from heaven, and God the Father spoke. Matthew said that when this happened, the disciples stopped talking and fell to the ground, terrified (see Matthew 17:6). The three disciples probably thought they were going to die.

Talk about It

:: Who appeared with Jesus during his transfiguration? *(Moses and Elijah)*

:: Can you remember something that Moses or Elijah did? *(Parents, you can remind your children what Moses did by giving them clues about leading the Israelites through the Red Sea. For Elijah, you can give clues about how he helped the widow, whose flour and oil didn't run out because she was willing to give him the last of her food.)*

:: For lack of a better idea, Peter suggested that they erect three tents there on the mountain. What would you have done if you had been there? *(Parents, there is no wrong answer, but you can help your children to understand that there was nothing to do but be amazed and worship God. If they had been there, they would have fallen to the ground in fear just as the disciples did.)*

:: What did Jesus' transfiguration tell the disciples about him? *(The disciples learned that Jesus was full of power; that he knew Elijah and Moses, who had lived a long time before then; and, most importantly, that God the Father called Jesus his beloved Son.)*

 ## Pray about It

Praise Jesus for all the things we learn about him through this story. We can praise him for his glorious power, for living forever, and for being willing to come down to earth to live a perfect life and to die for our sins.

DAY THREE _____

Connect It to the Gospel

Today is the day we connect this week's Bible story to the gospel. The gospel is the life, death, and resurrection of Jesus for our salvation. Can anyone guess how our story this week looks forward to or back at the gospel?

 Read Mark 9:9–13.

Think about It Some More

When you see something amazing the first thing you want to do is tell your friends about it. But in our story today, Jesus told Peter, James, and John not to tell anyone about what they'd seen—at least not until after he'd risen from the dead. But they didn't understand what Jesus meant by saying he would rise from the dead. The last thing they would have guessed was that Jesus was going to suffer and die on a cross.

They probably had other ideas. In their minds, the transfiguration was a great secret weapon. If Jesus ever did come up against the Romans, he could use it to fight them. That would scare them all right. The disciples knew that God had promised to deliver his people, but they thought the Messiah would deliver God's people from their earthly enemies. In that case, the transfiguration really would have been a great surprise weapon.

This helps us understand why Peter would have been so confident the night that Jesus was arrested and why he would have pulled out his sword. On that evening, Jesus didn't transfigure himself again; he allowed the soldiers to arrest him. (But in John 18:6 notice that Jesus did knock the guards to the ground by speaking three words, "I am he.") The reason Jesus didn't fight back with his power was that he didn't come to deliver Israel from the Romans—he came to save them from their sins. To do that, he had to go to the cross.

Talk about It

:: Whom did Jesus say Peter, James, and John could tell about what they saw? *(Jesus told them that they were not permitted to tell anyone, not even the other disciples.)*

:: The disciples didn't know what rising from the dead meant. What was Jesus talking about? *(Parents, this is an obvious question to us, but it is good to have our children repeat the story of Jesus' death and resurrection. See if they can tell you the story of what happened.)*

:: What do you think Peter, James, and John thought about Jesus' transfiguration? *(The Bible doesn't tell us what they thought, so draw out your children here. The disciples saw Jesus shine as bright as the sun, two men from the Old Testament appeared, and God the Father spoke. That would have made them believe that Jesus was powerful and that no one could defeat him.)*

 ## Pray about It

Praise Jesus for his glorious power and thank him for giving up his glory to suffer and die in our place.

DAY FOUR _____

Remember It

What has God been teaching you this week through our Bible story?

 Read Mark 9:14–29.

Think about It Some More

The disciples tried to cast the demon out of the boy by themselves, but they could not do it. Jesus didn't have any trouble doing it. The evil spirit obeyed Jesus' command to come out and never return. When the disciples asked why they were not able to cast out the demon, Jesus said they needed to pray. Praying is how we ask God for help. In this case, Jesus was telling the disciples that they couldn't do this without his help.

Jesus gave the disciples the authority to cast out demons, but they didn't have the power to do it on their own; they needed to pray. We need Jesus' help too. Every breath and step we take is possible only because of God's grace. Most importantly, none of us can get ourselves to heaven. Even after we place our trust in Jesus, we need his help to keep on living for him.

Talk about It

> ● ● KIDS, ask your parents to tell you a story of when
> ● ● they prayed to God for help with something they knew they couldn't do on their own.

:: Why did Jesus tell the disciples that they needed to pray when casting out demons? *(The disciples didn't have the power by themselves to cast out demons; they needed God's help. Praying is the way we ask God to help us.)*

:: Can you think of a time when you prayed for God to help you with something you couldn't do by yourself? *(Parents, try to help your children think of something they prayed for. It could be that they prayed for good weather for a sporting event or vacation or for protection on the highway during a trip.)*

 ## Pray about It

Make a list of things you could pray and ask God's help with. Then pray for those things.

DAY FIVE _____

Discover It

Today is the day we look at a different Bible passage—from the book of Psalms or one of the prophets—to see what we can learn from it about Jesus or our salvation.

 Read Psalm 72:11–13.

Think about It Some More

King Solomon wrote Psalm 72 about a king who would rule over the whole earth. In the part of the psalm we read today, Solomon said that the other kings of the earth would bow down to serve the one great king. Jesus is the only king who fits this description. Jesus rules over all the earth and is called the Lord of lords and King of kings (Revelation 17:14). When John the Baptist sent his disciples to ask Jesus if he was the Messiah, Jesus said to them, "The blind receive their sight and the lame walk, lepers are cleansed and the deaf hear, and the dead are raised up, and the poor have good news preached to them" (Matthew 11:5). Sounds a lot like the king described in Psalm 72!

Talk about It

:: What was King Solomon known for? *(Most people remember Solomon for his great wisdom.)*

:: How does Jesus fit the description of the king in this psalm? *(Jesus is the only king of all kings who hears when the needy call and saves them.)*

:: What kinds of things did Jesus do when he was alive to deliver the needy and help the poor? *(Jesus healed the sick and preached the good news to the poor.)*

 Pray about It

Praise Jesus for the way he cared for the poor, healing them and preaching the good news of the gospel to them.

Week 25

Jesus Cleanses
Ten Lepers

Story 103 – *The Gospel Story Bible*

Purchase a new pen or pencil for each of your children and a notepad if they are old enough to journal as part of their personal Bible study. As you pass them out, see if they say thank you without prompting. If they do, commend them. If they don't, ask them if it ever occurred to them to say thank you. Then let them know that you are going to be watching this week to see how well they do with saying thank you. Each day, give them an update. Say, "This week, we will learn about how Jesus healed ten lepers but how only one returned to say thanks."

DAY ONE

Picture It

Imagine that you let your younger brother (or sister) borrow your flashlight, but he didn't turn it off and the batteries died. Would you forgive him and lend him your flashlight again next time? Most people would forgive their brother and lend their flashlight again. But what if he forgot to turn it off a second time? And a third? And a fourth time? What if he borrowed your flashlight seven times and all seven times forgot to turn it off? Would you forgive him then? In our Bible story today, Jesus told the disciples that even if someone sinned against them seven times in one day they must forgive him.

 Read Luke 17:3–10.

Think about It Some More

The disciples were shocked when Jesus told them to forgive the same person seven times if he kept sinning against them. It was hard enough to forgive a person once, but seven times seemed too hard, so they asked Jesus to give them more faith. Jesus replied by saying that faith is so powerful a thing that even if a person has a tiny bit of it she could command a tree and it would obey her. But Jesus wasn't giving them instructions on how to transplant trees. He wanted them to put their faith in God.

When God told Moses to stretch out his hands over the Red Sea to open a pathway to cross it, Moses didn't stop to argue with God. He had faith in God's Word, and even though it seemed impossible, he believed. Likewise if God directed you to command a tree to jump into the sea, you can be certain that, if you obeyed God, the tree would jump into the sea. Since God said we should forgive a person seven times for sinning against us, we don't need a ton of faith to believe it—we should trust what God said and believe.

Talk about It

:: How many times did Jesus tell the disciples they should forgive someone? *(Seven times)*

:: What should we do if someone sins eight times against us? *(Jesus wasn't setting a limit for the number of times we should forgive; he was trying to tell the disciples they should keep on forgiving. We should keep forgiving people no matter how many times they sin against us.)*

:: What does it mean to forgive someone? *(When somebody hurts us or sins against us, we can forgive him, which means we will not count what he did against him but treat him as though it had never happened.)*

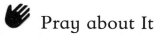 ## Pray about It

Ask God to help you forgive those who sin against you.

DAY TWO

Remember It

What do you remember about yesterday's story? What do you think is going to happen today?

 Read Luke 17:11–14.

Think about It Some More

Back in Jesus' day, leprosy was one of the most terrible diseases you could get, and there was no cure. Many people believed that those who got leprosy were being punished by God. Leprosy caused ugly sores on the face and body so that people were afraid to be near anyone who had the disease. Because it was contagious, people with leprosy were put out of the city to live with other people who had the disease.

If anyone came near someone with this disease, the leper would shout, "Unclean, unclean." Therefore, everyone would keep his distance. If a person with leprosy were healed, only the priest could say he was clean and give him permission to return to his family. Since a person with leprosy couldn't go into town to see Jesus, she had little hope of Jesus healing her unless Jesus were to happen to pass by her. So when the ten lepers heard that Jesus was coming, they got as close as they could and shouted out to him. But instead of shouting, "Unclean, unclean," they called out to Jesus for help, revealing the faith they had that Jesus could heal.

Talk about It

:: Why do you think there were ten lepers all together? *(Lepers could not live with healthy people, only with other lepers. The ten lepers in our story probably traveled together because of their disease. This was very common in Jesus' day. Whole colonies of lepers lived together, apart from the rest of the people.)*

:: Why did Jesus tell them to go and show themselves to the priest? *(The priest was the only one who could say that you were healed and could go back to living with healthy people.)*

:: If you were one of the lepers in the story and suddenly you were healed, what is one of the first things you would want to do? *(Parents, help your children connect to the emotional side of this story here. Think of it: These lepers had not been allowed to touch their children or their spouses for as long as they had been sick—maybe many years. They would have wanted to go to the priest, and then quickly find their families to give them hugs and kisses.)*

:: Do people still get leprosy today? *(Yes, people still get leprosy, but now we have medicines that can heal them from this terrible disease.)*

 Pray about It

Praise God for healing people back in Jesus' day and for giving us medicine so that we don't have to worry about this terrible disease.

DAY THREE

Connect It to the Gospel

Today is the day we connect this week's Bible story to the gospel. The gospel is the life, death, and resurrection of Jesus for our salvation. Can anyone guess how our story this week looks forward to or back at the gospel?

 Read Luke 17:15–16.

Think about It Some More

Jesus healed all ten of the lepers who called out for help. Then he sent them to the priest who could declare them clean so they could rejoin society. All ten of them turned to go, but one of them, a Samaritan, came back to say thank you. Because the Samaritans and the Jews did not get along, a Samaritan was the last person you would expect to come back to say thank you.

The Samaritans had once been a part of God's people too, but they had broken away to start their own country. And even worse, they worshiped idols on the hilltops of Samaria instead of God at the temple in Jerusalem. For this reason the Samaritans were rejected by the Jews. But Jesus wasn't like the other Jews. He was willing to forgive the Samaritans. Jesus didn't come to save the Jews only—he came to bring forgiveness and life to people from every tribe and nation. Even though the Samaritans broke away to worship idols, if they believed in Jesus, they could be welcomed back into God's family again.

Talk about It

:: What did the leper who returned to Jesus do on his way back? *(The leper came back to Jesus praising God.)*

:: Do you remember what country the leper came from? *(Samaria)*

:: Why didn't the Jews and the Samaritans get along? *(The Samaritans left Israel to go on their own. Instead of worshiping God at the temple, they made idols on the hills and worshiped there instead.)*

:: How does Jesus healing a Samaritan fit into God's promise to Abraham to make him a blessing to all nations? *(God planned to save people from every nation through one of Abraham's far-off grandchildren. Jesus is that far-off grandchild. By healing the Samaritan, Jesus was taking God's blessing to someone outside of the nation of Israel. That was the start of God keeping his promise to Abraham to make him a blessing to the nations.)*

 ## Pray about It

Praise God that his healing and forgiveness are good for all people, no matter what nation they come from, even if they have worshiped other gods.

DAY FOUR _____

Remember It

What has God been teaching you this week through our Bible story?

 Read Luke 17:17–19.

Think about It Some More

Jesus wondered why the other nine healed lepers did not thank him. We can know that the other nine were Jews because Jesus pointed out that only a foreign man, the Samaritan, had come back. If anyone should have forgotten Jesus, it should have been the man from Samaria, not the lepers who were a part of God's people. But this was not the only time Jesus was forgotten by his own people. Jesus would be rejected, arrested, and killed by his own people.

Talk about It

> KIDS, ask your mom or dad what they are most thankful to God for.

(Parents, make sure you start with thanking God for forgiving your sins, then also share something God has done for you in the course of your life.)

:: How many lepers were healed? *(Jesus healed all ten lepers.)*

:: How many lepers came back to thank Jesus? *(Only one)*

:: What did Jesus say was the reason the man was healed? *(The man was healed because he had faith in Jesus.)*

Pray about It

Make a list of at least five things you are thankful to God for, and then use your time in prayer to thank God for those things.

DAY FIVE _____

Discover It

Today is the day we look at a different Bible passage—from the book of Psalms or one of the prophets—to see what we can learn from it about Jesus or our salvation.

Read Zechariah 13:1.

Think about It Some More

When you read this prophecy, imagine a hot, dusty day when the travelers are all dirty from walking in the dust. When the people approach the town square, they find that the mayor of the town has opened up the fountain in the middle of the square for people to wash in. If you were a traveler on a hot day, think how wonderful it would feel to put your dirty, hot feet into a pool of clean running water overflowing from a fountain. Zechariah told of a day when a fountain would be opened for the house of David to cleanse away sin and uncleanness.

Jesus is that fountain. He cleansed the leper. But even more importantly, and in keeping with Zechariah's prophetic word, Jesus cleansed the leper of his sins. When Jesus told the leper, "Your faith has made you well," he was talking about a cleansing from sin, not just disease. Jesus is the fountain that is opened up to cleanse us from our sin and uncleanness. When Jesus healed the leper, he was fulfilling the prophecy that Zechariah gave long ago.

Talk about It

:: What does it mean to cleanse someone from sin? Read Psalm 51 for some clues. *(Psalm 51:2 gives us the answer: "Wash me thoroughly from my iniquity and cleanse me from my sin!" To cleanse means to clean away or remove. Our sin will be washed away by the fountain of Jesus.)*

:: What did Jesus do to clean away our sin? *(Jesus died on the cross to take the punishment for sin. He lived a sinless life, which he then gives to us. We receive Jesus' righteousness, and in exchange, he receives our sin and God's punishment that was meant for us because of our sin.)*

:: In what areas of your life do you most struggle with sin? *(Parents, help your children make a list of at least three of their struggles with sin, and lead by your own example of confession.)*

 Pray about It

Use the list you just made to call out to Jesus and ask for his forgiveness.

Week 26

Jesus Claims to Be God

Story 104 – *The Gospel Story Bible*

Record your voice saying the following sentence putting your child's name in the blank: "Hello _____, do you recognize my voice? I am so glad that God gave you to me." If you really want to make this fun, have another person your children don't know record the same message too before your own. Ask them if they know whose voice is in the first recording. Then move on to the recording of your own voice. Say, "This week we will learn how all those in the family of God will be able to recognize the voice of the Lord."

DAY ONE

Picture It

During World War I, both the Allies and Germany used radios and telephones to communicate in war zones. To keep the enemy from understanding what was said, the Allies used secret codes. But the German army kept breaking the codes—until the Allies got the great idea to start using Native Americans to talk over the radio in codes based on their native languages. The Germans could not figure out what they were saying.

During the Second World War's largest invasion—D-Day—Native Americans were used again to confuse the Germans.

Their code was simply to use everyday words from their own language to stand for things in the war. They called tanks *turtles,* machine guns were called *sewing machines,* and bazookas were called *stovepipes.* If a Native American code talker saw a row of tanks approaching, he could send a message back to the troops for them to "Get out the stove pipes, because the sewing machines are not strong enough, and we have a line of turtles coming." Of course they would use the words from their native language. This fooled the Germans every time.

In our story today, Jesus used his own code to pass along a message of the gospel. This confused the disciples. See if you can figure out what Jesus is talking about.

 Read John 10:1–6.

Think about It Some More

Did you pick up on the code words for God and his people in this story? The sheep are God's people and the shepherd is Jesus. It is easier for us to understand this code because we know all about Jesus' life from reading the rest of the Bible. Once you know the meaning of the code words, the picture of God as a shepherd in the code helps us to understand how God cares for us. Just as a shepherd cares for his sheep, so God cares for us. The people of Jesus' day knew all about shepherds and sheep, so that made it easier for them to remember and to teach others. But for the enemies of God—those who refused to believe—the code sounded like foolishness.

Talk about It

:: Who are the sheep and shepherd pictures of? *(Parents, we will come back to more of the code words tomorrow. For today, see if your children can understand that Jesus is the shepherd and those who believe in Jesus and follow him are the sheep.)*

:: Why did Jesus say the sheep would not follow a stranger? *(Jesus said the sheep would not follow a stranger because they would not recognize his voice.)*

:: Why did Jesus speak in stories instead of telling the people exactly what he meant? *(Jesus used parables to help those who wanted to believe to understand. But Jesus also said he spoke in parables so that people who refused to believe would not be able to understand [see Matthew 13:13–15].)*

 Pray about It

Ask God to open your mind and heart so that you can believe the message of the gospel.

DAY TWO

Remember It

What do you remember about yesterday's story? What do you think is going to happen today?

 Read John 10:7–10.

Think about It Some More

In our Bible passage today, Jesus explained some of the code. But he did not say what the sheepfold (John 10:16) stood for. Let's see if we can figure it out. We know from what Jesus said that the sheepfold is a place where a flock of sheep is protected and guarded. That sounds a lot like our salvation with Jesus in heaven, where we are safe from the punishment we deserve for our sins. It could also point to a day when we will go to heaven to be with God. The thieves and robbers were probably the false prophets and all people who try to get to heaven by their own works, like the Pharisees.

Talk about It

:: We know that *shepherd* is a code word for Jesus. What other code word did Jesus use to describe himself? *(Jesus is the door.)*

:: What does the sheepfold represent? *(The sheepfold refers to our salvation or to heaven where we will live with God.)*

:: How many doors are there in the sheepfold? *(There is only one door. That means Jesus is the only way we can be added to God's heavenly family.)*

 Pray about It

Thank God for giving us the Bible with secrets to the code so that we can understand and believe in Jesus.

DAY THREE

Connect It to the Gospel

Today is the day we connect this week's Bible story to the gospel. The gospel is the life, death, and resurrection of Jesus for our salvation. Can anyone guess how our story this week looks forward to or back at the gospel?

 Read John 10:11–18.

Think about It Some More

When Jesus said, "I lay my life down for the sheep," he was using the picture of a shepherd to teach the people the gospel. Not everyone understood the code, but we have the advantage of being able to use the whole Bible to help us break the code and understand what Jesus was talking about.

Here is what we learn: Jesus is the shepherd, and we who believe in him are the sheep who hear his voice. The shepherd's laying down his life for the sheep is a picture of Jesus dying on the cross for our sins. We also learn that Jesus wasn't forced to die on the cross for our sins, but that he gave up his life willingly for us. Finally, when Jesus said he would take his life up again, that is code for the last part of the gospel: his resurrection from the dead.

Talk about It

:: What did Jesus say the shepherd was going to do for the sheep? (*There are several answers within this passage, such as bring in the sheep and protect them, but the most important answer is that the shepherd will lay down his life for the sheep.*)

:: What did Jesus do to lay down his life for the sheep? (*Jesus died on the cross, in our place, so that our sins could be forgiven and we could go to heaven to live with God.*)

:: Jesus talked about two flocks of sheep. Do you know who the two flocks of sheep are pictures of? (*Parents, this is a tough question. Give your children some clues by reminding them that the sheep are people. That would then mean that Jesus came to die for two groups of people. The answer is the Jews, his own people, and the Gentiles, the non-Jews.*)

Pray about It

Praise Jesus for giving up his life freely for us out of his love. Doing this was his choice; he was not forced to do it.

DAY FOUR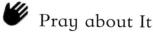

Remember It

What has God been teaching you this week through our Bible story?

Read John 10:19–42.

Think about It Some More

Even though Jesus explained the parable and went on to tell the Jews more about himself, they did not believe. Some said Jesus had a demon, while others said he was crazy. Finally, when Jesus said, "I and the Father are one" (v. 30), Jesus was telling them that he was God. But, instead of believing, the Jews picked up stones to kill him. Jesus tried to change their minds by reminding them of the miracles that he did. Yet they would not listen and tried to arrest him. It wasn't time for Jesus to die on the cross, so he escaped from them.

So you see, God's enemies cannot figure out the code. Even today, it is only people whose minds have been opened by God's grace who can understand the message of the gospel in the Bible. The rest think it is nonsense.

Talk about It

> ● ● KIDS, ask your parents if they ever knew a person
> ● ● who heard the gospel story about Jesus but rejected
> him.

(Parents, think of a person you know that rejected a clear gospel presentation. This should sober your children so that they call out to God to help them believe.)

:: Why did the Jews pick up stones to kill Jesus? *(They did not believe that Jesus was really God. For a normal man to claim he was*

God was a crime punishable by death. Since they did not believe Jesus, they hated him for saying he was God and were ready to kill him.)

:: How do we know that the Jews who were trying to stone Jesus were not a part of his flock of sheep? *(Jesus said that his sheep listen to his voice—they hear it and obey it. But the Jews did not like what Jesus was saying. The same is true today. Many people read the Bible, but not everyone believes. Those who hear his voice are those who hear the voice of God, or the call of God, in his Word and obey him. God's Word touches the heart of every believer. Those who do not believe are not affected by God's Word in the same way.)*

 Pray about It

Ask God to open up your ears so that you, like the sheep in the parable, can hear his voice and obey.

DAY FIVE

Discover It

Today is the day we look at a different Bible passage—from the book of Psalms or one of the prophets—to see what we can learn from it about Jesus or our salvation.

 Read Isaiah 45:17.

Think about It Some More

Isaiah said Israel would be saved with an everlasting salvation that would last for all eternity. That means that they would be saved forever. Jesus said something very similar when he talked about the sheep. Jesus said, "My sheep hear my voice, and I know them, and they follow me. I give them eternal life, and they will never perish, and no one will snatch them out of my hand" (John 10:27–28). Long before Jesus was born, Isaiah foretold the salvation that would come through him.

Talk about It

:: What does the word *everlasting* mean? *(Parents, the word actually tells you what it means if you reverse "ever" and "lasting." Something everlasting is something that lasts forever!)*

:: There is only one way to get everlasting salvation. Do you remember how Jesus used the sheepfold to teach that? *(Jesus said that he was the only door into the sheepfold. That means that there is no way to get everlasting salvation except through Jesus.)*

:: Isaiah said that Israel would be saved by the Lord. What did the Lord do to save Israel? *(Jesus lived a perfect life without sin and died in our place on the cross.)*

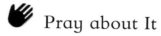 Pray about It

Thank God for his salvation, which is everlasting.

Week 27

The Pharisee & the Tax Collector

Story 105 – *The Gospel Story Bible*

Smear some chocolate frosting inside a clear glass, being careful not to get any on the outside. Take another glass and smear the outside, but make sure the inside is clean. Show your children both glasses and ask what is different about them. (Don't tell them it is chocolate frosting; let them think the glasses are soiled with something unpleasant.) Then ask which one they would rather drink out of and why. They should say they would rather drink out of the glass that is dirty on the outside. Tell them that Jesus described the Pharisees as people who wash the outside but leave the inside dirty. Say, "This week we will learn about the prayer of a Pharisee whose confidence came not from having a clean heart but from having a good-looking life."

DAY ONE

If you are ever pulled over by the police for driving through a red light, it won't help you to say that you were going slowly. Even if you were traveling under the speed limit, you would still be guilty of running a red light. You could have a valid driver's license, have your car inspected, and follow all the other rules of the road, but that would not excuse going through a red light. None of those good things would make your moving violation look any better. In the same way, we can't excuse our sins by saying we never committed really bad sins like murder or robbery. The Pharisee in our story today tried to make himself look good by listing all the sins he didn't do, instead of confessing those he did do.

 Read Luke 18:9–12.

Think about It Some More

When God, as judge, looks at all we have done in our lives, he does not compare us with other people; God compares us with himself. God is perfect and without sin, so when he compares us with himself, we all fall short. When we compare ourselves with God, it is easy to see how sinful we are. That helps us to see our need for God's forgiveness. But if we compare ourselves with other people, we can always find someone more sinful than we are to make us look good. That is what this Pharisee did. Because he compared himself with the tax collector, he never saw his need for forgiveness, and he missed the grace of God.

Talk about It

:: Who did the Pharisee compare himself with, God or others? *(The Pharisee compared himself with others.)*

:: What did the Pharisee think about himself? *(He thought he was good when compared with people who he felt had committed worse sins than he had.)*

:: What do you think the Pharisee would have thought if he'd compared himself with God? *(Since God is perfect, the Pharisee would have seen his sin.)*

:: Why should we compare ourselves with God? *(If you compare yourself with God, it helps you see your sin and your need for God's forgiveness.)*

 Pray about It

Praise God that he is perfect and spotless, without sin.

DAY TWO _____

Remember It

What do you remember about yesterday's story? What do you think is going to happen today?

 Read Luke 18:13.

Think about It Some More

Yesterday we learned about the Pharisee in the story, but today we see a very different prayer—from the tax collector. Most tax collectors in Jesus' day stole money from the Jewish people. Their job was to collect taxes to give the Romans, but if they were dishonest they could collect additional tax money to keep for themselves. Many tax collectors grew wealthy this way and were considered traitors and cheats by the Jews. Being convicted by God of his sins, the tax collector in our story was sorry for his sins and confessed them to God. Because he saw his sin, he realized he needed God's forgiveness.

Talk about It

:: How was the tax collector's prayer different from the prayer of the Pharisee? *(Draw the children out on the differences. The Pharisee compared himself with other men, but the tax collector compared himself with God and was convicted—and cleansed.)*

:: What can we learn from the tax collector's posture during his prayer? *(The tax collector was ashamed to look up to heaven. This is an indication that he realized he was unworthy before a holy God. It was a posture of humility.)*

:: Who are you more like: the tax collector or the Pharisee? *(Parents, help your children see that while we are all sinners, sometimes we think of ourselves as better than other people, just like the Pharisee did.)*

 Pray about It

Take turns confessing your sin and asking God for mercy. *(Parents, take the lead in confession. Then help each of your children to be specific.)*

DAY THREE _____

Connect It to the Gospel

Today is the day we connect this week's Bible story to the gospel. The gospel is the life, death, and resurrection of Jesus for our salvation. Can anyone guess how our story this week looks forward to or back at the gospel?

 Read Luke 18:14.

Think about It Some More

Jesus said that it was the tax collector who went home justified. *Justified* is a word that means that God forgave his sin. A good way to remember what justified means is to picture a judge in a courtroom. Instead of looking at our sin and saying, *"Guilty,"* the judge looks to Jesus, who lived a perfect life for us and then died for our sins. Then the judge declares us not guilty. Even though we deserve to be found guilty, we are declared righteous because of Jesus.

The Pharisee in the story had lived a good life and did a lot of good things, but none of those good works could save him. He needed to turn to God for salvation just as much as the tax collector did. None of our good works can earn us entrance to heaven. It is only by trusting in Jesus and what he did on the cross that we can be justified before God. It is only when we trust Jesus for our salvation, and Jesus takes away our sins and gives us his righteousness, that we are justified before God.

The Pharisee may have looked good on the outside, but on the inside he was a sinner who needed the gospel as much as the tax collector did. Even those who give their lives to Jesus need to watch out for the attitude of the Pharisee and be careful not to look down on others.

Talk about It

:: What does the word *justified* mean? *(Parents, help your children remember the picture of a judge saying not guilty.)*

:: Why couldn't the good works of the Pharisee get him to heaven? *(Even though the Pharisee was very good, he was still a sinner who needed God's salvation through Jesus. His good works could not cancel out his sins.)*

:: What was the Pharisee trusting in? *(The Pharisee was trusting in himself and the good works God helped him to do, instead of trusting in God.)*

 # Pray about It

Ask God to help you see yourself like the tax collector so that you always see your need to confess your sins to God so that you too can be forgiven.

DAY FOUR _____

Remember It

What has God been teaching you this week through our Bible story?

 Read Luke 18:15–17.

Think about It Some More

Some people think children are noisy and cause trouble, while other people enjoy having children around, laughing and playing. Isn't it great to know that Jesus loved children? Don't ever think that Christianity and going to church is just for parents. Jesus made it clear that church is for children too. The disciples didn't think the children were that important, but God has always loved children.

Talk about It

:: Who came to God more like a child: the tax collector or the Pharisee? (*The tax collector came more like a child because he was trusting in God for mercy. In contrast, the Pharisee was not trusting God. He was trusting in himself and his own good works; therefore, he felt he had no need for God, as expressed by his behavior.*)

:: What does it mean to receive the kingdom of God like a little child? (*Receiving God's kingdom means that we trust God, believe his Word, and come to Jesus, not trusting in our own good works. It means to receive his gospel in the same way a child receives a gift.*)

 Pray about It

Ask God to help you trust him for everything, the same way a little child trusts her parents for everything.

DAY FIVE _____

Discover It

Today is the day we look at a different Bible passage—from the book of Psalms or one of the prophets—to see what we can learn from it about Jesus or our salvation.

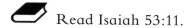 Read Isaiah 53:11.

Think about It Some More

In this verse, Isaiah told of a day when God's righteous servant would bear the iniquities (that means "carry the sins") of many, and they would be considered righteous. This simply means that one day God's servant would take away the sins of God's people so that they could be free from sin and be counted righteous, or good, in God's eyes. Jesus is the servant who did all that for us. He carried our sin to the cross and took the punishment we deserve so we could be forgiven. If we trust in Jesus, he declares us righteous.

Talk about It

:: What are iniquities? (*Iniquity is just another word for sin, or the things we do that are against God's law.*)

:: Where do you see Jesus in this passage? (*Jesus is the servant who bore the sins of many. Jesus did that by dying on the cross for our sins.*)

:: How does this one verse help us to know that God planned Jesus' death as the way to save his people from their sin? (*Isaiah was a prophet who spoke God's words many hundreds of years before Jesus was born. God used the prophet Isaiah to give his people clues to how he planned to rescue us. Looking back on these words gives us an appreciation of God's control over all things.*)

 ## Pray about It

Praise God for his wonderful plan of salvation to take away our sins through his Son, Jesus.

Lazarus

Story 106 – *The Gospel Story Bible*

You'll need a deflated balloon for this exercise. Gather your family and show them the balloon, and tell them you are going to demonstrate your command over the balloon. Say to the balloon, "Be filled up with the breath of air." Then blow the balloon up. Next say, "Be tied into a knot to hold your air." Then knot the end of the balloon so it does not deflate. Present the balloon to your children and ask them, "Isn't that amazing?" They are likely to say that it is not so amazing because all you did was blow up a balloon.

Explain that it was easy for you because you had the power and authority to do it. Then ask them if they think a frog could blow up the balloon. They will probably say no. Then finish up by saying, "A frog has neither the power nor the authority to blow up a balloon. This week, we will see Jesus demonstrate his power and authority, not over a balloon, but over death."

DAY ONE

Picture It

In 1912, Ehrich Weisz stood on the deck of a tugboat in the east river of New York City while a man wrapped his body in chains, locking them around his neck, arms, and legs. Then Ehrich was willingly locked into a crate. Slowly the crate was lowered into the river, as a crowd watched from a nearby pier. It looked as if he would surely die, but within minutes Ehrich Weisz had escaped, to the amazement of all.

Folks in the crowd knew him by his stage name, Harry Houdini, the world's greatest magician/escape artist. Mr. Houdini allowed what seemed like a terrible thing—to be chained, placed in a crate, and lowered into the river—for a greater end: the amazement of the crowd at his daring escape. It worked. The crowd was astonished. Because of his performance at the river that day, many people believed that he was the greatest magician of all time.

In today's Bible story, Jesus also allowed something terrible to happen so that he could perform an amazing sign to help people believe that he was the Son of God. But Jesus wouldn't use magic, and it would be no trick. Jesus would use his power to do something astonishing—he would raise a man from the dead.

 Readd John 11:1–16.

Think about It Some More

When strangers brought their sick friends and relatives to Jesus, he healed them. So you can imagine how difficult it must have been for Mary and Martha when Jesus refused to come to heal their sick brother, Lazarus. Jesus said Lazarus's sickness would not lead to death, but a few days later, Lazarus died. Strangely, Jesus told his disciples that he was glad he had not been there when Lazarus had died—that it would help the disciples believe and bring him much glory.

Even though the disciples had seen Jesus heal the sick, multiply the fishes and the loaves of bread, walk on water, and calm the wind and the waves, they still struggled to recognize that he was God and to put their complete trust in him. But through Lazarus, Jesus planned to give them an even more amazing sign. A sign that would show his power and authority over life itself. A sign that would show that he was God.

Talk about It

:: What was the name of Jesus' friend who died in our story today? *(Lazarus)*

:: Why didn't Jesus heal Lazarus? *(Younger children may answer that Jesus planned to raise Lazarus from the dead. If they answer that way, ask them why. Have your children look back at the text, or you can read it again and have your younger children raise their hands when they hear the answer. Jesus said it was for his own glory and for the sake of the disciples, to help them believe.)*

:: Why didn't the disciples want Jesus to go to Jerusalem where Lazarus was? *(The Jews wanted to stone Jesus. The disciples were afraid that if Jesus returned to Jerusalem, the Jews would kill him.)*

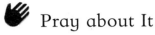 Pray about It

Thank God for his control over all things, even life and death.

DAY TWO _____

Remember It

What do you remember about yesterday's story? What do you think is going to happen today?

 Read John 11:17–24.

Think about It Some More

When Martha heard that Jesus was coming, she ran to greet him. She was upset that he was too late to help Lazarus. At first, Martha complained to Jesus, but then she softened her tone and said, "But even now I know that whatever you ask from God, God will give you." Little did she know that Jesus is God.

Jesus challenged her to believe that her brother would rise again. Martha thought Jesus meant that Lazarus would rise on the last day, the day of God's final resurrection when everyone who believes in God and died will rise again. That was correct, but Jesus had in mind that Lazarus would rise that very same day, for Jesus had the power and the authority over life and death.

Talk about It

:: Why was Martha upset? *(Because Jesus had not come in time to heal her brother.)*

:: What did Jesus tell her to comfort Martha? *(Jesus told Martha that her brother was going to rise from the dead.)*

:: When Jesus said Lazarus was going to rise again, what did Martha think he was talking about? *(Parents, if you have younger children, reread verse 24 and emphasize the words "resurrection on the last day." Martha thought Jesus meant he would rise at the last resurrection day, not on that same afternoon.)*

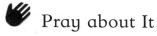 Pray about It

Praise God for the way he cares for us even when we are upset.

DAY THREE _____

Connect It to the Gospel

Today is the day we connect this week's Bible story to the gospel. The gospel is the life, death, and resurrection of Jesus for our salvation. Can anyone guess how our story this week looks forward to or back at the gospel?

 Read John 11:25–27.

Think about It Some More

Martha thought Lazarus would rise again on the last resurrection day. But Jesus said, "I am the resurrection and the life," showing Martha that he was God and had power over life and death. Then Jesus asked Martha one of the most important questions of all time: "Do you believe this?"

That is the same question God asks of every one of us today. We don't get to see Jesus in person, but we get to read all about him in the Bible, so God asks us the same question: "Do you believe?" Not only did Martha say, "Yes, I believe," but she went on to say that Jesus was the Christ, the Son of God. Even before Jesus had raised her brother from the dead, Martha was given the gift of faith. This story challenges us to ask ourselves, "Do we believe?"

Talk about It

:: What did Jesus call himself? *(Jesus called himself the resurrection and the life. Parents, if you have younger children, reread today's verses and ask them to raise their hands when they hear you come to the correct answer.)*

:: What important question did Jesus ask Martha? *(Jesus asked Martha, "Do you believe?")*

:: Why is that question so important for us today? *(We need to believe in Jesus and all he taught just as Martha did back then so that we can be saved from our sin. See Acts 16:31 and Romans 10:9.)*

 Pray about It

Praise God for giving Martha the faith to believe in Jesus. Ask God to give you faith to believe also.

DAY FOUR

Remember It

What has God been teaching you this week through our Bible story?

 Read John 11:28–53.

Think about It Some More

When Jesus commanded Lazarus to come out of the grave, he demonstrated that he had the greatest power of all. Jesus was more powerful than death. Jesus was God. Jesus waited for Lazarus to die, knowing that he would raise him from the dead to show his glory and to encourage his friends' faith. First, he rewarded Martha's faith by giving her back her brother. Second, he helped many who were not so sure about him believe that he was the Messiah.

There is something else that Jesus did with this great miracle. He made his enemies all the more angry. Earlier, the disciples were worried that the Jews might try to stone Jesus if he returned to Jerusalem. They were right. When the religious leaders heard about Lazarus, they made plans to kill Jesus—and Lazarus too. As a result of this sign, the religious leaders were afraid everyone would follow Jesus, and that could stir up trouble with Rome. They could lose their power. How sad to see the religious leaders give up the treasure of Jesus to hold on to their earthly power. That was a tragic mistake.

Talk about It

> KIDS, ask your parents how the raising of Lazarus affected the people who witnessed it.

(Parents, many Jews believed, just as Jesus predicted they would. Go on to talk about what it would be like if Jesus were alive today and raised a person from the dead.)

:: How did the raising of Lazarus affect the Pharisees? *(They became upset. They were afraid that so many believers following Jesus might result in trouble with Rome. They made plans to put Jesus to death.)*

:: How does the story of Jesus raising Lazarus affect you? *(Parents, draw out your children here.)*

 ## Pray about It

Praise God for the amazing miracle of raising Lazarus and for God's power over death. Pray for the unbelievers that you know, that God would give them faith to believe and trust in Jesus.

DAY FIVE _____

Discover It

Today is the day we look at a different Bible passage—from the book of Psalms or one of the prophets—to see what we can learn from it about Jesus or our salvation.

Read Hosea 13:14.

Think about It Some More

The apostle Paul quoted this verse from the prophet Hosea when he wrote to the Corinthian church (1 Corinthians 15:55). He said this verse pointed to Jesus' victory over death. Jesus was the one who ransomed us from the power of Sheol (death). Jesus raised Jairus's daughter from the dead (Luke 8:49–56), and in our story this week we see that Jesus raised Lazarus too. But the most important raising from the dead was when Jesus himself was raised from the dead. What Jesus said to Martha was very true—he is "the resurrection and the life" (John 11:25).

Now the sting of death (our fear of dying and being punished) is gone. Instead of punishment, all those who believe in Jesus receive everlasting life. So for believers, death is a doorway to a new life in heaven with Jesus. There is no need to fear, for the sting of death is gone.

Talk about It

:: Who else besides Jesus could Hosea's prophecy be talking about? *(There is no one else it could possibly be talking about. Only Jesus had victory over death because only Jesus could redeem us and ransom us from our sin.)*

:: What does it mean to redeem or ransom a person from death? *(Both words,* redeem *and* ransom, *speak of a payment that must be made to rescue a person from captivity or prison. Jesus rescued us from death and the punishment we deserved. He paid the price of his own life so we could be forgiven and set free from any punishment ourselves.)*

:: What is the sting of death that Jesus took away for anyone who believes in him? *(When believers die, our souls go to be with Jesus to live in heaven. Believers don't ever have to worry about the eternal punishment unbelievers receive. So the sting of death is gone. For a believer, death really means joy and life with Jesus.)*

 Pray about It

Praise Jesus for taking the sting of death away so that we don't have to worry about dying. When we die, we get to live again with Jesus in heaven.

Week 29

Jesus & Zacchaeus

Story 107 – *The Gospel Story Bible*

Collect one hundred pennies and lay them out on the table. Explain to your children that, in Jesus' day, tax collectors became rich by collecting extra tax money and keeping it for themselves. This practice was wrong, but they did it anyway. A man like Zacchaeus would have made a lot of money from cheating people. It is likely that at least ten out of every hundred dollars a tax collector made was from cheating people.

But after meeting Jesus, Zacchaeus was changed and said he would give half his money to the poor. (Separate fifty pennies and make a "give-back" pile.) He also said he would give back four times what he stole from people. That means if he stole ten, he would now give back forty. (Take forty and add them to the give-back pile.) But Zacchaeus probably stole even more than that. (Move nine more pennies to the give-back pile.) Hold up the remaining penny and say, "This week we will learn how, when Jesus touched a man's heart, he went from loving earthly riches to loving heavenly treasure instead."

DAY ONE

Picture It

Most people have good vision and don't know what it is like to be blind. Of all our senses, sight is probably the most difficult to live without. Imagine all the things you can't do if you can't see. A person who is born blind can't fully enjoy the magnificence of God's creation. Sure, he can touch plants or feel the fur of a dog, but he can't touch a rainbow or feel a butterfly flutter in the breeze. A person who cannot see will never drive a car to work, catch a touchdown pass, or watch a movie. So you can imagine how excited a blind person would be to discover a way to see.

Some researchers are working hard to discover a way to enable blind people to see. They are experimenting with implanting, in the back of a person's eye, an artificial retina that works with a camera on her nose. Although, so far, it has not given anyone sight, some people have begun to see light and shapes. In today's Bible story, one man discovered a way to get his sight back again. He called out to Jesus.

 Read Luke 18:35–43.

Think about It Some More

On his way to Jerusalem, Jesus came to the city of Jericho and was greeted by a blind man. Although the man had never met Jesus, he must have known about him. For as soon as he heard that Jesus was near, he called out to Jesus for help. When he called, he didn't just call Jesus by name, he called, "Jesus, Son of David." That meant he believed Jesus was the Messiah, the great far-off grandchild of David who was to come to save God's people.

When Jesus heard the man's cry, he stopped and healed him instantly. But Jesus did more than heal his eyes. Jesus said, "Recover your sight." Then Jesus added, "Your faith has made you well," which really meant, your faith has *saved* you. The crowd that had gathered around Jesus, when they saw what had happened, began to give praise to God.

Talk about It

:: When the blind man called out to Jesus, he used his name but he also called him something else. What did he call Jesus? *(The blind man called Jesus the Son of David, which meant he believed Jesus was the Messiah.)*

:: How can we tell from this story that the blind man believed in Jesus? *(As soon as he heard Jesus was near, he called out for mercy and called him the Son of David, a name that tells us he believed Jesus was the promised Messiah. Even after the people told him to stop calling out, he called out all the louder.)*

:: What are the two things Jesus said to the man just before he healed him? *(Parents, you may need to go back and reread verse 42 for younger children. As you read, ask them to raise their hands*

when they hear the correct answer. Jesus said, "Recover your sight"
and "Your faith has made you well." The word in the Greek for
"made you well" is the same word translated "saved" in other places.)

 Pray about It

Use the blind man's words in a prayer asking Jesus, the Son of David, to
have mercy on you and give your whole family faith to believe in Jesus.

DAY TWO

Remember It

What do you remember about yesterday's story? What do you think is
going to happen today?

 Read Luke 19:1–8.

Think about It Some More

The crowd accompanying Jesus must have been shouting as Jesus
approached Jericho. "Jesus is coming, and he just healed a blind man!"
Because he wanted to see Jesus, we know that Zacchaeus must have
previously heard about him. After Jesus raised Lazarus, everyone was
talking about this new prophet of Israel. Zacchaeus probably heard
about that amazing miracle too. Eager to see Jesus but too short to see
over the crowd, Zacchaeus climbed a tree.

Normally, grown men wouldn't climb trees, and it was certainly
not proper for a rich tax collector to scramble up a tree to see a Bible
teacher. But that is what Zacchaeus did. When Jesus saw Zacchaeus,
he commanded the tax collector to come down, and he invited himself
to his house for dinner. As a tax collector, Zacchaeus should have been
the one in authority. But this day Jesus was the authority, and his powerful call to Zacchaeus changed the man's life. Zacchaeus heard the
call of Jesus, obeyed at once, and was immediately changed.

As proof of that change, Zacchaeus turned away from his love of
money and offered to give half to the poor and pay back all those he
had cheated. One call from Jesus was able to cause a man to leave his
fishing nets to follow him. One command of Jesus was able to heal the
sick and open blind eyes. And one call of Jesus was able to soften the
hardest heart.

Talk about It

:: How did Jesus know Zacchaeus's name even though he never met him before? *(Jesus is God; he knows everything.)*

:: How long did it take for Zacchaeus, a tax collector, to be changed by Jesus? *(Zacchaeus was changed immediately as soon as Jesus called him by name.)*

:: Why was it a big deal for a tax collector to give away money to the poor and give back money to those he cheated? *(Tax collectors were supposed to collect tax money, not give it away. They grew rich by cheating the people, collecting more taxes than they were supposed to. By giving away his money, Zacchaeus showed that he was truly changed.)*

 Pray about It

Praise God for saving Zacchaeus and giving him grace to repent. Ask God to help you turn away from a love for money or your toys or anything else you might be tempted to love more than the Lord.

DAY THREE _____

Connect It to the Gospel

Today is the day we connect this week's Bible story to the gospel. The gospel is the life, death, and resurrection of Jesus for our salvation. Can anyone guess how our story this week looks forward to or back at the gospel?

 Read Luke 19:9–10.

Think about It Some More

Jesus connected the story of Zacchaeus to the gospel when he said, "Today salvation has come to this house." The word *salvation* means that even though Zacchaeus was an evil man, a tax collector who had become rich off the poor, God was saving him from punishment and adopting Zacchaeus into his family as one of his children.

What Zacchaeus didn't know was that Jesus was on his way through Jericho to go to Jerusalem, where soon he would be arrested, falsely charged, found guilty, beaten, and nailed to a cross. Then, while on that cross the holy anger of God was poured out on Jesus for Zacchaeus's sins.

Today, Jesus is calling out to us. He doesn't want to come to our house to dinner; he wants to come into our hearts to live and change us so that we, like Zacchaeus, can experience the life-transforming grace of God.

Talk about It

:: What did Jesus say had come to Zacchaeus's house? *(Parents, if you have younger children reread verse 9 emphasizing the word* salvation *when you get to it.)*

:: What does the word *salvation* mean? *(The word* salvation *means to be saved from something. See if your children can remember some of the benefits salvation brings.)*

:: Why did Jesus call Zacchaeus a son of Abraham? *(Zacchaeus was an Israelite, a Jew by birth, but Jesus didn't say that everyone who was born a Jew was a son of Abraham. The New Testament tells us that those who place their faith in Jesus— all those whom God calls—are sons and daughters of Abraham [see Galatians 3:29]. When God told Abraham that he was going to make his children as numerous as the stars in the sky, he was pointing Abraham to the day when God would call people from every nation through one of Abraham's far-off grandchildren, Jesus.)*

:: Once he believed, Zacchaeus reached out to the poor. What about you? What do you think God wants to help you do as you follow him? *(Parents, help your children consider how God may want to use them in his kingdom.)*

 Pray about It

Praise God for bringing salvation to Zacchaeus—and to us. *(Use the list of the benefits of our salvation to thank God: adoption into God's family, forgiveness of our sins, providing a place in heaven to be with God forever, etc.)*

DAY FOUR _____

Remember It

What has God been teaching you this week through our Bible story?

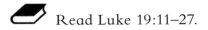 Read Luke 19:11–27.

Think about It Some More

When the people saw that Zacchaeus had turned away from his sin and offered to give half of all he had to the poor, they were amazed. Jesus had raised Lazarus from the dead and had just healed a blind man, and now Zacchaeus the tax collector was paying back everyone he'd cheated—four times the amount he'd stolen. The people had never seen anything like that before. That helped convince them that Jesus was the Messiah, the promised king from the family line of David who would rescue Jerusalem.

They expected Jesus to do what the heroes of old had done before him. They hoped he would call out to people of Israel to raise up an army and conquer the Romans, who ruled and oppressed them. And that was just what the religious rulers were afraid of. But Jesus wasn't going to Jerusalem to raise up an army and start a war against the Romans. Jesus was going to Jerusalem to give himself up to die. Jesus gave them a hint of this when he told the parable of the ten minas. The message of that parable was meant to show that Jesus (the nobleman) wasn't going to bring the kingdom of God in its fullness until he came a second time. But the people did not understand this.

Talk about It

> ●● KIDS, ask your parents what kind of changes they
> ●● made when they became a Christian.

(Parents, think back to when you first came to faith and what changes you made.)

:: Where was Jesus heading after he left Zacchaeus in Jericho? *(Jesus was traveling to Jerusalem, where he would die on the cross.)*

:: What did the people think Jesus was traveling to Jerusalem for? *(The people thought Jesus was going to bring God's kingdom, possibly by raising up an army to fight the Romans.)*

:: What did the parable teach the people who thought the kingdom of God was coming soon? *(It taught them that God wasn't going to bring the kingdom fully until Jesus came back a second time. Jesus introduced the kingdom of God, but it's not until he returns for his second coming that Jesus will bring the final judgment over sin and destroy all wickedness.)*

 Pray about It

Since Jesus has now gone back to heaven, we can pray that he returns soon to judge the world and put an end to all sin. This is the final prayer at the end of the Bible (see Revelation 22:20).

DAY FIVE _____

Discover It

Today is the day we look at a different Bible passage—from the book of Psalms or one of the prophets—to see what we can learn from it about Jesus or our salvation.

 Read Isaiah 11:10–16.

Think about It Some More

The apostle Paul said that when Isaiah talked about a root of Jesse, he was talking about Jesus (Romans 15:8–12). The root is a way to describe one of Jesse's descendants or far-off grandchildren. It comes from a picture of how some trees grow. Trees like the sassafras tree send out roots that sprout new trees along the way. Jesse is the tree, his roots are his children and their grandchildren, and Jesus is a shoot that pops up from the roots to form a new tree. Isaiah said that Jesus was going to stand as a signal or marker for the peoples and the nations. Notice it doesn't say a signal for Israel only but a signal for the nations. That is a hint of God's plan to rescue the Gentiles too.

Talk about It

:: What did Isaiah mean when he called Jesus the root of Jesse? *(That meant Jesus was one of Jesse's far-off grandchildren, which was a name for the promised Messiah.)*

:: Who are the two groups of people Isaiah said the root of Jesse would reach out to? *(The first group is the banished of Israel, the dispersed of Judah—the Jews. The second group is all the other nations—the Gentiles.)*

:: Which group does your family fall into, the Jews or the Gentiles? *(Parents, either way, help your children to see how your family is a part of God's saving plan.)*

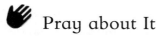 Pray about It

Thank God for bringing his salvation to people from every nation.

Week 30

The Triumphal Entry

Story 108 – *The Gospel Story Bible*

On a sheet of paper, draw the following: a crown, a palm branch, a cross, and a lightbulb. Don't be concerned if your drawings are not the greatest. Tell your children, "This week, you are going to read John chapter 12, the story of Jesus' triumphal entry into Jerusalem." Explain that you want them to guess what each drawing, taken from something in the chapter, has to do with Jesus. Here are the answers: crown (Jesus is the king of Israel [v. 15]); palm branch (the crowd waved palm branches at Jesus [v. 13]); cross (Jesus would be lifted up [on a cross; verse 32]); lightbulb (Jesus would be the light of the world [v. 35]).

Say, "This week we will learn how Jesus was celebrated in Jerusalem just days before the same people would demand that he be crucified."

DAY ONE

Picture It

The fireworks that are shot off in a large Fourth of July celebration can cost twenty thousand dollars or more. That is a lot of money for fifteen minutes of beautiful explosions in the sky. Most people, however, think the cost for these shows is worth the benefit because thousands of people come to watch them. But what if a town's fireworks committee knew that only one person were going to come to watch? They would not spend twenty thousand dollars on just one person unless that one person was very special, like the president of the United States. In our story today, a woman named Mary took a very expensive bottle of perfume, worth about a year's wages, and poured it out on Jesus. That is even more expensive than the whole fireworks show, and she used it up all on one person! That was because Jesus was very special.

 Read John 12:1–8.

Think about It Some More

Judas, the disciple who later betrayed Jesus, pretended to love Jesus, but really, lived for himself. In our story today, we learn that Judas was a thief who stole money from Jesus and the other disciples. On the one hand you have Mary, who is pouring perfume worth a year's wages on Jesus' feet. That means it would be worth over fifty thousand dollars today. On the other hand, Judas was complaining, thinking more about what the perfume was worth than he was thinking about Jesus.

Mary knew that Jesus was worthy of the highest honor, but Judas was blind to know how special Jesus was. When we turn away from the world and give our lives to Jesus, we follow Mary's example. When we believe in Jesus and commit to follow him, we are giving him something even more valuable than Mary's expensive perfume—we are giving Jesus our lives.

Talk about It

:: What was wrong with Judas' life? (*Judas acted like a follower of Jesus on the outside, but he was a thief who stole from the moneybag they all shared.*)

:: What did Mary do in our story that made Judas angry? (*Mary poured a large bottle of very expensive perfume on Jesus and wiped his feet with her hair.*)

:: What can we give Jesus to follow Mary's example? (*We can't pour perfume on Jesus, but we can give him the gift of our lives by turning away from the world and trusting and believing in him to save us.*)

 Pray about It

Ask God to pour out his Holy Spirit so that you might follow Jesus and give up your life to obey and serve him.

DAY TWO

Remember It

What do you remember about yesterday's story? What do you think is going to happen today?

 Read John 12:9–19.

Think about It Some More

If you have ever gone to a parade in which people lined the streets and cheered, then you know what it was like the day Jesus rode into Jerusalem on the donkey. Many of the people who saw Jesus raise Lazarus from the dead were following him into Jerusalem. They were celebrating Jesus as their new king. The people knew from the ancient prophecies that King David would always have a son on the throne (see Jeremiah 33:17). Matthew tells us that the crowd called Jesus the Son of David (Matthew 21:9) because they believed he was the one the prophecies talked about.

Everyone, filled with excitement, was waving palm branches—everyone, that is, except the religious rulers. They did not like what was going on. To them it looked as though the whole world was going after Jesus. If the Roman officials heard that Israel was crowning a new king, they would send in their soldiers and take what little power the religious leaders had left. Then the religious rulers would lose their positions. They might even be killed. Like Judas, they were blind to see who Jesus was. Instead, they were thinking about themselves.

Talk about It

:: Why did the crowd come to see Jesus? *(They wanted to see the person who had raised Lazarus from the dead. And they wanted to see Lazarus himself. It must have been exciting to talk with Lazarus and ask him what it felt like to be raised from the dead.)*

:: What did the chief priests plan to do with Jesus and Lazarus? *(They planned to kill them both.)*

:: Why did the people call Jesus a king? *(God had promised through his prophets that a deliverer would come to rescue his people and that there would always be a king on the throne. They believed that Jesus was the one the prophets said would come.)*

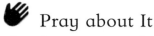 Pray about It

If you know a song with the word *Hosanna* in it, or a song about Jesus as king, sing it as a family. Pretend you are a part of the crowd welcoming Jesus, for he was and still is king.

DAY THREE _____

Connect It to the Gospel

Today is the day we connect this week's Bible story to the gospel. The gospel is the life, death, and resurrection of Jesus for our salvation. Can anyone guess how our story this week looks forward to or back at the gospel?

 Read John 12:20–33.

Think about It Some More

At the start of his ministry when he turned the water into wine, Jesus told his mother that his hour had not yet come. But now, on his way to Jerusalem, Jesus said something very different. Jesus said *the hour had arrived.* He knew that very soon he was going to be lifted up on a cross to die. There on that cross he would take our punishment. The Jews who waved palm branches as he rode the donkey, would soon be yelling, "Crucify him!" For now, they wanted Jesus as their king, but once Jesus was arrested and did not fight back, his own people would reject him.

Talk about It

:: What clue did Jesus give to let the people know how he was going to die? *(Jesus said he was going to be lifted up. Parents, feel free to reread verses 32 and 33 to give your children a clue.)*

:: Whose voice called out from heaven? *(God the Father's voice called out from heaven.)*

:: What did Jesus mean when he said, "Whoever loves his life loses it, and whoever hates his life in this world will keep it for eternal life" (v. 25)? *(Jesus was using strong words to make a point. Loving this life is when you love your life more than God.*

*Hating your life is when you are willing to give up anything to fol-
low God because you love him the most.)*

 Pray about It

Ask God to help you to love him more than anything in the world.

DAY FOUR

Remember It

What has God been teaching you this week through our Bible story?

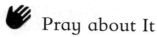 Read John 12:34–50.

Think about It Some More

When Jesus said he was to be lifted up, the people were confused
because they believed that the true Messiah would live forever. Jesus
tried to explain and called them to believe, but they did not, and those
few who did believe were afraid to tell anyone. They knew that if the
religious leaders heard them, they could be kicked out of the synagogue, so they chose the religious leaders over Jesus. Mary gave up
costly perfume when she poured it on Jesus' feet and didn't care what
people thought or said. These other people, who were fearful, were not
willing to follow Jesus. Soon they would join the religious rulers in
demanding that Jesus be crucified.

Talk about It

> ● ● KIDS, ask your parents if they can remember a
> ● ● time when they refused to believe in Jesus.

*(Parents, think back to before your conversion and share any hardness
of heart you experienced as an unbeliever.)*

:: In John 12:47, what did Jesus say he'd come to do? *(Parents,
   if you have young readers, have them raise their hands when they
   hear the correct answer. Repeat the question then reread verse 47 and
   see if they can answer that Jesus came to save the world.)*

:: In this Bible passage, what did Jesus compare himself to?
   (Jesus compared himself to light that came into the world so that

anyone who believes in him would no longer be in the darkness. Parents, if your children can't remember, reread verse 46.)

:: Why didn't those who believe tell anyone? *(They loved what other men thought and said about them more than what God thought about them, and they were afraid they would get kicked out of the synagogue for believing in Jesus.)*

 Pray about It

Ask God to help you believe in Jesus and not be afraid to tell people about him.

DAY FIVE _____

Discover It

Today is the day we look at a different Bible passage—from the book of Psalms or one of the prophets—to see what we can learn from it about Jesus or our salvation.

 Read Isaiah 6:9–10.

Think about It Some More

John quoted these words of Isaiah and included them in his gospel. John said that Isaiah understood that one day God would send his Messiah as our Savior (see John 12:41). Isaiah's writing predicted that the message of the gospel would be rejected and make the hearts of some even harder. Unless God softens our hearts and gives us the gift of faith, we would all act like those who rejected Jesus, and we would never believe.

Talk about It

:: What did Isaiah say happened to the people's hearts and eyes? *(Isaiah said their hearts became hard and their eyes blind. This means they didn't want to believe and could not see that Jesus was the one sent by God to save them.)*

:: Not everyone believed in Jesus when he came. What about today: Does everyone who hears the gospel believe? *(Just like in Jesus' day, not everyone believes when we share the story about Jesus. Many harden their hearts against it and do not believe.)*

:: How does Isaiah's description of blind eyes and hard hearts match the lives of the religious rulers in Jesus' day? *(The religious rulers refused to believe in Jesus. They could not see that Jesus was sent by God, and they planned Jesus' death.)*

 Pray about It

Ask God to give you eyes to see the light of Jesus and a heart that is soft to believe in him.

Week 31

The Widow's Offering

Story 109 – *The Gospel Story Bible*

Find two medium-size glass jars. Fill one with coins and dollar bills, and leave the other empty. Set them side by side on a table near where you gather for Bible study, and cover them with a cloth to hide them. In front of the empty jar, place two pennies. In front of the full jar, place six quarters. Ask your children to tell you which pile of coins is worth more? They should say the six quarters.

Explain that this money came from the savings of two people. (Take off the cover.) Tell them the person with the jar full gave the silver coins, and the person with the empty jar gave all she had. Then ask, "Which pile of coins would you say God thinks is more valuable, the two coins or the whole jarful?" Continue by saying, "Value doesn't just come from what the gift is worth, but from what it means to give it away. This week we will learn about a woman who gave away all she had."

DAY ONE

Picture It

There once was a watermelon farmer who left some of her watermelons in the field too long. On the outside they looked fine, but inside they were overripe and had begun to rot. The farmer picked them anyway, washed them all by hand, and put a shiny coat of wax on them. At the market she put the rotten melons out front with a sign that read, "Sun-Ripened Watermelons." On the rest of the crop, which were not rotten, she wrote another sign that simply read, "Watermelons."

When customers compared the fruit, most chose to purchase the rotten melons because they looked good on the outside and had a fancy name. By the time they were at home and cut them open to find a rotten core, the farmer was long gone. In our story today, Jesus warned the people against the Pharisees. Like the watermelons, they looked good on the outside but were wicked on the inside.

 Read Luke 20:45–47.

Think about It Some More

God is more interested in what is going on inside of us, in our hearts, than the good works we do to impress others on the outside. The Pharisees looked good in their long robes, greeting everyone warmly, but secretly, they were stealing from widows. On the outside their prayers sounded wonderful, but they prayed more for people to hear than for God to hear. But Jesus wasn't fooled. He knew what was inside their hearts, and he spoke out against them. That is one of the reasons the Pharisees didn't like Jesus and wanted to kill him.

Talk about It

:: What was wrong with the Pharisees? *(They did their good works only to look good, not because they loved God. Secretly, they were stealing from widows.)*

:: How did Jesus know about the sins of the Pharisees? *(Nothing is hidden from God; he knows all our sins. Jesus didn't have to spy on the religious leaders—he just knew.)*

:: Can you think of a time when you acted like the Pharisees? Perhaps you tried to hide your sins or appear better than you were just to impress others. *(Parents, lead in confession so your children will be more apt to share.)*

 Pray about It

Ask God to help you confess and not hide your sin, even when it makes you look bad to others.

DAY TWO _____

Remember It

What do you remember about yesterday's story? What do you think is going to happen today?

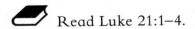 Read Luke 21:1–4.

Think about It Some More

If a person drops a quarter, a dime, or even a nickel, he will usually go hunting after it even if he is in a hurry. But if a person drops a penny he almost always lets it go, for a penny is not enough money to purchase the smallest piece of candy.

The two small copper coins the widow put into the offering were even smaller than one modern-day penny. Even so, Jesus said that the widow's coins were worth more to God than the big gifts the rich folks gave that day. As God told Samuel, "man looks on the outward appearance, but the Lord looks on the heart" (1 Samuel 16:7). The widow's offering was more valuable because it was given with a heart full of faith in God.

When it comes to giving, God looks at our heart, not at the outward amount of the gift. If you have a lot of money, it is easy to give away an expensive gold coin. That is not a sacrifice. But the widow gave God all she had. By giving the last of her money in the offering, she placed all of her trust in God. That is what made her small gift valuable to the Lord.

Talk about It

:: Who put the most money into the offering box? *(The rich people put the most money into the offering box.)*

:: How much money did the widow put into the offering? *(The widow put in two small copper coins; all she had to live on.)*

:: How was the widow different from the others who were giving? *(The widow was giving all she had to live on, while the others were giving from their wealth, with money to spare. While they gave more, it didn't cost them as much.)*

:: How should the widow's example affect the way we give? *(The widow's example doesn't mean we have to give all our money away. It does mean that we should give sacrificially. God blesses us so that we can give back to him and help others.)*

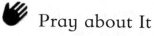 Pray about It

Pray that God would help you to live like the widow who loved God more than her money and trusted God to care for her.

DAY THREE

Connect It to the Gospel

Today is the day we connect this week's Bible story to the gospel. The gospel is the life, death, and resurrection of Jesus for our salvation. Can anyone guess how our story this week looks forward to or back at the gospel?

 Read Mark 12:41–44.

Think about It Some More

The story of the widow teaches us that we each have a choice to make. Will we be like the widow who entrusted her life to God or like the rich who trusted in their money instead? Remember, Jesus can see what is in *our* hearts too. But Jesus wants to remove our sin. He died on the cross so we could be set free from our sin and place our trust in him. When God saves us, he gives us the Holy Spirit to live inside our hearts and change us so that we can place our trust in God and obey his laws. The Holy Spirit makes it easier to trust God instead of worldly riches. By dropping into the offering box all she had to live on, the widow was entrusting her life to God and his plan. Jesus saw her faith and commended her. In the end, she got the best deal. She gave up a small treasure—two copper coins—and received a great reward: Jesus.

Talk about It

:: How much was the widow's offering worth? *(The widow's offering was worth one penny.)*

:: What did Mark include in his story of the widow's offering that Luke did not? *(Parents, you can read both accounts again. Start with Luke 21:1–4 then move to Mark to discover that he tells us Jesus sat down so that he could purposefully watch the people make their offerings that day and that the two copper coins together were worth about a penny.)*

:: What was Jesus trying to teach with the example of the widow? *(Jesus was trying to teach that it is not how much you give but the heart behind your gift. The widow's gift was all she had, so her gift showed that she was trusting God for her care. Jesus commended her.)*

 Pray about It

Ask God to help you trust him more so that, like the widow, you would trust him with your life.

DAY FOUR

Remember It

What has God been teaching you this week through our Bible story?

 Read Mark 13:1–2.

Think about It Some More

Have you ever seen a very young child open up a present but play more with the box it came in than the toy itself? The disciples were kind of like that. Jesus, the King of glory, was walking around with them in the temple. But instead of praising him, they began to praise the beautifully decorated temple building. They didn't understand that the earthly temple was meant to point to Jesus—the true temple, in whom the presence of God lived among them (John 2:21).

Jesus knew the temple wouldn't last. Even though some of the stones of the temple were more than thirty feet long, Jesus told them that it would all be destroyed. Sure enough, about forty years later, the temple was destroyed by the Romans. Today we have a new temple, but it is not one that is made up of stones or built by hand. The new temple of God is made up of everyone who trusts Jesus and has his Spirit living in them (2 Corinthians 6:16).

Talk about It

> KIDS, ask your parents in what areas they are most tempted to be drawn to the things of the world.

(Parents, we all have areas of weakness where we are drawn to the things of the world. Share what most captures your attention apart from Christ.)

:: What did one of the disciples say about the temple and the buildings? *(He said they were wonderful.)*

:: Why was Jesus the true temple? *(The temple is where God's presence lived. Jesus was God living among them. So wherever they walked with Jesus, the presence of God was with them.)*

:: What did Jesus say was going to happen to the temple? *(Jesus said it would be destroyed.)*

:: Where is God's temple today? *(God's temple today is made up of all the lives of the people who trust Jesus and are filled with the Holy Spirit with Jesus as the head. Together they become a living temple [2 Corinthians 6:16] where God's Spirit lives within their hearts and lives.)*

Pray about It

The disciples missed an opportunity to praise Jesus and praised the temple building instead. Ask your children to tell you things you can all praise God for, then take a moment and offer those items up in a prayer of praise to Jesus.

DAY FIVE

Discover It

Today is the day we look at a different Bible passage—from the book of Psalms or one of the prophets—to see what we can learn from it about Jesus or our salvation.

Read Isaiah 29:13–14.

Think about It Some More

Jesus quoted these verses from Isaiah when he spoke about the hypocrisy of the Pharisees (Matthew 15:8–9). Remember, hypocrisy is trying to look good on the outside while you are sinful on the inside. The Pharisees said they loved God, but on the inside they did not really love him. That's what was going on when the scribes were wearing beautiful robes, greeting people in the street, and offering up beautiful prayers with their lips—while secretly, they were stealing from widows. They thought they were wise and were following God, but while Jesus was performing wonders in front of them, few of them discerned that he was the Savior whom God had promised to send. Because of their sin and unbelief, Jesus was hidden from them (Matthew 11:25).

Talk about It

:: What does it mean to honor the Lord with your lips but have hearts that are far from him? *(Parents, help your children with each part of this. First, honoring with your lips is saying nice things. But when your heart is far from someone, it means that you don't really care about him. Jesus used this verse to show that the Pharisees said they loved God but didn't really.)*

:: Read Luke 20:45–47. Why are Isaiah's words a good fit for the scribes in Luke's gospel? *(The scribes' prayers are what Isaiah describes as "honoring me with their lips," but we can tell their hearts were far from loving God by the fact that they cheated widows.)*

:: How was the widow who put the two small coins in the offering different from the scribes? *(The widow trusted God in her heart and gave all that she had. She didn't try to draw attention to herself. It was Jesus who drew attention to her.)*

 ## Pray about It

Ask God to help you love him with your whole heart, soul, mind, and with your speech, as well.

Jesus Washes the Disciples' Feet

Story 110 – *The Gospel Story Bible*

Tell your children that you want to see who is the greatest person in your house. Have them stand one at a time against a wall to see how high they can jump from a standing position. Mark the spot of the highest jump. If you have only one child, invite your spouse to participate along with you. Congratulate whoever jumps the highest by telling her that she is the greatest person in the house. (This should be you or your spouse if you have only one young child participating.) Then ask your children if they think this test for greatness was fair. Help them to see that it really wasn't a very good test and explain that, this week, you will learn how Jesus taught that the greatest person is the one who serves. Take time this week to encourage true greatness (servanthood) in your children's lives.

DAY ONE

Picture It

Think what a crazy world this would be if everyone wanted to be in charge and no one wanted to be a servant. You would have everybody issuing commands with no one to carry them out. Imagine a king who orders his head chef to cook dinner. The head chef orders the assistant cook to do it. The assistant cook orders the baker to do it. The baker, who decides to take a stroll in the garden, tells the butler to do it. The butler tells the dish washer to do it. The dish washer tells the garbage man to do it. Finally, the garbage man, not too happy with the king for making him the trash collector, tells the king to fix his own dinner.

The problem is obvious. If no one is willing to be a servant nothing will ever get done. In our Bible story today, you will see that Jesus, the King of kings, lived as a servant to give us an example of how we should live.

 Read Mark 10:32–45.

Think about It Some More

Instead of thinking about Jesus, who had just finished explaining that he was on his way to suffer and die, the disciples were thinking of themselves and who was the greatest among them. James and John wanted to know if they could have the highest places of honor next to Jesus. They still didn't understand that, in the kingdom of God, the greatest honor goes to the one who serves. Although the other disciples got angry with the behavior of James and John, they were no better, for they also argued who among them would be greatest (Mark 9:34).

Talk about It

:: What did Jesus say you need to do to become the greatest? *(Jesus said you need to become the servant of all.)*

:: How did Jesus show that he was a servant? *(Jesus did what the Father asked him to do. Jesus served his Father in heaven, and the greatest service Jesus did was to die on the cross for our sins.)*

:: How should what Jesus said affect the way we live? *(Parents, help your younger children by asking them a simpler question like, should we think only of ourselves or should we serve one another? Then follow their answer up by asking them to explain why.)*

 Pray about It

Thank Jesus for being willing to become a servant and die on the cross for our sins.

DAY TWO _____

Remember It

What do you remember about yesterday's story? What do you think is going to happen today?

 Read John 13:1–5.

Think about It Some More

Back in Jesus' day, most of the roads were packed dirt, and none of the sidewalks were paved. So a person's feet got really dirty. When people came into a home for a meal, the household servant would normally wash their feet. But in our story today, there was no servant to wash feet. As they entered the house, the disciples all looked down at the washbasin, but no one offered to wash anybody's feet. So they all sat down to eat with filthy feet. At some point, when it was clear that none of his disciples were going to serve, Jesus rose from the table and took up the washbasin himself. Jesus had taught them on the way to Jerusalem that, if they wanted to be the greatest, they should be the servant of all, but the disciples still didn't understand.

It is easy to look down on the disciples for not serving here, but how many of us like to do the dirty work around the house? When was the last time you cleaned your bathroom without being told to do so?

Talk about It

:: Who washed the dirty feet that evening during the Passover meal? (*Jesus washed the disciples' feet.*)

:: Who should have offered to wash the feet? (*The disciples should have washed each other's feet or at least offered to wash Jesus' feet when they first came in the room to eat.*)

:: What can we learn from Jesus' example? (*Even though Jesus, the King of kings, was the greatest person at the Passover meal, he was willing to serve everyone. If Jesus can serve, then we should serve one another too.*)

:: What are some ways you could be a servant at home? (*Parents, draw your children out here and then help them put their ideas into practice.*)

 Pray about It

Ask God to help you live like a servant instead of thinking of yourself. Then pray for God to help you serve in some of the practical ways you talked about with your parents.

DAY THREE

Connect It to the Gospel

Today is the day we connect this week's Bible story to the gospel. The gospel is the life, death, and resurrection of Jesus for our salvation. Can anyone guess how our story this week looks forward to or back at the gospel?

 Read John 13:6–11.

Think about It Some More

When Jesus told Peter, "If I do not wash you, you have no share with me" (v. 8), Jesus wasn't talking just about Peter's dirty feet, he was talking about Peter's sinful life. Jesus was going to not only wash Peter's feet but also die on the cross to wash Peter's sins away. Paul tells us in Philippians 2:7–8 that Jesus made himself nothing and became a servant even to the point of dying on the cross for our sins. That was the greatest act of service anyone has ever done.

Talk about It

:: What did Peter say to Jesus when it was his turn to get his feet washed? *(Peter said he would never allow Jesus to wash his feet.)*

:: Why didn't Peter want Jesus to wash his feet? *(Peter probably felt that Jesus, the teacher, should not be washing feet.)*

:: What did Jesus' washing of the disciples' feet point to? *(Jesus' washing of the disciples' feet pointed to Jesus' washing the disciples' sins away by dying on the cross.)*

:: Can you think of any sins that you need Jesus to wash away? *(Parents, help your children come up with a few sins that will help them to see their need for Jesus to wash their sins away.)*

 Pray about It

Thank Jesus for coming to earth to die on the cross to wash our sins away, and ask him to forgive and wash away your sins.

DAY FOUR

Remember It

What has God been teaching you this week through our Bible story?

 Read John 13:12–17.

Think about It Some More

After washing their feet, Jesus challenged the disciples to follow his example. But he didn't mean only that they should wash each other's feet before eating. Jesus wanted the disciples to remember the bigger picture—that the greatest in the kingdom of God is the servant of all. If Jesus, who was God, could wash the feet of sinners, then we should be willing to serve one another too. Today when we look back at Jesus and how he served, we don't think only of how he washed the disciples' feet. We also remember how Jesus died on the cross to wash our sins away. Once we think of all that Jesus did for us, it seems silly for us to refuse to serve one another.

Talk about It

> ● ● KIDS, ask your parents what lesson Jesus wanted
> ● ● to teach the disciples by washing their feet.

(Jesus wanted to teach them that no one was too great to serve another. If he, the master, could serve, then they all could serve each other.)

:: Can you think of jobs around the house that you don't like to do? *(Parents, think of things like cleaning the bathroom or washing the dishes, and see if you can't get a reaction. Then compare those things with Jesus washing dirty feet to help them see that, if Jesus was willing to serve, we should also be willing to serve.)*

:: Think about how you have seen a family member serve others and thank them for doing so. *(Parents, try to help your children think of an example for each person. Then go around the room and allow time for each person to encourage someone else by thanking them for serving.)*

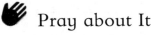 Pray about It

Ask God to fill you with his Spirit so that you can serve others like Jesus did.

DAY FIVE

Discover It

Today is the day we look at a different Bible passage—from the book of Psalms or one of the prophets—to see what we can learn from it about Jesus or our salvation.

 Read Psalm 40:4–10.

Think about It Some More

The writer of Hebrews quoted from Psalm 40 and said it was talking about Jesus. Jesus is the one who came to earth to do the will of God by dying on the cross for our sins as the final sacrifice (Hebrews 10:5–7). Back in King David's day (King David was the one who wrote this psalm), a person would sacrifice a lamb to atone (offer a sacrifice in place of his own life) for his sins. But in this Bible passage, we learn that God did not delight or find joy in those sacrifices. That is because they couldn't really take away any sin, but they did point forward to a day when Jesus came as the perfect sacrifice (Hebrews 10:10). Thousands of lambs were killed for sin in King David's day, and none of them could do the job of taking away sin.

Talk about It

:: Who did the lambs of King David's day point forward to? *(The lambs pointed to Jesus, the Lamb of God, who became the perfect sacrifice. Jesus died on the cross for all the sins of those who would trust in him.)*

:: What is in the heart of God's servant (see Psalm 40:8)? *(God's servant has God's law within his heart.)*

:: Where do you see the work of a servant hidden in this psalm? *(Parents, you are going to have to give your younger children clues. Remind them that a servant does the will of the person over her. Then read the passage again and, when you get to verse 8, emphasize, "I desire to do your will, O my God." The writer of the book of Hebrews tells us that Jesus is the one who did God's will by dying on the cross for our sins. Remind your children that it is God's Spirit, who comes to live in our hearts, who helps us to live for God so that we want to do his will.)*

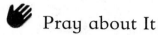 Pray about It

Ask God's Holy Spirit to help you be a servant like Jesus, who delighted to do God's will. Ask God to write his law within your heart.

Week 33

The Last Supper

Story 111 – *The Gospel Story Bible*

The Bible doesn't tell us what kind of coins Judas received for betraying Jesus, but most people think it was thirty silver shekels. One silver shekel is worth about three to four days' wages or about four hundred dollars in our money today. That means the thirty coins Judas received were worth around twelve thousand dollars. That amount sounds about right because, when Judas returned the money, the religious rulers used it to purchase a field. Take some time to think with your children about what can be purchased for twelve thousand dollars today, and consider that this is what Judas received for the betrayal of our Savior. Say, "This week we will learn about the last Passover meal that Jesus ate with his disciples. Judas left this meal to betray Jesus."

DAY ONE

Picture It

Imagine for a moment that you are a thief. When do you think would be the best time to rob someone's house? In the daytime, when everyone is up and can see you, or at night, when they are asleep and you can hide under the cover of darkness? The Bible gives us the reason why most crime happens at night: Sin loves darkness. The Bible also tells us that everyone who is evil hates the light and will not come into the light for fear that his sin will be exposed (John 3:20). In our story today, Judas made a plan to betray Jesus. When do you think he might try to pull off this crime, during the day or at night?

 Read Luke 22:1–6.

Think about It Some More

The religious rulers wanted to kill Jesus, but they were afraid to go after him in the daytime when everyone was around. But since Jesus didn't have a home and he went from place to place, they never knew where he would be. They'd probably heard stories of how, in broad daylight, he could mysteriously slip away (see Luke 4:28–30 and John 5:13). For this reason they were glad to pay Judas, one of Jesus' most trusted companions, to help them apprehend Jesus at a time when few people were around to see them.

Talk about It

:: What did the religious rulers give Judas to betray Jesus? *(They gave him money. We know from Matthew 26:15 that they gave Judas thirty pieces of silver.)*

:: What does it mean to betray someone? *(Parents, try to draw your children out here with this definition to help you. To betray someone means "to give someone over." In our story, the religious rulers gave Judas money to tell them when and where they could arrest Jesus. Instead of keeping Jesus safe, Judas was going to "give him over" or betray him to the chief priests.)*

:: Why didn't the religious rulers want to arrest Jesus in the daytime? *(Jesus didn't do anything wrong. Their plan was a wicked one that the people who were following Jesus would not support. Remember, the people wanted to crown Jesus king.)*

 Pray about It

Ask God for grace to always follow Jesus and never turn away.

DAY TWO _____

Remember It

What do you remember about yesterday's story? What do you think is going to happen today?

 Read Luke 22:7–13.

Think about It Some More

How would you like to be one of the disciples Jesus told to go meet a man with a water jar in the midst of a crowded city? Think about it, Jesus didn't say a short man with a blue water jar will be waiting for you sitting on a bench, or a gray-bearded man named Joshua will be waiting by a tree. There were thousands of people coming and going in the city. People carried water jars all the time. But the disciples didn't seem to mind—they trusted Jesus. They had seen him heal the sick, raise the dead, walk on water, and command the wind and the waves. If Jesus said a man with a water jar was going to meet them, then a man with a water jar was going to meet them. Without question they left to meet the man and prepare for the Passover.

The first Passover meal came on the night that the last plague, the plague of death, came upon Egypt. At that time a lamb was sacrificed in place of the firstborn son and the blood of the lamb was painted on the doorframe. Ever since that first Passover the people of Israel celebrate it once a year, in the spring, much like we celebrate Easter every year.

Talk about It

:: Why didn't the disciples ask questions to get more information? *(The disciples trusted that what Jesus said was true. Plus, Jesus didn't ask them to find the man with the water jar, he said that the man would find them. So all they had to do was go to the city and walk in. God had the rest all taken care of.)*

:: What meal were the disciples preparing for? *(The disciples were preparing for the Passover meal.)*

:: What did the Passover meal look back to, and what was the lamb for? *(The Passover meal celebrated God's rescue of Israel from the hand of the Egyptians back in Moses' day. When the angel of death moved through the country, all the firstborn sons in the homes with the blood of the lamb on the doorframe were spared God's judgment.)*

 ## Pray about It

Praise God for how he is in control of all things, even a man with a water jar, as was the case in our story.

DAY THREE

Connect It to the Gospel

Today is the day we connect this week's Bible story to the gospel. The gospel is the life, death, and resurrection of Jesus for our salvation. Can anyone guess how our story this week looks forward to or back at the gospel?

 Read Luke 22:14–22.

Think about It Some More

For hundreds of years, the people of Israel had followed the same Passover meal tradition. Back in Moses' day, God told his people to keep the Passover to remember their rescue from the Egyptians and the angel of death. But the Passover meal also pointed forward to Jesus, the Lamb of God. At the Last Supper, Jesus changed the tradition of the Passover meal. Instead of pointing back in time to God's rescue from Egypt, Jesus pointed his disciples to the future, when by his death on the cross he would rescue his people from sin.

Jesus referred to the bread he passed around as his body and said it would be given up for the disciples. Then he passed a cup of wine around, and he called it his blood poured out as a new covenant (promise). Although the disciples didn't know it, Jesus soon would be hanging on the cross for them (and for us). On the cross, Jesus was punished for our sin so that God's judgment could pass over everyone who believes. Today, we celebrate this new Passover each time we share the Lord's Supper—or Communion—during our Sunday service.

Talk about It

:: What did Jesus call the bread he passed to the disciples? *(Jesus said it was his body given up for them.)*

:: What did Jesus call the wine he passed around? *(Jesus said it was his blood poured out for them.)*

:: How do we obey Jesus' command to do what he did that night to remember him? *(When we take Communion, or the Lord's Supper, we are remembering what Jesus did when he died on the cross for our sins and his blood was poured out for us.)*

Pray about It

Thank Jesus for his willingness to take our sins upon himself so that we could be forgiven.

DAY FOUR _____

Remember It

What has God been teaching you this week through our Bible story?

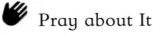 Read Luke 22:24–34.

Think about It Some More

Did you ever notice how crazy sin can be? Like when a Christian family argues and fights on the way to church or when we push and shove and get angry in line at a wonderful amusement park when we should be having fun. In our story today, Jesus breaks bread with the disciples, washes their feet to show them how to be a servant, and tells them that he is going to give his life up for them. But instead of enjoying Jesus, the disciples started to argue about which one of them was the greatest. Then when Jesus tried to warn Peter, he boasted all the more.

Talk about It

> ● ● KIDS, ask your parents if they can remember a
> ● ● time when sin came at a crazy time, when they
> should have been happy.

(Parents, think about your own trips to church, or how in marriage you can fight with the very person who loves you the most. It is good for every family to think about the way sin affects their lives and takes our focus off Jesus.)

:: Who did Jesus say was the greatest? *(Jesus said the greatest one was the one who served.)*

:: Can you think of a time when you argued with a brother or sister or friend about who was the greatest? *(Parents, children often argue about who runs the fastest or who has the best toys. Try to help your children identify with the disciples. So often we put ourselves first like they did. If they can't think of any examples, don't worry—you will be able to look back on this story the next time they boast about how great they are with each other or their friends.)*

:: Why was Peter so sure he would never deny Jesus? *(Peter thought Jesus would use his power to fight and bring victory, and he thought all he had to do was march with Jesus. Remember, he had seen Jesus transfigured in power. He had no idea that Jesus was not going to fight back. In all the Old Testament stories, those who trusted the Lord won the victory even when greatly outnumbered.)*

 Pray about It

Ask God to help you to think more about Jesus and less about yourself and to live as a servant, not as the greatest.

DAY FIVE

Discover It

Today is the day we look at a different Bible passage—from the book of Psalms or one of the prophets—to see what we can learn from it about Jesus or our salvation.

 Read Zechariah 11:12–13.

Think about It Some More

Hidden in the middle of Zechariah's prophecy is a clue about the betrayal price of Jesus, which Matthew pointed out in his gospel (Matthew 27:9–10). That means that although Judas thought his meeting with the religious rulers was secret, God knew about it hundreds of years before it happened. God even knew the price of the betrayal was going to be thirty pieces of silver.

Judas, like the other disciples, thought Jesus was going to be crowned as an earthly king. That would mean that anyone close to Jesus would get rich. But when Jesus started to talk about his death, Judas may have been listening more closely than the others. Judas couldn't get rich if Jesus died—unless he offered to betray him for money. Jesus knew about Zechariah's prophecy, and Jesus knew Judas's heart. Jesus said, "For the Son of Man goes as it is written of him, but woe to that man by whom the Son of Man is betrayed! It would have been better for that man if he had not been born" (Mark 14:21).

Talk about It

:: How many pieces of silver did Zechariah say Judas would be paid? *(Thirty)*

:: Why did God give the prophets a few details about how Jesus would die, for example, the thirty pieces of silver given for his betrayal? *(God wanted us to know that Jesus didn't die by accident, but that it was his plan for our salvation all along. That is why Jesus said that the Son of Man would go [or die] just as it is written in the prophets.)*

:: Can you think of any other Scriptures that tell us about God's control over all things? *(Parents, your younger children will probably not be able to answer without help. In that case, simply tell them that God is in control of all things and then read these verses to them: Ephesians 1:11; Romans 8:28; and Matthew 10:29–31.)*

 Pray about It

Praise God for the wonderful way God planned our salvation long ago. Jesus didn't die by accident; God sent him to die for us because he loved us.

Week 34

Jesus Promises to Send the Holy Spirit

Story 112 – *The Gospel Story Bible*

Bring a houseplant to Bible study. Point to a leaf on the plant and ask your children what keeps the leaf from drying out and turning brown. The answer is that the leaf is connected to the stem of the plant, which supplies it with nutrients and moisture. Ask your children what would happen to the leaves if you cut them off the plant? (They would dry up.) Cut off a plant segment with a few leaves and set it aside to watch over the next few weeks.

Use this as an illustration of how we need to remain in the vine (in Christ). Say, "If we reject Jesus, it is like being cut off the vine. We will dry up just like leaves separated from the stem of the plant. This week we will learn how Jesus supplies all that we need to live."

DAY ONE

Picture It

There once was a man who hiked deep into the wilderness to explore the wonders of nature. Suddenly a terrible snowstorm rolled in, and the man thought for sure he would freeze to death if he continued on. Rather than stop and set up camp, he decided to turn around and go home. But the way back was not so easy; it was growing dark and the falling snow had changed the look of the land.

The man did not panic because he had three items he needed to find his way home. First, he had a flashlight to light his way at night. Second, he had a compass, which showed him the correct direction to travel. Finally, he had food and water to sustain his strength on the way back. With these three tools, he made it safely home in the storm.

We also find ourselves lost in a world of sin. In our Scripture today, you will discover that Jesus is like the tools in this story. Jesus is the way (to light our path), the truth (the compass to show us the way to heaven), and the life (the bread and water we need to survive). If we turn from our sin and follow him, he will lead us safely home to heaven.

 Read John 14:1–14.

Think about It Some More

Windsor Castle in England has about one thousand rooms and is said to be one of the largest homes in the world. King Henry I was the first king to live there, and it is currently the largest castle in the world where people still live. But Windsor Castle can't compare to the mansion Jesus said that he is preparing for all of God's children. Now, don't expect that heaven will be one big house. Jesus used the idea of a house to help us understand that, once we die and Jesus returns again (v. 3), we will have a new home with him in heaven. One thing to remember is that there is only one way to get to heaven, and that is by believing and putting your trust in Jesus and his Word.

Talk about It

:: How many ways did Jesus say there are to get to the Father? *(There is only one way to God; Jesus is the way.)*

:: What did Jesus say heaven was going to be like? *(Jesus said that heaven is going to be like a mansion where there is plenty of room for all of God's children.)*

:: How are Jesus and the Father the same? *(Even though they are separate persons, they are one God. Jesus said, "If you have seen me, you have seen the Father." He also said that he was in the Father and the Father was in him. Parents, this is one of the Scriptures that theologians use to help us understand the Trinity, a word that means three in one—three persons in one God.)*

 Pray about It

Thank Jesus for preparing a place in heaven for us where we can live with him forever with no sickness, no sin, and no death.

DAY TWO

Remember It

What do you remember about yesterday's story? What do you think is going to happen today?

 Read John 14:15–20.

Think about It Some More

In yesterday's lesson, we learned how Jesus and the Father are one. In today's verses, Jesus tells us that he and the Holy Spirit are one. First, Jesus tells the disciples that the Holy Spirit will be in them, and then Jesus says that he himself will be in them. So, if the Father and the Son are one, and if the Spirit and Jesus are one, then all three must be one together. That is why we use the word *Trinity* (which means three in one) to describe God.

Talk about It

:: What two names did Jesus use to describe the Holy Spirit? *(Parents, if you have younger children, reread the passage and have them raise their hands when they hear the names* Helper *and* Spirit of truth.*)*

:: In verse 15, what two things did Jesus say we need to do? *(Jesus said that we need to love him and obey his commandments.)*

:: Can we get the Holy Spirit inside of us today like Jesus promised his disciples? *(Yes, whenever a person is born again and believes and places her trust in Jesus, the Holy Spirit comes to live inside of her.)*

 Pray about It

Thank Jesus for sending his Holy Spirit to be with us forever as our Helper.

DAY THREE

Connect It to the Gospel

Today is the day we connect this week's Bible story to the gospel. The gospel is the life, death, and resurrection of Jesus for our salvation. Can anyone guess how our story this week looks forward to or back at the gospel?

 Read John 14:21–24.

Think about It Some More

Here again in today's passage Jesus talked about the Trinity (that God is three in one). In verse 23, Jesus said that he and the Father would come to make their home in the life of anyone who loves Jesus. In yesterday's reading, Jesus said that the Holy Spirit was going to live inside believers (v. 17). So it seems that all three—Father, Son, and Spirit—are going to make their home in the lives of believers.

There is only one way that God, who is sinless, could come and make his home inside a sinful person: The person's sin must be taken away. God forgives our sins and comes to live inside of us when we believe and place our trust in Jesus. That is why Jesus said that he was *the way* and that no one comes to the Father except through him (John 14:6).

Talk about It

:: What is an orphan? *(An orphan is a child who doesn't have a father or mother.)*

:: What did God promise to do so that the disciples (and all of us) wouldn't become orphans? *(God promised to come live with us if we love him and keep his commands.)*

:: Who are the three persons of the Trinity whom God talked about as living inside each believer? *(Parents, if this question is too difficult for your smaller children, give them the first part of the answer—God the Father. Then ask them who the other two are.)*

 Pray about It

Praise God that he has promised to come and live with us so that we will never be alone.

DAY FOUR

Remember It

What has God been teaching you this week through our Bible story?

 Read John 14:25–31.

Think about It Some More

If you wanted to build a house but you were not sure how to do it, you could find an expert builder to help you—to double-check your plans, watch over your work, let you know when you were making a mistake, and be a valuable helper for you. In our Scripture today, Jesus called the Holy Spirit our *helper.* Like an expert builder can help you build a house to live in, the Holy Spirit helps us build our lives the right way, the way God wants us to. The Holy Spirit reminds us of God's instructions on how to live and build our lives. He lets us know when we sin, by reminding us of what Jesus taught in the Bible.

The best part of all is that the Holy Spirit is also at work in us, making us more like Jesus. That is like having a helper build your house while you are sleeping! The author of Hebrews said that, while we are working to do God's will, Jesus is "working in us that which is pleasing in his sight" (Hebrews 13:21). He does that through the Holy Spirit.

Even though Jesus went back to heaven after his resurrection from the dead, we are not alone. God gives his Holy Spirit to all believers to remind them of God's Word and enable them live for Jesus. This week, remember that putting your faith in Jesus means his Spirit lives in your heart so that you can be like him. We can ask the Spirit for help when we struggle with this.

Talk about It

> KIDS, ask your parents if they ever did something where having a helper made it a whole lot easier.

(Most people who learned to drive a car had a helper who showed them where to go and what to do next. Use that as an example if you can't think of another one.)

:: How is the Holy Spirit going to help us? *(He will remind us of what the Bible says and enable us to live the way God wants us to.)*

:: Can you think of an area in your life in which you need the Holy Spirit's help to be like Jesus? *(Parents, this is a great opportunity to help your children acknowledge the areas in which they have obvious struggles.)*

:: Can you remember a Bible verse that can help you to live for God today? *(Parents, help your children with this. They should be able to remember verses like, "Children, obey your parents" [Ephesians 6:1].)*

 Pray about It

Ask the Holy Spirit to enable you to live according to God's Word and help you remember Bible verses that will direct your lives.

DAY FIVE

Discover It

Today is the day we look at a different Bible passage—from the book of Psalms or one of the prophets—to see what we can learn from it about Jesus or our salvation.

 Read Joel 2:28–32.

Think about It Some More

Long before Jesus was born, the prophet Joel foretold a day when God would pour out his Spirit on all people. Back in Old Testament times, God poured out his Spirit on individual people; for example, the craftsman Bezalel who created the furniture for the tabernacle (Exodus 31:2–3), or the prophets like Ezekiel (Ezekiel 3:24), or the judges like Samson (Judges 14:6). But Joel saw ahead to a day when the Spirit of God would come upon everyone who calls upon the name of the Lord in faith. At Pentecost, Jesus kept the promise Joel spoke about, for it was then that the Holy Spirit came to all Christians (Acts 2).

Talk about It

:: According to the prophet Joel, who would be filled with the Holy Spirit? *(Joel said sons and daughters, young men and old men, and male and female servants would all be filled with the Spirit of God.)*

:: Whom did Joel say would be saved? *(Parents, if you have young children, you may want to ask the question and then reread verse 32 and have your children raise their hands when they hear the answer.)*

:: What does it mean to "call on the name of the Lord"? *(Calling on the name of the Lord is a way to say that a person knows he is a sinner, believes that Jesus died for his sins, and trusts in God for salvation.)*

 Pray about It

Pray for God to pour out his Spirit on you and give you the grace to call out to Jesus to rescue you from your sins. Pray this for people you know who don't yet believe.

Week 35

Jesus Is Arrested

Story 113 – *The Gospel Story Bible*

You will need a glass or cup for this activity. As you start Bible study explain to your family that you are going to pass a cup around and you want everyone, when they get the cup, to describe the worst thing they have ever had to drink. Some might say cough medicine, others might say sour milk or grapefruit juice.

When the cup comes back around to you, share your most terrible drink. Then say, "This week we are going to learn about the most terrible thing anyone has ever had to drink. It was the cup of God's wrath, and Jesus had to drink it. While Jesus was in the Garden of Gethsemane, he prayed: 'Father, take this cup from me.' The cup Jesus was talking about was not a normal cup filled with something like water. The cup Jesus drank from was filled with the wrath of God, which is his holy anger for our sins."

DAY ONE

Picture It

Did you ever try to stay up way past your bedtime? Some people like to stay up on New Year's Eve to be awake when twelve o'clock midnight strikes and the new year begins. Taking a nap that day makes it easier, but if you have a busy day and eat a big dinner, you might find it very difficult to keep your eyes open. That is what happened to the disciples in our story. First, they ate a big meal, then they listened to Jesus teach, and finally they went on a hike. By the time they reached the Garden of Gethsemane, it was past their bedtime, and they found it very hard to stay awake.

 Read Mark 14:32–42.

Think about It Some More

When Jesus went to the garden to pray, he talked about "the hour." The hour Jesus was speaking about was the hour, or time, of his death. Reread the passage inserting the phrase "the time of my death" for the word *hour*. This will help you understand why Jesus was so sad and wanted the disciples to stay up and pray with him. The disciples, however, had just finished the Passover meal and had hiked up the hill to the Garden of Gethsemane and were very tired. They had no idea what was about to happen.

Talk about It

:: Why was Jesus so sad? *(Jesus was sad because the hour of his death was soon to come. He knew that he would suffer and die on the cross, and that God the Father was going to punish him for our sins.)*

:: What did Jesus ask his Father to remove or take away? *(Jesus said that if possible he wanted God the Father to remove the cup—the cup of God's wrath—from him. But Jesus also said that he didn't want the cup removed for his own sake, only if it were what God the Father wanted.)*

:: What did Jesus tell Peter to do? *(Parents, if you have younger children, reread verses 37–38 to see if they can hear the answer and raise their hands to repeat it back to you. Jesus warned Peter to watch and pray so that he would not give in to temptation.)*

 Pray about It

Thank Jesus for not giving up on his mission. Even though it was hard, Jesus did not refuse to endure our punishment for sin.

DAY TWO

Remember It

What do you remember about yesterday's story? What do you think is going to happen today?

 Read Mark 14:43–50.

Think about It Some More

A kiss is supposed to be a special sign of your love for someone. But in this story, Judas's kiss was just the opposite—a sign of betrayal. When Peter saw the kiss and realized that the guards were there to arrest Jesus, he pulled out his sword to fight. Swinging his weapon he cut off a man's ear (John 18:10). But when Jesus told him to put away his sword and healed the man (Luke 22:51), and then gave himself up to be arrested, the disciples were shocked and confused. In their minds, Jesus was supposed to be the deliverer of Israel—a king. But their hopes for a new kingdom were crushed when Jesus gave himself up without a fight (see Luke 24:21). Fearing for their lives, they ran away and scattered into the night. The Old Testament prophet Zechariah said this would happen: "Strike the shepherd and the sheep will be scattered" (Zechariah 13:7).

Talk about It

:: What was evil about Judas's kiss? *(Judas used this sign of love and affection to betray Jesus. It was a betrayal that led to Jesus' death.)*

:: Why did Peter cut off the man's ear? *(Peter thought Jesus was going to fight too. When Jesus corrected Peter, he ran away, afraid.)*

:: Why did Jesus allow himself to be taken prisoner when he had the power to slip away? *(It was time for Jesus to die. He gave himself up and died for us so we could be forgiven. However, Hebrews 12:2 tells us that, in his suffering, Jesus was looking forward with joy to something—to the day when those he came to bring into his family would be fully redeemed.)*

Pray about It

Thank Jesus for not fighting back but for allowing himself to be arrested and be put to death to complete God's plan for our salvation.

DAY THREE _____

Connect It to the Gospel

Today is the day we connect this week's Bible story to the gospel. The gospel is the life, death, and resurrection of Jesus for our salvation. Can anyone guess how our story this week looks forward to or back at the gospel?

 Read John 18:1–11.

Think about It Some More

Each of the four Gospel writers—Matthew, Mark, Luke, and John—tell the story of Jesus' arrest a little differently. Here in John's Gospel, we catch one last glimpse of Jesus' power before his arrest. When the religious leaders and soldiers came to arrest him, Jesus came forward identifying himself by saying, "I am he." "I am" was the name for God that Moses received on the mountain. Hearing Jesus' statement, the soldiers drew back and fell to the ground. There would be no reason for them to fall down unless it was by the power of God.

Matthew's Gospel quotes Jesus as saying he could ask God to send legions of angels to fight for him, but that he wouldn't in order for the Old Testament prophecies and God's promise to be fulfilled (Matthew 26:53–56). Isaiah had compared Jesus to a lamb being led away to be killed. He would not fight back, so that he could die for the sins of God's people (Isaiah 53:7–8).

Talk about It

:: Why didn't Jesus fight back at his arrest? *(If Jesus had fought back, he would have won easily, but then there would be no way for us to be forgiven of our sins.)*

:: What two things did Jesus do to show that he was God—two things that Judas and the soldiers arresting him ignored? *(First, Jesus knocked his attackers to the ground by simply mentioning his name. Second, he miraculously healed the man's ear, which Peter had cut off.)*

:: Why did Jesus tell Peter to put his sword away? *(Jesus told Peter to put away his sword because he needed to drink the cup—the cup of God's wrath for our sin.)*

Pray about It

Thank Jesus for not calling down angels to defend him, even though it meant he would suffer and die. Ask Jesus to help you believe and place your faith and trust in him.

DAY FOUR

Remember It

What has God been teaching you this week through our Bible story?

 Read Mark 14:53–65.

Think about It Some More

Since Jesus had done nothing wrong, the religious rulers couldn't find anything bad to accuse him of. They had to ask people to lie about Jesus. But because they were lying, their stories didn't match. So the chief priest questioned Jesus himself. When Jesus admitted that he was the Christ and then called himself the Son of Man, he was identifying himself as God. That is why the priest tore his clothes and accused Jesus of blasphemy.

To the priest, Jesus looked like an ordinary man. When Jesus called himself the Son of Man, he was using a name from Bible passages like Daniel 7:13–14 and Psalm 8:4. The high priest knew that the Son of Man in Daniel was given authority and glory and that all the nations worshiped him. Because the high priest thought Jesus was a normal man like any one of us, and was only *claiming* to be God, he accused Jesus of blasphemy, a crime punishable by death.

Talk about It

> ● ● KIDS, ask your parents what they think they
> ● ● would have done if they lived in Jesus' day and had
> been in the courtroom during Jesus' trial.

(Parents, we can think that we would have acted nobly. The truth is we would have either sided with the religious rulers and accused Jesus, or sided with the disciples and deserted him. We should not look back at these men with judgment. They were all sinners, like us, in need of a Savior.)

:: What made the high priest so upset? *(Jesus claimed equality with God. By calling himself the Christ and the Son of Man, Jesus was saying that he was equal with God.)*

:: What punishment did the religious leaders say Jesus should get? *(They said he should die.)*

:: Whom do you know who, like the religious rulers, still does not believe that Jesus is God? *(Parents, help your children think about their friends and family who do not believe in Jesus.)*

 Pray about It

Pray that God would give the gift of faith to the people you know who do not believe that Jesus is God.

DAY FIVE

Discover It

Today is the day we look at a different Bible passage—from the book of Psalms or one of the prophets—to see what we can learn from it about Jesus or our salvation.

 Read Psalm 41.

Think about It Some More

Judas thought his plan to betray Jesus was secret, but Jesus knew all along what was going to happen. In fact, all the way back in King David's day, God gave David a prophecy that said Jesus was going to be betrayed by a close friend who ate bread with him (Psalm 41:9). Jesus quoted what King David said to the disciples to let them know that one of them was going to betray him. Then, just as Satan entered Judas on the night of the Last Supper, Jesus said, "What you are going to do, do quickly" (John 13:27). Every part of Jesus' arrest, death, and resurrection was known by God. Nothing happened by chance or accident, and Judas's evil plan was far from secret.

Talk about It

:: How do we know that Judas's betrayal of Jesus was not a secret? *(During the Last Supper, Jesus pointed back to Psalm 41, which prophesies that he would be betrayed by a friend. Jesus also told Judas, "What you are going to do, do quickly," knowing he was going to betray him.)*

:: Since we know that Psalm 41:9 is talking about Jesus, what do you think verse 10 means when it says, "But you, O

LORD, be gracious to me, and raise me up"? *(This seems to be a reference to Jesus' resurrection from the dead.)*

:: What other parts of this psalm sound like they could be talking about Jesus? *(Parents, go through verses 10–13 and ask your children how phrases about enemies not winning in the end and perfect integrity point to Jesus too.)*

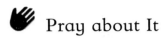 Pray about It

Thank God for his willingness to give up his Son so that we could be brought into God's family. He planned it all for us.

Week 36

Peter Denies Jesus

Story 114 – *The Gospel Story Bible*

Use a beach ball or some other large, lightweight ball for this exercise. Give the ball to your children and ask them to try to hide it so you cannot see it (while still holding on to it). The ball should be large enough to make this impossible. One might try to put it under his shirt, but its presence there would be obvious. Watch them and repeatedly say, "I can see it." Tell them that the ball is like our sin, which we can't hide from God. Say, "This week we will learn how Peter fell into sin even though he was a close follower of Jesus."

DAY ONE

Picture It

Imagine that you started to get really hungry about an hour before dinner. You knew you wouldn't be allowed to have a snack if you asked. So, rather than ask, you tiptoed into the kitchen, quietly opened the cookie jar, and gobbled down two chocolate chip cookies. But no sooner did you swallow the cookies than your sister came into the kitchen and asked, "Were you eating cookies?" Now if that really happened to you, what would you say? Would you tell the truth? Many people have found themselves lying in a situation like that. When we are afraid of getting into trouble, it is very easy to lie. That is what happened to Peter in our story today.

 Read John 18:12–18.

Think about It Some More

Peter never expected Jesus to be arrested. Until now, every time the religious rulers had wanted to hurt or capture Jesus, he had slipped away unharmed. Peter had seen Jesus transfigured, and he knew that Jesus was more powerful than anyone. So when the guards came to arrest Jesus, Peter was quick to draw his sword and fight back, cutting off a man's ear. But to Peter's surprise, Jesus did not fight back, show his awesome power, or even argue. Instead, he rebuked Peter, healed the man's ear, and gave himself up.

At Jesus' arrest, Peter and all the other disciples scattered in fear. Then, Peter turned and followed Jesus and his captors at a distance to see what would happen. His mind must have been filled with questions: Why did Judas betray Jesus? Why didn't Jesus fight back? What was he going to do now? Peter was afraid, for he could be arrested too—after all, he had attacked a man and cut off his ear. As he slunk into the courtyard outside the building where Jesus was being interrogated, Peter was asked by a servant girl whether he was one of the disciples. Only hours earlier, Peter had boasted that, even if all the other disciples fell away, he would not (Mark 14:29). But now he did the very thing he said he would never do: He denied Jesus.

Talk about It

:: Why did Peter lie and say he didn't know Jesus? *(Peter was probably afraid that he would be arrested.)*

:: If you had been Peter that night, what do you think you would have done? *(If we had been there that night, we would probably have lied just as Peter did.)*

:: Can you think of a time when you lied so that you wouldn't get into trouble? *(Parents, help your children identify with Peter. It is easy to look down on what he did, but in reality we would have done the same.)*

 Pray about It

Ask God to help you always tell the truth, even if it means that you might get into trouble.

DAY TWO _____

Remember It

What do you remember about yesterday's story? What do you think is going to happen today?

 Read John 18:19–24.

Think about It Some More

As we read the story of Jesus' arrest and how he was treated like a criminal by the religious leaders and struck by the soldiers, keep in mind that Jesus was no ordinary man. Jesus was God. Jesus was the Creator of the world who spoke things into being. The wind and the waves obeyed him. Jesus healed the sick, raised the dead, and commanded demons. Jesus could easily have destroyed the man who struck him, but Jesus took the blow and did not fight back. Jesus was on a mission to save us from our sins by dying on the cross and rising again. He loved us so much that he didn't defend himself against the terrible treatment he received.

Talk about It

:: Why did the official hit Jesus? *(The official accused Jesus of speaking disrespectfully, but Jesus was speaking truthfully.)*

:: How could Jesus have stopped the man who hit him if he wanted to? *(Parents, allow your children to speculate about how Jesus could have stopped the man, given Jesus' great power. We know from Scripture that Jesus could have called down angels, or he could have commanded the man to stop as he had commanded the wind and the waves.)*

:: In this story how did Jesus show his love for us? *(Jesus showed his love by not defending himself. He did that so that he could take upon himself the punishment that we deserved for our sins.)*

 Pray about It

Thank Jesus for not fighting back even when he could easily have done so.

DAY THREE _____

Connect It to the Gospel

Today is the day we connect this week's Bible story to the gospel. The gospel is the life, death, and resurrection of Jesus for our salvation. Can anyone guess how our story this week looks forward to or back at the gospel?

 Read Matthew 26:69–75.

Think about It Some More

On the night of Jesus' arrest, Peter carried a sword at his side. He boasted that he would fight to the death for Jesus. But when Jesus was arrested, Peter's courage turned to fear. Three times he denied ever knowing Jesus, and he even called down curses on himself to prove it. It wasn't until the rooster crowed that Peter realized what he had done. Peter discovered just how weak he was. When the rooster crowed, Peter realized his weakness and wept bitterly. He was a sinner who needed a Savior. The good news for Peter was that Jesus went to the cross, where he became his Savior by dying for Peter's sins.

Talk about It

:: How many times did Peter deny knowing Jesus? *(Three times)*

:: What reminded Peter of Jesus' warning? *(The rooster's crow)*

:: How are we like Peter? *(Parents, this is a more difficult question for younger children. Take them step-by-step through the answer. We are sinners, like Peter, who need the grace of God to follow Jesus. We cannot follow God in our own strength. If we try, we will fall away when we experience difficulty, just as Peter did.)*

 Pray about It

Ask God to pour out his grace to help you believe and never turn away from Jesus.

DAY FOUR _____

Remember It

What has God been teaching you this week through our Bible story?

 Read John 18:25–27.

Think about It Some More

Cutting off the ear of the servant of the high priest was a crime for which Peter could have been arrested. In the courtyard one of the men who had come to arrest Jesus recognized Peter. Peter knew this meant trouble. Perhaps Peter was recognized as the one who had cut off the servant's ear. If he'd said, "Yes, I was with him," it might've caused the man to take a closer look. Instead of telling the truth, Peter lied and denied Jesus again.

Talk about It

> KIDS, ask your parents if they ever had a time when they found it hard to share that they were a follower of Jesus.

(Parents, Peter is not the only one who found it difficult to share that he was a follower of Jesus. Most adults also struggle with the fear of man when it comes to sharing their faith in Jesus. We may not be threatened with persecution like Peter was that night, but we can worry about what people think of us, and, as a result, not share our faith with people around us.)

:: Why do you think Peter kept denying Christ? *(One lie often leads to another. Once we tell one lie, we often need to keep lying to cover up the first one.)*

:: Read Proverbs 16:18. How does "Pride goes before destruction" fit this story? *(Peter demonstrated his sinful pride when he boasted that he would not abandon Jesus even unto death. He said this in spite of the Lord's warning that all the disciples would fall away. Peter's pride caused him to think he was different from the other disciples, but when threatened, he failed and denied Jesus.)*

Pray about It

Ask God to help you never deny Jesus but always be willing to tell people about the gospel, even if you think they will reject you.

DAY FIVE

Discover It

Today is the day we look at a different Bible passage—from the book of Psalms or one of the prophets—to see what we can learn from it about Jesus or our salvation.

Read Isaiah 53:7.

Think about It Some More

The prophet Isaiah used the picture of sheep to explain how Jesus, the Lamb of God, would not fight back at the time of his arrest. When farmers shear their sheep (cut off their wool) the sheep do not fight or try to run away. They quietly allow the shearer to clip off their wool. In the same way, Jesus allowed his enemies to take his life without resisting. Even though Jesus was *afflicted*, which is a word that means he was hurt, he did not try to stop the men persecuting him. In the same way, a lamb being taken for a sacrifice does not fight back. Jesus did not fight back because it was God's plan for him to die upon the cross and take the punishment we deserved.

Talk about It

:: How does Isaiah's prophecy predict the way Jesus responded to the guards at the time of his arrest? *(Jesus did not resist arrest; he did not say even one unkind word.)*

:: How was Jesus oppressed and afflicted? *(Jesus was mocked, beaten, falsely accused, given a crown of thorns, and crucified.)*

:: How does the example of a lamb being led to die as a sacrifice fit what was happening to Jesus? *(A lamb doesn't fight back when led to be killed as a sacrifice. Jesus is called the Lamb of God. All the lambs that were killed as sacrifices pointed to Jesus, who died as a sacrifice to pay the penalty we deserved for our sins.)*

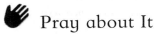 Pray about It

Thank Jesus for dying as a sacrifice for our sins so that we could be forgiven.

Week 37

The Crucifixion & the Criminals

Story 115 – *The Gospel Story Bible*

Put two glasses on a table. Place one securely in the middle of the table, but balance the second one on the table's edge so that it is in danger of falling. Ask your children which glass is in danger. They should answer that the glass on the edge is in danger of falling to the floor and breaking. Pick up both glasses, one in one hand and one in the other hand. Explain to your children that God can save someone wherever they are in life: in the middle of life (the glass in the middle of the table) or very near death (the glass balanced on the edge). No person is too far from God's saving hand. Say, "This week we will learn about a man whom God saved when he was just moments away from his death."

DAY ONE

Picture It

There once was a man who lost his job and had no money for food or rent. So he asked a friend to lend him one thousand dollars, which he promised to repay by the end of the year. The friend lent him the money, but at the end of the year, the man could not repay his debt. When he explained his troubles, the friend forgave the debt. By forgiving the debt, the friend assumed (took on himself) the loss. His one thousand dollars was gone. Every time we forgive a person, we bear the cost of that forgiveness. Because of our sin, we owed a great debt to God, but Jesus paid the cost of it for us with his own life so we could be forgiven.

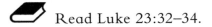 Read Luke 23:32–34.

Think about It Some More

There is always a cost to forgive someone. If someone owes you money and you forgive the debt, you lose that money. If a person hits you, you could hit back. But if you forgive him instead of hitting back, you are the one who is hurt, not him. Jesus could have punished the men who nailed him to the cross, but he forgave them instead.

We know that at least one of the soldiers present at Jesus' crucifixion believed. A centurion who saw Jesus breathe his last said, "Truly this man was the Son of God!" (Mark 15:39). It is amazing to think that even a soldier on duty at Jesus' crucifixion could believe and be forgiven. In Matthew 18:21–22, Jesus told Peter that even if a person sins against us seventy times seven times we should still forgive him. Jesus demonstrated that kind of forgiveness when he asked his Father to forgive those who nailed him on that cross.

Talk about It

- :: Who was crucified with Jesus? *(Two criminals)*

- :: What did our forgiveness cost Jesus? *(Our forgiveness cost Jesus his life; he took on himself the punishment that we deserved for our sins.)*

- :: What did Jesus say about those who crucified him? *(Jesus said, "Father, forgive them, for they know not what they do" [Luke 23:34].)*

- :: What lesson can we learn from what Jesus did? *(Remembering that Jesus died on the cross for our sins, we should be willing to forgive others who sin against us.)*

 Pray about It

Ask God to help you forgive those who sin against you and not hold their sins against them.

DAY TWO

Remember It

What do you remember about yesterday's story? What do you think is going to happen today?

 Read Luke 23:35–38.

Think about It Some More

After Jesus raised Lazarus from the dead, he traveled into Jerusalem for the Passover. The people shouted, "Hosanna!" and called Jesus the King of Israel (John 12:13). The people must have been very excited. They thought God was giving them a new king to help them fight against Rome. Zechariah had said the righteous king would rule from "sea to sea" and "to the ends of the earth" (Zechariah 9:10).

In our story today, things were very different from that exciting day. Now the people were looking at Jesus hanging on a cross with a sign above his head mocking his kingship. The religious leaders and soldiers mocked Jesus too, daring him to come down from the cross if he really was the Messiah. The disciples were without hope. They had thought that Jesus was the Messiah, but with him hanging on the cross, their hope was gone (Luke 24:21). Although the people mocking Jesus challenged him to come down from the cross, Jesus hung there and died. It appeared that Jesus was defeated, but secretly, his death was an overwhelming victory—not a victory over Rome, but a victory over Satan, sin, and death.

Talk about It

:: Who mocked Jesus? *(The soldiers and the religious leaders mocked him.)*

:: Why did they mock Jesus? *(Jesus had performed many miracles and had claimed to be God. Now he looked like any other man, bleeding on a cross. They mocked him because they thought he was finally defeated.)*

:: Why didn't the people speak out to defend Jesus? *(The people were disappointed and probably felt that Jesus had lied to them, or at least that they had judged him wrongly. They thought Jesus would be their king. They saw Jesus do miracles and save others, but now he looked just like the other two criminals hanging there.)*

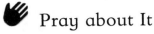 Pray about It

Thank Jesus for his willingness to be mocked on the cross for us.

DAY THREE _____

Connect It to the Gospel

Today is the day we connect this week's Bible story to the gospel. The gospel is the life, death, and resurrection of Jesus for our salvation. Can anyone guess how our story this week looks forward to or back at the gospel?

 Read Mark 15:25–32.

Think about It Some More

Mark tells us that, along with the soldiers and religious rulers, the people passing by also mocked Jesus. They challenged Jesus to come down from the cross, and they repeated Jesus' claim to rebuild the temple in three days. What they didn't realize was that Jesus *would* rebuild the temple—the temple of his body—for in three days he would rise again. If Jesus had listened to the mockers and come down from the cross, none of us could be forgiven. Although it is terribly sad to think about Jesus dying, it is good news that Jesus didn't come down from that cross. By remaining there, he made a way for all of us—even the mockers—to be rescued from our sin.

Talk about It

:: What did the sign above Jesus' head say? *(It read "The King of the Jews.")*

:: What did the people say Jesus would have to do before they would believe? *(They said Jesus would have to save himself and come down from the cross.)*

:: Why didn't Jesus just come down from the cross so they could see his power and believe? *(Jesus had to stay on the cross to die for our sins. By staying there on the cross, Jesus made a way for all of us to be forgiven our sins and to have our hearts changed so that we could believe. Remember, many of these people had heard about Jesus healing and raising people from the dead. They may have even seen this with their own eyes, yet they did not believe.)*

 Pray about It

Ask Jesus to help you believe and not doubt like those who mocked Jesus on the cross.

DAY FOUR _____

Remember It

What has God been teaching you this week through our Bible story?

 Read Luke 23:39–43.

Think about It Some More

When a skydiver straps on a parachute and jumps out of a plane, there is usually plenty of time to pull the ripcord, which sets the parachute free to open. But if the skydiver doesn't pull it soon enough and gets too close to the ground, the parachute won't have time to fully open and save the skydiver from crashing and being killed. Even though the ripcord is pulled while the skydiver is still falling, if it is pulled too late the parachute will do no good.

God doesn't work like a parachute. It is never too late for God to save a person. In our story today, one of the criminals crucified with him called out to Jesus only moments before his own death. Even so, it was not too late for him to call out to Jesus and be saved.

Talk about It

> ●● KIDS, ask your parents if they know anyone who, like the criminal, was saved late in life, and if they know someone who trusted Jesus from an early age. Have them tell you the stories.

(Parents, it is great to share stories of people we know and how they came to become Christians. If you know a person who waited a long time to trust the Lord, ask your children what would have happened if he had died before he had believed.)

:: What was the difference between the two criminals in our story today? *(One criminal joined in the mocking of Jesus, but the other one called out to Jesus for help.)*

:: What did Jesus say to the criminal who called out to him? *(Jesus said he would be with him in paradise—heaven.)*

:: Why is the present the only good time for someone to place their trust in Jesus? *(We don't know how long we have to live. We may think we will live to be seventy or eighty years old, but there are no guarantees. Only God knows how long a person will live. If someone offered you a valuable treasure, you would want to take it right away. You wouldn't wait for a few years to take it. Jesus is the most valuable of all treasures, so why should we wait to place our trust in him?)*

 Pray about It

Ask God to help unbelievers you know trust Jesus today.

DAY FIVE _____

Discover It

Today is the day we look at a different Bible passage—from the book of Psalms or one of the prophets—to see what we can learn from it about Jesus or our salvation.

 Read Psalm 22:17–18.

Think about It Some More

The words David wrote in these verses came true. People stared at Jesus hanging on the cross while the soldiers cast lots for his clothing. Many years before, God had revealed to David what would happen to Jesus. In fact, all of Psalm 22 is a prophetic look at how God's servant, Jesus, would suffer and die. Even though the religious rulers, the disciples, and the people had all read Psalm 22, they didn't connect the psalm to Jesus, so they never expected him to suffer and die. But Jesus himself knew because he prayed Psalm 22 from the cross (Matthew 27:46).

Talk about It

:: What does it mean to cast lots? *(Casting lots is like drawing straws. Each person gets a straw, but one of the straws is shorter. The one who picks the shorter straw is the winner or the loser, depending on the situation. That person is said to be the one who was chosen by the casting of lots.)*

:: Why did the soldiers cast lots for Jesus' clothing? *(They divided most of Jesus' clothing, but in John 19:23–24 we learn that they didn't want to tear the tunic woven in one piece, so they cast lots to see who would get it.)*

:: How do these verses help us to know that even the smallest details surrounding the crucifixion were a part of God's plan? *(There is no way that David, who wrote this psalm, could have guessed that Jesus' clothing would be both divided and taken by the casting of lots. The only way David could write that was if God planned it all that way and then had David write about what was going to happen.)*

 Pray about It

Praise God for his control over everything in the universe and the love he showed us by planning our salvation through his Son, Jesus.

Week 38

The Death of Christ

Story 116 – *The Gospel Story Bible*

Jesus died on the cross in our place—as our substitute. To better help your children to understand this concept, give them each an index card or piece of paper with the following words written on it: "I hereby redeem this card for one chore I don't want to do." Explain to them that they can save the card and redeem it (use it) by giving it to you. When you receive the card, you agree to serve in their place, as their substitute—to do that chore for them. When they redeem the card, remind them of how Jesus died on the cross in our place—for our redemption, so that we could be forgiven. Say, "This week we will read about the crucifixion of our Lord."

DAY ONE

Picture It

Have you ever pricked yourself with a thorn from a rose or some other thorny bush? If you have, then you know how much one little thorn can hurt. If you have ever run into a thorn bush while walking through a meadow, you know how the pain of the thorns biting into your skin can stop you in your tracks. So imagine what it would have been like for Jesus to have a crown of thorns pushed down onto his head. When you consider that the crown of thorns was the least of Jesus' punishments, you start to realize how much Jesus suffered so you could be saved.

 Read Matthew 27:27–31.

Think about It Some More

When the Roman soldiers assigned to whip the prisoners heard that Jesus was sentenced to death for claiming to be a king, they mocked him in front of a whole battalion of over one hundred soldiers. For a crown, they gave him thorns. For a staff or scepter, they gave him a wooden reed, and they spat on him and mocked him. Little did they realize that Jesus *was* a king—and not just any king, but King of kings and Lord of lords (Revelation 17:14). The only reason they got away with mocking Jesus is that he didn't fight back. Jesus stood there suffering as their substitute, taking the punishment they (and we) deserved.

Isaiah foresaw Jesus' suffering: "He was despised and rejected by men; a man of sorrows, and acquainted with grief; and as one from whom men hide their faces he was despised, and we esteemed him not. Surely he has borne our griefs and carried our sorrows; yet we esteemed him stricken, smitten by God, and afflicted" (Isaiah 53:3–4).

Talk about It

:: What did the soldiers do to make fun of Jesus? *(They dressed him up like a king with a crown of thorns, a reed for a staff, and a scarlet robe; then they mocked him in front of a whole battalion of soldiers. Parents, if you have younger children you might need to give them some clues such as saying, "A crown of _____ and a scarlet _____.")*

:: What would you have done if you had been standing among the soldiers mocking Jesus? *(We would have jeered and mocked right alongside them. It is important to remember that Jesus suffered and died because of our sins just as much as for the sins of the soldiers who mocked him.)*

:: Read 1 Peter 2:23–24. Why didn't Jesus fight back? *(Jesus offered no resistance because he entrusted himself to God, the judge, and willingly endured suffering for us.)*

 Pray about It

Take time to confess to God that you are a sinner. Then thank Jesus for being willing to be mocked and beaten as our substitute so he could deliver us from our sins.

DAY TWO _____

Remember It

What do you remember about yesterday's story? What do you think is going to happen today?

 Read Matthew 27:32–44.

Think about It Some More

Today's Scripture is Matthew's account of Jesus' crucifixion. Although we already read the same story from Mark, it is good to study how each of the Gospel writers tells the story, because each one shares it from a different perspective. Matthew, for instance, is the only one who mentions that the soldiers offered Jesus wine mixed with gall (a bitter herb thought to dull a person's pain) and that those who mocked him called Jesus the Son of God. So it is in reading all of the Gospel accounts of Jesus' death that we can see the full picture of what happened that day.

Talk about It

:: What was the name of the man whom the soldiers asked to carry Jesus' cross? *(Parents, if you have younger children who are not able to read, they may not remember the answer. In that case, reread the text and ask them to raise their hands when they hear the correct answer.)*

:: Why do you think Simon was asked to carry Jesus' cross? *(The Bible doesn't tell us why, but after Jesus had endured such a beating it is likely that he would not have been able to carry it on his own, and the soldiers didn't want him to die before being nailed to the cross and lifted up.)*

:: What did the mockers say to Jesus as he hung on the cross? *(The mockers said, "You who would destroy the temple and rebuild it in three days, save yourself! If you are the Son of God, come down from the cross" [v. 40]. Also, "He saved others; he cannot save himself. He is the King of Israel; let him come down now from the cross, and we will believe in him" [v. 42].)*

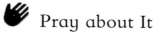 Pray about It

The people all mocked Jesus, but you can praise him for the very same things they mocked Jesus for. Praise Jesus as the Son of God who died and rose again to save us.

DAY THREE _____

Connect It to the Gospel

Today is the day we connect this week's Bible story to the gospel. The gospel is the life, death, and resurrection of Jesus for our salvation. Can anyone guess how our story this week looks forward to or back at the gospel?

 Read Luke 23:44–49.

Think about It Some More

As Jesus was dying, the whole land became dark. Then, at the moment of Jesus' death, the temple curtain was torn in two from top to bottom (Matthew 27:51). The temple curtain divided the Holy Place from the Most Holy Place, where God's presence lived. The curtain blocked people from freely entering into the Most Holy Place to spend time with God. But after Jesus died and the curtain was torn, the way to the Most Holy Place was opened. That symbolized that we can all go into God's presence if we believe and put our trust in Jesus' work on the cross. The death of Jesus is the heart of the gospel. The writer of Hebrews said that if Jesus hadn't shed his blood for us, there would be no forgiveness for our sins (Hebrews 9:22).

Talk about It

:: What happened to the temple curtain when Jesus died? *(The curtain was torn in two from top to bottom.)*

:: Why was there a curtain dividing the inner courts of the temple? *(The curtain protected the priests from the presence of God. Only once a year could the high priest enter the Most Holy Place, where God's presence lived. The rest of the year, the way was shut, and the people of Israel could not go into God's presence.)*

:: Why did God tear the temple curtain in two when Jesus died? *(God wanted to show that the way into his presence was opened now because Jesus had died for our sins. Now, instead of the high priest entering God's presence one day a year, we can all enjoy God's presence in our hearts every day. When we believe and place our trust in Jesus, the Holy Spirit of God comes to live in us. Jesus opened the way.)*

 Pray about It

Thank Jesus for tearing open the curtain that blocked us from the presence of God. Take time to praise God for all he has done.

DAY FOUR _____

Remember It

What has God been teaching you this week through our Bible story?

 Read Matthew 27:45–56.

Think about It Some More

While Jesus hung on the cross, he cried out, "My God, My God, why have you forsaken me?" Jesus said this because God his Father had turned away from him and punished him as a sinner. The Father poured out his full anger for our sins on Jesus, forsaking him as he hung on the cross. After taking the punishment for our sins, it did not take long for Jesus to die. He had been so tortured prior to being crucified that his body did not last long. His death was followed by earthquakes, the tearing of the temple curtain, and the resurrections of many. Those watching over Jesus were filled with awe, and there were some who realized in that moment that Jesus really was the Son of God.

Talk about It

> ● ● KIDS, ask your parents what touches them the
> ● ● most about the story of Jesus' death.

(Parents, give this question some thought and simply answer from your heart.)

:: What happened when Jesus died? *(Give younger children clues to help them with the list: the temple curtain was torn in two, the earth shook (earthquake), rocks split, tombs were opened, and people were raised from the dead.)*

:: What did the centurion say when the earth shook and people were raised from the dead? *(Parents, reread the passage for younger children and have them raise their hands when they hear the answer: "Truly this was the Son of God!" [v. 54].)*

:: Why did Jesus say God had forsaken him? *(God the Father had turned away from Jesus and poured out the wrath that we deserved for our sin on Jesus.)*

 Pray about It

Thank Jesus for dying on the cross so that we could be forgiven—for enduring the punishment we deserved, and for not calling out to God the Father to stop the punishment.

DAY FIVE

Discover It

Today is the day we look at a different Bible passage—from the book of Psalms or one of the prophets—to see what we can learn from it about Jesus or our salvation.

 Read Isaiah 53:5.

Think about It Some More

The words *transgressions* and *iniquities* from this verse are two more words for sin. The word *chastisement* means punishment. So Isaiah is telling us that Jesus was wounded and crushed for our sin and punished so that we could have peace with God. It is amazing how accurate Isaiah's prophecy was, especially when we consider how the soldiers mocked Jesus, how they struck him on the head, how they whipped him, and how God forsook him.

Talk about It

:: What do the words *transgressions* and *iniquities* mean? *(The words* transgressions *and* iniquities *are two words for sins.)*

:: How does Jesus' suffering show his love for us? *(Jesus wasn't just another man—Jesus was God. To think that God suffered and died to pay the price for our sin shows us just how deep his love for us is.)*

:: What are some of your sins that Jesus died for? *(Parents, take this opportunity to share some of the sins you have committed in your life as an example of confession for your children. Then help your children think of a few of their own. Finally, explain that Jesus can be their substitute too if they turn away from their sins and put their faith in him.)*

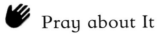 Pray about It

Thank God for making a way for our sins to be taken away.

Week 39

The Resurrection

Story 117 – *The Gospel Story Bible*

You will need to do a little work for this object lesson. Take a raw egg and using a pin, poke one hole in each end. Blow the egg out to leave an empty shell. Then, using food coloring or paints, decorate the egg as you would at Easter time, letting it dry with the hole down so it can drain. On a small slip of paper, write the sentence, "The tomb is empty, Jesus has risen." Roll the paper up tightly and slip it through the hole into the egg.

At Bible study, show the egg to your children and ask them what it is. Once they guess that it's an Easter egg, tell them it is a very special Easter egg. Crack the egg on the side of a table and open it in front of them. Pull out the paper, unroll it, and read it. The children should be very surprised to find that the egg is empty. Say, "This week we will be learning about Jesus' resurrection and how surprised the disciples were to find Jesus' tomb empty. This is the real reason we celebrate Easter every year."

DAY ONE

Picture It

If you met a street magician one day who said he could turn a tennis ball into a rabbit, you wouldn't believe him. But you might believe he could make it *look* like he turned a tennis ball into a rabbit. If he invited you to stay and watch him, you would probably start wondering where he was hiding the rabbit. You might look around his table or try to catch a peek up his jacket sleeve. In our story today, the chief priests and Pharisees didn't believe Jesus was going to rise from the dead, but they suspected that the disciples would try to make it *look* like he did. Let's see what they did to try to prevent this.

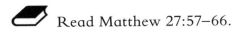 Read Matthew 27:57–66.

Think about It Some More

After Jesus died and was buried, the Pharisees remembered that Jesus had said he would rise again on the third day. They thought the disciples would try to steal the body and make it look like Jesus had risen from the dead. They explained this to Pilate, who gave them soldiers to guard the tomb. While Jesus was alive, the Pharisees had rebuked and corrected him for doing healing "work" on the Sabbath, the day of the week on which work was forbidden. But that didn't seem to stop them from going to Pilate on the Sabbath or ordering the soldiers to do the "work" of sealing the tomb and posting a guard on the Sabbath.

In the end, God used their sinful plan for good. When Jesus rose from the dead the next morning, no one could say that the disciples had come and stolen the body. By posting a guard and sealing the tomb, the Pharisees made sure that no one reading the Bible today would think the disciples stole the body.

Talk about It

:: What two things did the Pharisees do to prevent anyone from stealing Jesus' body? *(They sealed his tomb and posted a guard.)*

:: What were the Pharisees worried about? *(Parents, if you have younger children, reread the passage to help them remember that the Pharisees were afraid the disciples would steal the body and claim that Jesus had risen from the dead.)*

:: How can what the Pharisees did help us to believe that Jesus really did rise from the dead? *(By posting a guard, the Pharisees made sure that Jesus' resurrection was not faked. When we look back, we can see that God used even the Pharisees' unbelief to confirm that Jesus really did rise from the dead.)*

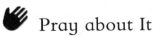 Pray about It

Praise God for the way he can use evil to accomplish his plan.

DAY TWO

Remember It

What do you remember about yesterday's story? What do you think is going to happen today?

 Read Matthew 28:1–10.

Think about It Some More

The soldiers guarding Jesus' tomb were told to watch out for the disciples, who might try to steal the body. But no one told them anything about powerful angels coming down from heaven and terrible earthquakes. That was more than the soldiers had bargained for. The guards were so afraid that they shook and fell to the ground. That is when the angel of the Lord gave one of the most famous announcements in the whole Bible: "He has risen, as he said!"

Today, Christians all over the world repeat the words of the angel on Easter Sunday as they celebrate the resurrection of Jesus. A wax seal and a Roman guard could not stop Jesus from rising from the dead. In fact, if the whole Roman army had been present, Jesus would have risen just the same.

Talk about It

:: What happened to the soldiers who were guarding the tomb when Jesus rose from the dead? *(They trembled and fell to the ground as dead men.)*

:: What did the women do when Jesus met them? *(Parents, if you have younger children, read the story again and have them raise their hands when they hear the answer. The women worshiped Jesus.)*

:: What did the angel tell the women to say to the disciples? *(The angel told the women to go quickly and tell the disciples that Jesus had risen from the dead.)*

 Pray about It

Do what the women did when they met Jesus: Worship him. Sing your favorite song about Jesus or simply praise him for rising from the dead.

DAY THREE

Connect It to the Gospel

Today is the day we connect this week's Bible story to the gospel. The gospel is the life, death, and resurrection of Jesus for our salvation. Can anyone guess how our story this week looks forward to or back at the gospel?

 Read Luke 24:1–12.

Think about It Some More

The resurrection is one of the most important parts of the gospel story. The apostle Paul said the resurrection is so important that if Jesus were not raised then our preaching is worthless, our faith is no good, and we are still in our sins (1 Corinthians 15:13–17). By rising from the dead, Jesus proved that everything he taught was true and won the greatest victory of all time. Jesus won the battle against sin and death by dying for our sin and then rising from the dead. Now all those who believe in Jesus will one day be raised from the dead too and live forever with the Lord in heaven.

Talk about It

:: What did the disciples do when the women told them Jesus had risen? *(They did not believe them. They said the whole thing sounded like an "idle tale"—a made-up story.)*

:: Which one of the disciples ran to the tomb? *(Peter ran to the tomb, and when he saw that Jesus was not there he marveled at what the women had said.)*

:: Why is the resurrection so important? *(With his resurrection, Jesus defeated sin and death and proved everything he had said was true. If he had not risen, he could not have been God.)*

 Pray about It

Shout joyfully to the Lord for winning the victory over death. (You may not be used to shouting joyfully to God, but when we root for a sports team and they win a victory we often shout. If you're still not sure, look up some of these Scriptures: Psalms 20:5; 47:1; 66:1.)

DAY FOUR

Remember It

What has God been teaching you this week through our Bible story?

 Read Matthew 28:11–15.

Think about It Some More

The religious rulers posted the guards at the tomb so that no one could steal the body and then start a rumor that Jesus had risen from the dead. But when the guards told them about the earthquake, the angel, and all that had taken place, they had a problem. If word got out that angels from heaven had broken Jesus out of the tomb, a lot of people would believe in Jesus. To prevent this, they paid the guards not to talk about it and had them tell a lie instead. But when Jesus started appearing to many in Jerusalem, the religious rulers' lie was exposed. By the time he went back to heaven, he had appeared to more than 500 people (1 Corinthians 15:6).

Talk about It

> ●● KIDS, ask your parents why they think the reli-
> ●● gious rulers paid off the guards.

(Parents, the religious rulers were desperate to hold onto their power. They looked good to the people on the outside, but were willing to lie to get what they wanted.)

:: What did the guards at the tomb tell the chief priests? *(They told them all that had taken place.)*

:: What did the chief priests decide to do to keep people from believing that Jesus had risen from the dead? *(They had the guards lie and say that the disciples stole the body while they were sleeping.)*

:: Why didn't the chief priests believe that Jesus rose from the dead? *(We don't know why, but they did refuse to believe, even though they heard the story from the guards. Not everyone who hears about Jesus believes. We need God to open our hearts to believe.)*

 Pray about It

Ask God to help the unbelievers you know to accept the truth that Jesus died on the cross for their sins and rose again from the dead.

DAY FIVE

Discover It

Today is the day we look at a different Bible passage—from the book of Psalms or one of the prophets—to see what we can learn from it about Jesus or our salvation.

 Read Psalm 34:19–20.

Think about It Some More

Dying on a cross was a slow and terrible way to die. As sad as it sounds, Roman soldiers would break the legs of those who were crucified to help them die faster. But when they came to Jesus, they found that he had already died, so the soldiers did not break his legs. Instead, they pierced his side with a sword. The apostle John said that the verses we read from Psalm 34 were a prophecy about Jesus, that none of his bones would be broken (John 19:36). This tells us that God was in control of every detail of Jesus' death. Long before Jesus was even born, God knew that none of Jesus' bones would be broken. Another verse, Psalm 16:10, talks about Jesus' resurrection.

Talk about It

:: Why didn't the soldiers break Jesus' legs when he was on the cross? *(Jesus had already died.)*

:: Read John 19:31–37. What did the soldiers do to Jesus instead of breaking his legs? *(They pierced his side.)*

:: How could God know that the soldiers were not going to break Jesus' legs long before Jesus was even born? *(God knows and controls all things, and he knows all that will happen and makes it work together according to his plan.)*

 Pray about It

Praise God for the way he controls all things and makes them work according to his plan.

Week 40

Doubting Thomas
Story 118 – *The Gospel Story Bible*

Bring a banana and an orange to Bible study and ask your children if they believe you can turn a banana into an orange. Tell them it is a magic trick that requires great powers. Ask them if they believe you could turn the banana into an orange without seeing you do it. They will likely say no. Explain that many people follow the policy that if they don't see it they don't believe it.

Say, "This week we will learn about Thomas, who refused to believe that Jesus rose from the dead unless he saw him with his own eyes." Then announce that you will now turn the banana into an orange. Say a bunch of made up "magic" words, and then dramatically and sharply rotate the banana so that it "turns into the orange" and collides with it. Stand up and take a bow and celebrate your wonderful achievement.

DAY ONE

Picture It

A family was going on vacation, but, due to the dad's work schedule, he was not going to be able to join them until the middle of the week. (At least that is what he told them.) Secretly, while his family drove the ten-hour trip, the dad flew ahead by airplane and checked into the hotel before his family. When it was close to the time they were to arrive, he called his wife to find out exactly where they were.

The dad's plan was to stand along the road just up the road from the hotel and hitchhike as his family drove past. When his family passed by, they saw him but didn't recognize him. When he ran after them waving his arms, they thought the poor hitchhiker was upset because he didn't get a ride. Finally the father ran to the hotel after his family calling his children and wife by name. It wasn't until they heard their names that they realized who he was. They hadn't recognized him on the road because they hadn't expected him to be there.

In our story today, two of Jesus' disciples walking on the road to Emmaus shortly after Jesus rose from the dead, had a similar experience.

 Read Luke 24:13–35.

Think about It Some More

Wouldn't it have been great to be on the road to Emmaus and have Jesus teach you how the Old Testament Scriptures pointed to him? Even though we can't go back in time to hear what he said, we do get to hear it secondhand from the disciples in the books and letters they wrote about Jesus. On the last day of these weekly studies, we review one of the Old Testament passages that points to Jesus. Think of the last day of each week as your personal "on the road to Emmaus" experience.

Talk about It

:: Why didn't the two disciples recognize Jesus? *(Even though they had heard that Jesus' body wasn't in the tomb, they did not believe he had risen from the dead. Luke adds that "their eyes were kept from recognizing" Jesus [v. 16]. Jesus could have said, "Hey, guys, it's me: Jesus," but he didn't.)*

:: What did Jesus explain in his conversation with the two men along the road? *(Jesus explained how the Scriptures, beginning with Moses and going through the prophets, pointed forward to him.)*

:: Can you think of a Bible verse from the Old Testament that points forward to Jesus? *(Parents, we learn one of these on the last day of each weekly study. As an example, substitute sacrifices point to Jesus [the ram instead of Isaac on the mountain or the lamb instead of the firstborn son on the first Passover].)*

 Pray about It

Praise God for how the whole Bible points to the gospel. The first part of the Bible—up to Jesus' cross—points forward to our salvation in Jesus. After Jesus' resurrection what we read in the Bible points back to what Jesus did for us.

DAY TWO

Remember It

What do you remember about yesterday's story? What do you think is going to happen today?

 Read John 20:19–23.

Think about It Some More

The soldiers spread rumors that the disciples stole the body of Jesus. With those rumors going around, the disciples, terrified, locked themselves in a room. Imagine their conversation: "What are we going to do? The chief priests are sure to be after us. The guards are spreading rumors that we stole Jesus' body. All they have to do is come up with one false witness to say they saw us near the tomb, and we will all be arrested and put into prison."

As they were huddled together in conversation, Jesus opened the locked door (or walked right through it), walked up behind them, and scared them half to death. Luke said they thought Jesus was a ghost (Luke 24:37). But as soon as Jesus showed them his hands and side and they touched him, they saw he was real, and they were glad. Then Jesus commissioned them to take the message of the gospel into the world.

Talk about It

:: Can you remember a time when you were startled by someone's sudden entrance into a room? Describe what it felt like? *(Parents, draw out your children here; this is just a fun way for them to identify with the surprise of the disciples.)*

:: Why did Jesus show the disciples his hands and side? *(Jesus showed them his hands and side to help them believe that he wasn't a ghost but was really alive. Luke 24:41–43 records that Jesus told the disciples to touch him and ate breakfast with them to help them believe he was alive.)*

:: Why did God the Father leave scars on Jesus from his wounds? *(Parents, draw out your children here. We know that Jesus used those nail marks to help his disciples believe it was really him. When we see Jesus in heaven, the nail marks on his hands and the scar on his side will remind us of Jesus' sacrifice for us on the cross.)*

Pray about It

Praise God that Jesus' wounds are an eternal, visible reminder of all that he did for us. If you know the hymn "Crown Him with Many Crowns," sing it together. Point out how the words in the last verse talk about the wounds of Jesus.

DAY THREE

Connect It to the Gospel

Today is the day we connect this week's Bible story to the gospel. The gospel is the life, death, and resurrection of Jesus for our salvation. Can anyone guess how our story this week looks forward to or back at the gospel?

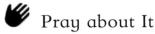 Read John 20:24–29.

Think about It Some More

"Seeing is believing" is a popular phrase people use when they doubt something they cannot see. If your friend told you that he found a hundred-dollar bill on the way to your house, you might say to him, "I'll believe it when I see it—seeing is believing." But if he pulled a damp, dirty, hundred-dollar bill out of his pocket, it would be easy to believe.

That's what happened to Thomas. Thomas said that unless he saw Jesus with his own eyes he would never believe that Jesus had risen from the dead. But when Jesus appeared to Thomas, he challenged the "seeing is believing" way of thinking. He said, "Blessed are those who have not seen and yet have believed" (v. 29).

Jesus is no longer with us on earth; he returned to his Father in heaven. Today, we all need faith to believe in Jesus. Faith is believing in something you cannot see. If we have faith in Jesus—that is, if we believe in him even though we don't see him—Jesus said we would be blessed. The Bible tells us that faith is a gift that only God can give (Ephesians 2:8). So asking God to give us faith to believe should be one of our daily prayers.

Talk about It

:: Why didn't Thomas believe? *(Thomas didn't believe because he was not there when Jesus visited the disciples earlier. He said he would not believe unless he saw Jesus for himself.)*

:: What happened to Thomas when the Lord appeared to him? *(Thomas believed.)*

:: What did Thomas call Jesus? *(Thomas called Jesus his Lord and God. This is one of the few places where someone called Jesus God directly. If what Thomas said were not true, Jesus should have rebuked Thomas. Instead, Jesus commended him.)*

 Pray about It

Ask God to bless each person in your family with faith to believe and trust Jesus.

DAY FOUR

Remember It

What has God been teaching you this week through our Bible story?

 Read John 20:30–31.

Think about It Some More

The last thing Jesus said to Thomas was, "Blessed are those who have not seen and yet have believed" (John 20:29). The bad news for all of us today is that we don't get to see Jesus until we go to be with him in heaven. But the good news is that God made sure his story was written down for all of us to read and believe.

Jesus, the living Word of God, showed his scarred hands to help Thomas believe. Although we don't have Jesus to show us his hands, we do have these wonderful eyewitness accounts of what happened, and we have the Holy Spirit, whom Jesus sent, to help us to know that Jesus is just who he said he was (John 15:26). The apostle Paul said that the gospel story in the Bible is the "power of God for salvation" (Romans 1:16). The writer of Hebrews tells us that the Bible is a living book that can cut to our heart and expose our sin and help us believe (Hebrews 4:12).

Talk about It

> :: :: KIDS, ask your parents how God has used the
> :: :: Bible to help them believe.

(Parents, think back to how you have been affected by your study of God's Word. You may not need to go back further than the last two weeks where you have been reading along with your children the story of the death and resurrection of Jesus.)

:: Why did John say God gave us the Bible? *(John said the Bible was written to help us believe that Jesus was the Christ, the Son of God.)*

:: What did John say all those who believe will have? *(Parents, if necessary reread today's verses aloud and have your children raise their hands when they hear the answer. John said that those who believe would have life in Jesus' name. That is a reference to living forever in heaven with God.)*

 Pray about It

Ask God to use the Bible stories to help you believe so that you too will have "life in his name."

DAY FIVE

Discover It

Today is the day we look at a different Bible passage—from the book of Psalms or one of the prophets—to see what we can learn from it about Jesus or our salvation.

 Read Psalm 80.

Think about It Some More

Jesus explained how the Old Testament pointed forward to him. Before you read through the following explanation, see if you and your children can find Jesus in this psalm.

Psalm 80 points forward to Jesus when it speaks of a shepherd who comes to save us. Jesus said that he was the Good Shepherd, who was going to lay down his life to rescue his sheep (John 10:11–15). Jesus was also called the Son of Man, the same name Asaph used in verse 17. Three times in this psalm, Asaph asked God to let his face shine upon his people. Today, we know that God answered Asaph's prayer when he sent his Son, Jesus. Jesus said, "I am the light of the world" (John 8:12). One day, when we go to heaven, we won't need any sunshine because Jesus will be our light and will shine upon us (Revelation 21:23).

Talk about It

:: How do we know the psalm is talking about Jesus when God is described as a shepherd who will save? *(Jesus told us that he was the Good Shepherd.)*

:: How did God answer Asaph's prayer for God to save Israel? *(God the Father sent his Son, Jesus, to save us.)*

:: What phrase did Asaph repeat three times in this psalm? *(He repeats three times the phrase, "Let your face shine, that we may be saved.")*

 ## Pray about It

Praise Jesus as the light of the world and the light of heaven, and thank God for answering Asaph's prayer to save us.

Week 41

Another Miraculous Catch

Story 119 – *The Gospel Story Bible*

You will need a teddy bear or other stuffed animal and a cookie for this exercise. Set the teddy bear and the cookie in front of your children. Ask your children if the teddy bear can eat cookies. They will say no. Then ask them why he can't eat cookies. They should answer that he can't eat cookies because he is not alive. Finally, ask your children what they would think if the teddy bear reached down, picked up a cookie, and ate it. Then explain to them that, after Jesus rose from the dead, he ate with his disciples, which was a great way to show them that he was really alive and not a ghost.

DAY ONE

Picture It

Imagine the life of a fisherman—every evening loading the net into the boat, rowing out to the middle of the lake, dropping it over the side of the boat, and then pulling it up to collect the fish in the boat. After fishing all night the fisherman must dock the boat, sort the fish, dry the nets, get something to eat, and, finally, go to sleep. A fisherman doesn't have much time for school or anything else. That is why, after Jesus died, the disciples who were fisherman went back to fishing. Fishing was pretty much all they knew how to do.

 Read John 21:1–4.

Think about It Some More

Jesus appeared to the disciples after he rose from the dead, but he didn't stay with them. He would visit briefly and then be gone again. You can see why the disciples struggled to believe. They must have been scratching their heads and wondering, "Did Jesus really appear to us?" Not knowing what else to do, they returned to their boats and fishing nets. When Jesus appeared to them on the shore, they didn't recognize him, nor did they remember that they were supposed to be fishers of *men*.

Talk about It

:: How many disciples went out fishing? *(There were seven disciples—Peter, Thomas, Nathaniel, James and John [the sons of Zebedee], and two others whose names we don't know.)*

:: Why didn't the disciples recognize Jesus? *(They were not looking for Jesus. It almost seems they had forgotten about him, and some were probably having a hard time believing he was really alive.)*

:: How do you think the disciples felt after fishing all night and catching nothing? *(It must have seemed to them that nothing was going right. Their whole lives had been turned upside down by Jesus, but now he had died. The disciples knew that Jesus had risen from the dead, but they were clearly uncertain about what it all meant.)*

 Pray about It

Thank God that even when we are not looking for him, he is looking for us.

DAY TWO _____

Remember It

What do you remember about yesterday's story? What do you think is going to happen today?

 Read John 21:5–14.

Think about It Some More

The disciples were so discouraged after fishing all night that they didn't recognize Jesus when they saw him. They didn't realize it was Jesus when he spoke and called them children, nor did they suspect it was Jesus when he told them to throw their nets out again, which was something Jesus had said to them before. But after they began to pull in their nets and saw that they were heavy with fish, they knew it was he. Any stranger walking by could have told them to throw out their nets again, but only Jesus could command large fish to fill the nets!

Talk about It

:: Which disciple first recognized Jesus? *(John, who refers to himself in his Gospel as "the disciple whom Jesus loved" [v. 7], is the one who first recognized Jesus.)*

:: Why did catching so many large fish help the disciples identify Jesus? *(First, Jesus had done the very same thing before, telling the disciples to cast their nets again after fishing without success. Second, catching so many large fish after a whole night without catching anything was clearly a miracle. Apart from God commanding the fish into their nets, it never would have happened. That helped them to know that it wasn't just anyone on shore: it was the Lord.)*

:: How did seeing Jesus eat, help the disciples believe Jesus was really there in person? *(If someone you knew died but suddenly reappeared, you might think she was a ghost or just a vision. But if you sat down with her and watched her eat a meal, then you would know she was real.)*

 Pray about It

Praise God for the way he cared for the disciples, giving them the miraculous catch of fish and not leaving them. Praise Jesus for never leaving us alone. Even though he doesn't eat breakfast with us, he is always with us.

DAY THREE

Connect It to the Gospel

Today is the day we connect this week's Bible story to the gospel. The gospel is the life, death, and resurrection of Jesus for our salvation. Can anyone guess how our story this week looks forward to or back at the gospel?

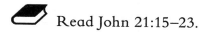 Read John 21:15–23.

Think about It Some More

Hours before Jesus' arrest, Peter boasted that even if everyone else deserted Jesus, *he* would remain by his side, even to the death (Luke 22:33). But when Jesus was arrested, Peter ran away. Like us, Peter deserved to be punished for his sins. But instead of condemning Peter, God condemned his Son, Jesus, in Peter's place so that Peter could be forgiven. In today's story, Jesus welcomed Peter back into ministry and told him to feed God's sheep. Just as Peter had denied knowing Jesus three times, so Jesus commanded him three times to care for the Lord's sheep. When we read this story, we should imagine that we are Peter with the Lord asking us, "Do you love me?" If we say *yes* and we really do love and trust the Lord, then we will be forgiven for our sins as Peter was.

Talk about It

:: How many times did Peter deny Jesus the night of his arrest? *(Three times)*

:: How many times did Jesus tell Peter to feed and care for his sheep? *(Just as Peter denied Jesus three times, so Jesus repeats his directions three times. It seems that Jesus wanted to make sure Peter got the message—he was welcomed back to do the Lord's work.)*

:: How did Peter show his faith in Jesus with his third answer? *(Peter understood that Jesus was God and knew all things, so he said, "Lord, you know everything; you know that I love you." Jesus didn't disagree, for Peter did love the Lord.)*

:: How does this story give us hope as sinners? *(Peter so completely denied the Lord that he even called down curses on himself [see Mark 14:71]. In spite of this, Jesus entrusted Peter with the care of his sheep. If Jesus can forgive Peter and trust him to care for his precious sheep, then we can be sure that he will forgive us and use us to build his church as well.)*

Pray about It

Ask God to forgive you for the sins you have committed; ask him to use you to care for and build his church.

DAY FOUR

Remember It

What has God been teaching you this week through our Bible story?

 Read John 21:24–25.

Think about It Some More

Did you know that there are hundreds, perhaps even thousands, of stories about Jesus that we don't know? John tells us that the stories we have about Jesus in the Bible are just a small sample of everything Jesus did while he walked the earth. One day, when we get to heaven, we will get to hear about all the other things Jesus did. Some people think of heaven as a place where we will float around with nothing to do. But there will be plenty to do and countless great stories to hear. Jesus healed thousands of people, and we will get to hear about them all. We'll probably meet many of them too! Then we will turn and worship Jesus for all that he has done for us.

Talk about It

> ● ● KIDS, ask your parents if they can remember a
> ● ● story from their childhood that they never told
> you.

(Parents, try to think of an interesting story you never told your children. Then remind them that when we get to heaven we will hear many stories about Jesus we never heard before.)

:: John said we could believe all that he had written was true because he was a witness. What is a witness? *(A witness is someone who personally saw the events in question. For example, when a crime is committed, the police ask if there were any witnesses—people who saw for themselves what happened.)*

:: How many books did John say would have to be written to hold all the stories of what Jesus did? *(Parents, if you have younger children, reread the verses for today and have your children raise their hands when they hear the correct answer: John said that the world could not contain the number of books that would need to be written to document everything that Jesus did.)*

:: If you were writing a story about what Jesus did for you, what would you put into it? *(Parents, help your children see that Jesus died for them, gave us the Bible so we could know all about him, and gave us the wonderful creation around us. Plus, since Jesus is God, all the good things we have are also gifts from him.)*

 Pray about It

Take time to thank Jesus for the things you mentioned in answering the last question.

DAY FIVE

Discover It

Today is the day we look at a different Bible passage—from the book of Psalms or one of the prophets—to see what we can learn from it about Jesus or our salvation.

 Read Isaiah 32:1–4.

Think about It Some More

When you read the prophets and they describe something no ordinary person could do, they are often talking about Jesus. For instance, today's passage describes a king who reigns in righteousness. Jesus is the only king who reigns with perfect goodness (righteousness). Every other ruler was a sinner. So we know that Isaiah couldn't be talking about anyone but Jesus, who rules perfectly and sinlessly.

Talk about It

:: What makes Jesus different from all the other kings over God's people? *(Jesus reigns in righteousness, which means he never sinned. All the other kings over God's people sinned, and some were very wicked.)*

:: But what does Isaiah say God will do in the day of the righteous King, for those whose eyes are closed and don't understand? *(Isaiah said that in that day, eyes will be opened to see and understand.)*

:: What is the most important thing that people need to see, hear, and understand? *(Parents, draw your children out here till they get the correct answer—the gospel; that Jesus died on the cross and rose again from the dead so that everyone who believes can be forgiven their sins. In our sin, we are blind to understand the truth about God's righteous king, but the Spirit of God opens our blinded eyes through the Word of God so that we can see Jesus and all he has done for us.)*

Pray about It

Praise Jesus as the righteous King who is perfect in every way. If you have friends or family who are still blind and cannot see the truth about Jesus, pray for them by name, and ask God to open their eyes to the truth about Jesus.

Week 42

The Great Commission

Story 120 – *The Gospel Story Bible*

Bring a globe or a world map to Bible study and point out Jerusalem to your children. Then point to Egypt and explain that Egypt is about two hundred miles from Jerusalem. That was the distance God's people traveled during Moses' time when they fled Egypt. Then find your home location on the map and show your children how far the message of Jesus traveled to get to you. This week, you will learn about Jesus' command to take the gospel to all nations.

DAY ONE

Picture It

Guinness World Records lists records for some unusual things: there's a man who balanced a small car on his head; a man who held ten live rattlesnakes by the tail; and the man who kept twenty-eight basketballs spinning at the same time. Even when people see photographs of these feats they often still say, "That's hard to believe." But the most amazing thing anyone has ever done was when Jesus rose again from the grave. No one had ever done that before, nor has anyone done that since. That is why some people find it hard to believe and why even after Jesus appeared several times to his disciples some of them still found it hard to believe.

 Read Matthew 28:16–17.

Think about It Some More

Even though Jesus appeared to all the disciples at least twice after he rose from the dead, it was still hard for some of them to believe he had risen. Remember, they thought Jesus would become the King of Israel. But at his arrest, when Jesus didn't fight back, and then after he died like an ordinary man, the disciples were confused. They had hoped Jesus was going to restore Israel to its former glory.

During Jesus' ministry he healed the sick, walked on water, and multiplied the fishes and the loaves, and yet at his arrest he did nothing. The disciples didn't understand Jesus' warnings that he would have to suffer and die, and they didn't understand God's plan to rescue us from the penalty of our sin by dying on the cross in our place. So you can understand why some still doubted.

Talk about It

:: Have you ever heard something you found hard to believe? *(Parents, help your younger children here if they can't think of anything. For instance, you could get a yardstick or tape measure and show them how long they were as babies, or you could tell them about some invention that is common today that didn't exist when you were a child.)*

:: Why do you think it was hard for some of the disciples to believe that Jesus had risen from the dead? *(Not only is rising from the dead unheard of, but when Jesus rose from the dead, all his wounds were healed. Only scars remained. That was so amazing it was hard to believe.)*

:: Why did the disciples worship Jesus? *(The disciples understood that Jesus was God. We are not supposed to worship anyone but God.)*

 ## Pray about It

Ask God to help each person in your family believe that Jesus really did die on the cross and rise again for our sins. Then ask God to help you place your trust in him.

DAY TWO _____

Remember It

What do you remember about yesterday's story? What do you think is going to happen today?

 Read Matthew 28:18–20.

Think about It Some More

Having won the battle against sin and death by dying and rising from the dead, Jesus prepared to send his disciples into the world to spread the message of his great victory. People call these verses the Great Commission. The word *commission* means to be given an important job or assignment. This commission (important assignment) was great because it was one of the most important jobs anyone has ever been given in the whole world. Jesus commissioned the disciples to spread the story about him into all the earth and then make disciples of those who believed. But even though the gospel story about Jesus went out from Jerusalem across the world, there are still billions of people alive today who have never heard about Jesus.

The Great Commission is not yet complete. There are still tribes of people who have never heard the gospel, and some people still don't yet have the Bible translated into their language. If you want to learn more about these people, do a search on the Internet for "unreached people groups." You'll discover that the Great Commission continues, and there is still a lot of work to do.

Talk about It

:: What job or commission did Jesus give the disciples? *(Jesus told them to go into all the world and make disciples by spreading the news about Jesus.)*

:: What were the disciples supposed to do for people who believed? *(Jesus told them to baptize people who became disciples and teach them the things he commanded.)*

:: Who did Jesus say would go with them? *(Jesus said he would be with them until the end of the age. That means Jesus is still with us as we go to tell people about him.)*

:: How can we join in the Great Commission today? *(When we share the gospel with people around us or invite people to church to hear God's Word, we are joining in the work of the Great Commission. We also are joining in the Great Commission when we teach one another about Jesus or give money to support the work of the gospel.)*

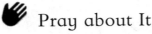 Pray about It

Ask God to help you live not for yourselves but for the Great Commission and the advance of the gospel.

DAY THREE

Connect It to the Gospel

Today is the day we connect this week's Bible story to the gospel. The gospel is the life, death, and resurrection of Jesus for our salvation. Can anyone guess how our story this week looks forward to or back at the gospel?

 Read Luke 24:46–49.

Think about It Some More

When we hear good news, we want to tell other people about it. Like when somebody gives birth to triplets or a friend of yours meets and shakes hands with the president of the United States. But the most exciting news of all time is the story about how Jesus died on the cross for our sins and rose victoriously from the grave on the third day. Once we understand how amazing the gospel is, we should tell everyone about Jesus.

Earlier in the week we read the Great Commission from Matthew's Gospel. Today, we read the same thing from Luke's Gospel. In this account, Jesus said he was sending the disciples to all nations but that they first had to wait until the Holy Spirit came upon them to give them power. Then, filled with the Holy Spirit, they would be able to spread the good news all across the world without fear.

Talk about It

:: What did Jesus want the disciples to tell people? (*Jesus wanted them to tell the story of his death and resurrection and to announce that, because of what Jesus did, we can be forgiven of our sins.*)

:: Whom did Jesus say he was sending the disciples to reach? (*Jesus said the message of the gospel was supposed to go to people of all nations.*)

:: What did Jesus say the disciples were supposed to wait for? *(They were supposed to wait for God's promise, which would bring them power from on high. Jesus was talking about waiting for the Holy Spirit.)*

 Pray about It

Pray that God would give you power and courage to spread the message of the gospel to people who still don't believe.

DAY FOUR

Remember It

What has God been teaching you this week through our Bible story?

 Read Genesis 18:17–19.

Think about It Some More

Since we have been reading New Testament stories about Jesus, you may have been surprised that today's passage is from Genesis. But the Great Commission had its start when God promised Abraham that he would be a blessing to all nations. Long before Jesus was even born, God knew that he would send his only Son, Jesus, to die on the cross for the sins of people from every nation. God kept his promise to Abraham by sending his Son, Jesus, to be from Abraham's family line. Abraham became a blessing to all the nations as the far-off great-grandfather of Jesus, the Savior of the world.

Talk about It

> KIDS, ask your parents whom your family could reach out to with the gospel.

(Parents, try to think of a neighbor you could invite over for dinner or to an outreach at your church.)

:: Who did God tell Abraham he wanted to bless through him? *(God wanted to bless people from every nation.)*

:: Who is the far-off great-grandson of Abraham that God used to bring the blessing that he promised? *(Jesus)*

:: What is the blessing God brought to us and to people of every nation through Jesus? *(The blessing Jesus brought is that we can have all of our sins forgiven and be brought back into a good relationship with God. Jesus did this by dying for our sins on the cross. All those who believe and trust in him, receive the blessing of forgiveness that God promised to Abraham long ago.)*

 Pray about It

Praise God for his wonderful plan to bless the nations by saving us from our sins.

DAY FIVE _____

Discover It

Today is the day we look at a different Bible passage—from the book of Psalms or one of the prophets—to see what we can learn from it about Jesus or our salvation.

 Read Micah 5:4–5.

Think about It Some More

Micah's prophecy is about Jesus. He is the prophet who foretold that Jesus would be born in Bethlehem (see verse 2). In our verses today, Micah goes on to call Jesus the shepherd who will be our peace. Jesus said to his disciples, "Peace I leave with you; my peace I give to you. Not as the world gives do I give to you. Let not your hearts be troubled, neither let them be afraid" (John 14:27).

Jesus also said that he was the Good Shepherd (John 10:11). As our Good Shepherd, Jesus brought us the greatest peace of all—peace with God. Because of our sin, we were God's enemies. But when Jesus took our punishment on the cross, he made a way for us to be forgiven, so that we are no longer God's enemies. If we believe in Jesus, instead of being God's enemy, we become his children and enjoy peace with God forever in heaven. God fills us with his Holy Spirit, who transforms our lives. He places his Word in our hearts (Jeremiah 31:33) and day by day transforms us to be like Jesus (2 Corinthians 3:18).

Talk about It

:: What did Micah say Jesus was going to give us? *(Micah said that Jesus, the ruler of Israel who would be born in Bethlehem, would give us peace. Parents, if you have younger children, you may want to read this section of Scripture again and change the tone of your voice when you get to the word* peace *so your children can answer correctly.)*

:: Why did we need peace with God? *(When we sinned against God we became God's enemies. By taking our punishment on the cross Jesus restored our relationship with God so that we were no longer his enemies.)*

:: Micah called the ruler in his prophecy a shepherd. Why does that help us to know he was talking about Jesus? *(Jesus said that he is the Good Shepherd, and he said that we are his sheep that he came to protect and lead.)*

 # Pray about It

Praise God for the amazing way he planned to save us and bring us peace through Jesus long before Jesus was even born.

Week 43

The Ascension

Story 121 – *The Gospel Story Bible*

Buy a helium balloon for this illustration. Just for fun, put a self-addressed card with a stamp on your balloon in a plastic baggie along with a note asking the finder to please indicate where it landed on the card and mail it back to you. You can also include an invitation to your church! (Note: make sure your balloon is hand-tied, with no tails (ribbon, string, etc.). A released latex balloon is biodegradable, but often the tail is not. Plus, it can easily become tangled in trees and power lines.)

Take your children outside to release the balloon, and watch it ascend into the clouds just like Jesus ascended. Later, if someone returns your card, take time to see if your children remember the lesson you were learning when you watched the balloon go up into the sky. This week, you will learn about the day Jesus left the disciples and returned to his Father in heaven.

DAY ONE

Picture It

Have you ever watched a two-part movie? Most people will watch the second part the next day because of how long it would take to watch them both together. But if you watched part one in the movie theater you might have to wait a year or more to see part two. Books in a series are like that too. The moment you finish one, you want to read the next book in the series to find out what happened. If the next book isn't published yet, you have to wait.

The books of Luke and Acts were like that. Luke wrote book one, his Gospel, for a man named Theophilus. But Theophilus had to wait for book two, the book of Acts. When it finally came, he must have been very excited to read the rest of the story about Jesus. As we start the book of Acts today, imagine what it was like for Theophilus to be the very first person to read it.

 Read Acts 1:1–5.

Think about It Some More

Some people don't believe that Jesus rose from the dead. But Luke tells us that, after Jesus rose from the dead, he walked among the people for forty days to prove that his resurrection was real. Jesus showed the disciples his hands and side, so they could see his scars. He gave seven of his disciples another miraculous catch of fish, and Jesus talked and ate with them. Shortly before Jesus left earth, he reminded the disciples of his promise to send the Holy Spirit. Even though he wanted them to go out to be witnesses and tell his story to everyone, they had to wait for the Holy Spirit to fill them and give them the power they needed to be his witnesses (Luke 24:49).

Talk about It

:: What were some of the ways Jesus proved that he rose from the dead? *(The most important way Jesus proved that he rose from the dead was that he showed himself to people so they could see that he was alive. He ate with them and allowed them to touch him.)*

:: What did Jesus want the disciples to wait for in Jerusalem? *(Jesus wanted the disciples to wait to be baptized with the Holy Spirit.)*

:: Can you remember how Jesus said the Holy Spirit would help them? *(Parents, give your older children these Scriptures to look up, or read them to your younger children and have them raise their hands when they come up with an answer—Luke 24:49, John 14:26.)*

 Pray about It

Thank Jesus for sending the disciples and all of us his Holy Spirit to help us, teach us, and give us power to tell everyone about Jesus.

DAY TWO

Remember It

What do you remember about yesterday's story? What do you think is going to happen today?

 Read Acts 1:6–8.

Think about It Some More

When young children go with their parents on a long drive, they soon ask a very common question, "Are we there yet?" Even if their parents told them the trip was going to take six hours, before the first hour is up they usually start asking, "Are we there yet?" The disciples were like that with Jesus. Only they were not talking about a long car ride: They wanted to know when Jesus was going to restore the kingdom of Israel. Before Jesus died, the disciples thought he was going to win a victory against Rome, but that didn't happen. Now that Jesus was alive, they got their hopes up again and thought, *Maybe this time Jesus will restore Israel and defeat the Romans.*

The disciples still did not understand. They thought Jesus would quickly restore the nation of Israel, but God had a different plan. God's plan was to use them to spread the gospel to all people and give new life to people from every nation. God's plan was much bigger than defeating the Romans and saving the nation of Israel. God wanted to use them to help him reach the whole world.

Talk about It

:: What did Jesus say the disciples would receive when the Holy Spirit came upon them? (*Jesus said they would receive power to be his witnesses.*)

:: What is a witness? (*A witness is someone who saw something happen and can tell others what she saw. The disciples were witnesses of Jesus' ministry, death, and resurrection.*)

:: Where did Jesus say they were going to go to be his witnesses? (*They were going to go to Jerusalem, which was where they were at the time. He also said they were going to go to Judea and Samaria, which was the land around Jerusalem. Finally, Jesus said they would be his witnesses to the ends of the earth—everywhere else. Jesus wanted everyone in all countries to learn about him and his salvation. This is good for us since most of us live in countries beyond Judea and Samaria.)*

 Pray about It

Praise Jesus that he wanted the gospel to go to the ends of the earth so it was able to reach us all the way across the ocean.

DAY THREE

Connect It to the Gospel

Today is the day we connect this week's Bible story to the gospel. The gospel is the life, death, and resurrection of Jesus for our salvation. Can anyone guess how our story this week looks forward to or back at the gospel?

 Read Acts 1:9–11.

Think about It Some More

In the three years the disciples lived with Jesus they watched him open the eyes of the blind, raise the dead, and teach thousands about God. They ran in fear at his arrest, cried at his death, and rejoiced at his resurrection. In our story today, the disciples watched Jesus float up into the heavens and disappear, just as we might watch a helium balloon fly away. But Jesus wouldn't leave the disciples alone for long. Soon the Holy Spirit would come and fill the disciples. Then, because the Holy Spirit and Jesus are one, Jesus would be with them again.

Jesus told his disciples he would not leave them as orphans, but he would come to live inside of them (John 14:20). Today, we too have the Holy Spirit, and through him all Christians have, immediate, instant, and uninterrupted access to God—as was promised by the tearing of the temple curtain at Jesus' death. Even so, we still wait for Jesus to one day come back to earth, as the angel promised. Jesus will return when the job of reaching the nations with the gospel is complete. Nobody knows the day of Jesus' return, but the apostle Paul said that we should encourage one another with the hope that one day Jesus will return from heaven with a blast from God's trumpet, just as he said (1 Thessalonians 4:16–18).

Talk about It

:: Where did Jesus go? *(Your children might say that Jesus went up into the sky, which is true. But Jesus went back to heaven to be with his Father.)*

:: What did the two angels tell the disciples to encourage them? *(The angels told the disciples that Jesus would return again the same way he left.)*

:: Read Luke 24:50–53. What do we learn from these verses about how the disciples felt after Jesus left them. *(After Jesus was lifted up into heaven, the disciples worshiped him and then left with great joy, and afterward they spent night and day praising God.)*

 Pray about It

Take time to do what the disciples did after the ascension: praise and worship God. Parents, help your children praise the Lord. You might try using a psalm (Psalms 9, 19, or 30) as a guideline for things you can praise God for.

DAY FOUR

Remember It

What has God been teaching you this week through our Bible story?

 Read Acts 1:12–14.

Think about It Some More

The disciples returned from the Mount of Olives filled with joy (Luke 24:52) and met together in a place called the upper room. They were joined by Mary, Jesus' mother, and Jesus' brothers. (This is the last we hear in the Bible of Jesus' mother.) It is exciting to see that Jesus' mother and his brothers kept their faith and were there with the disciples waiting for the Holy Spirit to come. One day, when we go to heaven, we will be able to talk to Mary and Jesus' brothers, along with all the disciples who waited in that upper room.

Talk about It

> :: :: KIDS, ask your parents who they are most looking
> :: :: forward to meeting in heaven one day.

(Parents, share your favorite Bible character who demonstrated his or her faith in Jesus.)

:: Why were the disciples and Jesus' family all together in the upper room? *(Jesus told them to wait for the Holy Spirit to come to them and said the Holy Spirit would come soon.)*

:: What did the disciples and Jesus' family devote themselves to while they were waiting for the Holy Spirit? *(They devoted themselves to prayer.)*

 Pray about It

We can devote ourselves to prayer, as well. Most families are not used to praying for more than a few minutes. Make a list of prayer requests, and use a clock to time yourselves. Try to spend fifteen minutes praying. Include praying for Jesus to return soon.

DAY FIVE

Discover It

Today is the day we look at a different Bible passage, either from the book of Psalms or from one of the books of the prophets, to see what we can learn from it about Jesus or our salvation.

 Read Zechariah 12:10–11.

Think about It Some More

The apostle John wrote about how the soldiers pierced Jesus' side. He connected Zechariah's prophecy to that part of the gospel story (John 19:37). That tells us that long before Jesus died, God knew that his Son would be pierced with a sword. Zechariah's prophecy also tells us that even though the people were going to kill Jesus, God planned to pour out his grace so that the very people who killed him would have a change of heart and call out for mercy. In these verses, Zechariah was prophesying about our salvation. Jesus died to take the punishment for our sins too—so, in a real sense, we too are responsible for his death. Jesus was killed because we were sinners.

When the Holy Spirit opens our hearts and minds to believe, we join with the people of Zechariah's prophecy who mourn the death of Jesus and call out to God for mercy. The good news of the gospel is that God promises to forgive everyone who calls out to him.

Talk about It

:: Why are the people sad in Zechariah's prophecy? *(The people are sad because they killed the Lord.)*

:: Have one of your children read John 19:37. How is this similar to Zechariah's prophecy? *(Parents, if your children are too young to read the verse, do it for them. You can also read John 19:37 with Zechariah 12:10 to help the children see that the words are almost identical.)*

:: What did God say he was going to pour out on the people? *(Parents, if you have younger children, reread verse 10 and have them raise their hands when they hear the answer to the question: that God is going to pour out a "spirit of grace and pleas for mercy." That means that God was going to help the people to see that what they did was wrong.)*

:: Why do we also need God's grace to help us? *(We are all sinners. God sent his Son, Jesus, to die for our sins too. So it was also because of our sin that Jesus was nailed to the cross. The problem is that apart from God opening our eyes to see our sins, we think we are pretty good. Once God opens our eyes to see that we are sinners, we can call out to him for forgiveness.)*

Pray about It

Ask God to forgive you for your sins. Remember that Jesus died because of your sins.

Week 44

Pentecost

Story 122 – *The Gospel Story Bible*

For this exercise you will need a straw for each person. Before Bible study cut one inch off of one straw. Show the straws to your children. Explain that, if you hide the ends of the straws in your fist, with the opposite ends even, you can't see how long they are. Have everyone pick a straw to see who gets the short one. This demonstrates how the disciples picked lots to choose the replacement for Judas the betrayer. Say, "This week we will learn how the disciples used lots to choose a replacement for Judas. After the new disciple was chosen, the Holy Spirit came upon them."

DAY ONE

Picture It

When a baseball player is injured during a game and can't play, the coach will put in a replacement because it is important to have a full team. For instance, if you didn't have a pitcher, who would throw the ball? If you tried to play without a right fielder, all the batters would try to hit the ball into that opening in the field. In our story today, it was important for the disciples to have a full team too.

First, the disciples were known as the "twelve." However, after the death of Judas who betrayed Jesus, their number had been reduced to eleven. It just wouldn't do for a group of eleven to be called the twelve. There was also a lot of meaning behind having a group of twelve lead the church. Historically, Israel had been divided into twelve tribes. We learn from Revelation 21:12–14 that the names of the twelve apostles are written on the twelve foundations of the walls of the new Jerusalem, the holy city.

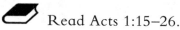 Read Acts 1:15–26.

Think about It Some More

As the disciples were considering someone to fill Judas's spot, Peter said there were two qualities that this person must have. First, he had to have been with Jesus since the very beginning of his ministry. From the baptism of Jesus all the way until his ascension into heaven. The second requirement was that he had to be a witness of the resurrection. That meant he had to have seen Jesus after he'd risen from the dead. Only two men were recommended who met these qualifications. The apostles could have taken a vote to see whom *they* wanted to join their group, but instead they cast lots and allowed God to choose. Jesus chose all the other apostles when he was alive, so it seemed good that this choice should be God's as well.

Talk about It

:: Which disciple was chosen to replace Judas? *(Matthias)*

:: What were the two qualities Peter said a replacement apostle had to have? *(Parents, if you have younger children, reread verses 21 and 22 and have your children raise their hands if they think they know the answer. The man had to have been with Jesus from the beginning all the way through his ascension, and he had to have seen Jesus after he rose from the dead.)*

:: What did Peter say God knows about all of us? *(Peter said that God knows the hearts of all, so God would know which of the two men was best qualified.)*

:: How can remembering that God knows the hearts of all men help us to live for God? *(It is easier to sin if we think no one would know what we did. Remembering that God sees everything we do can help us not sin.)*

 ## Pray about It

Ask the Lord to help you remember that he knows your heart and everything you do so that you will not want sin against him.

DAY TWO

Remember It

What do you remember about yesterday's story? What do you think is going to happen today?

 Read Acts 2:1–6.

Think about It Some More

People who have been near a tornado say that the winds are so strong they sound like a freight train. That must have been what it sounded like the day the Holy Spirit came upon the people, for the wind is described as a mighty rushing wind. The people outside the building must have heard that sound, because by the time Peter explained what was going on a little later in our story, there was a great crowd gathered.

If the sound of the wind didn't get everyone's attention, then the flames of fire in the shape of tongues that appeared over the heads of the disciples surely did. It seemed that God wanted a large audience when he poured out his Spirit. Imagine what you would have thought, first hearing a mighty wind, then seeing tongues of fire, and finally hearing people speak praises to God in a language you know they didn't normally speak.

Talk about It

:: What happened when the Holy Spirit came? *(There was a mighty rushing wind, tongues as of fire fell on all of them, and they began to speak in other languages.)*

:: Why were the Jews, who had gathered in Jerusalem for the feast of Pentecost, surprised at what they heard? *(They were surprised because they heard in their own language what the people were saying even though they were all Galileans and couldn't possibly know all those other languages.)*

:: How can we receive the Holy Spirit? *(When we turn away from our sins and trust Jesus, the Holy Spirit comes to live with us as our guarantee that we will live with Jesus in heaven forever. See 2 Corinthians 1:22.)*

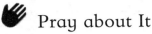 Pray about It

Thank Jesus for keeping his promise to send the Holy Spirit to be our helper.

DAY THREE _____

Connect It to the Gospel

Today is the day we connect this week's Bible story to the gospel. The gospel is the life, death, and resurrection of Jesus for our salvation. Can anyone guess how our story this week looks forward to or back at the gospel?

 Read Numbers 28:26–31.

Think about It Some More

The Holy Spirit came upon the disciples on the celebration of a holiday called Pentecost. That celebration began back in Moses' day, when it was called the day of the firstfruits. Back then, God told Moses to offer sacrifices to the Lord to cover the sins of the people. But on Pentecost, the day the Holy Spirit came upon the disciples, there was no need to sacrifice animals anymore. That is because Jesus, the Lamb of God, had died on the cross as the last sacrifice. He paid the penalty for our sins upon the cross once and for all. After Jesus' death, no more bulls needed to be killed, nor any more rams or lambs. The time of sacrificing animals to the Lord was over.

Talk about It

:: What animals did God tell Moses he should kill for the day of the firstfruits? *(Parents, if your younger children can't remember, reread the passage and have them raise their hands when they hear the answer. God told Moses to sacrifice two bulls, one ram, and seven lambs.)*

:: God told Moses the animals were to be perfect, with no blemishes. Why do you think God wanted perfect animals to be sacrificed? *(The animals represented his Son, Jesus, who would live a perfect life without sin and then be sacrificed for us.)*

:: Why don't we need to kill these animals every year like Moses did? *(We don't have to kill animals to pay for our sin anymore because Jesus died to pay the penalty for our sin once and for all. Jesus was the perfect sacrifice, who covered all the sins of all who place their trust in him. These animal sacrifices pointed to Jesus, but once Jesus came, there was no need for them anymore.)*

 Pray about It

Thank Jesus for becoming our perfect sacrifice. Praise God that he accepted Jesus' sacrifice for our sins and that no more sacrifices are needed.

DAY FOUR

Remember It

What has God been teaching you this week through our Bible story?

 Read Acts 2:7–12.

Think about It Some More

When the Holy Spirit came upon the disciples and they began to speak in other tongues, the people around them heard them in their own different languages. On that day, there were people visiting Jerusalem from over a dozen different countries, yet they all understood what the disciples were saying. Way back at the tower of Babel, because of the people's sin, God had confused the workers and scattered them by making them speak in different languages. Here at Pentecost, God began his work of regathering those who were scattered. God promised Abraham to bless the nations of the world through his offspring. Pentecost was the beginning of God keeping that promise.

Talk about It

> ● ● KIDS, ask your parents if the Holy Spirit lives in them and what it is like to have the Holy Spirit with you.

(Parents, if you have given your life to Christ and he has changed your heart, the Holy Spirit lives in you. It can be hard to describe

what the Holy Spirit is like, but do your best to describe the inner joy of knowing Jesus and the confidence or assurance you feel that you are one of God's children.)

:: What happened when the Holy Spirit came upon the disciples? What did they do? *(The disciples started praising God in different languages.)*

:: God scattered people and confused their languages at the tower of Babel. How is what God did at Pentecost different? *(At Pentecost, God gathered people of different languages together again.)*

 Pray about It

Praise God for making a way to bring people from every nation together into his family.

DAY FIVE _____

Discover It

Today is the day we look at a different Bible passage—from the book of Psalms or one of the prophets—to see what we can learn from it about Jesus or our salvation.

 Read Ezekiel 36:24–28.

Think about It Some More

Long before Pentecost, the prophet Ezekiel spoke of a day when God would gather his people from the nations. Ezekiel said God would cleanse them, which is another way to say God would take away their sins. He said God would take away their hard hearts and give them new hearts, and put his Spirit inside of them to live. That is a great description of what happened to the disciples gathered at Pentecost.

Talk about It

:: Sin makes us dirty in God's eyes. What did Ezekiel say God was going to do for us? *(Ezekiel said that God was going to sprinkle water on us to cleanse us and take away our idols. That is a picture of God's forgiveness through Jesus' sacrifice.)*

:: What did Ezekiel say God was going to do to the hard, stony hearts of sinners? *(God said he would take away our hard hearts and give us new soft hearts.)*

:: Describe the difference between a hard heart and a new soft heart of flesh. *(A hard heart is a heart that rejects God and his laws, but a soft heart is a heart that obeys God's laws. Think of soft clay compared with hard, dried-out clay. You can't put an impression of something into the hard clay because it is too hard and won't be shaped. But soft clay will take the impression of whatever you press into it. A soft heart for God allows God's Word to be pressed into it and shape it.)*

 Pray about It

Pray and ask God to take away your hard stony heart and give you a new soft heart so that you will want to obey God's Word.

Peter & the Prophet Joel

Story 123 – *The Gospel Story Bible*

The prophet Joel lived over five hundred years before Jesus was born, yet he predicted that God would one day pour out his Spirit on all people. To see just how amazing this prophecy is, have your children try to guess what meal they will have for dinner on Day Three this week, what the weather will be like on Day Five, and how many items you will get in today's mail. Say, "This week we will hear how God fulfilled Joel's prophecy about the outpouring of the Holy Spirit at Pentecost."

DAY ONE

Picture It

What would you think if you got up one morning and your whole family was speaking in a language you couldn't understand? Imagine that when you got up, your mother said, "God morgon. Vill du ha frukost?" What would you say if your brother asked, "Vill du leka utomhus med mig?" *(Parents, get your children's impression here and see if they can guess what is being said. The first line is Swedish for "Good morning. Do you want some breakfast?" and the second is "Do you want to play outside with me?")* In our story today, not everyone understood what the disciples were saying at Pentecost—some thought the disciples were drunk.

 Read Acts 2:13–20.

Think about It Some More

While most of the people were amazed to hear the disciples speaking in their own language, not everyone could tell what was going on. Some people thought the disciples were drunk. When Peter saw their confusion, he spoke out boldly. The Spirit of God helped him explain what was happening from the Scriptures. In past times, God poured out his Spirit only on a few people, like Joseph (Genesis 41:38), who saved God's people during the famine, or Bezalel the craftsman, whom God filled with his Spirit to help him create the furniture for the tabernacle (Exodus 31:2–3). But now that Jesus had opened up a way for everyone to be saved, God was pouring out his Spirit on all people.

The same is true for us today. God wants to pour out his Spirit on all of us. When anyone believes and trusts in Jesus, God's Spirit comes and lives in them. In days past, God's Spirit lived in the temple made of stone. Today, God's Spirit lives in his people, who all together make up the church, which is the new temple of God.

Talk about It

:: What did the people who were making fun of the disciples think had happened to them? *(They thought the disciples were drunk.)*

:: On whom did the prophet Joel say God was going to pour out his Spirit? *(On all people—those from every nation, young and old, and both men and women.)*

:: In days of old, God's Spirit lived in a temple made of stone. What kind of temple does God's Spirit live in today? *(God's Spirit lives in the hearts and lives of all his children. Peter called those who believe in Jesus a temple of "living stones" [1 Peter 2:5].)*

 ## Pray about It

Ask God to help unbelieving family and friends place their trust in Jesus and be filled with the Holy Spirit.

DAY TWO

Remember It

What do you remember about yesterday's story? What do you think is going to happen today?

 Read Acts 2:21.

Think about It Some More

Some verses in the Bible are so simple that even a small child can understand them. And some verses are so important you have to think about them all by themselves. This is one of those verses. It tells us that every single person who calls out to Jesus to rescue him will be saved. It is both easy to understand and carries a powerful message—all you have to do is call out to Jesus and repent of your sin to be given new life. When you realize you are a sinner and need to be saved, call out to Jesus.

The youngest child and the oldest person can call out to Jesus. There are no hard words to learn; the call is a simple one—"Jesus, I am a sinner. Please save me." We can be sure that God will deliver us when we call out to him because he cannot lie. If he said that everyone who calls upon the name of the Lord will be saved, he cannot turn back from his Word.

Talk about It

:: What do we need to do to be rescued from our sins? *(We need to call out to Jesus and ask him to save us.)*

:: Do our words save us, or are we saved because we trust and believe in Jesus? *(The verse we read is not made of magic words. Just repeating the words, "Lord, save me," is not enough. The apostle Paul explained that we need to say the words with our mouth but we must also believe them in our heart [Romans 10:9].)*

:: How do we know if we have truly believed in our heart? *(God places his Holy Spirit in the hearts of all genuine believers. The Holy Spirit helps us obey and helps us to love Jesus and his Word more and more each day.)*

Pray about It

Ask God to help you believe and put his Spirit in your heart to change you to be like him.

DAY THREE

Connect It to the Gospel

Today is the day we connect this week's Bible story to the gospel. The gospel is the life, death, and resurrection of Jesus for our salvation. Can anyone guess how our story this week looks forward to or back at the gospel?

 Read Acts 2:22–24.

Think about It Some More

Peter told the crowd something important about Jesus. Long before Jesus was nailed to the cross, God planned that Jesus would die for our sins. While it's true that people were guilty of killing Jesus, God actually planned Jesus' death for the purpose of taking the punishment we deserved. God even planned the way Jesus would die. God knew Jesus would die on a cross. That is why people couldn't kill Jesus any other way. When people tried to throw Jesus off a cliff, he slipped away (Luke 4:29–30), and when they picked up stones to stone him, Jesus escaped (John 8:59).

Talk about It

:: Who planned that Jesus would die on the cross? *(Peter said that Jesus was killed according to God's definite plan.)*

:: What kind of people crucified Jesus? *(Parents, if you have younger children, you may want to reread the passage and change your tone of voice when you read the answer, "lawless men." Then explain that* lawless *is a word used to describe people who do not follow the law. In this case, men disobeyed God's command not to kill. Jesus didn't do anything wrong and did not deserve to die. The men who killed Jesus were guilty of murder.)*

:: What happened to Jesus after he died? *(Jesus was raised from the dead. Since Jesus was God, death had no power over him. God is the one who gives life and takes it away. Jesus had the power to give up his life and take it up again [John 10:17–18].)*

 Pray about It

Thank Jesus for agreeing to die on the cross and be cursed by God for our sin so that we could be forgiven.

DAY FOUR

Remember It

What has God been teaching you this week through our Bible story?

 Read Acts 2:25–32.

Think about It Some More

When Jesus promised to send the Holy Spirit to the disciples, he told them that the Holy Spirit would guide them into all truth (John 16:13) and help them remember all that Jesus had taught (John 14:26). In our passage today, the Holy Spirit helped Peter explain how the Old Testament pointed to Jesus. Filled with the Holy Spirit, Peter remembered and quoted from Psalm 16 and explained how it described Jesus rising again from the dead. Not only was Peter filled with courage again, but he also spoke to the crowd like a man who had been preaching about Jesus for years. But that was not the case—it was the Holy Spirit helping him, for this was the first sermon Peter had ever given about Jesus.

Now we know that apart from abiding in Christ we can do nothing (John 15:5). And yet in God's plan he sent the Holy Spirit to work with us. That is what was happening with Peter. The Holy Spirit came upon him in power, but Peter still had to open his own mouth and obey the command Jesus gave him to be his witness (Matthew 28:19–20).

Talk about It

> ● ● KIDS, ask your parents how the Holy Spirit has
> ● ● helped them in their lives.

(Parents, God places his Spirit into everyone who believes in Jesus. In fact, without the Holy Spirit to open our minds to the truth of the gospel, none of us would believe. The Holy Spirit helps us understand the Bible, and the Holy Spirit gives us courage to share the truth with others. Think through your life, and tell your children how the Holy Spirit has changed you.)

:: How is Peter different from when he denied Jesus the night Jesus was arrested? *(Then, Peter lied about even knowing Jesus. But here, Peter is not afraid to tell the whole crowd about Jesus.)*

:: What other way, besides giving him courage and boldness, did the Holy Spirit help Peter that day? *(The Holy Spirit helped Peter understand how Psalm 16 pointed to Jesus and helped him explain the gospel to the crowd.)*

:: How could the Holy Spirit help you? *(We all need boldness to tell others about Jesus, and we all need the Holy Spirit to help us understand the Bible. God still pours out his Spirit on people to help them, just as he did with Peter.)*

 Pray about It

Ask God to help you believe and to pour out his Spirit on you so that you can tell others about Jesus with boldness.

DAY FIVE

Discover It

Today is the day we look at a different Bible passage—from the book of Psalms or one of the prophets—to see what we can learn from it about Jesus or our salvation.

 Read Isaiah 49:7–13.

Think about It Some More

Peter explained in his sermon that when David talked about the Holy One in Psalm 16 he was talking about Jesus. Once we know that the Holy One is another name for Jesus, it helps us understand other passages of the Bible where the name Holy One is also used. In our passage today, the prophet Isaiah also uses the name Holy One. Isaiah said that the Holy One would save his people; he would free the prisoners, feed the people, protect them from danger, and bring them salvation. Isaiah was talking about Jesus.

Talk about It

:: Who is the Holy One Isaiah is talking about? *(Jesus)*

:: Read verse 13 again. What does it say we should do? *(We should sing for joy and praise God for all that he has done for us.)*

:: What has God done for you? *(Parents, help your children see that everything we have comes from God, and that God has given *us his Word so we can learn about him. Jesus has died on the cross so that if we place our trust in him we can be forgiven and enjoy the blessings of peace and joy in heaven with God forever.)*

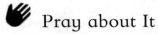 ## Pray about It

Parents, lead your children in a joyful song that praises Jesus.

Week 46

New Believers

Story 124 – *The Gospel Story Bible*

Beforehand, talk with your spouse about how much money you as a family could give to help someone. At Bible study, involve your children in the discussion about who to bless. Don't limit your ideas to those with larger needs. You might think of several people who have smaller needs so that you are able to bless more than one person or family. Write out a card as a family and send it along with your gift. Say, "This week we will be learning how the early church shared their possessions with one another."

DAY ONE

Picture It

Imagine that you received a phone call from a woman who says that you were related to a billionaire who has recently died and left you his inheritance. She goes on to explain that one hundred billion dollars has been placed in a bank account where you and your children after you can take out one million dollars each year, and that the account will never run out of money. That means that your children, your grand-children, your great-grandchildren, and all those great-great-grand-children to be born in the distant future will all get a million dollars every single year of their lives.

If you are thinking you will never get a call like that, you are prob-ably right. But God has offered us an inheritance that is even more valuable. Today in our Bible story, you will see that God's inheritance is so valuable that all of our children, our grandchildren, our great-grandchildren, and all those great-great-grandchildren who are far off can enjoy it as well.

 Read Acts 2:36–39.

Think about It Some More

Jesus died to pass on the greatest inheritance of all time: the forgiveness of our sins and the gift of the Holy Spirit coming to live inside us. If you had all the money in the world, you could not buy either one of these things. Nor could all the gold in the whole world pay the penalty for your sin, so that you could be forgiven. But Jesus paid the price of his own life, so that all those who trust in him can be forgiven and receive the Holy Spirit. Peter said that this promise was not for the disciples and their children only but also for everyone the Lord calls to become a Christian.

When the crowd of people gathered around heard this good news, they were sorry for their sin and wanted to know what they had to do. Peter replied that they should turn away from their sin and trust Jesus for forgiveness. Then they would receive the Holy Spirit and could be baptized as followers of Jesus Christ.

Talk about It

:: What is an inheritance? *(An inheritance is a gift you receive from a person at his death. Usually a person writes down who will receive his possessions in a document called a will. After he dies, the will is read to announce who receives the inheritance. Jesus didn't need a will, because he came back to life and could tell the disciples himself.)*

:: What did Peter say we could receive if we repent of (turn away from) our sin to trust in Jesus? *(Peter said that if we repent and turn away from our sins to trust in Jesus, we would be forgiven and receive the Holy Spirit.)*

:: How do we know this promise is for us too? *(Not only did Peter say the promise was for all the people gathered and their children after them, he also said that the promise would be given to everyone whom the Lord calls to himself to become a Christian. So if God draws us to believe, the promise is for us too.)*

Pray about It

Thank the Lord for giving us the most valuable inheritance of all time, the forgiveness of our sins and the Holy Spirit to live within us and enable us to live for Jesus.

DAY TWO

Remember It

What do you remember about yesterday's story? What do you think is going to happen today?

 Read Acts 2:40–41.

Think about It Some More

Before Jesus went back to heaven, he told the disciples something that seemed hard to believe at the time. Jesus told them that once he went back to heaven the disciples would do even greater things than he did (John 14:12). Through the work of the Holy Spirit in them, the disciples would draw even more people than Jesus ever did while he was alive. Remember, Jesus preached to large crowds and healed many, but there were only about one hundred twenty believers who waited in the upper room for the promised Holy Spirit. But after the Holy Spirit came and Peter preached the gospel for the first time, three thousand believed the very first day!

Talk about It

:: From what did Peter say the people needed to save themselves? *(Parents, if you have younger children, reread verse 40 and have them raise their hands when they hear the answer. Then explain to them that the word* crooked *is another word for sinful and* generation *is a word used to describe the present time. So Peter warned them to save themselves from the terrible sin of those days.)*

:: What happened to those who received Peter's words and believed in Jesus? *(They were baptized and added to the church that day.)*

:: What would happen in your church if three thousand new people came this Sunday all at once? *(Parents, this is a fun exercise to think about. Remember that the disciples didn't have a large building in which to hold services. Talk through this with your children to try to figure out what you would have to do. You will find out later in the story that the people started meeting in their homes, going from house to house.)*

Pray about It

Pray that God would save a lot of people around where you live and bring them into your church. Ask God to give you boldness to share with the unbelievers you know so that you can be a part of bringing them in.

DAY THREE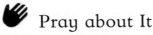

Connect It to the Gospel

Today is the day we connect this week's Bible story to the gospel. The gospel is the life, death, and resurrection of Jesus for our salvation. Can anyone guess how our story this week looks forward to or back at the gospel?

Read Acts 2:42–45.

Think about It Some More

When the Holy Spirit uses the gospel to touch a person's life, he or she is instantly changed. After sharing the gospel, Peter called the people to repent of their sins—turn around and walk away from their sins. That is exactly what the people did. Before, they were selfish, greedy, and did not believe in Jesus. But after they believed in Jesus and repented, they thought about others, shared all they had, and put their hope and trust in Jesus.

A person can say she believes, but if her life is not changed, there is no evidence that she really does believe. But when you see people changed by the gospel like the people were in this story, there is plenty of evidence of the Holy Spirit's presence in them empowering them to live for Jesus.

Talk about It

:: What changed in the peoples' lives once they believed in Jesus and were filled with the Holy Spirit? *(They devoted themselves to the apostles' teaching, and they shared their possessions with those in need. They even sold things and gave the money to people in need.)*

:: What was the apostles' teaching? *(The New Testament had not been written yet. The only way the people could learn about Jesus was to listen to the apostles tell about the things they remembered Jesus saying and doing. In time, that teaching was written down as the Gospels.)*

:: When we trust in Jesus, should we sell our things to help people in need too? *(Christians should never love their things more than they love God, and they should always be willing to give to those in need. If we remember that everything we have is a gift from God, then when we see someone in need, we can pray and ask God to show us how we can help. That could mean selling something we own to help them get the money they need.)*

 Pray about It

Ask God to help you love him more than things of the world so that when you see a person in need, you willingly share what you have.

DAY FOUR

Remember It

What has God been teaching you this week through our Bible story?

 Read Acts 2:46–47.

Think about It Some More

During Jesus' earthly mission, he told his disciples that if they loved one another, the world would know they were his disciples (John 13:35). Jesus knew that our love for one another is the best way we can show people that God has changed our lives with the gospel. When people see that our lives are different from the rest of the world and they ask us why that is, we can share the gospel and tell them about Jesus. That was one of the ways the early church grew. Everyone was sharing with one another, and they were visiting each other in their homes and enjoying meals together. As people around them saw what was going on, they wanted the same kind of life and probably asked them why they were so different. That provided an avenue for them to share the gospel message. Because of the love these early Christians had for each other, people believed in Jesus and became a part of the early church.

Talk about It

> KIDS, ask your parents how they were affected by the joy or generosity of other Christians when they were first saved.

(Parents, try to remember how the lives of other Christians affected you when you were newly saved.)

:: How would you describe the lives of the new Christians in our story today? *(Parents, help your younger children see that their lives were filled with joy as they shared with others.)*

:: Who can you invite over from your church for a meal in the next three weeks? *(Parents, the busyness of life can crowd out time we should be spending with other believers. Take time to invite someone from church over to your house. Pick folks you've never had over so that you can get to know someone new. Take time to pray or sing a few praise songs as families. You may be surprised at how wonderful it is to share the Lord with people in your home.)*

 ## Pray about It

Pray that God would bless the relationships among the people in your church.

DAY FIVE

Discover It

Today is the day we look at a different Bible passage—from the book of Psalms or one of the prophets—to see what we can learn from it about Jesus or our salvation.

Read Isaiah 35:4–7.

Think about It Some More

Long before Jesus was born, Isaiah described his ministry when he said that God would come to save us, and the eyes of the blind would be opened. We know that Jesus did open the eyes of the blind, restored hearing to the deaf, and made the lame leap like the deer. Jesus also forgave our sins and poured out his Spirit into the hearts of everyone who believes. Isaiah's prophecy points to a future day when Jesus will return again, and every blind and sick believer will be made well. When Jesus came the first time, he gave us a taste of heaven. But one day Jesus will come back again, and everyone who trusts in him will be completely healed. Then he will come and re-create the earth and live with us here (Revelation 21:1–3).

Talk about It

:: What did Isaiah say in this prophecy that reminds you of things Jesus did? *(Jesus opened the eyes of the blind and caused the lame to walk.)*

:: When will all the Christians who are blind or lame be healed? *(When Jesus comes back again, all the Christians will go to heaven where there is no more sickness, and we will all get new bodies. See Philippians 3:21.)*

:: How did God keep the promise Isaiah spoke about in verse 4 when he said, "He will come and save you"? *(God the Father sent his Son, Jesus, to die on the cross for our sins so that if we repent of, or turn away from, our sins and believe in Jesus, we will be delivered from the punishment we deserve for our sins and be forgiven.)*

 Pray about It

Praise God the Father for sending his Son, Jesus, to die for our sins so that the promise of Isaiah, that God would come and save us, would come true.

The Lame Beggar Walks

Story 125 – *The Gospel Story Bible*

You will need a small whiteboard and red marker for this exercise. Ask your children to share the sins they have committed in the past week. You can help them here. Then add a few of your own. Perhaps you can remember a time this week when you were impatient with them or got angry. Go ahead and list that on the whiteboard. Then explain that to go to heaven we need to live perfect lives without sin . . . but everyone has sinned.

Say, "When we trust in Jesus, God blots out our sins. Isaiah wrote, 'though your sins are like scarlet, they shall be as white as snow' (Isaiah 1:18)." As you explain this, erase all the sins from the board. Say, "This week we will learn how Peter healed the lame beggar and called the people to repent so their sins could be blotted out."

DAY ONE

Picture It

Think back to a time when you felt really ill, perhaps a day when you got a stomach virus or the flu. When you get sick like that, you feel achy and your stomach feels like you are going to get sick at any moment. Then, if a fever comes, you start shivering and feel like you are freezing. Now try to remember what it felt like the moment your fever broke and you didn't feel sick anymore.

The first morning after your sickness is gone, when you wake up well again, you feel like you could conquer the world, like all your troubles are over. You might even go around your house running and jumping with energy and excitement. Today in our story, God used

Peter and John to heal a man who had lived his whole life with crippled legs. Let's see how he reacts to being healed.

 Read Acts 3:1–8.

Think about It Some More

With legs that didn't work, the crippled man would have lived his whole life as a beggar at the temple because he couldn't work to earn money. When Peter and John came by, he called to them asking for money. Peter, filled with the Spirit, did something the man did not expect. Instead of giving him money, Peter took him by the hand and commanded him to stand up and walk. In an amazing display of God's power, the man rose and started dancing around.

Jesus had returned to heaven, but through his Spirit and by his name, the power to heal continued. Imagine the amazement of the crowd as they saw the crippled man, who had sat begging at the gate for years, stand to his feet and start jumping around.

The Pharisees thought they could stop Jesus by killing him. But they were wrong. Jesus rose from the dead, went back to heaven, and sent his Holy Spirit to touch the lives of thousands. With the Holy Spirit on the move, the message of the gospel could not be stopped. Imagine what the Pharisees and priests heard as they came out to see what the commotion was all about. They would have heard people exclaiming, "Did you see that? He healed the crippled man in the name of Jesus." "Oh, no!" they must have said. "Jesus is back, healing through his disciples!"

Talk about It

:: What did the man do after he was healed? *(The man jumped to his feet and started walking and leaping and praising God.)*

:: Read Luke 5:23–26. How are these two stories similar? *(Peter healed a man much like Jesus did.)*

:: What do you think the religious rulers thought about a man being healed in Jesus' name? *(The religious rulers were trying to get people to forget about Jesus. Someone being healed in Jesus' name would be the last thing they would want.)*

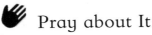 Pray about It

Praise God the same way the crippled man did when he was healed. Parents, if you have smaller children, allow them to pretend they are the man who was healed. Have them jump up, walk around with their hands over their heads, and jump up and down as they praise God.

DAY TWO _____

Remember It

What do you remember about yesterday's story? What do you think is going to happen today?

 Read Acts 3:9–16.

Think about It Some More

When the crippled man was healed, Peter spoke out to make sure everyone knew that it was Jesus who had healed the man. Peter didn't want them telling everyone that he, Peter, had healed him in his own power. Peter wanted them to know that it was Jesus, the one they had killed but who had risen again, who healed the man and made him walk again, and that by believing in the name of Jesus, they could be healed too! Before Jesus left, he told the disciples, "You will receive power when the Holy Spirit has come upon you, and you will be my witnesses in Jerusalem and in all Judea and Samaria, and to the end of the earth" (Acts 1:8). Through the healing of the crippled man, we can see that the power Jesus promised had fallen upon the apostles, just as he said.

Talk about It

:: When the people at the temple saw the crippled man healed, what did they think? *(They were amazed and thought that Peter had healed the man in his own power.)*

:: What did Peter tell the crowd so they didn't think the power to heal had come from him? *(Peter told the crowd that it was the man's faith in the name of Jesus that had healed him. It did not happen by Peter's own power.)*

:: Read verse 16 again. What does Peter tell us about the man who was healed? *(Peter reveals to us that God gave the man faith to believe and trust in the name of Jesus, and that it was his faith in Jesus that had healed him.)*

 Pray about It

Thank Jesus for giving us these wonderful Bible stories to help us believe.

DAY THREE

Connect It to the Gospel

Today is the day we connect this week's Bible story to the gospel. The gospel is the life, death, and resurrection of Jesus for our salvation. Can anyone guess how our story this week looks forward to or back at the gospel?

 Read Acts 3:17–26.

Think about It Some More

Since the crippled man had lived most of his life begging at the temple, listening in on the conversations, he must have heard about Jesus and how Jesus healed the sick. He may even have wanted to meet Jesus so that he himself could be healed. If so, he would have been disappointed to hear that Jesus was crucified. That would have been big news among the people walking by him at the temple. Remember, a lot of things happened around the death of Jesus. For instance, the temple curtain was torn in two and people were raised from the dead (Matthew 27:51–53). Everyone would have been talking about this.

The man must have known about Jesus, for when Peter said, "In the name of Jesus Christ of Nazareth," the man was filled with faith and believed and was healed. The crippled man never asked, "Who is Jesus?" He simply believed. Then Peter used the healing as an opportunity to explain the gospel to the crowd and invite them to believe.

Talk about It

:: What did Peter tell the crowd would happen if they repented of (turned away from) their sins and put their faith in Jesus? *(Peter told the crowd that their sins would be blotted out, which means taken away or forgiven, and that the presence of the Lord would come upon them.)*

:: Why did Peter talk about the prophets so much? *(We need to remember that the New Testament had not yet been written. Peter was simply using Scripture as his authority so the people's faith did not depend on his testimony alone, but on the testimony of God through the prophets.)*

:: Where do you see the gospel mentioned in Peter's message? *(Help your children locate the gospel in the passage. We never want to tire of making sure they know and can clearly recognize the gospel message.)*

 ## Pray about It

Thank God for keeping his promise to Abraham that all nations would be blessed through his descendants. Jesus is the fulfillment of that blessing.

DAY FOUR _____

Remember It

What has God been teaching you this week through our Bible story?

 Read Acts 4:1–22.

Think about It Some More

It did not take long for the religious rulers to hear the commotion and find out that Peter and John were telling everyone that Jesus had risen from the dead. The religious leaders didn't like that very much, so they arrested Peter and John—but that only provided another opportunity for the gospel. Peter wasn't the same fearful man he'd been at the time of Jesus' arrest. Though in the courtyard he fearfully denied Jesus three times, now, filled with the Holy Spirit, Peter boldly proclaimed that Jesus was alive. He accused the religious rulers of killing Jesus and told them that believing in Jesus was the only way to be saved.

Sadly, the religious leaders refused to put their trust in Jesus even though the crippled man who was healed was standing before them.

They rejected the gospel message and commanded the disciples never to mention the name of Jesus again.

Talk about It

> KIDS, ask your parents if they can remember a
> time when they refused to believe.

(Parents, did you ever reject the message of the gospel? Even if you became a Christian at a young age, you may be able to recall a time when you didn't believe. If so, share it with your children and praise God for his mercy in continuing to reach out to you.)

:: Why didn't the religious rulers punish Peter and John? *(They were afraid of what the people would think. On the one hand they wanted to stop the spread of the word about Jesus, but on the other hand they wanted to do it in a way that would not make them look bad. They were more interested in pleasing man than pleasing God.)*

:: Where did Peter get the courage to speak to the rulers and elders? *(Peter was filled with the Holy Spirit, who emboldened him and helped him [Acts 4:8].)*

:: Why does the gospel keep getting repeated? *(The gospel is the power of God unto salvation for everyone who believes. See Romans 1:16.)*

Pray about It

Pray and ask God to help you believe like the crippled man and not reject Jesus like the religious rulers did.

DAY FIVE

Discover It

Today is the day we look at a different Bible passage—from the book of Psalms or one of the prophets—to see what we can learn from it about Jesus or our salvation.

 Read Psalm 49:7–15.

Think about It Some More

This psalm tells us that no one can ransom (pay the penalty for) another's life. Even if you paid all the money in the world, it would not be enough to pay for even one person's sins. There is only one way to pay the ransom price: someone perfect needs to die in our place. Since we are all sinners, none of us could do that. That is why the person who wrote this psalm said that we will all see the pit—we will all die. But we know that there is someone who was perfect and never sinned. His name is Jesus. Jesus lived a perfect life so he could pay the penalty for our sin.

In his letter to Timothy, Paul said that Jesus gave his life as a "ransom for all" (1 Timothy 2:6). Not only was Jesus sufficient as a ransom for one man, himself, but he also paid the ransom price for all who trust in him! That is why Peter told the religious leaders, "There is salvation in no one else, for there is no other name under heaven given among men by which we must be saved" (Acts 4:12). There is hope found in this psalm. Verse 15 says that God himself will pay the ransom price for our souls. He did this by sending his own Son, Jesus, to die in our place.

Talk about It

:: Who was the only one who could pay the ransom price for our lives so that we could go to heaven? *(Jesus)*

:: What was different about Jesus that he could pay the price that no one else could pay? *(Jesus never sinned. Only a perfect person could redeem the life of a sinner. That is why Jesus had to live a life without sin.)*

:: What do we need to do for Jesus to pay for our sins? *(All we have to do is believe that Jesus died for our sin and rose again from the dead and place our hope and trust in Jesus. Since there is no other way to get to heaven, Jesus is our only hope.)*

 ## Pray about It

Thank Jesus for coming to earth, living a sinless life, and dying on the cross to pay the penalty for our sin. Ask God to help the people you know believe and place their trust in him.

Week 48

Ananias & Sapphira

Story 126 – *The Gospel Story Bible*

For this exercise you will need a clear food storage container and enough small cookies for each child to have two. Before Bible study, explain to the children that you have some cookies for them in your container and you are going to give them all away, every last one.

Open the container, give each of them one cookie, then tell them that there are no more; you gave them all away. When they object and say that you didn't give them all away, ask how they know. They will say that they can see more snacks inside the container. Explain to your children that, to God, our lives are like the see-through container. We might think we can hide things from God, but he knows everything. Say, "This week we will learn about people who tried to hide their sin from God."

DAY ONE

Picture It

Pretend for a moment that your family car was destroyed in an accident and you didn't have enough money to buy another. How much more difficult would it be for your family if you had to walk to the supermarket and carry your groceries home in a wagon? Then imagine that a person in your church heard you lost your car and decided to give your family one of her extra cars completely free. She drove it to your house, knocked on your door, and said that she wanted to give it to your family because you needed it more than she did. Wouldn't that be amazing? That is the kind of generous giving that the Christians in the first church were showing each other.

 Read Acts 4:32–37.

Think about It Some More

When we realize what an awesome treasure we have in Jesus, worldly possessions lose their value and are not as special to us anymore. The Bible tells us that earthly treasures can be destroyed or stolen (Matthew 6:19–20), but nobody can take Jesus away from us. Remembering this can make giving our things away to those in need much easier. After God poured out his Spirit upon the first church in Jerusalem, the Holy Spirit helped them generously give away their things to those in need.

The early Christians didn't just give small things away; some even sold land and gave the money to the apostles to distribute to those in need. This money was given joyfully out of gratitude for what Jesus had done for them. That is how the Holy Spirit works in us when we become Christians. He fills us with joy as we follow God. Obeying God becomes easy because the law of God is written on our hearts!

Talk about It

:: What two great things came upon the people in the early church? *(Parents, if your younger children don't get the answer, reread verse 33 and have them raise their hands when they hear the answer. The Holy Spirit came with great power, and the people received grace to selflessly and joyfully give to one another.)*

:: What did the apostles do with the money they collected from the people who sold their land? *(The apostles gave the money to help those in need. In the end, there was enough money for everyone who needed it.)*

:: What things of yours could you give away to help others? *(Parents, help your children think of what they could give away to help someone else.)*

Pray about It

Ask God to pour out his grace upon you to enable you to live for Jesus and not for the things of this world.

DAY TWO

Remember It

What do you remember about yesterday's story? What do you think is going to happen today?

 Read Acts 5:1–6.

Think about It Some More

Yesterday we learned about a man named Barnabas who sold some land and gave the money to the apostles to help the poor. In today's story, a man named Ananias also sold some land and said that he would give all the money to the poor. But secretly, after the land was sold, he decided to keep some of the money for himself. Then he lied and pretended that he was giving all the money away. Ananias didn't think anyone would know he'd kept some for himself. Everyone would think he was just as generous as Barnabas, who gave all the money from the sale of his land. But Ananias forgot that God would know— and God was not going to let dishonesty hurt the growing church. If he had told the truth, he could have kept the money for himself.

Talk about It

:: What did Ananias do wrong? *(Ananias told Peter that he was giving all the money he received from the sale of his property, but he lied. Secretly he kept some of the money for himself.)*

:: How did Peter know that Ananias lied to him? *(The Bible doesn't say, but the Holy Spirit made sure that Peter discovered the truth.)*

:: Whom did Peter say Ananias had lied to? *(Peter said that Ananias lied to the Holy Spirit. When we lie, even though we might lie to a person, our lies are first and foremost against God.)*

 Pray about It

Ask the Lord to help you live truthfully and transparently.

DAY THREE _____

Connect It to the Gospel

Today is the day we connect this week's Bible story to the gospel. The gospel is the life, death, and resurrection of Jesus for our salvation. Can anyone guess how our story this week looks forward to or back at the gospel?

 Read Acts 5:7–11.

Think about It Some More

Jesus had said that he was going to build his church and that nothing would stand in his way, not even the evil powers of hell (Matthew 16:18). This is why God took Ananias's sin so seriously. The newly formed church was growing as people showed each other the love of Jesus by helping each other out. Ananias's sin threatened to ruin the good witness of the church and of the gospel. Ananias and Sapphira thought they could get away with a lie and keep some of the money for themselves while claiming to have given all of it, but God wasn't going to let anything hamper the growth of his church. Instead of getting away with their lie, both Ananias and Sapphira died. When people heard what happened, they became afraid of sinning against God, which helped the new church grow stronger.

Talk about It

:: What did Sapphira do wrong? *(Like her husband, she lied about how much money they'd received for the sale of the land.)*

:: Why did God kill Ananias and Sapphira? *(It can sound harsh to say that God killed Ananias and Sapphira, but we need to remember that God is the Lord over life. He is the one who decides how long a person will live. God can allow a person to live a long life or take his life away when the person is young. He was not going to allow Ananias and Sapphira to hurt the reputation of the church by their lies.)*

:: Verse 11 tells us that great fear came upon the church. What were they afraid of? *(The people feared God and they were afraid to sin against God. They realized that God had to punish sin and that he was going to protect the church.)*

:: Do we need to be afraid to sin against God too? *(Yes, the Bible tells us that the "fear of the LORD is the beginning of wisdom" [Proverbs 9:10]. That doesn't mean that we should be afraid to pray to God. It means that we should be afraid to willfully sin against God who has redeemed us at such a great cost—the cost of the life of his Son.)*

 Pray about It

Ask God to help you fear the Lord so that you will honor him by staying away from sin.

DAY FOUR

Remember It

What has God been teaching you this week through our Bible story?

 Read Acts 5:12–16.

Think about It Some More

The sinful lie of Ananias and Sapphira could have hurt the growing church. That is why the Lord judged them so quickly. Ananias and Sapphira loved the praise of men but not so much that it made them want to give away their money. They also loved money more than they loved God. As a result, they missed the joy of seeing God move in grace and power. Soon after they died, God poured out his power for healing upon the growing church. Verse 14 tells us that, more than ever, believers were added to the Lord. The church, which was only a few weeks old, was fast approaching ten thousand members! People outside the church saw the genuine love that the folks in the early church had for one another. They saw sinful, greedy people become generous after becoming Christians. Those changed lives made it easy for them to see that Jesus has the power to change a person's life.

Talk about It

> ● ●   KIDS, ask your parents to tell you a story of how
> ● ●   God saved and added someone to your church.

(Parents, remember what seems like a routine story is very educational to our children. Think of a person who became a Christian and was added to your church. Share their testimony with your children.)

::   How many people were healed? *(Parents, if you have younger children, reread the passage and have them raise their hands when they hear that everyone who came was healed.)*

::   What do you think the religious leaders thought about all healings? *(This passage doesn't tell us what they thought, but you can guess that they were not too happy. They wanted to stop the followers of Jesus from growing in number.)*

::   Why did people want Peter's shadow to fall on them? *(They wanted to be healed. The power of God for healing was so strong that it seems that even Peter's shadow was enough to heal those who came by faith.)*

 Pray about It

Praise God for the miraculous way he poured out his power on the early church.

DAY FIVE _____

Discover It

Today is the day we look at a different Bible passage—from the book of Psalms or one of the prophets—to see what we can learn from it about Jesus or our salvation.

 Read Isaiah 56:7.

Think about It Some More

In Matthew 21:13 Jesus quoted today's verse from Isaiah as he rebuked the money-changers in the temple and overturned their tables. At the time, the temple was thought of as the place where God lived among his people. Jesus said that it should be kept as a house of prayer and not be turned into a marketplace. But after Jesus died, the Holy Spirit came to live inside the people, and they became the temple of God. So when Ananias and Sapphira lied, they were hurting the reputation of God's temple, the church. When God killed Ananias and Sapphira, he was making sure the new temple of God would be kept clean, free of sin that could destroy the church.

Talk about It

:: Why did Jesus chase the money-changers and people selling animals out of the temple? *(The temple was supposed to be a place where people could pray, not a market.)*

:: How was what Jesus did in cleansing the temple like what he did to Ananias and Sapphira? *(God wanted to make sure no one was going to spoil his house.)*

:: Why does God judge sin? *(God is all good, and sin is evil. God fights sin because sin is against God.)*

 Pray about It

Praise God for being all good and thank him for sending Jesus to take our sins away so that we don't have to be judged like Ananias and Sapphira were.

The Death of Stephen

Story 127 – *The Gospel Story Bible*

You will need a small cup filled to the brim with either water or dry rice. (Choose the one that will be easier for you to clean up in your home.) Hand the cup to one of your children, and explain that the cup represents his life, and the rice or water represents the gospel. Have him stand and hold the cup without moving. Note that very little of the gospel is being spread around. Now tell him you are going to count to three and then come after him. Give him a three-second head start and then run after him. As he runs he will spill some of the rice or water. When you have apprehended him, take a look back and help everyone to see how the gospel spread as a result of your chasing him. Explain that this is what happened to the early Christians when persecution broke out. Say, "This week we will learn about Stephen and the persecution of the early church."

DAY ONE

Picture It

Imagine what it would be like to live in a country where it is against the law to be a Christian. In a country like that, you can be thrown into prison or even killed for sharing the gospel story about Jesus. Imagine how sad it would be if your mom or dad were sent to prison for sharing the gospel. That is the kind of sacrifice that men and women are still making in some places around the world today. In fact, some people are still killed for telling others about Jesus. In the story we are about to read, we will learn how Stephen gave his life for the gospel.

 Read Acts 6:8–15.

Think about It Some More

While still with his disciples, Jesus warned them saying, "If they persecuted me, they will also persecute you" (John 15:20). His words came true, for Peter and John were arrested after healing the crippled man. The religious rulers had let them go because of all the people who were rejoicing at the crippled man's healing, but they warned them not to talk about Jesus anymore. Some of the Jews hated the Christians. That is why, when Stephen shared the gospel, they arrested him. Like Jesus at his arrest, people lied about Stephen to get him into trouble.

As for Stephen, you might think he would be afraid at his arrest and be quiet, but that is not what Stephen did. The Holy Spirit came upon him and helped him trust God. He wasn't afraid, and while he spoke his was like the face of an angel. When we give our lives to Jesus, the Holy Spirit fills us and gives us boldness too (Ephesians 3:12).

Talk about It

:: How was Stephen's ministry like Jesus' ministry? *(Stephen did great wonders and signs among the people. Like Jesus, Stephen shared the gospel with such wisdom that the leaders could not argue against him. And as with Jesus, they wanted to kill Stephen.)*

:: Who helped Stephen defend himself when he spoke? *(The Holy Spirit helped Stephen and gave him great wisdom so that those who were arguing with him couldn't win.)*

:: What did the evil men do to get Stephen in trouble? *(They asked people to lie and say that Stephen was speaking against the temple and God's law.)*

 # Pray about It

Pray for the people around the world who are persecuted, or hurt, for believing in Jesus. *(Parents, for your older children, do an Internet search on the persecuted church and find modern-day examples of people who are experiencing persecution. Pray for the people you read about.)*

DAY TWO

Remember It

What do you remember about yesterday's story? What do you think is going to happen today?

📖 Read Acts 7:1–50. *(Parents: This is a longer reading than usual, but Stephen gives a wonderful summary of Israel's history that is worth sharing with your children.)*

Think about It Some More

False witnesses lied about Stephen and said that he spoke against God's law. When it was Stephen's turn to speak, he defended his love for God's law by sharing the story of Israel. By doing so with such honor and accuracy, he showed that he wasn't against the Jews who accused him. He called them his brothers and Abraham his father (v. 2). Stephen wanted them to see that following Jesus didn't mean forming a new religion. Jesus came to fulfill the promise God had given Abraham. In the past, the Jews had had to sacrifice lamb after lamb after lamb to try to cover their sin, but Jesus had come as the final Lamb of God to take away their sins once and for all. Yet these Jews were rejecting Jesus.

Talk about It

:: What was the promise God gave Abraham? *(God told Abraham that his children would be more numerous than the stars of the sky and the sand of the seashore, and that through his offspring all nations would be blessed. Jesus fulfilled that promise. He was the far-off great-grandchild of Abraham who brought the blessing of salvation to people of every nation. Now anyone who believes in Jesus becomes a child of Abraham and takes part in God's promise.)*

:: In verse 37 Stephen quoted Moses, who said, "God will raise up for you a prophet like me." About whom was Moses speaking? *(Moses was speaking about Jesus. Jesus even said that Moses wrote about him. See John 5:46.)*

✋ Pray about It

Thank God for keeping his promise to Abraham by sending Jesus to rescue us—and people from every nation.

DAY THREE

Connect It to the Gospel

Today is the day we connect this week's Bible story to the gospel. The gospel is the life, death, and resurrection of Jesus for our salvation. Can anyone guess how our story this week looks forward to or back at the gospel?

 Read Acts 7:51–60.

Think about It Some More

When Stephen was finished sharing the story of Israel, he gave a warning to the men who had arrested him. He said they were just like their fathers, who had killed God's prophets. That was the whole point of Stephen's message: The Savior of Israel had lived with them, and yet instead of worshiping Jesus, they had killed him. It is likely that some of the men who arrested Stephen had been involved in killing Jesus too. When they heard Stephen's rebuke, the men got terribly angry. Instead of turning away from their sin, they rushed at Stephen in anger. But Stephen was not afraid—God gave him a vision of heaven with Jesus standing next to his Father.

No matter what the Jews did, Stephen knew that Jesus was with him. They grabbed Stephen, dragged him away, and stoned him to death. With Stephen's last words, he forgave his attackers, much the same way as Jesus forgave those who had crucified him. Jesus had said, "Father, forgive them, for they know not what they do" (Luke 23:34). Jesus' last words demonstrate the grace and forgiveness that come to us through the gospel. Because Jesus forgave us, we have the grace to forgive others. Although we are commanded to forgive others (Colossians 3:13), true Christian forgiveness springs up out of a Spirit-directed love for our Savior.

Talk about It

:: Stephen said the men did not keep God's law. Which commandment did they break? *(They broke the commandment not to murder, for they had killed Jesus, an innocent man.)*

:: Stephen called the religious rulers stiff-necked. What do you think that means? *(It means they were stubborn and refused to* believe in Jesus. The term comes from farming when an ox refused to take a yoke upon its neck for plowing and had to be forced to bend.)

:: How did God help Stephen? *(God gave Stephen a vision of Jesus standing next to God the Father in heaven.)*

:: Who watched the coats of Stephen's murderers? *(The coats were laid at the feet of Saul, a Pharisee whom God would later call to preach the gospel to the Gentiles. We know him best by his other name, Paul, the man who ended up writing many of the books of the New Testament.)*

Pray about It

Pray that God would help you love Jesus like Stephen did instead of turning away from Jesus like the Jews in our story did.

DAY FOUR

Remember It

What has God been teaching you this week through our Bible story?

 Read Acts 8:1–8.

Think about It Some More

After the religious rulers had killed Stephen, their anger spilled out toward other Christians. Saul took the lead and went from house to house arresting other believers. Because of this persecution, Christians fled Jerusalem and were scattered throughout the surrounding towns. The Jews who participated in the persecution thought they had to protect their religion by stopping the Christians, but God used the persecution to accomplish his plans. The Christians who were scattered took the gospel story with them and told the people in the surrounding countryside all about Jesus. So, many people heard the gospel and were saved (Acts 11:19–21).

Talk about It

> KIDS, ask your parents if they can remember a time when God turned something bad that happened into a blessing.

(Parents, many folks have gone to the doctors complaining of some small pain only to discover a treatable cancer. Perhaps you know of a person who was late to leave for work, only to discover that there had been a terrible accident on the road at the very same time they were planning to be on it.)

:: How did God turn the evil persecution into good? *(When the Christians were scattered, they began to tell the gospel to the people they met, and many believed.)*

:: Why didn't many of the Jews like the Christians? *(When Jesus died, the temple curtain was torn in two to show that a way was opened up for all people to come into God's presence. God wouldn't live in the temple anymore; he would live in the hearts of Christians by his Holy Spirit. The Jews didn't believe in Jesus and didn't like this new teaching. They didn't want to give up their sacrifices and laws. That is why they started to persecute the Christians.)*

Pray about It

Praise God for the way he can use evil for good and how God is in control of everything that happens. He can even take a wicked man like Saul and save him and turn around his life for good.

DAY FIVE

Discover It

Today is the day we look at a different Bible passage—from the book of Psalms or one of the prophets—to see what we can learn from it about Jesus or our salvation.

Read Isaiah 24:10–16.

Think about It Some More

Isaiah spoke of two different groups of people in this passage: First, the sinful people of the world who have wasted their lives on too much wine; and second, the people who gave great praises to a person called the Righteous One. In our story this week, Stephen said that Jesus was the "Righteous One" (Acts 7:52), and he was stoned for it. The Righteous One in Isaiah's prophecy was worshiped and exalted in glory. By calling Jesus the Righteous One, Stephen was saying that Jesus was worthy of worship. That made the Jews angry enough to stone him, for they did not believe that Jesus was God.

Talk about It

:: Who is the Righteous One who Isaiah spoke about in this passage? *(Jesus)*

:: Why is Jesus called the Righteous One? *(Jesus never once committed sin. Jesus kept the whole law perfectly.)*

:: Why was it so important that Jesus never sinned? *(Perfect righteousness, or goodness before God, is what God requires of all of us. But because we all sin, we are all under God's judgment. The only way we could be forgiven is if Jesus lived in our place, and never sinned. Then Jesus died to take our punishment. Jesus now offers both forgiveness and perfect righteousness as a gift to everyone who believes. You see, Jesus was already perfectly righteous and good in heaven. So, when he came as a man and lived a perfect life, he didn't do it for himself—he did it for us.)*

Pray about It

Thank Jesus for the two things he did for us: First, he lived a perfect life for us; and second, he died on the cross to take the punishment we deserved.

Week 50

Saul Is Knocked to the Ground

Story 128 – *The Gospel Story Bible*

Blindfold one of your children, turn her around a few times, then ask her to do something blindfolded like walk over to the sofa or pick up the book on the table. In order to complete the task, she will need to feel her way. Say, "This is a picture of what we are like in our sin without God. It also gives you an idea of what happened to Saul when God blinded him, as we will hear in our story this week."

Now give your child a second assignment, this time, not blindfolded. Say, "It is obviously so much easier to do things when we can see. When God gives us new life, he opens our blinded eyes to see our sin, so we can repent. Living for Jesus also becomes a lot easier too. When the Spirit opens our eyes to see the beauty of Christ and gives us a desire to follow him, we start wanting to do what is right. That is what happened to Saul."

DAY ONE

Picture It

Imagine what it would be like to see an angel and have him tell you to go to a certain place. That is what happened in our story today with Philip. An angel appeared to him and told him to go down a certain road. Philip must have thought something special was going to happen on that road. What would you think if an angel appeared to you in your bedroom and said, "Go outside to your backyard and stand under the large tree that is growing there"? You would go out expecting something to happen or someone to be there for you to meet. In our story today, an angel of the Lord sent Philip down a particular road. Let's see whom he met along the way.

 Read Acts 8:26–40.

Think about It Some More

Once Saul started arresting them in Jerusalem, Christians fled the city for their lives so they would not be captured by Saul and thrown into prison. As they traveled to places outside of Jerusalem, they told the story of Jesus to the people they met along the way. Philip, for example, left Jerusalem and went to Samaria. While in Samaria he told the people there about Jesus, and he healed the sick. As a result, many people believed in Jesus.

After that, the angel of the Lord appeared to Philip and sent him on his way again, this time along a desert road. Philip was probably wondering why God sent him there. But then he saw an Ethiopian eunuch reading from Isaiah 53. Before Philip could think what to do, the Spirit of God told him to go over to the man. Once Philip explained that the prophecy was about Jesus, the Ethiopian believed and wanted to be baptized. If it hadn't been for the persecution, Philip might never have met the Ethiopian.

Talk about It

:: What was the Ethiopian doing when Philip saw him? *(The Ethiopian was reading from the Old Testament book of Isaiah. He was reading about the lamb of God who was going to die for the sins of God's people.)*

:: What did the Ethiopian do after Philip explained that Isaiah was talking about Jesus dying on the cross for our sins? *(The Ethiopian believed and asked to be baptized.)*

:: What happened to Philip soon after the Ethiopian man was baptized? *(God took Philip away to preach the gospel along the coast. We don't know how God did it, but Philip seemed to disappear!)*

:: What do you think happened to the Ethiopian? *(He probably went back to his country in Africa, and told his people about Jesus. He may have been the very first African to be saved.)*

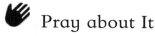 Pray about It

Praise God for the way he used the persecution to reach more people with the gospel so they would have a chance to believe in Jesus and be forgiven.

DAY TWO

Remember It

What do you remember about yesterday's story? What do you think is going to happen today?

 Read Acts 9:1–9.

Think about It Some More

It didn't take long for Saul to realize that the Christians had fled Jerusalem. So he planned to go after them. They were spreading the story of Jesus all across Judea, and Saul was determined to stop them. Finding the Christians was easy. All Saul would have to do is ask around in the towns to find out who was talking about Jesus, arrest them, and bring them back to Jerusalem for trial. As a Pharisee, Saul thought he was protecting the Word of God by arresting and killing the Christians, but Saul was actually fighting against God. After Saul left the city to chase after the Christians, God stepped in to stop him. With one flash of his glory, God knocked Saul off his horse and blinded him. When Jesus spoke to Saul, he didn't accuse him of persecuting the Christians; instead, Jesus accused Saul of persecuting *him*.

Talk about It

- :: Why did Saul leave Jerusalem? *(Saul left Jerusalem to chase after the Christians who had fled the city. He wanted to arrest them and bring them back to prison in Jerusalem.)*

- :: Who stopped Saul? *(Jesus stopped Saul. With a flash of his glory, he knocked Saul to the ground and blinded him.)*

- :: Whom did Jesus say Saul was persecuting (hurting)? *(Parents, if you have younger children, you may want to reread verses*

4 and 5 and have them raise their hands when they hear the correct answer: Saul was persecuting Jesus.)

 Pray about It

Thank Jesus for the way he protected the church and the gospel so that one day we too could hear about Jesus and believe.

DAY THREE _____

Connect It to the Gospel

Today is the day we connect this week's Bible story to the gospel. The gospel is the life, death, and resurrection of Jesus for our salvation. Can anyone guess how our story this week looks forward to or back at the gospel?

 Read Acts 9:10–22.

Think about It Some More

Jesus could have killed Saul to punish him for all that he had done in persecuting the Christians. But he didn't. Instead, Jesus did something no one would expect—something that people would be talking about for millennia: Jesus saved Saul from his sins. When Jesus was on the cross, he died for Saul's sins, and he knew that one day Saul would become one of his most well-known followers. Jesus went after Saul, not to kill him but to save him, and he chose Saul to be the one to preach the gospel to the Gentiles.

Once God opened his eyes, Saul stopped persecuting Christians. Instead, Saul began preaching the gospel. Before, Saul had traveled about persecuting the Christians, now he would travel about preaching the gospel to the Gentiles. God even used Saul's training as a Pharisee and his knowledge of Scripture to prove to the Jews that Jesus was the promised Messiah.

Talk about It

:: How did Saul's life change after he believed in Jesus and became a Christian? *(Saul went from fighting against Jesus by persecuting Christians to living for Jesus by preaching the gospel. That is an amazing change.)*

:: If Jesus had not come after Saul, do you think Saul would have ever become a Christian? *(If Jesus had not gone after Saul, Saul would not have believed. Saul was interested only in stopping the Christians.)*

:: How are we like Saul? *(We need to be rescued from our sins too. If Jesus didn't send people to preach the gospel to us, we would stay sinners all our lives like the other unbelievers around us. Just as God sent Ananias to Saul, God sends people to us. God uses pastors, Sunday school teachers, parents, brothers, sisters, and even people we don't know to share the message of the gospel. We can also be saved and changed like Saul was! When we believe in Jesus, the Holy Spirit transforms our hearts of stone to hearts of soft flesh and writes God's law upon our hearts so that we grow in our desire to obey. In fact, many new believers experience an amazingly transformed life just like Saul did. They are terrible sinners one day, and they start serving the Lord the next.)*

 ## Pray about It

Thank God for saving Saul and for sending people to preach the gospel to us. Ask God to help the unbelievers you know, believe in and follow Jesus.

DAY FOUR

Remember It

What has God been teaching you this week through our Bible story?

 Read Acts 9:23–31.

Think about It Some More

Imagine what it would have been like for the new believers to hear that Saul was coming to their church meeting. Remember, he was the one who had been arresting Christians. People must have thought he was trying to trick them, pretending to be a Christian to find out where they met and then, at the last moment, arresting them all and taking them off to prison in Jerusalem.

That is why the Christians were afraid and many did not believe that Saul's conversion was real. But it didn't take the Jews long to turn against Saul. When they heard that Saul was defending Jesus, *they* believed he was converted and planned to kill him. God used that to help the Christians believe that his conversion was real.

Talk about It

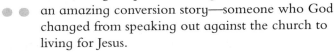

> KIDS, ask your parents if they know someone with an amazing conversion story—someone who God changed from speaking out against the church to living for Jesus.

(Parents, think about the members of your church. Nearly every church has a person who at one time spoke out boldly against Christianity but who was then changed by the power of the gospel and started living for Jesus. If you know someone like that, you might consider having him over for dinner so he can share his testimony with your children personally.)

:: Why was it hard for the Christians to believe that Saul was a Christian? *(Saul had done such terrible things against the Christians that they thought he was trying to trick them.)*

:: Why did the Jews want to kill Saul? *(The Jews hated the Christians. Saul was a well-trained Pharisee who knew the Scriptures so well they could not argue against him. Now he was helping the Christians. With him on their side, more and more people would come to know Jesus.)*

:: How did God use Saul? *(Saul became the apostle Paul, who wrote many of the books of the New Testament and preached the gospel to thousands who became Christians.)*

 Pray about It

Praise God for the amazing way he can change our hearts with the gospel. One day we are living only for ourselves, and the next, for him. When God transforms us by his Spirit, we can say no to sin and start living for God.

DAY FIVE

Discover It

Today is the day we look at a different Bible passage—from the book of Psalms or one of the prophets—to see what we can learn from it about Jesus or our salvation.

 Read Psalm 130.

Think about It Some More

A watchman patrolling the wall of a city at night would be glad to see morning come, for dawn meant that his work was finished and he could go home and rest. Without a clock to tell the time, a watchman looked in the sky for the morning star rising on the horizon. The morning star—the planet Venus—signaled that night was almost over, so the watchman looked eagerly to see it. The psalmist compared a watchman waiting for the morning with how he eagerly waited for God to forgive his sin. As a sinner, he realized that his only hope—that *Israel's* only hope—was for God to forgive them and redeem them from their sins.

Looking back, we know that God answered the psalmist's prayer by sending Jesus. Jesus said that he is our bright morning star (Revelation 22:16). Jesus is our hope that soon we too will have rest from our work battling with sin on earth. Peter said, "And we have the prophetic word more fully confirmed, to which you will do well to pay attention as to a lamp shining in a dark place, until the day dawns and the morning star rises in your hearts" (2 Peter 1:19).

Talk about It

:: What was the psalmist asking God for? *(Parents, if you have younger children, you may want to reread the psalm and have them raise their hands when they hear the answer: The psalmist is asking God to forgive his sins.)*

:: Why does the psalmist hope God will save him from his sins? *(The person who wrote this psalm hopes that God will save him from his sins because there is no other way to be saved. He realizes that if God must judge everyone, no one will be able to stand because everyone is a sinner.)*

:: The psalmist tells us that he is waiting for God's forgiveness like a watchman waits for the morning. Why would a watchman be excited to see the morning? *(The night watchman eagerly awaits morning, because when morning comes, his labor is over and he can rest.)*

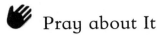 Pray about It

Pray through Psalm 130. Pray that God would forgive your sins and help you put your hope in the Lord.

Week 51

The Gentiles Are Converted

Story 129 – *The Gospel Story Bible*

Use this exercise to help your children understand how Peter would have felt about eating unclean animals. Have your children come over to the kitchen table and tell them you want to try to come up with a new kind of sandwich.

Start by spreading some jelly over a slice of bread on a plate. Ask them what they think so far. Then go to your refrigerator and pull out mustard, and squirt a bit on top the jelly. You can really play this up by complimenting your creation as you go. Then add a few other condiments, whatever you have on hand, and finish it off by cracking a raw egg on top. Then smear it all together and add a second slice of bread. Pick up the plate and hold it close to their faces. They should react in disgust.

Explain to them that this week they will learn how God called Peter to eat kinds of food he thought were not good to eat and how God used that to teach Peter to share the gospel with the Gentiles.

DAY ONE

Picture It

One day in his science class, Brian's teacher asked him to pick up the toad from the terrarium and bring it to the front of his class. "I can't do that," Brian replied. "My brother said toads give you warts." The teacher smiled and explained that although toads look like they have warts all over them, they are perfectly safe, and you can't get warts from them. Still Brian was afraid. His teacher had to ask him three times before he built up enough courage to pick up the toad. In the end, he trusted his teacher. Later, he looked up *toad* in a book at the school library and found that his teacher was correct: You cannot get warts from a toad.

In our Bible story today, God showed Peter that something he had been taught was wrong. Peter was told that you shouldn't eat with—or even touch—Gentiles (people who were not Jews) because doing so would make you unclean. But God had never said that Gentiles were unclean. God said only that some of the foods they ate were unclean. To show Peter that God loved the Gentiles, he gave Peter a vision of some of the unclean animals they ate and told Peter to eat them. Let's see how Peter responded.

 Read Acts 10:1–23.

Think about It Some More

Back when God gave Moses the law, he gave him a list of foods that his people were not supposed to touch or eat—like lizards, pigs, and certain birds, like seagulls and hawks. God called these animals unclean. You can find the whole list in Leviticus 11. The religious rulers stretched God's command. They told the Jews that it wasn't just the food the Gentiles ate but the Gentiles themselves that were unclean. That is why the Jewish people would not even go into the house of a Gentile. But God had never forbidden that. In fact, God planned to reach people from every nation.

To teach Peter that the good news of the gospel was for the Gentiles too, God gave him a vision of the unclean animals and told Peter to kill and eat them. That was hard for Peter because from his childhood he had been taught that it was wrong to eat those things. That is why God reminded Peter that *he* made the rules—and if God made something clean, then it was clean. To make sure Peter got the message, God repeated the vision three times. God wanted to teach Peter to preach the gospel to everyone, including the Gentiles, whom the Jews thought were unclean.

Talk about It

:: Why did Cornelius send men to find Peter? *(God told Cornelius to send for Peter.)*

:: Why didn't Peter want to obey God and kill and eat the animals in the vision? *(The animals on the sheet were unclean. They were animals that God had forbidden his people to eat.)*

:: What was God trying to teach Peter with the vision? *(God was trying to teach Peter that if God called something clean, it was clean. In this case, God was going to use the vision to help Peter understand that God wanted to save Gentiles too.)*

:: Why did Peter agree to go to Cornelius's house? *(God told him to go.)*

 Pray about It

Thank God for the way he answered Cornelius's prayers by sending Peter to him with the gospel.

DAY TWO _____

Remember It

What do you remember about yesterday's story? What do you think is going to happen today?

 Read Acts 10:24–35.

Think about It Some More

To make absolutely sure the people of Israel obeyed all God's law, the Pharisees took God's law and made it even more strict. So when God said that a person should not work on the Sabbath, the Pharisees added a rule that said a person could not even touch a tool on the Sabbath or carry anything. That way, there was no way a person could break God's law by working on the Sabbath.

Another rule they made up was that Jews were not permitted to even go into the house of a Gentile. Since the Gentiles ate unclean foods, the religious rulers said the Gentiles themselves were also unclean. That is why when the Jews went to Pilate to accuse Jesus, Pilate had to come out of his house to talk to them (John 18:28). But God had never said Gentiles were unclean. Jesus died for all people, which means that the gospel message was for Gentiles too.

Talk about It

:: What did God teach Peter? *(If you have younger children, reread verse 28 and have them raise their hands when they hear the answer: God showed Peter that he should not call any person unclean.)*

:: Why did God send Peter to Cornelius? *(God sent Peter to Cornelius to tell him about Jesus. That is why Cornelius asked Peter to tell him all that he was commanded by the Lord to say. If you remember, Jesus told the disciples to go and make disciples of all nations [Matthew 28:19].)*

:: Is your family Jewish or Gentile? *(Parents, if your family is Gentile [non-Jewish], help your children realize that if God had not corrected Peter, your family might not have understood that the gospel was for you too.)*

 ## Pray about It

Thank God for making a way for people from every nation to be brought into God's family. Thank God for making a way for your family to know the story of Jesus and how he came to save us.

DAY THREE _____

Connect It to the Gospel

Today is the day we connect this week's Bible story to the gospel. The gospel is the life, death, and resurrection of Jesus for our salvation. Can anyone guess how our story this week looks forward to or back at the gospel?

 Read Acts 10:36–44.

Think about It Some More

Once Peter realized that God wanted the gospel to go to the Gentiles too, he proclaimed the gospel message—that Jesus died and rose again to save us—to Cornelius and his household. At first, Peter probably thought the Gentiles would reject the message of the gospel. But God touched the hearts of the Gentiles and poured out his Holy Spirit upon them, just as he had upon the Jews, showing that God wanted to save people of all nations. As a result, the Gentiles accepted the message and believed. The apostle Paul wrote, "For I am not ashamed of the gospel, for it is the power of God for salvation to everyone who believes, to the Jew first and also to the Greek" (Romans 1:16).

Talk about It

:: What did Peter share with Cornelius and his household? *(Peter shared the story of Jesus—the gospel—with Cornelius and his household.)*

:: What did Peter say God would give everyone who believes in Jesus? *(Peter said that God would give forgiveness to everyone who believes in Jesus.)*

:: Reread Peter's words to Cornelius. How does what he said help us to know what we need to believe? *(We need to believe the very same things. We need to believe that Jesus died and that he was raised from the dead so that we can be forgiven for our sins.)*

 Pray about It

Thank Jesus for dying on the cross to save people from every nation.

DAY FOUR

Remember It

What has God been teaching you this week through our Bible story?

 Read Acts 10:45—11:18.

Think about It Some More

When Peter returned to Jerusalem, some Jewish believers were not happy that he had gone to eat with the Gentiles. They felt Peter had broken God's laws. But when Peter explained that the Holy Spirit had fallen upon the Gentiles so that they believed in Jesus and spoke in tongues, the men rejoiced and worshiped God. They could not argue with what God had done.

It took a while for the Jews to get used to having Gentiles in the church. Some Jews wanted to require the Gentiles to follow the Jewish laws as a requirement to be saved. But the apostle Paul said that that would be "adding to the gospel," so he spoke strongly against forcing the Gentiles to obey the Jewish law (Galatians 2:15–21).

Anytime we make good works a requirement for salvation, we destroy God's gospel of grace. Paul said, "For by grace you have been saved through faith. And this is not your own doing; it is the gift of God, not a result of works, so that no one may boast" (Ephesians 2:8–9).

Talk about It

> KIDS, ask your parents if they were ever surprised at someone God saved.

(Parents, think of someone whom you thought would never turn to the gospel, but whom God saved. If you can't think of anyone, remind your children of the thief on the cross who was saved. No living person is out of reach of the gospel.)

:: What happened to the Gentiles when Peter preached the gospel to them? *(God gave them new life in him and filled them with the Holy Spirit, and they began to speak in tongues. [Parents, for a description of tongues, see 1 Corinthians 14:2.])*

:: Why were the Jews amazed when they saw the Holy Spirit fall upon the Gentiles? *(The Jews had been taught that the Gentiles were unclean, so they were surprised to see God saving them.)*

:: What did Peter command when he saw the Holy Spirit fall upon the Gentiles? *(Peter commanded them to be baptized.)*

Pray about It

Praise God that he doesn't have favorites when it comes to the gospel. Thank him for dying for all people and offering all people the gift of his Holy Spirit.

DAY FIVE

Discover It

Today is the day we look at a different Bible passage—from the book of Psalms or one of the prophets—to see what we can learn from it about Jesus or our salvation.

 Read Zechariah 9:10–11.

Think about It Some More

Earlier in this chapter, Zechariah said that the king would one day come into Jerusalem riding on a donkey. We know that he was talking about Jesus. In our verses today, Zechariah went on to explain that this king would bring peace to the nations.

When the Jews read these verses, they assumed the king in Zechariah's prophecy would bring peace by winning a great battle over the enemies of Jerusalem. But Jesus didn't come to win an earthly war for the Jews. Jesus came to win a victory over sin and death by taking the punishment we deserved for our sins so that we could have peace with God.

When Zechariah talked about the "blood of my covenant," he was pointing to the day when Jesus was going to shed his blood on the cross to make a way for people of every nation to be saved. Even back in Zechariah's day, God planned to save both Jew and Gentile.

Talk about It

:: To whom did Zechariah say the king would bring peace? *(Parents, for your younger children, you may want to reread this passage, and when you get to the word* nations *change your tone of voice to give the children a verbal clue that God would bring peace to the nations and rule to the ends of the earth.)*

:: How does this Bible passage fit with our story in which we learned that God wanted to deliver the Gentiles along with the Jews? *(Israel was only one nation. If God was going to bring peace to all nations, he was going to save the Gentiles too.)*

:: Zechariah talks about the "blood of my covenant." What is the "blood of my covenant" about? *(The phrase "blood of my covenant" points forward to the day when Jesus shed his blood on the cross.)*

 Pray about It

Praise God for coming up with a plan that would rescue people from every nation.

The Fruit of the Spirit

Story 130 – *The Gospel Story Bible*

Note: This lesson contains several references to circumcision. Given the key role of circumcision in the Bible, it might be good to tactfully explain its meaning to your grade-school children. Once your children learn to read, they will discover references to circumcision throughout the Bible.

Beforehand, collect at least three types of fruit that come from trees (e.g., an apple, an orange, and a pear). Gather your children and show them the fruit, one by one. As you hold up the different kinds of fruit, ask your children to tell you what kind of tree it grows on. Then ask them how they can tell fruit trees apart. Help them get to the conclusion that you can tell the kind of tree by the fruit that it bears. For example, you will never find an apple growing on an orange tree. Then explain that it is the same in our lives. Say, "You can tell if the Spirit of God lives in a person by the fruit of the Spirit at work in their lives. This week we will learn to recognize the fruit of the Spirit."

DAY ONE

Picture It

During the Civil War, Abraham Lincoln and the Union army freed the slaves of the South. But even though tens of thousands of slaves were given their freedom, they didn't all walk away from slavery. Many had been slaves all their lives and didn't know any other way to live. They had to be taught what freedom from slavery was all about and how to live as free people. The same is true for new Christians who had always lived as slaves to the law trying to get to heaven by doing good deeds.

In our Bible passage today, Paul is trying to teach the new Christians about God's grace—that Jesus has set them free from the law.

 Read Galatians 5:1–15.

Think about It Some More

Some of the Jews were confusing the new Gentile Christians, telling them that believing in Jesus was not enough. They said a man also had to be circumcised before God would accept him into his family. But Paul knew that was wrong. They didn't need to add circumcision to what Jesus did—Jesus' death was all they needed. To fight this false teaching, Paul told the new believers that Jesus had set them free from their slavery to the law and that if they went back to circumcision, it would be like giving up their freedom to go back into slavery.

Talk about It

:: What is circumcision? *(Parents, you can skip this question if you feel your children are too young, but remember that you will continue to hear it throughout the Bible. Consider telling your younger children that circumcision was when they cut off a little flap of skin off a man to show that he was a part of God's family. Most of the time they did this while he was an infant, but that mark remained there for the rest of his life. For older children, you can give them more detail if you want.)*

:: Some were saying that Jesus' death was not enough; that the law had to be added to it. Why is that bad? *(If we say we have to add the law to what Jesus did, it means Jesus failed to take away our sins.)*

:: Paul said that circumcision doesn't count anymore because it can't save us. What *does* save us? *(Parents, if you have younger children, reread verse 6 again and have them raise their hands when they hear the answer: faith working through love. Then explain that faith is believing in Jesus.)*

 Pray about It

Thank Jesus for setting us free from the law by following the law perfectly, then dying for our sins and rising again in victory.

DAY TWO

Remember It

What do you remember about yesterday's story? What do you think is going to happen today?

 Read Galatians 5:16–23.

Think about It Some More

Just like an apple tree bears apples, Christians filled with the Holy Spirit should bear the fruit of the Spirit in their lives. But because we are still sinners, we can ignore the Holy Spirit and live for ourselves instead. When we do that, we bear bad fruit. It is kind of like an apple tree with rotten apples. The Holy Spirit is at work enabling us to bear good fruit, while our sinful nature (Paul calls this our *flesh*) wants us to turn away from God to enjoy the things of the world instead. When we follow our sinful nature, all kinds of bad fruit—like anger, jealousy, and idolatry—show up in our lives. That is why Paul encouraged new believers to walk by the Spirit so that they would see the fruit of the Spirit.

Talk about It

:: What is the fruit of the Spirit? *(Parents, this is a great list for young children to memorize. If you have younger children, you might want to reread verses 22–23 and then ask them again if they can remember one of the things Paul lists as the fruit of the Spirit. They are love, joy, peace, patience, kindness, goodness, faithfulness, gentleness, and self-control.)*

:: Can you name at least one of the bad fruits of sin in our lives that Paul calls works of our flesh? *(Parents, many of the sins listed are hard to explain to young children. Focus on anger, jealousy, or idolatry [loving something more than God].)*

:: Which fruit of the Spirit do you most need the Holy Spirit to help grow in you? *(Parents, draw out your children and help them look at their own lives.)*

 Pray about It

Ask God to help you walk by the Spirit—to love God and obey his commands—so that you will see the fruit of the Spirit in your life.

DAY THREE

Connect It to the Gospel

Today is the day we connect this week's Bible story to the gospel. The gospel is the life, death, and resurrection of Jesus for our salvation. Can anyone guess how our story this week looks forward to or back at the gospel?

 Read Galatians 5:24.

Think about It Some More

When you read through the list of the fruit of the Spirit, nothing on the list seems too difficult to do. Everybody wants to be loving and joyful and patient. The problem is that we are all sinners. Sin spoils our fruit just like rot and worms can spoil an apple. So, instead of loving freely, we expect people to give us love. If they don't, we get impatient and angry because our love is selfish. That is why we need the Holy Spirit.

The Holy Spirit reminds us of what Jesus did in giving up his life for us (John 14:26), and he empowers us to do the good works God planned for us to walk in even before we were born (Ephesians 2:10). The Holy Spirit also helps us to see that sin is trying to destroy us (Galatians 6:8). Once we clearly see the truth about our sin, we can turn to God and away from sin. As we turn from sin and walk by faith, the Holy Spirit fills our hearts with his fruit, enabling us to do the good works God planned for us. That is what Paul meant when he said "Those who belong to Christ have crucified [killed] the flesh."

Peter said, "Make every effort to supplement your faith with virtue, and virtue with knowledge, and knowledge with self-control, and self-control with steadfastness, and steadfastness with godliness, and godliness with brotherly affection, and brotherly affection with love" (2 Peter 1:5–7). Notice how he mentions the fruit of the Spirit here in his encouragement for us to live for God.

Talk about It

:: To whom did Paul say we need to belong in order to kill our sin? (*Paul said we need to belong to Jesus. That means we give our lives to him and then trust him to show us our sin, to give us the grace to repent, and to enable us to walk by faith.*)

:: Paul said we need to crucify our sinful desires and passions. What does it mean to crucify our sin? *(Parents, give your children a clue by asking them what happened to Jesus when he was crucified. Jesus died. So then what does it mean when we crucify our sin? It means that we kill it.)*

:: Who enables us to kill sin in our lives? *(The Holy Spirit enables us to kill sin. Without the Holy Spirit, we would not have good fruit in our lives. But when we believe in Jesus, when we belong to Jesus, he sends his Holy Spirit to live inside of us, and it is the Spirit of God who changes our desires so that we love God more than the world and live for God instead of living for ourselves.)*

 ## Pray about It

Ask the Holy Spirit to help you kill sin and live for Jesus.

DAY FOUR

Remember It

What has God been teaching you this week through our Bible story?

 Read Galatians 5:25—6:1.

Think about It Some More

If we remember that we are all sinners, it will help keep us from thinking we are better than other people when they sin. When we do see others sin, we should correct them gently, remembering that the next time it might be we who need correction. Sadly, it is easy to correct others harshly. That is why Paul warned us to keep a watch over our own lives so that we don't fall into the same sin ourselves.

Talk about It

> ● ● KIDS, ask your parents whom God has used to
> ● ● help them in their fight against sin.

(Parents, think of whom God has placed in your life to gently correct you. Pride would want us to hide our weaknesses from our children, but it is very helpful for them to know you are a sinner who needs the help of others.)

:: What does it look like to correct a person with gentleness? *(Parents, help your children here. They will be better able to demonstrate this than explain it. Ask them to pretend their brother, sister, or friend was selfish and grabbed a toy away from another child. Act out how they could correct them gently.)*

:: What does it feel like when someone corrects you harshly? *(When someone corrects us harshly it makes us feel sad, and it is not encouraging. That is why, when we correct others, we should correct with gentleness.)*

:: When are you most tempted to be harsh in your corrections? *(Parents, take the lead and confess first, then draw out your children.)*

 Pray about It

Ask God to help you correct with gentleness when people around you sin.

DAY FIVE

Discover It

Today is the day we look at a different Bible passage—from the book of Psalms or one of the prophets—to see what we can learn from it about Jesus or our salvation.

 Read Jeremiah 9:23–26.

Think about It Some More

When God changed Abram's name to Abraham, he told him that every son should be circumcised when he was eight days old (Genesis 17:12). Abraham obeyed God, and for hundreds and hundreds of years the people of Israel circumcised their sons as a reminder that they were a part of God's people. But when Jeremiah spoke, he said a time was coming when circumcision was not going to be good enough.

Jeremiah said that God's people would also need to be circumcised in their hearts. In Romans 2:29, the apostle Paul tells us that Israel's circumcision pointed to the day when Jesus would circumcise hearts by saving them and sending the Holy Spirit to come and live inside of them. Jeremiah was trying to tell Israel that an outward mark on their body was not enough to change them on the inside.

Talk about It

:: What does the word *boasting* mean? *(Parents, younger children will have no idea what boasting is. The best way to show them is to demonstrate boasting by saying, "I am the greatest person. Nobody is as good as I am. I can do everything better than everyone else. I have a nicer house, a nicer car, more money, and I am smarter than anyone else." You can use the words* bragging *and* pride *to help them understand what boasting means.)*

:: Jeremiah said there were some things about God that we could boast about. What were some of the things he listed? *(Parents, if you have younger children, reread verse 24 and have them raise their hands when they hear the answer. Jeremiah said we can boast that our God practices steadfast love, justice, and righteousness.)*

:: What is the most amazing thing God did that we can boast about? *(The most amazing thing we should boast about is that Jesus died on the cross so that we could be forgiven, and that he then sent his Holy Spirit to enable us to live for Jesus.)*

✋ Pray about It

Praise God for his steadfast love, justice, and righteousness. His steadfast love never ends, his judgments are always good, and he is perfectly righteous.

Week 53

The Body of Christ

Story 131 – *The Gospel Story Bible*

Tell your children the following story. "There once was a baseball team where no one wanted to play in the outfield. They all wanted to play the bases and pitch. When their coach tried to correct them, they told him they didn't need a coach, and they chased him away. For some games they had three first basemen and two pitchers with no one in the outfield. The pitchers fought over every ball returned by the catcher, and the first basemen would push each other off and say, 'I don't need you here.' When the opposing team hit the ball into the outfield, no one wanted to chase it. As a result of their foolishness, they never won a single game. What was wrong with this team? This week we will learn how Christians are to work together as a team."

DAY ONE

Picture It

A beehive is a little bit like the church. God gave different bees different gifts and jobs to make the hive run smoothly. There is a queen bee, which lays the eggs, and drones, which take care of the queen. The nurse bees feed the babies, while the workers go out looking for food. There are bees that guard the hive and there are air conditioning bees that stay at the entrance of the hive and buzz their wings to keep the hive cool. God ordered all honeybee hives to work this way. The bees have different jobs and gifts to bless the whole hive and help it run well. Today we will learn how God, by his Spirit, is at work in the church in much the same way. The Holy Spirit is the one who gives different people different gifts. When we all work together, the church runs smoothly.

 Read 1 Corinthians 12:1–11.

Think about It Some More

The apostle Paul wrote to the Corinthian church because there was a lot of arguing going on in that church. (See 1 Corinthians 1:11–12; 3:1–4; and 6:1–11.) Instead of encouraging one another and working together, the Corinthians loved to boast about themselves. That was probably why Paul reminded them that all our gifts come from the Holy Spirit. If God is the one who gives out gifts, and if he gives them as he wants, then we shouldn't think we are special for having a certain gift, and we shouldn't look down on others who have other gifts.

Talk about It

:: Who did Paul say gives all the gifts to the people in the church? *(Paul said the Holy Spirit is the one who gives the gifts to people in the church.)*

:: Why did Paul say God gave spiritual gifts to the church? *(Parents, if you have younger children, reread verse 7. When you get to the words "common good," change the tone of your voice so they will know that is the answer. Then explain that God gave the gifts of the church to bless everyone in the church, not so that the person with the gift would boast or think he or she was better.)*

:: Why is it important to remember that spiritual gifts are given by God for the good of the church? *(It would be very easy for a person to think he is better than others because of his gifts. People often use these gifts to exalt themselves and not Christ. This is what was happening in the Corinthian church. People were boasting that they were more spiritual than others because of their gifts.)*

:: How have you been tempted to boast in your gifts or accomplishments? *(Help your children see how they might have boasted in a gift or achievement so they can identify with the challenges the Corinthians were facing.)*

 Pray about It

Pray that God would help you always remember that all our gifts are meant to serve the body of Christ for the glory of God, not for our own glory.

DAY TWO

Remember It

What do you remember about yesterday's story? What do you think is going to happen today?

 Read 1 Corinthians 12:12–26.

Think about It Some More

Paul's description of the church as a body can really help us see how we need to work together to help one another. What if on Sunday, twenty different people wanted to preach the sermon but no one wanted to work on the sound board? What if none of the choir members wanted to sing because they all wanted to be the director? With people unwilling to serve one another, the church would not run smoothly.

That is why Paul reminded the Corinthians that God gave us each a place in the church to serve. Instead of wanting the important jobs or looking down at those who serve in the lesser jobs, we should remember that we are all called to serve each other, working together like the parts of the body to help the church run well. Instead of boasting or competing against each other, we should be serving one another.

Talk about It

:: How does the picture of a body help us to see that we need each other in the church? *(Imagine a leg trying to walk around without the rest of the body, or an eye trying to take hold of something it sees. The only way the body works is if all its parts work together.)*

:: Paul talks about two different problems in the body. Can you figure out what they are? *(Parents, if you have younger children, feel free to give them some clues. The first problem is when people don't like the part of the body they are and want to be a different part. This speaks of jealousy or self-pity among members who long to be a different part of the body. The second problem is when a part of the body does not think it needs the other parts. This speaks of a person's pride in thinking he doesn't need others.)*

:: How does God want us to work as a body? *(Parents, draw out your children here. Paul gives the answer in verses 24–26. If your children don't remember, reread those verses and have them raise their hands when they hear a way God wants us to work together in the church.)*

 Pray about It

Ask God to help you look for a place where you can serve in church so that you can become an active part of the body.

DAY THREE _____

Connect It to the Gospel

Today is the day we connect this week's Bible story to the gospel. The gospel is the life, death, and resurrection of Jesus for our salvation. Can anyone guess how our story this week looks forward to or back at the gospel?

 Read 1 Corinthians 12:27.

Think about It Some More

The apostle Paul compared the Corinthians to a body with different parts that contribute in different ways—eyes see, ears hear, and feet carry us places. We need all the parts to make the body work. In the verse we read today, Paul revealed a wonderful mystery—that the body of the church is the body of Jesus Christ. Paul was not trying to say that one person is the foot of Jesus while another is the elbow of Jesus. We don't make up a real physical body; we make up a spiritual body, because Jesus lives in us. We represent Jesus when we reach out to the world with our hands in service, when we speak out to the world with the message of the gospel, and when we walk alongside them so they can see Christ in our lives. Sports teams identify themselves with a city, like the Dallas Cowboys or the Pittsburgh Steelers, but we identify ourselves by Jesus Christ, who sacrificed his life in our place to take the punishment for our sins and who now lives inside of us by his Spirit. That is why we are called Christians.

Talk about It

:: What body did Paul say all Christians are a part of? *(We are all a part of the body of Christ.)*

:: When we all work together as the body of Christ, what things can we do? *(We can help each other, like a hand washes another part of the body; and we can speak God's Word, as a mouth speaks words of encouragement.)*

:: What part does your family play in the body of Christ? Where do your parents or brothers and sisters serve and use their gifts? *(Parents, tell your children how you are connected to the church in service and ministry.)*

 Pray about It

Ask God to show your family, as part of the body of Christ, ways you can serve, help one another, and reach out to the lost.

DAY FOUR

Remember It

What has God been teaching you this week through our Bible story?

 Read 1 Corinthians 12:27–31.

Think about It Some More

There are a lot of gifts at work in the body of Christ, the church. We need pastors to teach, administrators to help the church run smoothly, and people to pray for the sick. All of these gifts are important. Just as a baseball team can't do well if everyone wants to be the pitcher, a church won't do well if everyone wants to be a teacher. A church will also do poorly if nobody wanted to lead because everyone wanted to serve. Paul said we should ask God to bless us with more gifts to help the church grow stronger and be able to reach more people for Jesus.

Talk about It

> KIDS, ask your parents what gifts they think God has given you and how they think you might use them in church.

(Parents, take some time to encourage your children and help them see how God might want to use them as part of his body. There are ways our children can serve, teach, and encourage in the church right now.)

:: Why wouldn't it be good if everyone in the church had the same gift? *(There are a lot of different jobs to do. Remember, Paul said that if the whole body were an eye we wouldn't be able to hear. If everyone wanted to preach, who would serve? If everyone wanted to serve, who would preach?)*

:: Which gifts would you want God to give to you? *(Parents, encourage your children to seek after the gifts of the Spirit here. Perhaps you can already see a hint of how God might want to use them. If so, encourage your children with what you see.)*

 Pray about It

Ask God to pour out his gifts upon your family.

DAY FIVE _____

Discover It

Today is the day we look at a different Bible passage—from the book of Psalms or one of the prophets—to see what we can learn from it about Jesus or our salvation.

 Read Hosea 2:14–20.

Think about It Some More

Did you know that the body of Christ, the church, is also called the bride of Christ? That is the way God describes the church in Revelation 21:2. Hosea used the word *betrothed,* a word that describes the promise a man makes when he pledges to marry a woman. God promised to be married to his people forever. Hosea also said that, once the wedding day comes, God would help his people turn away from idols like Baal and turn to the Lord and call him their husband instead. In that day, all of our sin will be taken away so that we can love God in faithfulness and righteousness forever. And God will take away all fighting so we can live with one another and with God in peace.

Talk about It

:: Who is the husband in this Bible passage? *(God)*

:: Who is the bride who marries the husband? *(God's people)*

:: Why do you think God chose the image of marriage to help us understand his love for us? *(Marriage is for life, so that tells us God will love us forever. Marriage is about love, so that tells us that if God wants us to be his bride he must love us very much.)*

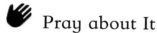 Pray about It

Thank God for loving us so much that he wants us to be his bride in heaven forever.

Week 54

Love

Story 132 – *The Gospel Story Bible*

Gather some large pot lids and wooden spoons. If your spouse is available to help you, he or she can grab a lid or two, as well. After announcing it is time for Bible study, bang the lids with the spoons, making as much noise as you can. After a brief pause, choose a familiar song to sing and go at it again even louder. After your children have had enough, stop and ask them what they think of your music. Once you draw them out, explain that God compares the noise of a clanging gong or cymbal to a person who does not love. Say, "This week we will read and study Paul's famous chapter on love."

DAY ONE

Picture It

Imagine that you were an inventor who created a mighty robot that could do amazing feats if you programmed it with information. You could program it to lift up your car so you could change a tire without using a jack. You could program it to carry the groceries in from the car and put them away.

But there is one thing your robot could never be for you: He couldn't be a friend to show you love. You could program it with a voice to say, "I love you" or to hold out its arm to shake your hand, but something would be missing. Without the ability to feel and express love from the heart, a robot is just a machine and could never truly be a friend. Today and all week long we are going to learn how important love really is.

 Read 1 Corinthians 13:1–3.

Think about It Some More

God had blessed the Corinthians by giving them the gifts of tongues and prophecy, but rather than using these gifts with humility, they boasted about their gifts and how special they were to have them. Paul compared the use of their gifts to noisy gongs and clanging cymbals. When a gong or cymbal is played at the right time in a song, it adds beauty to the music. But if you play it in the wrong place, it just makes noise and ruins the song. That is what was happening with gifts in the Corinthian church. Instead of using them to bless the other believers, they were using them to boast.

Talk about It

:: Why is love the most important gift of all? *(Parents, draw your children out here; there is no one right answer to this question. Love can be used alongside all other gifts.)*

:: Why did Paul use the example of a noisy gong or clanging cymbals to represent a person who isn't showing love? *(Gongs and cymbals can be loud and jarring when not played correctly. If a person is not showing love to others, he is hard to live with. He annoys and hurts the people around him.)*

:: List at least three gifts that you see among your family members. Then talk about how a person could use those gifts in a loving way. *(You could come up with talents like running fast, jumping high, or singing, as well as biblical gifts like wisdom, hospitality, leadership, or other spiritual gifts, for all of these can be used in loving or unloving ways.)*

 Pray about It

Ask God to help you use all your gifts and talents in loving ways.

DAY TWO

Remember It

What do you remember about yesterday's Bible passage? What do you think we will learn about today?

 Read 1 Corinthians 13:4–7.

Think about It Some More

The word *love* is overused. We love pizza. We love a favorite toy. We love sports teams, the beach, and a million other things. But Paul described love differently. He didn't say that love is like your favorite flavor of ice cream or a trip to an indoor pool in the winter. Paul also didn't say that love is something we *feel*. He didn't call love wonderful, delightful, or passionate. Paul wanted us to see that true biblical love is all about serving, forgiving, and sacrificing ourselves for others. If you were to look at his list, you would have to say that love is not about what we get, but what we give to others.

Talk about It

:: In this passage, what are some of the ways Paul tells us to love? *(Parents, if your younger children can't remember, reread the passage and have them raise their hands when they hear the answer.)*

:: Why can't we use God's description of love to love something like ice cream? *(Even though there is a sense in which you can enjoy ice cream, you can't be patient or kind toward ice cream, like Paul is talking about. God's love is something we show people, not objects or food.)*

:: What on Paul's list do you think is hardest for you to do in loving your family? *(Parents, go back over the list and explain some of them. For example, many kids insist on getting their own way and have a difficult time being patient. Try to help your children see their weaknesses. Then later on in the week remind them to ask the Holy Spirit to help them love those around them if they fall back into that same sin pattern.)*

Pray about It

Ask God to help you love the people in your family his way.

DAY THREE _____

Connect It to the Gospel

Today is the day we connect this week's Bible story to the gospel. The gospel is the life, death, and resurrection of Jesus for our salvation. Can anyone guess how our story this week looks forward to or back at the gospel?

 Read 1 John 4:10–20.

Think about It Some More

The best way to learn how to do something is to watch someone who is better at it than you are. John knew that the best way for us to learn how to love one another was look at the way God loved us. God loved us so much that he sent his only Son to die on the cross for our sins (John 3:16).

John said that God sent his Son to be a *propitiation* for our sins. That means that Jesus took our place and our punishment so we could be right with God. Remembering that God gave up his only Son so that we could be forgiven should help us to be more willing to forgive others. That is why John said, "If God so loved us, we also ought to love one another" (1 John 4:11). This is only possible if we have been united with Christ and if we abide with Christ (1 John 4:13). *Abiding* means "staying with" or "remaining with."

Talk about It

:: What did God do to show us his love? *(God gave up his only Son, Jesus, to die on the cross to show us his love.)*

:: What did John call someone who says she loves God, but doesn't love her brother? *(Parents, reread verse 20 if your younger children don't remember that John called that kind of person a liar. The reason he calls her a liar is that if you really love God then you should want to be like him and show love to others.)*

:: Can you think of a way we can love others like God loved us? *(We can forgive others when they sin against us, because that is what God did for us.)*

 Pray about It

Thank God for showing his love by giving up what he loved the most, his only Son, Jesus. Ask him to help you love others by forgiving them when they sin against you.

DAY FOUR

Remember It

What has God been teaching you this week through our Bible story?

 Read 1 Corinthians 13:8–13.

Think about It Some More

Love is the one gift in the Bible that will never end. Paul says that when Jesus comes back one day, we won't need gifts like prophecy or tongues because Jesus himself will teach us and lead us into truth. But love is different. Every time we look at the nail marks in Jesus' hands and feet, we will remember the love he showed for us, and we will want to worship him to show him love in return. That is why Paul wanted the Corinthians to make sure, if there was one gift they got right, it should be the one that will last forever—love.

Talk about It

> KIDS, ask your parents what was the greatest demonstration of love they have ever seen or heard about.

(Parents, try to think of a sacrificial act that parallels the gospel, such as a father giving up something for his child. Or think of a wonderful act of forgiveness a person extended toward another. Then connect your story to the gospel. Remind your children that we love because God first loved us. See 1 John 4:19.)

:: What is the one gift God said is going to last forever? *(love)*

:: What did Paul say was going to happen to the gifts of prophecy and tongues and knowledge? *(Parents, if your younger children can't remember, reread verse 8, changing your voice a bit when you say* prophecies, tongues, *and* knowledge. *Then see if your children can repeat them back to you.)*

:: What is the greatest gift of all? *(love)*

Pray about It

Thank God for giving us the best gift of all—everlasting love.

DAY FIVE

Discover It

Today is the day we look at a different Bible passage—from the book of Psalms or one of the prophets—to see what we can learn from it about Jesus or our salvation.

 Read Psalm 31:1–8.

Think about It Some More

Just before Jesus died, he spoke the words of this verse, "Father, into your hands I commit my spirit!" (Luke 23:46). The centurion who heard him said, "Certainly this man was innocent!" (Luke 23:47). Jesus' death on the cross was the greatest demonstration of love of all time. David, the writer of this psalm, didn't know all about what Jesus was going to do. But he did know that God's love was a steadfast love that never gives up and never fails.

Because of God's steadfast love, David knew that God would not give him over to his enemies. Instead, King David believed that God would take care of him. He placed his faith in God's salvation. Even though he didn't know all the details of how God would save through Jesus, he trusted by faith God's plan just the same.

Talk about It

:: What was Jesus' attitude when he was dying on the cross? *(Jesus was loving and forgiving.)*

:: What does it mean when the Bible tells us that God's love is steadfast? (Steadfast *means that God's love doesn't run out or end. Parents, a great psalm to read that talks about God's steadfast love is Psalm 136, which uses the phrase, "his steadfast love endures forever," twenty-six times, once in every verse.)*

:: Read aloud Luke 23:46–47 where Jesus quoted part of David's psalm. How did Jesus' words affect the centurion? *(The centurion saw that even with Jesus' very last breath, he wasn't bitter or angry and did not speak an unkind word. He could tell that Jesus was no ordinary man and that he was innocent.)*

 Pray about It

Thank God that his love for us never ends and ask him to help us to love others like he loves us.

Week 55

Paul's Work in Ephesus

Story 133 – *The Gospel Story Bible*

You will need several of one type of seed for this lesson: for example, kernels of popcorn, sunflower seeds, or kidney beans. Let your children examine the seeds. Ask them what they are. If they say popcorn or sunflower, keep drawing them out to see if they can come up with the idea that it is a seed. Ask, "What do you need to do with a seed to sprout it?" The answer is that you have to plant it and water it.

Then ask, "Who makes the seed grow?" The answer is that only God can make it grow. Say, "Paul used this same illustration to explain how the church grows. Paul planted seeds by sharing the gospel. Teachers like Apollos watered the seed by continuing the work of ministry after Paul left. But only God could make it grow; God is the one who gives faith to make the seed of the gospel in someone's heart grow." (See 1 Corinthians 3:6.)

DAY ONE

Picture It

There once was a very young girl whose father gave her a balsa wood airplane kit. The next day, the girl opened the plastic packaging and put the airplane together. But because she hadn't yet learned to read, she couldn't follow the directions. She put all the wooden pieces together following the picture on the front label, but left off the long rubber band, which was meant to power the propeller. To fly the plane she threw it by hand, though it didn't go very far.

When the father came home, he noticed the plane and asked about the rubber band. The little child explained that the picture didn't show the rubber band so she left it in the package. The father smiled and said that the rubber band was meant to power the propeller. Within minutes the rubber band was in place and the little girl shouted with excitement as the plane soared through the air, the propeller powered by the tightly twisted rubber band. Things were much different now that the plane had power.

Today in our story you will read about a group of people in a city called Ephesus. They heard about John the Baptist and the ministry of Jesus, but they didn't have the full teaching of the gospel and the power of the Holy Spirit. Let's see how they were changed by the power of God.

 Read Acts 18:24—19:7.

Think about It Some More

Apollos taught people about Jesus, but he didn't have the whole story. His message was like the balsa wood plane without the power of the rubber band. He didn't have the full teaching of the gospel—the story of Jesus' death and resurrection, which is the power of God for our salvation. In the same way, the disciples whom Paul met in the city of Ephesus had been taught about Jesus but they didn't have the power of the gospel either, and they didn't know anything about the Holy Spirit. Once Paul explained the gospel to them, they believed and were filled with the Holy Spirit in great power and began to speak in tongues and prophesy.

Talk about It

:: Apollos and the disciples in Ephesus knew only about John's baptism and the beginning of Jesus' ministry. What were they missing? *(They were missing the most important components of the gospel, that Jesus had died on the cross for their sins, risen again, and sent his Holy Spirit to live in his people.)*

:: What happened to the disciples in Ephesus once they understood the gospel? *(They were baptized and filled with the Holy Spirit and began to speak in tongues and prophesy.)*

:: What part of the story of Jesus has the power to save us? *(We can know all about Jesus as a good teacher or a miracle worker and still not be saved from our sins. For it is believing that Jesus died for our sins and rose again in victory that has the power to change our hearts by the Holy Spirit.)*

Pray about It

Thank Jesus for giving us the power of the gospel so that everyone who believes can be saved from their sins.

DAY TWO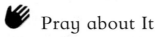

Remember It

What do you remember about yesterday's story? What do you think is going to happen today?

Read Acts 19:8–12.

Think about It Some More

Paul was patient with the Jews of Ephesus, for he loved the Jewish people and desperately wanted them to believe and be forgiven. Later, in Paul's letter to the Romans, he wrote that he was very sad that the people of Israel had rejected Jesus. He said that if it were possible to trade away his salvation so that they could be saved, he would do it (Romans 9:2–4). But after three months of preaching and explaining, the Jews still refused to believe. So Paul took his disciples and began to reach out to the Gentiles instead. God blessed Paul's ministry and used Paul to perform powerful healings and touch many with the gospel.

Talk about It

:: Why did Paul stop teaching the Jews in the synagogue? *(The Jews refused to believe and spoke evil things against the Christians.)*

:: How did God turn the unbelief of the Jews into a blessing for others? *(After Paul left the synagogue, people from all over Asia heard the gospel, and many believed.)*

:: How long did Paul stay in Ephesus teaching the church after he left the synagogue? *(Parents, reread the passage for your younger children and have them raise their hands when they hear the correct answer: two years.)*

:: Who did the extraordinary miracles? *(God did the miracles through Paul. We always need to remember that God is the power behind all the miracles performed in the Bible. This passage tells us how God was behind the scenes working through men like Paul.)*

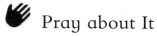 Pray about It

Praise God for the way he uses ordinary people to do extraordinary things.

DAY THREE

Connect It to the Gospel

Today is the day we connect this week's Bible story to the gospel. The gospel is the life, death, and resurrection of Jesus for our salvation. Can anyone guess how our story this week looks forward to or back at the gospel?

 Read Acts 20:17–27.

Think about It Some More

After leaving Ephesus to take the gospel to the land of Macedonia, Paul returned for one last visit with the pastors of the Ephesian church on his way back to Jerusalem. When the Ephesian pastors (elders) arrived, Paul thought back to how their church had first begun. Paul reminded them how he had preached the gospel in public and from house to house to both Jews and Gentiles. Every chance Paul got, he made sure that everyone remembered that the gospel is the message that can change people's lives. Paul taught that men should repent of, or turn away from, their sins and put their faith in Jesus Christ. That simple gospel message has never changed, and it is the same message we teach today.

Talk about It

:: We learn from verse 21 that there were two things Paul said he'd taught the Ephesians. What were they? *(Parents, if you have younger children, reread the verse and have them raise their hands when they hear the correct answer. Paul taught that people should repent of their sins against God and have faith in Jesus.)*

:: What did the Holy Spirit say was going to happen to Paul in Jerusalem? *(The Holy Spirit told Paul that imprisonment and afflictions awaited him in Jerusalem.)*

:: Why would Paul go to Jerusalem if he knew it was going to be dangerous? *(Paul said that preaching the gospel was more important than being safe from the danger he would face.)*

 Pray about It

Ask God to give you courage to share the gospel with people you meet and not be afraid of what they might say or think about you.

DAY FOUR _____

Remember It

What has God been teaching you this week through our Bible story?

 Read Acts 20:28–32.

Think about It Some More

A brand new bicycle costs over one hundred dollars. A brand new car costs thousands. A brand new house costs hundreds of thousands. A brand new jet airplane costs millions of dollars. But it cost Jesus his priceless life to buy back the people of God—the church—from the curse of sin and the punishment we deserved. All the gold and all the money of the whole world put together was not enough to buy salvation for one soul. By dying on the cross for our sins, Jesus paid the cost of forgiveness for everyone who believes in him. That is why Paul wanted the Ephesian pastors to take special care of the people of God.

Talk about It

> ● ● KIDS, ask your parents what the most valuable
> ● ● item in your whole house is and why it is so valu-
>   able.

(Parents, think of your china or crystal or a valuable piece of furniture, then tell your children why it is valuable.)

:: Why did Paul say the church was so valuable? *(The church cost Jesus his life. Jesus shed his blood on the cross to purchase the salvation of all those who believe.)*

:: What did Paul say the Ephesian pastors should do to protect the church? *(Paul said they should watch out and be alert for false teachers. Paul called these false teachers wolves who would try to twist the Word of God to lead the people away from the truth.)*

 Pray about It

Thank Jesus for giving up his priceless life, so that we could be delivered from our sins and brought into the family of God.

DAY FIVE

Discover It

Today is the day we look at a different Bible passage—from the book of Psalms or one of the prophets—to see what we can learn from it about Jesus or our salvation.

 Read Isaiah 45:21–22.

Think about It Some More

Jesus is the only Savior. Jesus said, "I am the way, and the truth, and the life. No one comes to the Father except through me" (John 14:6). Compare Isaiah's words with those recorded in Acts 4:12 by Luke: "There is salvation in no one else, for there is no other name under heaven given among men by which we must be saved." Surely Isaiah's prophecy points forward to Jesus.

Talk about It

:: What did Isaiah say is the only way we can be saved? *(Isaiah said the God of Israel was the only God who can save us.)*

:: How can we tell that this passage points to Jesus? *(Jesus Christ is called our Savior in the New Testament. That is what the angel called the baby Jesus when announcing his birth to the shepherds [Luke 2:11]. Jesus also said that he came to "seek and to save" [Luke 19:10].)*

:: What do Isaiah's words tell us about all the other religions in the world that follow other gods like Buddha, Allah, and Vishnu? *(All other gods are false. Jesus is the only way for us to be saved.)*

:: What do we need to do to turn to God and be saved? *(Parents, help your children remember what Paul said he preached to the Ephesians—that we should repent of our sins and believe in Jesus. You can reread Acts 20:21 for younger children to see if they can remember the two things Paul said we need to do to be saved.)*

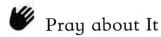 Pray about It

Ask God to help unbelievers you know to repent of (turn away from) their sins and trust in Jesus.

Week 56

A New Creation

Story 134 – *The Gospel Story Bible*

Take a look through your loose change to identify the oldest, most corroded penny and the brightest, shiniest penny you can find. Pass around the old corroded penny and have your children describe it. Tell them that when the penny was new it was bright and shiny but that it has become corroded. Explain that this is what happened to mankind after Adam and Eve sinned, and that when God forgives our sins and comes to live inside us, he makes us brand new like the second penny. As you speak, show them the new penny and pass it around. Say, "This week we will learn that when God saves us, he makes us brand new."

DAY ONE

Picture It

When you sit behind the steering wheel of a car and drive, *you* decide where that car will go. If you want to go left, you turn the wheel to the left. If you want to go right, you turn the wheel to the right. Our lives can be compared to a car that is driven by sinful desires or by our love of God. If our sinful desires are behind the wheel, we drive as fast as we can, heading directly into sin. But if the love of Christ controls that wheel, then we want to go places and do things that honor God.

 Read 2 Corinthians 5:11–15.

Think about It Some More

If you had an uncle who gave you a really great present for your birthday, you would want to please him when he came to visit you. In the same way, when we realize that God gave us the best gift of all, his Son, Jesus, we want to live to please him. That is what Paul meant when he said that Christ's love controls us (v. 14). When God opens our eyes to understand the great gift God gave us and fills us with his Spirit, God moves in our hearts so that our desire to live for God grows. Even though we still sin, the love that God had for us in sending us his Son pushes us to live for him. Day by day we grow to love and obey God more.

Talk about It

:: What did Paul say controlled him? *(the love of Christ)*

:: How did Paul say that the death of Jesus should change us (v. 15)? *(Paul said that Jesus' death should change us so that instead of living for ourselves we live for Jesus.)*

:: What was missing in the people who were boasting about their outward appearance? *(Parents, you may want to reread verse 12 to your youngest children or give your grade school kids a clue that the answer is in that verse. The people who were boasting of their outward appearance didn't have a heart that was changed to love God on the inside.)*

 Pray about It

Ask God to open your eyes to see what a wonderful gift God gave us in Jesus, and pray that God would help you to live for God and not for yourself.

DAY TWO _____

Remember It

What do you remember about yesterday's Bible passage? What do you think we will learn about today?

 Read 2 Corinthians 5:16–17.

Think about It Some More

Yesterday we learned that God's love is so amazing that it should affect the way we live. Today, Paul tells us that God changes a person so much when she becomes a Christian that he calls her a new creation.

Think of it this way: If you take a ball of clay, you can mold it into anything you want. You can create a clay pot; a snake; or a face with eyes, nose, and mouth. If, after making a clay pot, your younger brother squashes it, you could make it new again by re-creating it.

The Bible tells us that we are God's clay, and that he created us. But our lives were ruined by sin. When God forgives us, he reshapes our lives by his Holy Spirit and re-creates us to make us brand new. That is why Paul called Christians new creations, and that is why Paul said the old was gone and the new had come.

Talk about It

:: What did Paul call anyone who believes in Jesus? *(a new creation)*

:: When God makes us a new creation, what happens to the old creation? *(Parents, if you have younger children, reread verse 17 and have them raise their hands when they hear the correct answer: it passes away. God takes it away so that it is gone.)*

:: What does God put into the heart of everyone who believes in Jesus to change us so that we are a new creation? *(the Holy Spirit)*

:: Do you know anyone whose life changed radically when God made them into a new creation—from going in the direction of self and sin to going in the direction of God and his glory? *(Parents, help your children here. If they can't think of someone, remind them of your own life and how that happened to you.)*

 Pray about It

Ask God to make each person in your family one of his new creations.

DAY THREE _____

Connect It to the Gospel

Today is the day we connect this week's Bible story to the gospel. The gospel is the life, death, and resurrection of Jesus for our salvation. Can anyone guess how our story this week looks forward to or back at the gospel?

 Read 2 Corinthians 5:18–20.

Think about It Some More

The apostle Paul used forms of the word *reconciliation* five times in today's Bible passage. When two people end their fight and "make up and shake hands," you could say they reconciled. Reconciliation simply means to bring back together two people who were against each other.

As sinners, we are enemies of God. Because sin is evil, God must destroy sin, and because we are sinners, God must punish us. Our sin makes us God's enemies. But Jesus died for our sin so we can be reconciled with God. Now, instead of being God's enemy, we are God's friend. That is what the gospel does for us if we believe.

After we are saved, we become ambassadors for Christ (2 Corinthians 5:20)—we take this message of reconciliation to others. That is how God's kingdom grows.

Talk about It

:: What does the word *reconciliation* mean? (*Reconciliation means to bring together two people who were against each other.*)

:: Why do we need to be reconciled to God? (*God is holy and completely righteous. Our sin is an attack on his holiness. God must destroy sin. As sinners, we need help to change from being God's enemies to being God's friends.*)

:: Who makes it possible for us to be reconciled with God? (*Jesus does, by dying on the cross to take the punishment for sin that we deserved. That is what makes it possible for us to be reconciled to God.*)

 Pray about It

Thank Jesus for making a way for us to become God's friend instead of his enemy.

DAY FOUR _____

Remember It

What has God been teaching you this week through our Bible story?

 Read 2 Corinthians 5:20—6:2.

Think about It Some More

There are over 175 countries in the world today. That is too many countries for a leader of any one country to keep up with. That is why presidents choose ambassadors to help them talk with the officials in other countries. An ambassador's job is to be a spokesperson for the president. So if the president wanted to pass on a message to all the other countries, all the ambassadors would be gathered together, given the message, and told to deliver it to their assigned countries.

In our Bible passage today, Paul tells us that Christians are ambassadors for Christ to the world. God has a message he wants everyone to hear. It is called the gospel, the story of Jesus. Jesus, who lived a sinless life, took our sin and gave us his righteousness so that we could be forgiven, adopted into God's family, and one day go to heaven. That is the best trade anyone in the world could ever make: our sin for the righteousness of Jesus. Yet the only way for people all over the world to hear about this good news is for us to tell them.

Talk about It

> KIDS, ask your parents to tell you about a time when they were ambassadors for Christ.

(Parents, think of a time when you shared the gospel with someone who didn't know it. This could be a time when you shared your testimony with a family member, friend, or coworker.)

:: What is an ambassador? *(An ambassador is a spokesperson for another. In a country, an ambassador is chosen by the president to speak on behalf of the president to the leaders of other countries.)*

:: Why does Paul call Christians God's ambassadors? *(Paul calls us ambassadors for Christ because we have been chosen by God to speak the message of the gospel to people of all nations.)*

:: What is the wonderful trade Paul tells us we get when we trust in Jesus? *(We get to trade our sinfulness for Christ's righteousness.)*

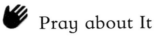 Pray about It

Ask God to use you as an ambassador to take his message to the world. Pray that he would put people in your path who need to hear his message so that you can share it with them.

DAY FIVE

Discover It

Today is the day we look at a different Bible passage—from the book of Psalms or one of the prophets—to see what we can learn from it about Jesus or our salvation.

 Read Psalm 31:9–16.

Think about It Some More

We learned last week that Jesus quoted from this psalm just before he died. So, as we continue reading this psalm, it is important to look for other clues that might point to Jesus. Although King David wrote this psalm a long time ago when *he* was suffering, his words also seem to describe the suffering of Jesus. Jesus was filled with grief and sorrow on his way to the cross, and his strength failed him to the point that the soldiers made Simon of Cyrene carry the cross for him (Mark 15:21). His disciples ran away, and the Jews spoke against him from every side.

Long before Jesus was born, God was giving prophets like David hints of how he was going to save us from our sins. Now we can look back and see how all these clues fit together to point to Jesus.

Talk about It

:: What was one way Jesus suffered while he was on the cross? (*Jesus was struck, spat upon, and had a crown of thorns pressed into his head. He was whipped, mocked, and nailed to the cross.*)

:: Verse 14 says, "I trust in you, O LORD." What does it mean to trust God? (*Parents, trust is an important word to explain to your children. Tell them that trust can mean you are giving something to someone else to take care of. So when you go on vacation you might trust a friend to take care of your pet. When you drive in the car with your parents, you trust them to get you safely home.*)

David, who wrote this psalm, trusted God to save him from his sin. Jesus trusted his Father's plan to die on the cross for our sins, and in the end he rose again from the dead in victory.)

:: Why do we need to trust God? *(We are all sinners who can't get to heaven on our own. But God promises in the Bible that if we trust Jesus, who died on the cross to take our sins away, we can get to heaven.)*

 Pray about It

Ask God to help each person in your family trust in Jesus, who suffered on the cross in our place so that we could become God's children.

Week 57

God Loves a Cheerful Giver

Story 135 – *The Gospel Story Bible*

Bring a bag of snack crackers or some other treat to Bible study. Put on your best grumbling countenance and voice, show the treats, and say something like, "I guess nobody here wants what I have. I don't know why I'm giving these to you anyway. It's a waste of money. You're just going to eat them, and then they'll be gone. For what? Spending all my money on treats. Well, go ahead, take some. Come on."

Quickly change your tone and tell your children what you were just doing wrong. Help them to see that it is not only important to do kind things like sharing, it is also important to do them with a good attitude. Say, "This week we will learn that God loves it when we give with a cheerful heart."

DAY ONE

Picture It

Imagine that you received two birthday presents from your friends. When you opened the first card, it read, "Happy Birthday, I hope you like your gift. I picked it out for you myself. Your friend, John." The second card sounded very different. It said, "Happy Birthday, my mom made me get you a present, otherwise I would not have gotten you anything. I hope you're happy. Your friend, Bob." Now in real life, a person would never write down his bad feelings in a card to you like the second person here. But sometimes people feel that way in their heart. We should always remember that God can see what is in our heart.

 Read 2 Corinthians 9:1–9.

Think about It Some More

As the gospel spread to the Gentiles, the Christians back in Jerusalem were struggling. The Jews were persecuting them, so many of them were poor and in need of help. That is why the apostle Paul decided to take up an offering for them among the Gentile churches in Asia, Macedonia, and Rome. In an earlier letter to the Corinthians, Paul told each person to set aside some money every Sunday so that when he came to visit, everyone would be ready with an offering to send to the Christians in Jerusalem. But Paul didn't tell them how much they should give. He didn't want them to feel forced to give. He wanted them to give cheerfully, motivated by all that God had done for them.

Talk about It

:: What things has God given to us? *(Parents, to help your children see that everything we have is a gift from God, keep suggesting items when they can't think of anything else. The Bible tells us that every good and perfect gift comes from God [James 1:17].)*

:: How can remembering all that God has given us, help us to give to others? *(If we remember that everything we have is a gift from God, we will be willing to share freely.)*

:: Can you think of someone you could give a gift to as a family? *(Parents, work with your children to try and think of someone who is in need and something you could give to him or her.)*

Pray about It

Pray for the person you mentioned above and ask God to help you give your gift with a cheerful heart.

DAY TWO _____

Remember It

What do you remember about yesterday's Bible passage? What do you think we will learn about today?

 Read 2 Corinthians 9:10–12.

Think about It Some More

When a farmer plants a crop, she sows more than she needs for food. This is so extra grain seeds can be collected to plant next year. But if the farmer has a bad year and a small harvest, she is faced with a difficult decision: either eat the grain meant for next year or save the extra grain as planned and go hungry this year. In a really bad year, the entire harvest might have to be eaten. Then the only way to get seeds for next year would be to buy them. But if she gave money away to the poor, there might not be enough to pay for seeds if they were needed.

Paul knew those fears weighed on the hearts of the Corinthians, so he encouraged them by reminding them that it is God who blesses a farmer with both the harvest for food and enough seeds to sow for next year's crop. They didn't have to worry, for the Lord would take care of them.

Talk about It

:: Why does a farmer have to save some grain for next year? *(The farmer uses the grain to sow the next crop.)*

:: What did Paul say God provides for the farmers? *(Paul said that it is God who provides both bread to eat and seeds to sow the next crop.)*

:: In verse 12, Paul said the Corinthians' offering for the poor would bring two blessings. What are they? *(Parents, if you have younger children, reread verse 12 and have them raise their hands when they hear the answer. The two blessings are that the needs of the poor would be met and that God would be praised.)*

:: Can you think of something you need that you could ask God to provide for your family? *(Parents, try to come up with a need your family has that you can lift up to God. God doesn't give us everything we want, but praying as a family for the things we need provides many opportunities to see God move on our behalf.)*

 ## Pray about It

Pray and ask God to provide your family with what you mentioned in answering the question above.

DAY THREE

Connect It to the Gospel

Today is the day we connect this week's Bible story to the gospel. The gospel is the life, death, and resurrection of Jesus for our salvation. Can anyone guess how our story this week looks forward to or back at the gospel?

 Read Romans 6:23.

Think about It Some More

Eternal life through the sacrifice of Jesus on the cross is the greatest gift anyone could ever receive. Eternal life means we get to live forever in heaven with God as a part of his family. All our sins are forgiven, and God takes away all the bad things of the world like sin, sickness, disease, and pain. Once we understand how amazing a gift eternal life is, giving our money to help others is a lot easier. All the treasures of this world are one day going to pass away, but our joy in heaven will last forever.

Talk about It

:: What is the free gift Paul said God offers to us? (*God offers the free gift of eternal life with Jesus in heaven.*)

:: What does Paul mean when he says the wages of sin is death? (*Everyone who sins will die and go to hell, which is described here as death. The opposite is true for everyone who believes in Jesus: They get eternal life.*)

:: What gifts are better than the gift Paul is describing? (*Parents, help your children see that there are no gifts better than living with Jesus in heaven forever. You can do this by comparing things; for example, would you rather have a new bike or live forever in heaven with Jesus?*)

:: What are all the different blessings we receive from God because of what Jesus did? (*Because of what Jesus did, our sins are forgiven and we are adopted as sons and daughters into God's family. We are given Jesus' perfect life. We get to live forever in heaven. We get to see God face-to-face. Jesus becomes our brother. God's Spirit comes to live inside of us. God gives us the power to say no to sin.*)

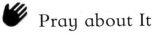 Pray about It

Pray and thank God for the blessings he has given you through the sacrifice of his only Son, Jesus.

DAY FOUR

Remember It

What has God been teaching you this week through our Bible story?

 Read 2 Corinthians 9:13–15.

Think about It Some More

To provide drinking water, sometimes rivers flowing between mountains are dammed up to make large lakes. During a drought, the people who live in the towns below the lake are blessed by the water flowing out of the lake, and they give thanks to God. That is what Paul told the Corinthians that their generous giving was like. But instead of a lake supplying water, Paul said their giving flowed out of the gospel. Did you know that the grace to give generously is a gift from God? Paul lists it in Romans 12:8 as one of the gifts God bestows on his people!

By believing in Jesus and being reminded by the Holy Spirit of all we have been given, generosity, the desire to share with others, fills our hearts like water filling a lake formed by a dam. When people need help downstream, our love for the gospel and all that Jesus did moves us to help them any way we can.

Talk about It

> ● ● KIDS, ask your parents if they can remember a
> ● ● time when God provided for them through the
> giving of others.

(Parents, try to remember a time when you were helped financially by either a family member or someone in the church. If you can't think of a time, then perhaps you could share a story about a gift you gave someone in need.)

:: What good gift did the Corinthians receive from God that made them want to give generously to others? *(God gave the Corinthians his only Son, Jesus, to die on the cross for their sins. That most wonderful gift made them want to give to others.)*

:: What did Paul say the poor saints in Jerusalem would do when they received the Corinthians' gift? *(Parents, for younger children, reread the verse and emphasize the words "glorify God." Then ask the question again.)*

:: Why do you think the saints in Jerusalem would thank God for something that the Corinthians gave them? Why not thank the Corinthians themselves? *(God is the one who gives us everything we have. It was God who gave the Corinthians what they had to be able to give, and it was God who gave the Corinthians the gospel, which made them want to give. So we could say that it was God working through the Corinthians who gave the gift to the needy in Jerusalem.)*

 Pray about It

Praise God for all of the blessings he has given us. We are like giant lakes filled with blessing that God can use to bless others.

DAY FIVE

Discover It

Today is the day we look at a different Bible passage—from the book of Psalms or one of the prophets—to see what we can learn from it about Jesus or our salvation.

 Read Isaiah 53:9.

Think about It Some More

Long before Jesus was born, God spoke through Isaiah and said that Jesus would be buried in the tomb of a rich man. After Jesus died, a rich man named Joseph of Arimathea gave up his family tomb for Jesus (Matthew 27:57–60). Even though a tomb cut into the rock was very expensive, Joseph gave it gladly because of all that Jesus had done for him. Joseph was one of the few rich men who followed Jesus. He also displayed great courage to go before Pilate and ask for the body of

Jesus. While others deserted Christ, Joseph, a rich man who believed in Jesus, cared for our Savior's body.

Talk about It

:: What did Joseph give to Jesus? *(Joseph gave Jesus his tomb.)*

:: Isaiah said that Jesus was buried with sinners even though he was not violent and never lied. Why was it important for Jesus to never sin? *(If Jesus had sinned, he would deserve to be punished himself, so he couldn't die for us, and he couldn't give us the gift of his perfect life. But because Jesus was God, he was able to say no to every temptation and never sin.)*

:: Jesus said it was very hard for a rich man to enter heaven. What was different about Joseph of Arimathea as compared with other rich men in the Bible? *(Joseph loved Jesus more than he loved his riches. He was willing to go before Pilate and risk being himself arrested, and he was generous to give up his expensive tomb for Jesus. That showed he loved Jesus more than money.)*

 Pray about It

Ask God to help you love Jesus more than anything in the whole world.

Week 58

A Gift of Righteousness

Story 136 – *The Gospel Story Bible*

Prepare five index cards by scribbling with markers on the white side of the cards. At Bible study, show the cards one by one, excitedly explaining that you drew some really nice pictures. Before you show the first card, tell them it is a drawing of a beautiful princess, then show them the card. Repeat this with the other cards but change the subject of the drawing. You might that you've drawn a delicate flower, a cute little kitty, a majestic sunset, and a handsome knight on a tall horse.

Then ask which drawing they would describe as a good drawing. The children should look confused. Help them get to the place where they honestly tell you that none of them are good, not even one. Say, "This week we will learn how in our sin we are like the drawings: Not one of us does good."

DAY ONE

Picture It

What is the grossest thing you have ever seen in your life? Now that sounds like a crazy question to ask when you are studying the Bible, but you will see that the Bible verses we are about to read today mention some pretty gross things. For instance, Paul compares our sinful mouths, which speak all kinds of lies, curses, and insults, to open graves.

There is a good reason we bury people under the ground when they die. Dead bodies can be full of bacteria, they smell terrible, and they can be full of bugs. The reason Paul would use such a gross example is that he wanted to show us how terribly sinful we all are, apart from God's grace.

Read Romans 3:9–20.

Think about It Some More

The apostle Paul is trying to pass on a simple message: every single person in the world is a sinner who needs to be rescued. Notice how many times the word "no" shows up in today's passage. When God wants to get our attention, he repeats himself. In this passage, God wants to make sure we understand that there is *no way* we can get to heaven without his help.

Think of it like this: If you wanted to put on your brand new white sneakers and go outside to play on a muddy day, your dad might tell you, "No, no way, never, nada, ain't gonna happen, so you better stop asking." Some people want to know if there is a way to get to heaven by doing good deeds. Paul answers the question like a dad telling his son not to wear his white sneakers in the mud. He said, "None, no, no, no, not even one." That is because everyone, Jew and Gentile alike, is a sinner and will be judged by God. Apart from God's grace, we are doomed.

Talk about It

:: Who is good enough to get to heaven? *(No one can get to heaven by doing good deeds.)*

:: Can you think of some way you have sinned? *(Parents, you can help each of your children identify with the fact that they are sinners by having them think of a way they sinned. Then confess that you too are a sinner. You might say, "Paul was right: We are all sinners who need to be saved. None of us is good.")*

:: What did Paul say to make sure we understand that none of us can get to heaven by doing good works? *(Paul used the word "no" many times to make the point that there are no exceptions. Everyone is a sinner who cannot go to heaven to be with God.)*

:: If we can't trust our own good works to get to heaven, how can we get there? *(Parents, understanding that we are all sinners who can't get to heaven is the "bad news" of the gospel. We need to understand the bad news so that we hunger for the good news of the gospel. The good news is that Jesus lived a perfect life in our place and died to take the punishment for our sins. If we trust in Jesus, he makes a trade: our sin for his goodness.)*

 Pray about It

Take time to pray around, confessing your sins, and asking God for forgiveness.

DAY TWO _____

Remember It

What do you remember about yesterday's Bible passage? What do you think we will learn about today?

 Read Romans 3:21–24.

Think about It Some More

Yesterday, we heard the bad news—not one of us is righteous. We are all sinners. No one can stand before God and say, "I deserve to be allowed into heaven because I have been good." Today we hear the good news. Even though we are not righteous, Jesus can take away our sin in exchange for his righteousness—his perfect obedience—so that we can stand before God and not be punished for our sins. If we believe by faith and trust in Jesus, he takes away our sin and declares that we are righteous because of what he did.

We call that declaration by God *justification*. Justification is God's announcement that we are not guilty because of what Jesus did. Instead of looking at our sin, God looks at Jesus' righteousness and forgives us. That is what it means to be justified.

Talk about It

:: What is the good news Paul shares with us in this passage? *(The good news is that even though we are all sinners, we can get to heaven by trusting in Jesus, who never sinned even once.)*

:: What does the word *justified* mean? *(The word* justified *describes God's "not guilty" announcement over our lives when he looks at Jesus' righteousness instead of our sin.)*

:: Can you remember what the word *righteousness* means? *(The word* righteousness *means perfect goodness without sin. This too is an important Bible word to know. An easy way to understand what it means is "right in God's eyes." The only way we can be right in God's eyes or perfectly good is if Jesus gives us his perfect righteousness.)*

 Pray about It

Thank Jesus for living a sinless life in our place and giving us his righteousness so we could be justified.

DAY THREE _____

Connect It to the Gospel

Today is the day we connect this week's Bible story to the gospel. The gospel is the life, death, and resurrection of Jesus for our salvation. Can anyone guess how our story this week looks forward to or back at the gospel?

 Read Romans 3:25–26.

Think about It Some More

Yesterday we learned two big words, *righteousness* and *justified*. Today, Paul gives us another big word, *propitiation*. *(Parents: some Bibles substitute the phrase "sacrifice of atonement" for the word* propitiation. *You might think that words like* propitiation *or* sacrifice *or* atonement *are too difficult for young children to learn. But when you understand what they mean, it is not too hard.)*

When you see the word *propitiation*, just think of three simple words that Jesus spoke on the cross: *"It is finished"* (John 19:30). You see, the worst part of the cross for Jesus was not the terrible pain of the thorns on his head or the nails in his hands and feet. The worst part of the cross was when God the Father turned against his Son, giving him the punishment we deserved. Propitiation is the word that describes Jesus taking that punishment until it was all gone. When he said, *"It is finished,"* there was no more punishment left, the propitiation for our sin was complete; the punishment we deserved was all poured out—it was finished!

Talk about It

:: What does the word *propitiation* mean? *(Parents, help your children remember this definition by going back to it later in the day. Propitiation means that Jesus took our punishment on the cross until it was all gone. Help your children remember the words "It is finished," which indicate there was no punishment left to take.)*

:: Paul said we receive God's propitiation (Jesus taking our punishment until it was finished) as a free gift by something called faith. What is faith? *(Faith means believing that something is true—usually something we can't see. Since Jesus lived and died before we were born, we have to trust God's Word and believe it by faith.)*

:: What did God do for all the people who had faith but died before Jesus ever lived on earth? *(God passed over their sins knowing that Jesus was going to die on the cross for them. God gave them credit for their faith in his saving plan even though Jesus was not born yet [see Romans 4:5].)*

 ## Pray about It

Ask God to help you have faith that Jesus was a propitiation for your sin—that he took your punishment for sin—so you could be forgiven.

DAY FOUR

Remember It

What has God been teaching you this week through our Bible story?

 Read Romans 3:27–31.

Think about It Some More

Yesterday we learned that *propitiation* is the word that describes Jesus taking our punishment. That is why, in our Bible passage today, Paul said that none of us can boast or brag about our own good works. Remember, none of us is good. Apart from Jesus, the only thing we have to boast about is our sin. Jesus lived a perfect life for us, died in our place, and took our punishment. Now he offers to give us his righteousness so that we can be right in God's eyes and justified, for he declares that Jesus' righteousness is ours. Since Jesus did all the work, there is no way to boast in our own work. Our only job is to believe in Jesus—our only boast is in him.

Talk about It

> KIDS, ask your parents to explain what the word *boasting* means and if they have ever been tempted to boast about something.

(Boasting is a form of pride in which a person tells everyone how good he is because of something he has done. If a person wins a race and then brags about how fast he is and how he beat everyone else, he is boasting about the race.)

:: Why would it be wrong to boast about going to heaven because of something that you did? *(We can't boast about going to heaven based on our works, because if it were not for Jesus dying in our place, we couldn't go to heaven. None of our good works can get us there.)*

:: What do you think it means to boast in Jesus? *(When we celebrate or tell others about what Jesus did for us, we are boasting in Jesus. When we tell them we are weak without his strength and we are lost without the cross, we are boasting about Jesus.)*

 Pray about It

Ask God to help you always remember that when it comes to heaven, we did nothing and Jesus did everything. Ask God to help you believe in what he did and give you the gift of faith.

DAY FIVE

Discover It

Today is the day we look at a different Bible passage—from the book of Psalms or one of the prophets—to see what we can learn from it about Jesus or our salvation.

Read Isaiah 52:14–15.

Think about It Some More

This week we learned a big word, *propitiation*. Propitiation means that Jesus took our punishment. In Old Testament times, before Jesus was born, lambs were killed as a sacrifice for sin. The lamb's blood was sprinkled on the altar to show that a sacrifice had been made in place of the people who sinned. The Bible passage we read today is about Jesus and his terrible suffering. It says that he shall sprinkle many nations. That points back to the sprinkling of the blood of the lamb that died in place of the people of Israel as a propitiation for their sins.

Isaiah tells us that Jesus' appearance would be marred. That means that his body would be cut and scarred so badly that he wouldn't even look like a man. The blood that poured from his wounds is the blood that was shed for us. Because his blood was sprinkled out as a propitiation for our sin, we can draw near to God with our hearts sprinkled clean (Hebrews 10:22). That is why we sing the song that says the blood of Jesus washes away our sin.

Talk about It

:: Why did Jesus have to die such a terrible death? *(Jesus died a terrible death because our sin against God is so terrible.)*

:: Read Exodus 29:15–16. What did God tell Moses to do with the blood of the ram that was sacrificed? *(God told Moses to sprinkle it on the altar.)*

:: Whose blood was poured out for us? *(Jesus' blood was poured out for us. God tells us that Jesus' blood covers our sins because Jesus took our punishment on the cross.)*

 # Pray about It

Thank Jesus for dying on the cross in our place and for shedding his blood to cover our sins so that we could be justified—declared righteous by God.

Abraham: Father to All by Faith

Story 137 – *The Gospel Story Bible*

Beforehand, pick up a gift card to your local ice cream shop for each of your children. Hide a gift card in your hand or hands and approach your youngest child. Say, "I have an ice cream cone in my hand for you to enjoy." Then ask if he believes you. Explain that since he cannot see the ice cream, and he knows an ice cream cone would not fit in your closed hands, the only way to believe you is by faith. Faith is believing even when we cannot see that it is true. Then surprise him with the gift card.

If you have more than one child, repeat the exercise. It will be much easier for the second child to believe once she has seen the first gift card. Say, "That is the same way faith operates in our lives with God. By reading in the Bible all that God has done in the past, we gain faith for the future. This week we will learn that we must follow the example of Abraham, who believed what God told him even though it seemed impossible."

DAY ONE

Picture It

Matt and Tim were sitting on the front step when their dad asked if they would like to earn a trip to their local candy store by helping to rake leaves. They gladly agreed and quickly set to work. Their younger brother, Jason, who was only three years old, wanted to help too, but he made more of a mess than anything else. As the older boys raked the leaves into a large pile, Jason ran into the pile, scattering the leaves.

His older brothers chased him out of the pile, chiding him for making a mess. Then they finished the job.

When their dad came out and saw the job complete, he told Matt and Tim to get into the car. Jason stood looking up at his dad, waiting for his invitation. His dad said, "You didn't earn a trip to the candy store for working, but I am going to let you come anyway. Think of it as a free gift." On the way to the candy store, Matt and Tim were a little upset, but their dad explained how, even though none of us can work our way to heaven, Jesus offers us heaven as a free gift to anyone who believes and trusts in him.

 Read Romans 4:1–5.

Think about It Some More

Abraham did not earn the righteousness (good standing before God) that God gave to him. Abraham was a sinner, and there was nothing he could do by himself to become righteous. But when God called Abraham and told him to move away from home, Abraham believed God by faith and trusted in God's plan. Although Abraham didn't know it at the time, the most important part of God's plan would come later when he sent his Son, Jesus, to die on the cross to take our sins away. So when Abraham was trusting in God's plan for his life, he was actually trusting in Jesus. That is why, when God saw Abraham's faith, he credited (gave) him the righteousness of Jesus and justified him.

Talk about It

:: What free gift did God give Abraham? *(Parents, your children may correctly say that God saved Abraham. But help them use the words* righteousness *and* justified. *God gave Abraham righteousness [a right standing before God] and justified him [declared or announced that he was given the free gift of Christ's righteousness].)*

:: What did Abraham do to earn the free gift? *(Abraham didn't do anything to earn God's gift. You can't earn a gift: a gift has to be free to be a gift. Abraham didn't even know about Jesus living a perfect life and dying for our sins, since that was still in the future. Abraham only trusted God's plan. It was that faith that God saw, and it pleased God to give Abraham the free gift of Jesus' righteousness.)*

:: What can we do to earn God's free gift? *(There is nothing we can do to earn God's free gift, either. But if we trust in God's plan to deliver us through Jesus dying on the cross, God promises to justify us and adopt us into his family too.)*

 Pray about It

Thank God for his free gift of righteousness that he gives to everyone who believes and trusts in him and his plan to save us from our sin through Jesus.

DAY TWO

Remember It

What do you remember about yesterday's Bible passage? What do you think we will learn about today?

 Read Romans 4:6–12.

Think about It Some More

The Jewish people called themselves children of Abraham because Abraham was their far-off great-great-grandfather. But God's promise to Abraham was to save people from every nation, not just from Israel. God counted Abraham's faith as righteousness before circumcision or the law. So Abraham wasn't counted righteous for following the law but because he had faith in God's plan. That is why Paul said that Abraham wasn't the father of only the Jews—Abraham was the father of everyone who believes in Jesus.

Abraham is our father, not because we are Jewish (related to him as family, by blood), but because we are related to him by faith. So, if you believe in Jesus, you are a child of Abraham.

Talk about It

:: Why did the Jews call Abraham their father? *(They called Abraham their father because they were related to him by blood. He was their far-off great-grandfather.)*

:: What did God count as righteousness for Abraham: his good works in following the law or his faith in God's plan?

(Parents, if your children say the law, remind them that the law wasn't written yet, and let them guess again.)

:: What made Abraham the father of everyone who believes: his good works in following the law or his faith in God's plan? *(Parents, your children should get this answer correct after the last one. Point out that Abraham becomes our father too when we put our faith in Jesus. Abraham is our father but not because we are related to him as family, by blood. Abraham becomes our father because we are related to him by faith.)*

:: What do we need to do to become a part of Abraham's family, the family of God? *(Everyone who has faith in God's plan through Jesus becomes a part of the family of God and can say, "Abraham is my father too.")*

 ## Pray about It

If you have younger children who know the song "Father Abraham," consider singing it together to reinforce today's lesson. If your children are older, thank God for opening a way for all of us to become children of Abraham and a part of the family of God.

DAY THREE _____

Connect It to the Gospel

Today is the day we connect this week's Bible story to the gospel. The gospel is the life, death, and resurrection of Jesus for our salvation. Can anyone guess how our story this week looks forward to or back at the gospel?

 Read Romans 4:13–17.

Think about It Some More

The gospel story of Jesus runs through this Bible passage—hidden in one little word called *faith*. Faith in God means that we believe and trust God and his saving plan. We all know today that God planned to send his only Son, Jesus, to die on the cross for our sins. Although Abraham didn't know Jesus by name, he still had faith in God's saving plan. That was good enough for God, who then counted Abraham's faith as righteousness and didn't count his sins against him. God knew that Abraham couldn't know Jesus' name. What God wanted then—and still wants today—are people who believe that the only way to be saved from sin is to trust in God's saving plan.

And we don't need faith just to join God's family; we need faith to continue walking the Christian life too. Paul tells us that while we wait for our heavenly home, "We are always of good courage. We know that while we are at home in the body we are away from the Lord, for we walk by faith, not by sight" (2 Corinthians 5:6–7). We need faith—a trust in God's plan—to first believe and we need faith as we continue following Jesus.

Talk about It

:: What Bible story should we remember anytime we see the word *faith* in the Bible? *(We should remember the story of Jesus dying on the cross, because that is the story we believe by faith to be saved.)*

:: Why is Abraham called the father of many nations? *(Abraham is called the father of many nations because people can believe in Jesus no matter what country they come from. The Jews thought Abraham was only their father. But God promised to bless all the nations through him.)*

:: How can Abraham become our father? *(Abraham can become our father if we believe and have faith in Jesus, who died on the cross so that our sins would not count against us, and so that Jesus' good works would be counted for us.)*

 Pray about It

Thank God for making a way for Abraham to become our father by believing in Jesus.

DAY FOUR

Remember It

What has God been teaching you this week through our Bible story?

 Read Romans 4:18–25.

Think about It Some More

All week Paul has been talking about how faith is "counted" for us. The best way to understand what that means is to think of scoring in a sports game. If your team hits a home run in a baseball game when you have a runner on second base, two runs are counted for your team. If your football team kicks a field goal, three points are counted for your team. On the other hand, if you fumble the football and the other team scores a touchdown, six points are counted against you. At the end of a game, if you have more points counting for you than the other team has, you win the game.

When it comes to sin and faith, you don't get points, you get either sin or Christ's perfect righteousness counted to your score. If we have faith in Jesus, God counts our faith as righteousness, and he doesn't count our sin against us. It is like having Jesus on your team. Even though you are a sinner, Jesus scored the best victory of all when he died on the cross for your sins and then rose again from the dead. When you believe in what Jesus did, it is like God putting Jesus onto your team. By trusting in his victory over sin, he becomes a part of our team, and we win the game.

Talk about It

> ● ● KIDS, ask your parents if they can remember a
> ● ● time when their sports team won or lost an important championship game.

(Parents, if you can remember a game, use the "counted" language to describe the loss or victory to help your children understand the concept that points your team scores are counted for them, and points the other team scores are counted against you.)

:: What did Paul say was counted to Abraham as righteousness? *(Parents, if you have smaller children, reread verse 22 emphasizing the word* faith *to help your children get the correct answer.)*

:: What did Paul say we have to believe about Jesus? *(Parents, if you have smaller children, reread verses 24 and 25 and have them raise their hands when they hear the answer. The answer has three parts. First, we are to believe in God, who raised Jesus from the dead. Then we need to believe that Jesus died for our sins. Third, we have*

*to believe that Jesus was raised from the dead so that we could be justi-
fied [declared righteous] by God because of what Jesus did for us.)*

 Pray about It

Ask God to help you believe the three answers from the last question.
That God sent his Son, Jesus, to die for our sins, and be raised in victory
so that our sins could be taken away.

DAY FIVE

Discover It

Today is the day we look at a different Bible passage—from the book
of Psalms or one of the prophets—to see what we can learn from it
about Jesus or our salvation.

 Read Isaiah 53:10.

Think about It Some More

Isaiah 53 is all about Jesus dying on the cross. Verse 10 tells us that it
was God's plan to crush his Son to make him an offering for our sin. In
the Old Testament, lambs were killed to make an offering for people's
sins. In a sense, the lamb was killed as a replacement for the person. An
innocent animal took away the sin of the guilty person. In the same
way, Jesus, the Lamb of God, is our substitute, the one who died in our
place. He is our sin offering. Long before Jesus died on the cross, God
planned Jesus' death as the way he would remove our sins. If you look
carefully in this passage, you will also see the resurrection in Isaiah's
prophecy. Even though it says God would crush Jesus, it also says that
he will see his offspring. That verse points to Jesus rising from the dead
in victory.

Talk about It

:: Why did God crush his Son? *(Parents, if you have younger
children, reread the passage emphasizing the phrase "an offering for
sin." Then ask your children the question again. Isaiah tells us God
crushed his Son to make an offering for sin.)*

:: What is an offering for sin? *(An offering for sin is a sacrifice
made and offered up to God [like the killing of a lamb] in place of*

the person who sinned. Jesus was killed in our place as our offering for sin.)

:: How does this passage from Isaiah fit into our lesson this week about faith being counted as righteousness? *(The faith God counts for us is our faith in Jesus dying on the cross for our sins.)*

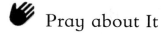 Pray about It

Thank God for his plan to send Jesus to die as an offering for our sin so that we could be declared righteous.

Week 60

Believe and Confess

Story 138 – *The Gospel Story Bible*

Gather three opaque (non-see-through) plastic containers with lids. Place kidney beans, small screws, or beads inside each of the containers and close the lids. Then place a label on the top of the container with the names of three types of candy, such as M&M's, Skittles, and jelly beans. When your children come to Bible study, shake the containers to give a clue about the contents and ask them to guess what they think is inside.

One container at a time, look at the label and say, "This one says on the label that it is jelly beans." Open each container to reveal what is inside. When your children voice surprise, explain that words on the outside of something don't always tell the truth about what is on the inside. Say, "This holds true for people too. People can say they love Jesus, but in their heart they might really love the world instead. This week we will learn how we need to do more than say we believe in Jesus, we need to believe it in our hearts."

DAY ONE

Picture It

Imagine that it is Christmas morning and John was opening his biggest present. John tore open the paper to reveal a large, bright red fire truck. But instead of playing with the fire truck, John gave it back to his mom and dad and said that he would have to pay them for it before he could play with it. They were both shocked, and they explained to him that a gift is free—you don't have to pay for it or earn it. You just have to accept it as a free gift. But John would not budge. He refused to accept it freely, and insisted he work for it before he could have it.

In our story today, you will read how the Jews largely rejected God's free gift of righteousness because they insisted on trying to earn their own way to heaven through the law—something that was impossible to do. The Gentiles, on the other hand, were glad to receive God's free gift by faith, and they greatly enjoyed knowing Jesus.

 Read Romans 9:24—10:4.

Think about It Some More

The Jews thought that by obeying the law they would be righteous (good in God's eyes) and accepted by God. When Jesus came, he explained that no one was able to keep the law without sinning. Even the Pharisees broke the law. That is why Jesus taught that he is the only way to the Father. To be accepted by God, we must put our faith in Jesus, who lived a perfect life and then died on the cross to take our sin away and to give us his righteousness.

But even though Paul and the other apostles preached this message, many of the Jews refused to give up the law, and they rejected God's free gift. Many of the Gentiles, though, were glad to hear about Jesus, and they believed in him. Once the Christians started welcoming in the Gentiles, some of the Jews rejected Jesus all the more.

Talk about It

:: What does the word *righteous* mean? *(Parents, this is a review question. Righteousness is goodness before God. All of us are sinners which means we are not perfectly righteous, but Jesus offers his righteousness to everyone who believes in him.)*

:: Paul explained that there were two ways people tried to get to God. The correct way was by believing in Jesus. What was the wrong way to try to get to God? *(Parents, if you have younger children, reread verse 32 and emphasize the word* works. *The Jews thought they had to work for righteousness by following the law.)*

:: Why can't we be made righteous by keeping the law? *(We can't be made righteous by keeping the law because we sin. If you sin even once, you are not perfect. You have to be perfect in order to stand in God's holy presence in heaven.)*

:: How did Paul feel about the Jews who refused to believe in Jesus? *(Paul really wanted the Jews to believe, and he prayed that God would save them.)*

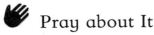 Pray about It

Thank God for sending Jesus to put an end to the law so that we don't have to try to work our way to heaven. Instead, we can trust in Jesus who obeyed the law perfectly in our place.

DAY TWO

Remember It

What do you remember about yesterday's Bible passage? What do you think we will learn about today?

 Read Romans 10:5–13.

Think about It Some More

If you ever got a toy that needed to be assembled, you know how important the instructions are. The instructions tell you how to assemble it correctly. Romans 10:8–10 is like God's instruction sheet for how to become a Christian. There are only two main steps: First, believe that God raised Jesus from the dead after he died for our sins on the cross; and second, speak out with our mouths that Jesus is our Lord.

Just saying the words is not enough, for anyone can say he believes in Jesus on the outside while trusting himself on the inside. To become Christians, people must believe the gospel message by faith inside their heart. They must believe that Jesus died on the cross for their sins and rose again in victory so they could be saved. These instructions apply to every person in the whole world. It doesn't matter if you are a Jew or a Gentile, we all become Christians the very same way, and God promises to save everyone who believes and calls out to him.

Talk about It

:: What are the two instructions God gave us to help us know how to become a Christian? *(We need to believe in our heart that the gospel is true, and we need to confess with our mouth that Jesus is our Lord.)*

:: Why do we have to believe in our heart? Why can't we just say we believe with our mouth? *(Anyone can say something and not really mean it. God wants words that come from a heart that believes.)*

:: Who did Paul say could be saved by following these instructions? *(Paul said that anyone can be saved by following these instructions.)*

:: Why do we need the Holy Spirit's help to believe in our heart? *(We are sinners who reject God and do not want to believe. The Holy Spirit must open our eyes so that we can see the ugliness of our sin and the beauty of what Jesus did on the cross for us.)*

 Pray about It

Ask God to help all the people in your family see how ugly sin is so that they will want to believe in Jesus down deep in their heart and put their faith in him.

DAY THREE _____

Connect It to the Gospel

Today is the day we connect this week's Bible story to the gospel. The gospel is the life, death, and resurrection of Jesus for our salvation. Can anyone guess how our story this week looks forward to or back at the gospel?

 Read Romans 10:14–15.

Think about It Some More

In order to be saved and become a Christian, we need to believe the good news of the gospel in our heart and confess—speak or declare—that Jesus Christ is our Lord. Many people are dying in their sins and don't even know they need to be forgiven. They are like people happily sleeping in a building with a blazing roof. In order for them to be rescued from the fire, someone has to wake them up and tell them about the fire. God wants us to help others understand they are sinners in danger of the fires of hell, and the good news that God provided a way to be saved through Jesus. Then they too can experience the joy of knowing and loving Jesus and living a life in service to our great King.

All they need to do is follow God's instructions—believe in their heart that God raised Jesus from the dead and confess with their mouth that

Jesus is Lord—and they will be saved. If we don't tell them, they won't know. That's why we are called to go and preach the gospel to all people.

Talk about It

:: What is the good news Paul is talking about? *(The good news is that Jesus Christ died in our place and took the punishment we deserved for our sins so that we can go to heaven. We call that the gospel, which means "good news.")*

:: Why did Paul say the feet of people who share the good news are beautiful? *(The feet of those who share the gospel are beautiful because it is a life-saving message. If you were in a house that was on fire and someone knocked at your door to tell you to get out, and your whole family was saved from certain death, you would think their feet were pretty beautiful for bringing you that message.)*

:: Who do you know who still needs to hear the good news of the gospel? *(Parents, help your children think of unsaved friends or neighbors, and come up with a plan to invite them over to your home for an activity with the hope of sharing the good news of what Jesus did for them.)*

 Pray about It

Pray for the people you know who still need to hear the good news of the gospel, and ask God to give your family an opportunity to share the good news with them.

DAY FOUR

Remember It

What has God been teaching you this week through our Bible story?

 Read Romans 10:16–21.

Think about It Some More

When scientists discovered that Mt. Saint Helens was going to erupt, they warned all the people in the valley below to move far away. Most of the people listened, but one man, named Harry, who lived at the base of the mountain, refused to listen. Harry died when the volcano exploded. Other people were glad for the good news of the warning and made it safely away. But not Harry: He got angry with people who tried to convince him to leave. In the end, only those people who believed the scientists and left the mountain were saved.

In the same way, not everyone to whom we tell the gospel will believe in Jesus. Still, it is very important to tell everyone about the danger of sin and the good news about Jesus, for sometimes God will give faith to the most stubborn people.

Talk about It

> KIDS, ask your parents if there is a person they have been sharing the gospel with who refuses to believe.

(Parents, if there is a person to whom you've been reaching out with the gospel who does not believe, take some time to pray for that person with your children at the end of your Bible study.)

:: What is the message that the Bible calls the good news? *(Parents, this is a review question, but it is important that we make sure our children can articulate the gospel: that Jesus Christ died for our sins and rose again from the dead so we could be forgiven and be with God in heaven.)*

:: Why is the message about Jesus called the good news? *(The message is good news because it tells us how to be rescued from God's terrible judgment and provides a way: believing in Jesus.)*

:: Why don't some people believe that message? *(People refuse to believe because they don't want to turn away from their sin and what they love about the world.)*

✋ Pray about It

Pray for those you know who refuse to believe the gospel message. Pray that God would soften their hearts to believe.

DAY FIVE _____

Discover It

Today is the day we look at a different Bible passage—from the book of Psalms or one of the prophets—to see what we can learn from it about Jesus or our salvation.

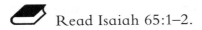 Read Isaiah 65:1–2.

Think about It Some More

Way back before Jesus was born, Isaiah prophesied that not everyone was going to believe the good news of the gospel. He said that even though God spread out his hands to welcome Israel to believe, they would not believe. Then, once Israel rejected him, God was going to turn to the Gentiles (a people not called by his name) and say, "Here I am." That meant that God would give the Gentiles a chance to believe.

Jesus went to the Jews, but they rejected him. So God sent the message of the gospel through others like Paul to the Gentiles, and many of them believed. Today, God is opening his arms to us and saying, "Here I am" through the gospel message about Jesus. Each of us has the chance to either welcome the message into our hearts and believe or reject him.

Talk about It

:: What does it mean that God spread his arms out to us? *(Parents, help your children by demonstrating this. Open your arms wide, welcoming them to come and give you a hug. "What does it mean when a father opens his arms like this to his children?" Then follow up with the question again: "What does it mean for God to spread his arms out to us?" The answer of course is that he wants us to come to him.)*

:: How does God call out to us today saying, "Here I am"? *(God calls out to us today through the Bible. Parents, if your children don't know, give them a clue by holding up your Bible.)*

:: What keeps people from believing the good news God gives to us in the Bible? *(Anything people love more than God can keep them from believing the gospel. God wants us to love him more than anything else in our lives.)*

 Pray about It

Ask God to help you run to his arms and believe, and ask him to help you give up anything you love more than God.

Week 61

Paul in Chains

Story 139 – *The Gospel Story Bible*

In preparation, do a search on the Internet for the words persecuted church. Several sites will come up that can provide up-to-date information on where the church is currently under attack. Look for a few stories to tell your children. When you gather for Bible study, ask your children the meaning of the word persecution (inflicting suffering on a person because of his or her beliefs). Then share with them some of the information you have gathered. Take some time to pray for the persecuted church. Say, "This week we will learn how Paul endured imprisonment for his faith with courage, and how he shared the gospel in spite of his persecution."

DAY ONE

Picture It

Imagine that you had a classmate who accused you of stealing the teacher's purse. To make the lie believable, she emptied the money out of the teacher's wallet and hid the purse in a bathroom trashcan. When the teacher complained that her purse was missing, your classmate lied and said she saw you carrying something like a purse toward the bathroom.

If that happened to you, and you were charged with stealing and expelled from school, you could ask for a trial. In a trial, a jury of twelve people would listen to the facts and decide whether or not you were guilty.

If you asked for a trial, you would have to be granted one. The same was true in ancient Rome. In our Bible story today, Paul demanded a trial before Caesar, the ruler of the Roman Empire. He was afraid the Jews would kill him even if he were set free. Once he appealed to Caesar

for a trial, the law said he must be taken to Rome, away from the Jews
who meant him harm.

 Read Acts 26:19–32.

Think about It Some More

Paul's imprisonment began when he went to Jerusalem to deliver the
offering the Gentile churches had collected. Soon after his visit, he
was opposed by some Jews from the province of Asia, who stirred up
a mob against him (Acts 21:27–29). Before long, the whole city of
Jerusalem was in an uproar (Acts 21:30), and the Jews tried to kill
Paul. This riot prompted Roman soldiers to arrest Paul.

The Jews planned to kill Paul while he was under arrest. More
than forty men vowed not to eat or drink until he was dead. But Jesus
appeared to Paul and encouraged him, telling him that he would be
preaching the gospel in Rome (Acts 23:11). Therefore, when charges
were brought against Paul, he appealed to Caesar. By appealing to
Caesar, the law said he had to be sent to Rome, away from the angry
Jews in Jerusalem who wanted to kill him. That is why, even though
King Agrippa didn't think Paul was guilty of a crime, he said he must
remain a prisoner and be sent to Rome.

Talk about It

:: What name did Paul go by before his ministry to the Gentiles? *(While he was persecuting the church, before he became a
Christian, Paul was known as Saul. He was a Jewish Pharisee who
was arresting Christians and putting them in prison.)*

:: What did Paul do to make the Jews so mad? *(They thought
he was a traitor, and they did not want him to preach the good news
about Jesus in Jerusalem.)*

:: Why did Paul ask for a trial before Caesar, since the rulers
in Jerusalem wanted to let him go? *(Paul knew the Jews wanted
to kill him, and Paul also knew that Jesus wanted him to go to
preach the gospel in Rome. By asking for a trial before Caesar, they
would have to send Paul by ship to Rome. That way, Paul could
escape the Jews who wanted to kill him.)*

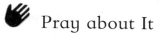 Pray about It

Thank God for the way he protected Paul, and thank God for the way he watches over and protects us.

DAY TWO

Remember It

What do you remember about yesterday's Bible passage? What do you think we will learn about today?

 Read Acts 27:39—28:16.

Think about It Some More

Paul's trip from Jerusalem to Rome was not an easy one, but God protected Paul and provided for him. While he was sailing across the Mediterranean Sea, a storm caused his ship to crash on the reef off a small island called Malta. Paul and the crew all survived the crash and spent time on Malta until they could get another ship to finish their journey.

While on Malta, Paul had the opportunity to heal the sick and preach the gospel. By the time he left, the people were so affected by him that they honored Paul and gave him all the food he needed to make the journey on the next ship to Rome. When Paul finally arrived in Rome, God provided another group of Christians to meet Paul, which encouraged him greatly. Best of all, Paul was not sent to a prison but was allowed to remain under house arrest. That meant that Paul could live in a house with a guard—and have visitors—instead of being alone in a cold prison cell.

Talk about It

:: How did God use the terrible events of Paul's shipwreck for good? (*Paul was able to heal people on the island of Malta and preach the gospel to them.*)

:: Whom did God send to encourage Paul? (*Some Roman Christians came to visit Paul when they heard he was under house arrest.*)

:: Why was house arrest better than prison? *(Prisons were usually dark, cold, and smelly places. But house arrest is simply remaining chained in your house, with a guard assigned to watch you. People can come to visit you, and you can make whatever food you want for dinner.)*

 ## Pray about It

Thank God for the way he worked all things together for good in Paul's life. He protected the men on the ship, he protected Paul from the poisonous snake, he healed the people of Malta, and he allowed Paul to be held under house arrest instead of prison.

DAY THREE _____

Connect It to the Gospel

Today is the day we connect this week's Bible story to the gospel. The gospel is the life, death, and resurrection of Jesus for our salvation. Can anyone guess how our story this week looks forward to or back at the gospel?

 Read Acts 28:17–31.

Think about It Some More

Once in Rome, it didn't take Paul long to start sharing the gospel. It was only three days after he arrived that he sent for the Jewish leaders and shared his whole story challenging them to believe. Most people who went through all the hardships Paul did would have complained, but not Paul. He was more interested in talking about Jesus. But like the Jews back in Jerusalem, not everyone believed. Paul rebuked the Jews for not believing and told them that because of their unbelief he would take the gospel to the Gentiles.

But Paul remained in chains for the next two years. In spite of his arrest, God made a way for Paul to spread the gospel anyway. Because he was only under house arrest and could receive visitors, Paul was able to continue to preach the gospel boldly with anyone who came to visit—and every soldier who came to guard Paul heard the message of the gospel too.

Talk about It

:: How much time did Paul spend talking to the religious leaders and other Jews trying to convince them about Jesus? *(Parents, if you have smaller children, reread verse 23 and ask them to raise their hands when they hear the correct answer: Paul talked to them from morning until evening. Paul loved to talk about Jesus with others.)*

:: What good came out of Paul's two years under house arrest? *(Parents, if your younger children need some help, reread verses 30–31 and repeat the question. The good that came of Paul's house arrest was his opportunity to share the gospel with all those who came to visit him.)*

:: Paul said it was because of the hope of Israel that he was wearing his chains (v. 20). What was the hope of Israel? *(Jesus was the hope of Israel. Paul was arrested for teaching about Jesus.)*

 Pray about It

Thank God for using Paul's imprisonment to spread the gospel, and ask God to give you more courage to tell others about Jesus.

DAY FOUR

Remember It

What has God been teaching you this week through our Bible story?

 Read Philippians 1:12–18.

Think about It Some More

When Paul was imprisoned in Rome, he wrote a letter to the Christians in the city of Philippi. Even though it was sad that Paul was imprisoned in Rome, Paul wanted the Philippians to know how God used his imprisonment to spread the message about Jesus. He told them how he shared the gospel with the Roman soldiers who were guarding him so that the whole palace guard knew about Jesus. When other Christians saw Paul's boldness, they grew in their own courage to share the gospel with the people they met. In the end, the message about Jesus spread across Rome because of Paul's imprisonment.

Talk about It

> KIDS, ask your parents who in your church is a
> great example of a person who loves to share the
> gospel with others.

(Parents, it is good to hold in front of our kids, people who do a great job sharing the gospel with others.)

:: What did Paul talk about with the soldiers who were sent to guard him? *(Paul shared the gospel with them.)*

:: How did Paul's example while under house arrest encourage the Christians in Rome? *(Paul's boldness in sharing about Jesus helped embolden other Christians and give them courage to talk about Jesus outside the prison.)*

:: How are you doing in spreading the gospel as a family? Who can you be reaching out to? *(Parents, draw out your children and come up with a plan to reach out to one of your neighbors or someone you know who does not know the Lord.)*

 Pray about It

Ask God to give you and your whole family boldness and courage to tell others about Jesus.

DAY FIVE _____

Discover It

Today is the day we look at a different Bible passage—from the book of Psalms or one of the prophets—to see what we can learn from it about Jesus or our salvation.

Read Psalm 22:22–31.

Think about It Some More

Psalm 22 is prophetic song that David wrote to tell the story of Jesus. The psalm begins by describing the terrible suffering that Jesus endured on the cross. The later part of the psalm speaks of the wonderful salvation that Jesus' death provides for us. The writer of the book of Hebrews repeated verse 22 and explained that it is Jesus talking

(Hebrews 2:11–12). Jesus is the one who will one day look at everyone who believes and call them his brothers. When we believe and trust in Jesus, God adopts us into his family, and Jesus becomes our brother. That means that everyone who believes and places his or her trust in Jesus becomes his brother or sister. That is why, when Paul reached Rome, the Christians who first came to visit him were called his brothers (Acts 28:14–15).

Talk about It

:: Why does Jesus call us his brothers and sisters when we believe in him? *(When we believe in Jesus, we become a part of the family of God. That is why the Bible calls believers, brothers and sisters in Christ.)*

:: Where do you see the promise God gave Abraham in this psalm? *(Parents, first ask your children what the promise God gave Abraham was. Then, see if they can find it. If you have younger children who are not strong readers, reread the passage and have them raise their hands when they hear the correct answer: God promised Abraham that all the peoples or nations of the earth would be blessed through him [Genesis 12:3].)*

:: How does David describe the people who become a part of God's family? What are they like? *(Parents, if you have younger children, reread the passage and have them raise their hands when they hear the correct answer: God's people praise, worship, and serve him.)*

 Pray about It

Praise the Lord and worship him. Pick a favorite hymn or song and sing together as a family. If it makes it easier, sing along with your favorite worship music.

Week 62

The Supremacy of Christ

Story 140 – *The Gospel Story Bible*

Cut up an apple into about six equal wedges. Put the apple back together and bring it to Bible study in the palm of your hand holding the slices together. The cuts in the apple should be nearly invisible to your children. Have a plate ready as well. Tell your children to look at the apple in your hand, then say that it is being held together in your hand. Drop the apple onto the plate so that it separates into the slices. Pass around the pieces.

Explain that you have the power to hold together a sliced apple, but Jesus has the power to hold all of creation together. Also explain that scientists know that everything we see is made up of tiny particles, molecules, that are actually moving around but are also held together. It is amazing to think that the molecules of a solid oak table are actually moving around while the table holds together. Say, "This week, you will learn that Jesus is the one who holds everything together."

DAY ONE _____

Picture It

Imagine that you are under house arrest like Paul was. If you were under house arrest, you could not leave your house to run around outside or go for a walk. You would be guarded by a soldier, who would watch your every move. Since there were no phones in Paul's day, you couldn't make a phone call or send a text to talk to your family. Unless your family and friends visited you, the only thing you could do is write letters. So if you were locked up for two years like Paul was, you probably would write a lot of letters. That is what Paul did. In fact, some of his letters have survived and are part of the Bible today. The book of Colossians we are reading this week is one of the letters Paul wrote while he was under house arrest in Rome.

 Read Colossians 1:1–12.

Think about It Some More

One day during Paul's house arrest, a soldier brought another Christian prisoner to stay with him. His name was Epaphras (Philemon 23). Epaphras loved to tell people about Jesus. He started the church in the city of Colossae by preaching the gospel there. While with Paul under house arrest, he shared the story of how the Colossians first became Christians. After that, Paul and Epaphras prayed together for the Colossian church, along with Timothy, who came to visit Paul. One day when Timothy was with Paul, Paul decided to send the Colossian church a letter like he did for some of the churches he'd begun. That way, even though he had to remain in prison, he could greet the church, encourage them, and teach them with his letter. Paul hoped that his instruction would help them fight against the bad teaching that some false teachers were spreading in the churches in Asia.

Talk about It

:: How did Paul feel about the Christians he was writing to in Colossae? *(Paul cared about them. Even though he'd never met them, Paul seemed to have come to love them just from the stories Epaphras told him.)*

:: How often did Paul pray for the Colossian church? *(It doesn't say exactly how often Paul prayed, but verse 9 does say that he never stopped praying for them. That probably means that Paul prayed for them every day.)*

:: Reread verses 9–10. What are some of the things Paul prayed for? *(Paul prayed that the Colossians would be filled with the knowledge of God's will and for wisdom and understanding so they could please the Lord in everything they did.)*

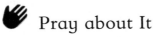 Pray about It

Take time and ask God to fill you with the knowledge of God's will and for wisdom and understanding so that you can also please the Lord in everything you do.

DAY TWO _____

Remember It

What do you remember about yesterday's Bible passage? What do you think we will learn about today?

 Read Colossians 1:13–18.

Think about It Some More

After a short introduction to let the Colossians know that he was praying for them, Paul jumped right in with some very important teaching about Jesus. He taught them that Jesus is God; that Jesus had existed before creation; that it was Jesus who created all things, both in heaven and on earth; and that all things are held together by Jesus. Our sins are forgiven through Jesus, and Jesus is the head of the church and ruler over all. We get to read Paul's letter today because somebody, perhaps the pastors of the church in Colossae, saved his letter so that copies could be made and passed around for everyone to read. God protected those copies so they could become a part of our Bible today.

What a joy it is for us to read about our great Savior. We learn things from Paul's letter that are completely new and had to be revealed by the Holy Spirit. Isn't it amazing to think that Jesus, God the Son, was the one who created the earth in the first place? As Christians, we should read the Bible every day to learn all we can about our great God!

Talk about It

:: What is one thing Paul taught the Colossians about Jesus? *(Parents, feel free to give your children clues. After they name one thing, see how many more they can remember. If your children can read, allow them to review the verses.)*

:: In what two ways was Jesus involved in the creation of the world? *(Paul tells us that Jesus created the world and that he holds the whole creation together.)*

:: What does it mean to have your sins forgiven? *(Parents, this is a simple but wonderful question. Hebrews 8:12 gives us a short answer: "I will remember their sins no more." Forgiveness begins by Jesus shedding his blood and taking the punishment we deserved. When we believe in Jesus, our sins are covered by what Jesus did on the cross, and God gives us Jesus' perfect record so that we can stand justified, just as if we never sinned, before God.)*

 Pray about It

Praise God for his forgiveness—for putting our sins as far away as the east is from the west and remembering them no more.

DAY THREE _____

Connect It to the Gospel

Today is the day we connect this week's Bible story to the gospel. The gospel is the life, death, and resurrection of Jesus for our salvation. Can anyone guess how our story this week looks forward to or back at the gospel?

 Read Colossians 1:19–23.

Think about It Some More

It is not hard to find the gospel in today's Bible verses. Paul said that Jesus, who was born a man, was also fully God. He opened the way for us to have peace with God by the blood he shed when he died on the cross (Colossians 1:20). That is the way we can be reconciled (brought back into a relationship) with God.

Paul reminded the Colossians of what they used to be like. Before God saved them, they were alienated (separated) from God and were enemies of God, doing evil deeds. What a contrast that is from how Paul described the Colossians in the opening of his letter when he said, "We always thank God, the Father of our Lord Jesus Christ, when we pray for you, since we heard of your faith in Christ Jesus and of the love that you have for all the saints" (Colossians 1:3–4).

Talk about It

:: What did Jesus do to bring peace between us and God? *(Jesus died in our place, taking our punishment. Once God's anger for our sin was poured out on Jesus, there was none left for us.)*

:: How were the Colossians changed by the gospel? *(The Colossians started out doing evil deeds as enemies of God, but when they were changed by the gospel and they believed in Jesus, they started loving one another.)*

:: Like the Colossians, before we are changed by the gospel, we are enemies of God, doing evil deeds. How have you seen the gospel change people you know? *(Parents, try to remind your children of the testimonies they have heard. If they are young and haven't heard many testimonies, then share your own story with them.)*

 Pray about It

Thank God for all that Jesus did so that we could become holy and blameless before God.

DAY FOUR _____

Remember It

What has God been teaching you this week through our Bible story?

 Read Colossians 1:24–29.

Think about It Some More

Try this exercise: While everyone's eyes are closed, place an object on a table, under a tablecloth. Then have them open their eyes. They can see a part of the shape of what is hidden, but what it is exactly remains a mystery. If you put a ball under the tablecloth, you would see that something round was hidden there. You might even guess that it was a ball. But you wouldn't know how heavy it was or whether it was a bouncy ball or a bowling ball. You couldn't tell what color it was or if it was smooth or maybe bumpy like a basketball. But once you removed the tablecloth, the mystery would end, and you could see exactly what was hidden.

In our passage today, Jesus is the mystery that God revealed. God told his people that he would one day send the Messiah to rescue them, but God's people didn't know when, who it would be, or how exactly he would do it. Those facts remained hidden as a mystery until Jesus was born, died on the cross, and rose again from the dead. Then Paul said God sent men like himself to tell everyone about Jesus and end the mystery.

Talk about It

> KIDS, ask your parents to tell you their favorite mystery story.

(Parents, think of your favorite mystery. It could be a Sherlock Homes or Hardy Boys story, or even something like Lord of the Rings *where the mystery is not knowing what will happen to the ring in the end.)*

:: What is a mystery? *(A mystery is something that is hidden.)*

:: What mystery is Paul explaining? *(Paul explained the mystery of how people were going to be saved from their sins through Jesus. God gave hints to his people, with things like sacrificing lambs and with prophecies like Isaiah 53, where he talks about a suffering servant. But it wasn't until Jesus died and his story was told that the mystery was fully revealed.)*

 Pray about It

Praise God for opening our eyes and giving us the answer to the biggest mystery of all, how a person can be saved from his sins through Jesus.

DAY FIVE _____

Discover It

Today is the day we look at a different Bible passage—from the book of Psalms or one of the prophets—to see what we can learn from it about Jesus or our salvation.

Read Psalm 22:14–16.

Think about It Some More

God gave us Psalm 22 to help us figure out the mystery of how God was going to rescue people from their sins. This psalm describes how a person was going to suffer and die at the hands of evil men. Although David wrote this long before Jesus was born, it is a prophetic picture that gave a clue to how Jesus would suffer. The psalm predicts the piercing of Jesus' hands and feet.

Remember that Thomas said he wouldn't believe until he saw and touched the nail marks in Jesus hands (John 20:25)? Looking back, we see that even the way Jesus died was not an accident but all a part of God's plan. Although angry men killed Jesus, it was God who planned his death as a sacrifice for our sin so we could be forgiven.

Talk about It

:: How do the verses we read today point to Jesus' death on the cross? *(These verses describe how a person would feel who was crucified. The piercing of the hands and feet would have been caused by the nails used to hold Jesus to the cross.)*

:: Why do you think God would describe the way Jesus would die as a clue to the mystery long before it happened? *(By giving a detailed description of the cross, God helps us to know that Jesus didn't die by accident, but that it was God's plan by which he would join us to his heavenly family.)*

:: How does reading about Jesus' death make you feel? *(Parents, give your answer to this question first, then draw out your children. It is also helpful to remember that Jesus was God, who had no sin at all and who died in our place.)*

Pray about It

Thank Jesus for suffering on the cross in our place so that we didn't have to suffer God's punishment for our sins.

Week 63

Chosen before the World Began

Story 141 – *The Gospel Story Bible*

Collect baby photos of you and each of your children. If you have more than one child, have the children guess who is in each photo. Then ask, "Who was the first to know you?" This is a bit of a trick question. They will likely answer Dad and Mom. Follow up by asking, "What about before us?" After a moment give them the correct answer by telling them that God knew them even before they were born, which is what they will learn in this week's lesson.

DAY ONE

Picture It

The first step in constructing a building is laying a foundation. A foundation is the underground support that a building stands on. Most buildings are constructed on a foundation of stone or cement, which is very strong and keeps the building from collapsing. But before a foundation can be laid, there is something needed: there must be a building plan. Without a plan, you won't know how long or wide to make the foundation. In our Bible passage today, Paul tells us that long before God made the foundations of the earth, he made a plan, and each one of us were made a part of his plan before he started creating anything.

 Read Ephesians 1:1–6.

Think about It Some More

Some people think the world was created by accident and that life on earth sprang up all by itself. But we know from reading the Bible that it was God who created the earth. It was also God who sent Jesus to die so that we could be forgiven of our sins. All of it was planned out by God before the world began. God knew that Adam and Eve would eat the forbidden fruit, and that he would need to send Jesus to die on the cross for their sins and ours. God also knew each person he planned to save and adopt into his family. Nothing happens by accident.

Talk about It

:: Why is it good to have a plan before you start building a foundation? *(A plan helps you to know what size and shape the foundation should be and where to build it.)*

:: What did Paul say God planned to do before he started to create the world? *(Even before God made the world, he planned to save sinners like us and adopt us into his family.)*

:: How did God know us before we were born? *(God knows everything, even things that have not happened yet.)*

 Pray about It

Thank God that he is in control of everything, and that he planned to rescue us and bring us into his family even before we were born.

DAY TWO _____

Remember It

What do you remember about yesterday's Bible passage? What do you think we will learn about today?

 Read Ephesians 1:7–12.

Think about It Some More

From the very beginning, before the world was created, Jesus' death on the cross was the way God planned to rescue us from sin. After Adam and Eve sinned, God didn't have to scramble to come up with a plan. God never said, "Oh, no! Adam and Eve disobeyed. Now what am I going to do?" Even before Adam and Eve, God planned to send his Son into the world. God chose the exact time (the fullness of time [Galatians 4:4]) for Jesus' birth, and through the prophets, God announced his coming before Jesus was born.

One special part of God's plan was to give an inheritance to everyone who believes in Jesus. An inheritance is the money, treasure, or land that a person passes on to his ancestors. God saves and adopts into his family everyone who believes in Jesus. Once we are a part of his family, we share in his inheritance—living forever in heaven with Jesus.

Talk about It

:: Why doesn't anything that takes place surprise God? *(God knows everything that is going to happen, and it all takes place according to his plan.)*

:: How long ago did God plan to rescue us from our sin by sending his Son, Jesus, to die on the cross? *(Even before God made the earth, the stars, and all that we see, he planned to send Jesus as the way to save us from our sins.)*

:: What is an inheritance? *(An inheritance is the money, treasure, or land that a person passes on to his children.)*

:: As God's adopted children, what do we receive as our inheritance? *(We receive Jesus living in our hearts by his Spirit, and we get to live with God in heaven forever.)*

 Pray about It

Praise God for giving us Jesus as our inheritance, and for providing a future for us with him in heaven.

DAY THREE _____

Connect It to the Gospel

Today is the day we connect this week's Bible story to the gospel. The gospel is the life, death, and resurrection of Jesus for our salvation. Can anyone guess how our story this week looks forward to or back at the gospel?

 Read Ephesians 1:13–14.

Think about It Some More

If you buy a brand new car, it comes with a guarantee. A guarantee is a sure promise. Some car companies will guarantee that for five years your engine won't break. If it does, they promise to fix it or give you a new car. A guarantee like that helps a car dealer sell more cars because people know the car company will stand behind its product. If something expensive breaks, they will take care of it. When we believe in Jesus, God sends his Holy Spirit to live inside of us as our guarantee. We know that if the Holy Spirit is living in our hearts here on earth, we will be able to live with God when we get to heaven. That is God's guarantee to us.

Talk about It

:: What is a guarantee? *(A guarantee is a sure promise. If someone guarantees to give you something, she is promising to give it to you for sure, and it can't be taken away.)*

:: Who did Paul say is our guarantee? *(Parents, reread verses 13–14 if your children don't remember the answer. You can empha-size the words* Holy Spirit *to give your children a clue. Then explain to them that, when a person believes in Jesus, the Holy Spirit comes to live inside him. The Holy Spirit living inside us is our guarantee that we will always live with God in heaven.)*

:: What did the Ephesians hear that helped them believe in God? *(The answer is found in verse 13. They heard the "word of truth, the gospel," which is the story of Jesus' death and resurrection for the forgiveness of our sins.)*

 Pray about It

Thank God for giving us the word of truth so that we can believe and be filled with the Holy Spirit as our guarantee that we will always be with God.

DAY FOUR _____

Remember It

What has God been teaching you this week through our Bible story?

 Read Ephesians 1:15–23.

Think about It Some More

The apostle Paul loved to pray for the churches. He often told them in the letters he sent that he was praying for them. Today we read one of

Paul's prayers. It is wonderful to see the kind of things Paul prayed for so that we can pray them for our church family too. Paul said that he wanted God to help them understand how to know Jesus better and to help them see the hope they had in heaven and the inheritance they would get as sons and daughters adopted into God's family. Paul wanted them to know that, even though Jesus went back to heaven, he was still ruling over everything, especially his church.

Paul's prayers for the Ephesian church are wonderful prayers for us to pray too. As Christians, we never stop learning about the great inheritance God has given us in heaven. We never stop learning more about the amazing, awesome God who saved us. So pray that God can give you more wisdom and knowledge of himself so that you can better know the immeasurable greatness of his power that was at work when he raised Jesus from the dead and seated him at his right hand.

Talk about It

> KIDS, ask your parents what kind of prayers they pray for you.

(Parents, share the prayers you pray for your children.)

:: Why do you think Paul told the Ephesians how he prayed for them? *(When we hear people are praying for us, it encourages us. Paul wanted to encourage the Ephesians. He also wanted to teach them. By hearing what he prayed for, they would know how to pray for one another.)*

:: Can you remember one of the things that Paul prayed for the Ephesians? *(Parents, Paul's prayer was pretty advanced for younger children, but if you read the passage slowly like a prayer it might help them pick out a part of Paul's prayer. The idea here is to help them listen carefully to what they read so they can take away something to use in their own life.)*

 ## Pray about It

Pray Paul's prayer for the Ephesians for your family. Pray that God would help you to know Jesus better; that he would open your eyes to how wonderful heaven will be; that he would help you remember that Jesus is always with us; and that we will know that we can rely on his power to help us to live for him.

DAY FIVE _____

Discover It

Today is the day we look at a different Bible passage—from the book of Psalms or one of the prophets—to see what we can learn from it about Jesus or our salvation.

 Read Zechariah 9:10–11.

Think about It Some More

Just before Jesus was arrested, at the Last Supper, Jesus broke the bread, which represented his broken body; then he took the cup of wine, gave thanks, and said, "Drink of it, all of you, for this is my blood of the covenant, which is poured out for many for the forgiveness of sins" (Matthew 26:27–28). Long before Jesus was ever born, Zechariah told of a day when the "blood of the covenant" would set the prisoners free. The blood of the covenant is the blood of Jesus poured out on the cross, which set us free from the punishment of hell. Hell is what Zechariah described as a waterless pit—a deep, deep hole you can't ever climb out of, with nothing at all inside to drink.

Talk about It

:: Whose blood was Zechariah talking about? *(Zechariah was talking about the blood of Jesus.)*

:: What does the waterless pit represent in this Bible passage? What is it like? *(The waterless pit is like hell—a place of suffering that you cannot escape by yourself.)*

:: What did Zechariah say God would bring to the nations? *(Parents, if your children are younger and not strong readers, reread verse 10 and emphasize the word* peace. *Have your children raise their hands when they hear the correct answer.)*

 Pray about It

Thank God for sending Jesus to die for our sins so that we would not have to spend eternity separated from God.

Week 64

From Death to Life

Story 142 – *The Gospel Story Bible*

Bring a stuffed animal to Bible study and lay it on the floor facedown. Ask your children to speak to it and tell it to roll over. They will likely say that it can't move by itself. Draw them out until they explain that it is not alive. Use this illustration to ask them what the difference is between someone who is alive and someone who is dead. The answer, of course, is that a dead person can't breathe, move, or do anything at all. Say, "This week, you will learn that before God saves us, we are dead in our sins and can do nothing to respond to God, just like the stuffed animal could do nothing to move itself."

DAY ONE

Picture It

Imagine that you are on a trip somewhere in a car with your parents, and your car battery dies. You are in a remote area with no one to help for hundreds of miles. You know that once the battery is dead, your car will not start. You try turning the key again and again, but nothing happens. The car still looks like a car. It still has an engine. But without the spark that makes the engine go, you could sit for hours and the car would not move anywhere. Unless you were to jump-start the battery or get a new one, you are stuck. That is what we are like in our sin. We are dead, and there is nothing we can do to save ourselves.

 Read Ephesians 2:1–3.

Think about It Some More

Before God saves us and makes us alive in Christ, we are dead in our sins. Our body is alive and we can walk around, but there is no way for us to get to heaven when we are dead in our sins, because inside we cannot believe in God or trust in Jesus. We do what we want instead of obeying God. Every person starts out that way, dead in sin—an enemy of God. Satan, who Paul calls the "prince of the air," tempts all of us to reject God and follow our own desires.

If it were not for God breathing spiritual life into our hearts, we would never turn to God and believe. Without the Holy Spirit, we would continue to live all our lives dead in our sins, refusing to believe, living with God's wrath (his holy anger) against us.

Talk about It

:: Why is the word *dead* a good way to describe a person before God saves them? *(Parents, help your children think about the analogy of a dead person. He can't do anything at all to help his cause. He can't get up. He can't breathe. That is a picture of us apart from God's saving grace.)*

:: Who is the "prince of the air"? *(Satan is the "prince of the air." He tempts us to live to please ourselves instead of living to please God.)*

:: What is God's wrath? *(God's wrath is his holy anger against sin. God must punish sin because sin hurts people, and sin is rebellion against God.)*

 Pray about It

Ask God to pour out his Spirit on each member of your family so none of you stay dead in your sin.

DAY TWO

Remember It

What do you remember about yesterday's Bible passage? What do you think we will learn about today?

 Read Ephesians 2:4–10.

Think about It Some More

Yesterday we learned the bad news that all people are dead in their sin. Today we hear the good news of the gospel—God can make us alive again. God gives new life to us by his grace, which means it is a free

gift we don't work for or earn. Jesus did the work when he lived a perfect life in our place and then died on the cross taking the punishment
we deserved for our sin. Since God did all the work, we have nothing to
boast or brag about. We can't take any of the credit. All the praise and
glory for making us alive and saving us goes to God.

Talk about It

::   What is the bad news? *(The bad news is that we all start out
dead in our sin.)*

::   What is the good news? *(The good news is that Jesus died on the
cross for us, so that even though we are dead in our sins, God can
make us alive again.)*

::   What does it mean to boast? *(Boasting [bragging] is when we
speak proudly about something we did.)*

::   Why does Paul say that no one can boast about getting
saved? *(Parents, if your children can't get the correct answer, give
them a clue by asking, "Who did the saving? Did God save us or
did we rescue ourselves?" Since God did the work, we have nothing
to boast or brag about.)*

 Pray about It

Thank God that he did all the work necessary to deliver us from sin
and to bring us into his family. His offer of salvation to all comes as a
free gift.

DAY THREE _____

Connect It to the Gospel

Today is the day we connect this week's Bible story to the gospel. The gospel is the life, death, and resurrection of Jesus for our salvation. Can anyone guess how our story this week looks forward to or back at the gospel?

 Read Ephesians 2:11–18.

Think about It Some More

Yesterday we learned the good news of the gospel. Today we learn
that the good news of the gospel is for all people. When God called
Abraham, he promised to bless all the people of the earth through him.

Yet it wasn't until Jesus died for the sins of all people that a way was opened up for Gentiles to come to God.

By trusting in Jesus, the Gentiles, who were once separated from God, can also join God's family. God kept his promise to Abraham through Jesus, who was born into Abraham's family line. So, way back when God promised to give Abraham a son and bless the nations, he was thinking of Jesus dying on the cross so that everyone, both Jew and Gentile, could be rescued from their sins.

Talk about It

:: What is a Gentile? (Gentile *is a name given to people who were not Jews—who were not a part of God's nation of Israel.*)

:: What opened the way for the Gentiles to join God's family? (*Jesus dying on the cross for their sins opened the way for the Gentiles to be forgiven and join God's family.*)

:: What did Jesus preach to those who were both far off and near? (*Parents, if you have younger children who are not strong readers, read the passage again and emphasize the word* peace *each time you come to it in verses 15–17.*)

 Pray about It

Thank God for opening a way for people from every nation to join the family of God.

DAY FOUR _____

Remember It

What has God been teaching you this week through our Bible story?

 Read Ephesians 2:19–22.

Think about It Some More

When you are driving toward a large city you will see signs along the road pointing the way to get there. You can't get lost if you follow those signs. In the same way, there are signs in the Old Testament that point to Jesus. For example, in Solomon's day the people of Israel built a temple made of stones, and God's presence came to live inside that temple. To take away the punishment for their sin, they killed lambs and sprinkled the blood on the altar. The temple and the sacrifices of the old covenant were like road signs pointing to Jesus.

Today, we don't have to sacrifice lambs because Jesus, the perfect Lamb of God, died for our sins. The lambs of old were like signs pointing to Jesus. Instead of God's presence filling a temple made of stones, God's Holy Spirit fills the hearts and lives of all believers. The temple of old was a sign that pointed to the day when God's people have become his temple with the Spirit of Christ living in their hearts.

Talk about It

> KIDS, ask your parents if they ever felt the presence of God in their heart or among God's people when they went to church.

(Parents, share what it feels like to have God's Spirit living inside you. Share the joy you experience on Sunday when hundreds of other people who also have God's Spirit come together to worship God.)

∷ The old temple foundation was made of hard, cold stones. What is the new temple foundation made of? *(Jesus, the apostles, and the prophets make up the foundation of the new temple. They are not really lying on the ground with the rest of us piled up on them, like you would lay bricks. Jesus and the apostles are called the foundation because the church is built upon the teachings of Jesus, which the apostles taught and passed on to us and that are preserved in the Bible.)*

∷ What does a person need to do to become a part of God's temple and have the Holy Spirit live inside? *(A person must turn away from sin and trust Jesus for salvation.)*

Pray about It

Pray that all members of your family turn away from their sin and believe in Jesus so they can become a part of God's temple with the Spirit of God living inside them.

DAY FIVE

Discover It

Today is the day we look at a different Bible passage—from the book of Psalms or one of the prophets—to see what we can learn from it about Jesus or our salvation.

 Read Isaiah 53:6.

Think about It Some More

There is no clearer verse in the whole Old Testament than Isaiah 53:6 to tell us the bad news about our sin and the good news of the gospel. Isaiah said that, as sinners, we have all gone astray and turned away from God to do what we want. He didn't say that some have turned away. He didn't say that many have turned away. Isaiah tells us that each and every one of us has turned to his own way. But Isaiah didn't leave us hopeless with only the bad news; he also spoke about the good news when he said that God would put our sin (our iniquity) on Jesus.

Talk about It

:: What is the bad news Isaiah shared in today's Bible verse? *(Parents, if you have younger children, reread Isaiah 53:6 and have them raise their hands when they hear the bad news: all of us have turned away from God just like sheep wander away from their shepherd.)*

:: What does the word *iniquity* mean? *(Iniquity is just another word for sin.)*

:: What is the good news that Isaiah shared in today's Bible verse? *(The good news is that, instead of punishing us, God placed our sin on Jesus and punished him in our place.)*

 Pray about It

Thank God for putting our iniquities—our sins—on Jesus. Thank Jesus for taking our iniquities on himself. Praise God that everyone who believes in Jesus, though they are dead in their sins, can be made alive.

Week 65

The Gift of Men

Story 143 – *The Gospel Story Bible*

Bring to Bible study a blank thank-you card to give to your pastor. Together, come up with ways your pastor cares for your family. Then write a thank-you note that details the items on your list. Have each of your children sign their name, and send the card to your pastor in the mail. Say, "This week we will learn that God gives us leaders in the church as gifts to help us grow in Christ."

DAY ONE

Picture It

When a boy joins the Scouts he makes a promise to do his best to serve God and country, obey the Scout laws, help people in need, and do good. If he breaks his pledge while wearing his uniform, the whole Boy Scout organization looks bad because of his poor behavior. Once a person joins the Army and puts on the uniform, she represents the country she serves. Whatever she does, good or bad, affects the way people think about her country. The same is true for Christians. We don't live just for ourselves; we live for Christ and represent the church.

When we trust and believe in Jesus, the Bible says we are clothed with Christ (Galatians 3:27). That is another way to say that we have been completely changed by Jesus and that God's Spirit has come to live inside us. Even the name *Christian* represents Jesus. We also have a pledge. When we turn away from our sins, we promise to live for Jesus. So if a Christian breaks his promise to follow Jesus and lives a sinful life, he makes Jesus and the whole church look bad.

 Read Ephesians 4:1–6.

Think about It Some More

In our Scripture today, Paul reminds the Ephesians to keep their promise to live for Jesus. Just as a Scout has a code of conduct or a way to behave, so does a Christian. As Christians, we are called by God to live like Jesus lived. We can't earn our way to heaven by doing good deeds—Jesus paid the way for us. But once the Holy Spirit helps us understand all that Jesus did for us and we put our faith in him, we want to live for Jesus and turn away from our sin. Even so, because sin remains, we sometimes forget the gospel and don't listen to the Spirit of God. That is why Paul reminded the Ephesians to walk in a manner worthy of the calling they had received (Ephesians 4:1). Paul knew that the Holy Spirit would help the Ephesians as they worked to live together in unity and peace.

Talk about It

:: How did Paul remind the Ephesian Christians to live? *(Paul reminded the Ephesians to live in humility, gentleness, patience, love, and unity.)*

:: How would it affect unbelievers if they saw all Christians living the way Paul described—in humility, gentleness, patience, love, and unity? *(If we all lived that way, people who don't believe would see that we were very different from the rest of the world, and they would want to know what enables us to live that way. Then we could tell them about Jesus.)*

:: How does it affect people when Christians don't live like Jesus and are proud, mean, impatient, angry, and divided? *(When Christians don't follow Jesus, we look the same as all the other people in the world, and people are not attracted Jesus.)*

:: How can we live the way Paul described? *(Only God can enable us to be loving and kind to one another. First, we need to give our lives to Jesus and be born again and filled with the Holy Spirit. Then we need to turn away from the world and live a life of repentance and faith, trusting that the Holy Spirit will make us like Jesus.)*

 Pray about It

Ask Jesus to open the eyes of all the members of your family to believe and fill them with his Holy Spirit to enable them live in humility, gentleness, patience, love, and unity.

DAY TWO

Remember It

What do you remember about yesterday's Bible passage? What do you think we will learn about today?

 Read Ephesians 4:7–13.

Think about It Some More

Yesterday we learned that God wants us to live in humility, gentleness, patience, love, and unity. But God knew we couldn't do that all by ourselves, so he gave us some very special people as gifts to help us. God gave us church leaders, for example, our pastors, to remind and teach us. Our pastors teach us from the Bible to remind us of all that Jesus did. Then they show us how to live by their example so that we grow up in our faith to be more like Jesus. That way, we won't fight with one another or be led astray by false teaching.

Talk about It

:: What gifts did Paul say God gave the church to help us to grow in our faith to be more like Jesus? *(Paul said God gave the church gifts of leaders, like our pastors, to help us to grow in our faith to be more like Jesus.)*

:: What are two ways that pastors help us to be more like Jesus? *(Pastors teach from the Bible and they lead by their example.)*

:: Can you remember a time when a pastor taught you to live like Jesus? *(Parents, help your children identify with the teaching of your pastor. Remind them of the last time the pastor addressed them on a Sunday morning.)*

 Pray about It

Thank God for the gifts of leaders in your church and pray for them by name.

DAY THREE

Connect It to the Gospel

Today is the day we connect this week's Bible story to the gospel. The gospel is the life, death, and resurrection of Jesus for our salvation. Can anyone guess how our story this week looks forward to or back at the gospel?

 Read Acts 20:17–32.

Think about It Some More

Yesterday we learned from Paul's letter to the Ephesians that God gives leaders to the church as gifts to care for the people. In today's passage, as we read Paul's encouragement to the Ephesian pastors, we get an inside picture of how a pastor cares for the people of his church. Paul reminded the Ephesian pastors how he himself cared for the Ephesian church because he wanted them to remember and follow his example. He told the Ephesian pastors that the message of the gospel was the most important message a pastor could teach his people. Paul said that teaching the whole Bible ("the whole counsel of God" [v. 27]) would protect the church from false teachers who wanted to lead them away from the truth. Those are the same things our pastors do for us today. They teach us about the gospel and the whole counsel of God so we will not be led away from the truth by anyone.

Talk about It

:: What message did Paul say he taught from house to house? *(Parents, if you have younger children, reread verses 20–21 and emphasize the words* repentance toward God *and* faith in our Lord Jesus Christ *and see if your children can pick up the answer.)*

:: Paul told the Ephesian pastors to teach the whole Bible. From whom did he say that would protect the people? *(Paul said that if the pastors taught the people the whole Bible [the whole counsel of God] that it would protect them from fierce wolves—false teachers who would say twisted things to lead the people astray. If the people of the church knew what the Bible said, they wouldn't believe the lies of the false teachers.)*

:: Can you think of a way the pastors of your church are the same as the pastors God gave the Ephesians? *(Parents, help your children to see that all pastors have the same job: to preach the gospel and care for the people so that false teachers don't lead them away from the truth.)*

 Pray about It

Pray for your pastors as they teach you the whole Bible and help you to grow.

DAY FOUR

Remember It

What has God been teaching you this week through our Bible story?

 Read Ephesians 4:14–16.

Think about It Some More

If a small child fell off a ship into the ocean, she would be helpless against the waves and the wind. Even a life jacket wouldn't help her to fight the wind and the huge waves, and she would float away wherever they took her. That is the picture Paul uses to show us what it is like to live without good teaching from the Word of God. If we don't know what is true, we will believe almost anything. That is why God gave gifts of leaders to teach us the truth.

Yesterday we learned that Paul told the Ephesian pastors that preaching the whole Bible would protect the people from false teachers. In today's Bible passage, Paul is saying the same thing to warn the people in the church about deceivers who would come to try and lead them astray. Knowing the truth of God's Word helps us to recognize the lies of false teachers.

Talk about It

> ●● KIDS, ask your parents if a false teacher ever tried
> ●● to lead them astray.

(Parents, you don't have to go much further than advertisements that want us to believe we need to buy things to make us happy. You may, however, have a story about a person who tried to spread false teaching in your church. If you do, share that.)

:: How can learning the Bible protect us against false teaching? *(The Bible tells us what is true. If what a preacher says is different from what the Bible says, we know not to follow him.)*

:: What did Paul say we can do to help each other grow? *(We can speak to each other the truth that we learn from the Bible [v. 15]. Although God gave pastors as gifts to teach the church, we can also remind one other what the Bible teaches.)*

:: What is something the Bible teaches that you could share to help remind your family of the truth? *(Parents, help all your children remember something they learned from the Bible. Help them know how to use it to encourage each other. John 3:16 and Ephesians 6:2 are good verses to remind the children of.)*

 Pray about It

Ask God to help you to love and learn his Word so that you will be protected from false teaching.

DAY FIVE

Discover It

Today is the day we look at a different Bible passage—from the book of Psalms or one of the prophets—to see what we can learn from it about Jesus or our salvation.

 Read Psalm 68:1–20.

Think about It Some More

When Paul wrote to the Ephesians, he quoted Psalm 68:18 and said that that verse was talking about Jesus (Ephesians 4:8). This psalm is a picture of a victorious king who won a great battle and then leads away the prisoners (the captives). Jesus is the king who descended (the word *descended* means to go down) when he came to earth as a man. Then, after defeating sin and death by rising from the dead, Jesus ascended (went back up) to heaven.

Talk about It

:: How do verses 19–20 describe God? *(Parents, if your children are younger, read the verses and have them raise their hands when they hear the description of God as our salvation.)*

:: In Psalm 68:1–4 what does David say we should do? *(Parents, if you have younger children, reread the verses and have them raise their hands when they hear the correct answer: David said we should be glad and filled with joy and should sing to God.)*

:: Why should we be glad and filled with joy today? *(We should be glad and filled with joy because Jesus has won a great victory. He descended from heaven and died for our sins, and then he rose again and ascended back into heaven, where he sits as the victorious king. One day we will all join him there. Through Jesus, God has saved us and given us a share in his victory!)*

 Pray about It

Thank Jesus for giving up heaven to descend to earth as a man and die for us.

Week 66

Putting Off the Old Self

Story 144 – *The Gospel Story Bible*

Take an old, ragged shirt and mark it up with spray paint or markers. Then tear it in multiple places without ruining the integrity of the cuffs, collar, or sleeves so it can still be worn. Wear the shirt to Bible study. Your children will comment for sure. Tell them it was an old shirt that you should throw away, but you thought you could still get some wear out of it. Ask them if they think it would be okay to wear it to work or church.

When they object to the torn shirt, draw them out and ask why. See if they can tell you that it would be foolish to wear an old, torn shirt when you have brand new shirts to wear. Say, "This week we will learn how the shirt is a great illustration of our spiritual lives. Paul told the Ephesians to put off their old self and put on the new."

DAY ONE

Picture It

If you commit a crime and are sentenced to a prison term, your everyday clothes are taken away and you are given prison clothes to wear. That way, the guards can immediately tell if someone is a prisoner by their clothes. If a convict escapes from prison, anyone who sees them on the road will know they are an escapee and call the police. One of the very first things a prisoner does when released from prison is to take off the prison clothes and throw them away. Imagine how joyful it is for a prisoner to remove the old prison clothes, put on a T-shirt and jeans, and walk out into freedom.

Before we believe and trust Jesus, we are all prisoners bound by the chains of sin, wearing the clothing of sin. But when God, by his Spirit, sets us free from the power of sin, he calls us to put off the prison clothes of sin and put on the righteousness of Christ. Although we can still sin like we did as unbelievers, God calls us to live in our salvation with the life-transforming power of the Holy Spirit working in us (Philippians 2:12–13).

 Read Ephesians 4:17–24.

Think about It Some More

Once God saves us, and sends his Spirit to live inside of us, we grow in our desire to put off the old prison clothes of our sinful lives by saying no to sin. Then, when we live for Jesus by doing good works, it's like putting on new clothes. These outward good works match who we are on the inside where God, by his Spirit, has made us brand new. Paul called this putting off the old self of our former sinful life and putting on the new self so that our lives show the glory of God, who created us to be like Jesus. Before God sets us free from the power of sin, we live sinful lives and are not only unwilling, but also unable, to live for God. But when God makes us born again and puts his Spirit into our hearts, he breaks the power of sin over us and sets us free.

Once God's Spirit lives in us, the desires of our heart begin to change so that we begin to want to live for God. Sometimes though, we fall back into our old sinful patterns. That is why Paul encouraged the Ephesians to put that old way of life off and to put on their new lives in Christ. We can't obey in our own strength, trusting in ourselves. But by "walking by the Spirit" (Galatians 5:16), Paul assures we can live without giving in to our sinful desires.

Talk about It

:: What does Paul mean when he talks about the old self? *(When Paul talks about the old self he is talking about what a person's life is like before he becomes a Christian, when he is a prisoner of sin.)*

:: What does Paul mean when he talks about the new self? *(When Paul talks about the new self, he is talking about a person who has become a Christian and God has changed her life to be brand new. God forgives her sins and sets her free from her former sinful life, so she can obey God.)*

:: When do we first get our new self that allows us to say no to sin and yes to God? *(Our new self comes when we believe and*

God changes our hearts and puts his Spirit inside of us. The Bible calls this being born again [John 3:3].)

 Pray about It

Ask God to fill you with the Holy Spirit so that you can live a life of repentance and faith, trusting him to make you like himself.

DAY TWO _____

Remember It

What do you remember about yesterday's Bible passage? What do you think we will learn about today?

 Read Ephesians 4:25–32.

Think about It Some More

Yesterday Paul taught us to put off the old self of sin and put on the new self, which is a life being changed by the Holy Spirit to be like Jesus. In our passage today, we see a whole list of examples of what that looks like. You could call it a put-off-and-put-on list. Think of your sin as a heavy old coat that is worn and dirty, and think of your new self as a brand new coat. You can't put the new one on until you take the old one off. The trouble is that only God can take off the old coat of sin. That is why Paul said that the Holy Spirit sealed us (v. 30) and Christ forgave us (v. 32). Without Jesus dying on the cross for our sins and giving us the Holy Spirit to live inside us, we would not be able to take off that old coat of sin—nor would we want to.

Talk about It

:: How many items on Paul's put-off-and-put-on list can you remember? *(Paul said we should put off falsehood, anger, stealing, corrupting talk, bitterness, wrath, and anger. And he said we should put on truth, hard work, building one another up, kindness, and forgiveness.)*

:: Why do we need God's help to put off sin? *(We need God to save us and change us on the inside or else we will love sin more than we love God. We don't want to take off the old coat of our sin until God opens our eyes to see that it is dirty and worn.)*

:: What sins on Paul's list are big struggles for you? *(Parents, this is a great opportunity to talk with your children about sin and get into a conversation about whether they trust Jesus. Watch them and look for evidence of the fruit of the Holy Spirit in their lives. Anyone can say he is a Christian, but it is over time that we prove our repentance is genuine by the fruit of a life changed by Christ.)*

 ## Pray about It

Ask God to help each person in your family want to put off their old coat of sin and put on a new life of believing in Jesus and turning away from sin.

DAY THREE

Connect It to the Gospel

Today is the day we connect this week's Bible story to the gospel. The gospel is the life, death, and resurrection of Jesus for our salvation. Can anyone guess how our story this week looks forward to or back at the gospel?

 Read Ephesians 5:1–2.

Think about It Some More

Sometimes people try to live for God out of their own strength. When they fall into sin they feel condemned as a failure without hope, and when they do well they become proud and feel they are finally worthy of God. But even our good works can't get us into heaven. That is why, after his put-off-and-put-on list in Ephesians 4, Paul wanted to make extra sure that we are not, in our own strength, trying to put off the old self of sin, and why Paul reminded them of Jesus. Jesus lived a perfect life in our place, and Jesus died on the cross to take away our sin. We don't put off our old self as a way to earn a ticket to heaven. Just as sin cannot keep out of heaven a person Jesus died for, neither can our good deeds get us in. All our hope is in Jesus.

Talk about It

:: What did Paul say was the reason Jesus died for us? *(Paul said that Jesus died for us because he loved us.)*

:: How should Jesus dying on the cross affect the way we treat others? *(Paul said that we should want to love others because of how Jesus loved us when he gave up his life for us.)*

:: Who did Paul say we are imitating when we put off the old self and put on the new? *(God)*

 ## Pray about It

Ask God to always help you remember that Jesus dying on the cross for our sins is the reason we do good things.

DAY FOUR

Remember It

What has God been teaching you this week through our Bible story?

 Read Ephesians 5:3–21.

Think about It Some More

After reminding us of the gospel, Paul continued on with his put-off-and-put-on list. He compared sinning to walking in the dark, while he said that following Jesus was like walking in the light. Jesus taught the very same thing to his disciples. He said, "I am the light of the world. Whoever follows me will not walk in darkness, but will have the light of life" (John 8:12). The only way we can walk in the light is if we are children of the light. That means the only way we can say *no* to sin and *yes* to God is if our eyes have been opened to the truth of the gospel—that Jesus died for us and has taken our sins away.

Talk about It

> ●● KIDS, ask your parents how what Jesus did for
> ●● them makes them want to please him.

(Parents, share how Jesus dying for you opened your eyes and made you want to please him by daily repenting and walking by faith.)

:: What does Paul mean when he called the Ephesians "children of light" (v. 8)? *(God, in Jesus, is the light of the world. When God saves us, we become his adopted children. We then are children of light, which is just another way to say we are God's children.)*

:: What did Paul say we are supposed to put on instead of drunkenness? *(Paul said we should put off drunkenness and put on being filled with the Spirit of God.)*

:: What kind of things did Paul say we should do once we are filled with the Holy Spirit? *(Paul said we should sing with all our heart to one another, giving thanks to God while we submit to one another, which means we should not fight but rather give up what we want to bless one another.)*

 Pray about It

Ask God to fill each person in your family with his Holy Spirit that you may sing with joy and live in peace with one another.

DAY FIVE

Discover It

Today is the day we look at a different Bible passage—from the book of Psalms or one of the prophets—to see what we can learn from it about Jesus or our salvation.

 Read Psalm 44:11–22.

Think about It Some More

Paul quoted today's Bible passage in Romans 8:35–36 to describe the persecution that comes to Christians when they follow Jesus. *Persecution* is a big word that means to cause someone to suffer because of what they believe. Jesus said, "If they persecuted me, they will also persecute you" (John 15:20). Some people don't like to hear that Jesus is the only way to be saved. When we tell others about Jesus, some will reject what we say. Some people may laugh at us, and some will even get angry and say bad things about us. All of that is persecution. But in some countries around the world, Christians are put in prison and even killed for believing in Jesus and telling others about him.

Talk about It

:: What does the word *persecution* mean? *(Persecution means to cause someone to suffer because of what they believe.)*

:: Why would people want to persecute Christians? *(Some people hate Jesus and don't like anyone who follows Jesus either.)*

:: From Psalm 44:11–22, list some of the ways the people of God have been persecuted? *(Parents, if your children are not strong readers, reread the passage and have them raise their hands when they hear a way the people of God were persecuted by others. The people of God were laughed at, mocked, and even killed.)*

 ## Pray about It

Pray for the Christians around the world who are being persecuted for their faith in Jesus.

Week 67

The Armor of God

Story 145 – *The Gospel Story Bible*

Collect an opened, empty metal can; two potatoes, each of which can fit inside the can; a cutting board; and a kitchen knife that you're not afraid to dull. Prior to Bible study, gather your children around the kitchen table and tell them you are going to give them an armor demonstration. Place the first potato on the cutting board and, making sure your children are at a safe distance, give the potato several sharp downward chops with the knife. You should be able to cut it to pieces easily. Explain that this is what would happen in battle to a person not wearing armor.

Now lay the metal can down on the cutting board and slip the second potato inside. Repeat the cutting motion with the same force as before, but this time onto the metal can. Then pass the can around to see how it took the blows of the knife, leaving the potato inside without a mark. Say, "This week we will learn how the armor of God protects us against the schemes of the devil and the temptations of the world."

DAY ONE

Picture It

In the year 1513, after discovering gold on an island he named Puerto Rico, a famous explorer named Ponce de León left the island in search of a new treasure: the Fountain of Youth. After a short time at sea, he discovered the coast of Florida and left his ship anchored to go ashore and explore the new land in search of the fountain. He first learned of the Fountain of Youth from Puerto Rican natives who said that a drink from the Fountain of Youth would give you long life or, if you were old, make you young again.

Ponce de León never found the fountain. But if he had read his Bible, he would have discovered the true secret to long life. Today in our Bible story, we will learn the special promise of long life God gave to all children.

 Read Ephesians 6:1–4.

Think about It Some More

In today's passage, Paul repeated a commandment that God had given to the children of Israel. Paul wanted children to know that the reason children must obey their parents is because God said to, not just because their parents want them to. But even children need Jesus to help them. That is why Paul added the words "in the Lord." It is only by believing in Jesus that a child wants to obey. This goes back to Paul's teaching about putting off the old self and putting on the new. Unless a child puts on the new self and becomes like Jesus, he will keep disobeying his parents, and life won't go well for him.

As for parents, Paul wanted us to be understanding and not provoke our children to anger. We need to remember that until they give their hearts and lives to Jesus, it is impossible for them to obey consistently. Rather than get angry when they sin, we need to point them to Jesus, their Savior.

Talk about It

:: What did God say we need to do to receive the promise of long life? *(God promised that if we obey our parents we will live long in the land.)*

:: What is the most important instruction a parent can teach his children? *(Parents, let your children keep guessing until they guess the gospel. If you need to give them some clues, the most important thing a parent can teach their child is that they need believe in what Jesus did on the cross. Without Jesus living inside of us by his Spirit and giving us a desire to obey, we would just keep doing what we want—sinning against God.)*

:: Whose help do we need to obey your parents? *(The only way to obey parents is by trusting the Lord. That is why Paul said children should obey their parents "in the Lord.")*

Pray about It

Ask God to help each child in your family believe and trust in Jesus so that they will have the help and strength they need to follow Jesus.

DAY TWO

Remember It

What do you remember about yesterday's Bible passage? What do you think we will learn about today?

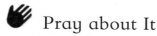 Read Ephesians 6:10–13.

Think about It Some More

During the time Paul was awaiting trial in Rome and writing his letter to the Ephesians, he lived under house arrest, chained to an armor-clad Roman soldier. Inspired by the Holy Spirit, Paul got an idea. He could use the example of the armor to teach the Ephesians how to defend themselves in the battle against sin and evil. Satan, our enemy, loves to try to make us feel bad, whispering lies to us like, "You are too bad—Jesus can't save you." He also likes to tempt us to sin by telling us to lie, steal, and cheat to get what we want. Remembering that we have armor, which is the truth of the gospel, helps us to stand against his temptations and lies. Each of us, Paul said, must put on the armor of God. The picture of armor became an easy way to help the Christians remember to stand firm, trusting in the gospel when Satan attacked them with lies or tempted them to sin.

Talk about It

:: How does armor protect a Roman soldier in battle? *(Parents, draw out your children here. If an enemy attacked an armor-clad soldier, the enemy's weapon would hit the armor instead of the soldier's body.)*

:: What does the armor of God protect us from? *(Parents, if your children are not strong readers, reread the passage asking them to raise their hands when they hear something that the armor of God protects us from. Paul said the armor of God protects us from attacks of evil and the scheming lies of the devil.)*

:: What is the armor of God made out of? (*The armor of God is not made from leather or steel. The armor of God is a way for us to remember the truth of God's Word so we can use it to fight against the enemy's lies.*)

:: Can you remember a story where Satan attacked Jesus with lies, and Jesus used the truth of God's Word like armor to stand against Satan? (*Parents, see if your children can remember the story of Jesus' temptation. That story [Luke 4:1–13] is a great illustration of how Jesus used God's Word like armor to defend against the enemy's attacks.*)

 Pray about It

Ask God to help you diligently study the Bible so that you will be able to stand against the enemy's lies.

DAY THREE

Connect It to the Gospel

Today is the day we connect this week's Bible story to the gospel. The gospel is the life, death, and resurrection of Jesus for our salvation. Can anyone guess how our story this week looks forward to or back at the gospel?

 Read Ephesians 6:14–15.

Think about It Some More

Each piece of God's armor points us to trust the gospel, the story of what Jesus did for us when he died on the cross.

Our belt is a belt of truth. We can be sure that everything we read in the Bible is true. Knowing the gospel is true gives us the confidence we need to stand our ground and fight against the enemy's schemes.

Our breastplate is the righteousness of Jesus. When we trust in Jesus, he forgives our sin and gives us his righteousness. That way, when the enemy tries to discourage us by saying we are terrible sinners, we remember that Christ's righteousness covers our sin.

Leather shoes protected the Roman soldier so he could boldly run into battle and not worry about hurting his feet on sharp objects. The

gospel gives Christians the same confidence to run into battle. For
when we run with the gospel, we have God to protect our every step.

Talk about It

:: What parts of the armor of God did we learn about today?
*(We learned about the belt of truth, the breastplate of righteousness,
and the shoes of the gospel of peace.)*

:: What does the belt of truth represent? *(The belt represents the
Bible. Everything in the Bible is true. That is why we can stand
firm in battle. If anyone tells us something that is different from
what the Bible says, we can know that the Bible is always right.)*

:: What does the breastplate of righteousness represent? *(The
breastplate of righteousness is the sinless life of Jesus that he gives us
when we trust in him. Even though we are sinners, the righteousness
of Christ covers our sin.)*

 ## Pray about It

Thank God for giving everyone who believes in Jesus his own righteousness—his sinless life—so we can have peace with God and run
into battle with God at our side.

DAY FOUR _____

Remember It

What has God been teaching you this week through our Bible story?

 Read Ephesians 6:16–20.

Think about It Some More

God's armor has a shield of faith, which Paul said we must always
carry. A shield is the first defense against the weapons of the enemy.
When the devil sends his flaming darts of lies and doubt, we can hold
up our faith in Jesus and his victory on the cross as a shield to protect
us. We wear God's promise to save all those who believe as our helmet.
Paul called it the helmet of salvation.

In addition to the armor protecting us against the enemy's attacks,
Paul also said we carry a weapon to fight and strike back with. Every
Christian has a sword, the Word of God. That is what Jesus used to fight

against Satan and the attacks of the Pharisees, and we can use God's Word the same way.

Talk about It

> KIDS, ask your parents to tell you how the armor of God has protected them against the attacks of the enemy.

(Parents, see if you can remember a time when you felt condemned or discouraged and the gospel encouraged you, or a time when you faced temptation and did not give in because God's Word strengthened you.)

:: Why is a shield a very important piece of the armor? *(A shield gives you double protection. An arrow, for instance, would have to get through your shield before it could even touch the armor of your breastplate.)*

:: Paul called our shield a shield of faith. What does the word *faith* mean? *(Parents, you may need to help your younger children with this one. Feel free to give them a few clues. Faith means believing something is true. Our faith is in God and the gospel. If we have faith and believe that Jesus died to forgive us and we are going to heaven, then the enemy's lies won't get past the shield.)*

:: What did Paul say God gave us as a sword? *(The Word of God is our sword. A sword is an offensive weapon we can use to attack the enemy just like Jesus did.)*

Pray about It

Thank God for giving us his armor, especially the sword—his Word, which helps us to remember all of the other pieces of the armor and what they stand for.

DAY FIVE _____

Discover It

Today is the day we look at a different Bible passage—from the book of Psalms or one of the prophets—to see what we can learn from it about Jesus or our salvation.

Read Psalm 69:19–25.

Think about It Some More

When David wrote Psalm 69, he was probably writing about his own life and how he called out to God in his suffering. But when we look back at this psalm, we see that it paints a picture of Jesus and his suffering on the cross. For instance, when Jesus was crucified, he was offered sour wine (wine vinegar) to quench his thirst (Matthew 27:48) and gall, a poisonous herb (Matthew 27:34). This matches what David wrote (v. 21). Also, Peter quoted verse 25 to describe Judas, who died after betraying Jesus, leaving an opening among the twelve apostles (Acts 1:20).

Talk about It

:: What in this psalm points to Jesus? *(Psalm 69 points to the suffering of Jesus on the cross when he was offered sour wine and poisonous gall.)*

:: Who helped David write things about Jesus long before Jesus was even born? *(The Holy Spirit helped all the writers of Scripture to write down just what God wanted them to write.)*

:: How do verses 19–20 also point to Jesus? *(Jesus was mocked and shamed at the cross, and no one came to help him. Even God his Father turned away from Jesus and punished him for our sin. Jesus died on the cross, alone.)*

 ## Pray about It

Thank Jesus for dying on the cross for our sins, alone, rejected even by God his Father.

The Humility of Christ

Story 146 – *The Gospel Story Bible*

Beforehand, list five skills or activities your children are good at. These could be athletic skills like throwing a baseball, or school subjects like math, or gifts and talents like drawing or playing the piano. Gather the children and ask them to name someone who is skilled in each of the five areas you read. Make a list of the names they mention.

If they mention their own name, explain that you are not going to put their name on the list because this week we are going to consider others over ourselves. If none of your children mention their own names, commend them for their humility and use that as an opportunity to introduce this week's topic, which is considering the interests of others over our own. Then encourage your children to consider others as more important than themselves this week.

DAY ONE

Picture It

Imagine a world where everyone wanted to be first all the time and nobody cared about other people. In a world like that, no one would hold the door for anyone, and everyone would fight to be first in line all the time. Cars would crash at intersections because all the drivers refused to stop to let others go through. Team sports would change because all the players would want the ball so they could score points for themselves. In a world where everyone thought of only themselves, no one would share or give to others. That kind of world would not be a very nice place to live. In our Bible passage today, God teaches us something very different: we should think of others as more important than ourselves.

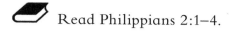 Read Philippians 2:1–4.

Think about It Some More

What would you do if someone were giving away ice cream, but there were more people in line than there was ice cream for? Would you try to push to the front the line to make sure you got some? Or would you volunteer to give yours up for someone else? Paul said that as Christians we should consider others more important than ourselves because of what Jesus did for us. Remember, as Christians, we are called to put off our former way of living and "put on the new self, created after the likeness of God in true righteousness and holiness" (Ephesians 4:24).

Considering others' interests over our own is simply living out the truth of who God created us to be. When we consider others more significant than ourselves, we are using our lives to show that we were made in the image of God. Paul tells us that if we have "any participation in the Spirit" we should live this way. It is only by the power of the Holy Spirit that we can live for God.

Talk about It

:: Whose example are we following when we think of others as more important than ourselves? *(Once your children say Jesus, follow up by asking what Jesus did to show that he was thinking more about us than himself. Jesus, as the Son of God, put aside his glory and became a man and died for us.)*

:: Can you think of a time in the past week when you considered someone more important than yourself? *(Parents, help your children if you can remember an example. Remind them that, apart from the Holy Spirit changing our hearts, we don't want to think about others' needs.)*

:: What kinds of things could you do for your parents, brothers, sisters, and friends to consider them above yourself? *(Parents, help your children think of how they could share with and serve one another or their friends.)*

 Pray about It

Ask God to help you grow in your desire to be more like Jesus and consider others more important than yourself.

DAY TWO

Remember It

What do you remember about yesterday's Bible passage? What do you think we will learn about today?

 Read Philippians 2:5–7.

Think about It Some More

Before Jesus was born in Bethlehem, he had lived in heaven as God the Son with his Father. The Son was fully and completely God, just like his Father. But the Son of God did not stay in heaven, for the Father gave him a job that required a huge sacrifice. He asked his Son to put aside his glory in heaven to go to earth and die a painful death as a man. The Son of God said *yes* to his Father and was born as Jesus in a smelly stable, leaving the glories of heaven behind.

As a baby, Jesus was unable to care for himself, and had to depend on his mom and dad like any other human baby. God the Son, all-powerful and full of glory, humbled himself to become a baby who couldn't even take care of himself. Jesus could have stayed in heaven and held onto his glory, but he became a servant and gave up his glory so that one day he could die for us.

Talk about It

:: Where was God the Son before he was born as a man? *(God the Son lived together with God the Father and God the Holy Spirit in heaven.)*

:: What did the Son of God give up when he became the baby Jesus? *(God the Son gave up his throne and the display of his glory as God, and he put on the helplessness of a baby.)*

:: Paul said, "Have this mind among yourselves," and then pointed to Jesus. That was just another way to say we should follow Jesus' example. Since Jesus was willing to give up all the glories of heaven to come to earth as a baby, what can we do to follow his example? *(Parents, explain to your children that while they might be able to try and follow God's example, they need the Holy Spirit to change their hearts and cause them to be born again. If your children are believers, help them think of practical things they can do to follow Jesus' example.)*

Pray about It

Ask the Holy Spirit to change your heart so that you will be more willing to give up things for others.

DAY THREE _____

Connect It to the Gospel

Today is the day we connect this week's Bible story to the gospel. The gospel is the life, death, and resurrection of Jesus for our salvation. Can anyone guess how our story this week looks forward to or back at the gospel?

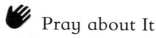 Read Philippians 2:8.

Think about It Some More

It is amazing that God the Son would put aside his glory in heaven to become a man to live among us. On top of that, it is even more astonishing that Jesus came to die a terrible death on the cross. But that is not the worst of his suffering. While Jesus was dying on the cross, God poured out his anger for our sin upon Jesus and rejected his only Son. That is why Jesus cried out, "My God, my God, why have you forsaken me?" (Matthew 27:46). Jesus' death on the cross is the greatest sacrifice and demonstration of humility and servanthood of all time. Paul uses Jesus' example to remind us how to live. If Jesus gave up his life, suffering a terrible death and rejection of his Father for us, then surely we can humble ourselves and serve one another with joy in day-to-day life. The problem is that without the Holy Spirit to change us and help us, we can't do this on our own. But, once the Spirit of God comes to live in us, he opens our eyes to see the joy and delight of following God. Then we really can try and be more and more like Jesus.

Talk about It

:: What does the word *humble* mean? (*A good way to explain humility is "to make yourself low."*)

:: What did Jesus do to humble himself? (*Jesus left his throne in heaven to become a man, and then died as a criminal.*)

:: How much did Jesus know about the cross and dying before he came to earth? (*Jesus knew everything. When Paul said that Jesus became obedient to death on a cross, he was telling us clearly that Jesus knew that God the Father was asking him to give up his life for our sins. Jesus gave up his glory knowing he was going to die.*)

 Pray about It

Thank Jesus for giving up his position in heaven to die for us on the cross.

DAY FOUR _____

Remember It

What has God been teaching you this week through our Bible story?

 Read Philippians 2:9–11.

Think about It Some More

Parents love to celebrate when their kids make good choices and serve others, like when you give up your seat on a bus for someone or give up the last cookie for your brother or sister. When parents celebrate the things their kids do, they are following God the Father's example. After Jesus died on the cross, God the Father made Jesus the King of kings and declared that everyone—all the angels in heaven, all the people on the earth, and even all the demons of hell—would one day bow down to him.

One day, at the final judgment, all the people who refused to believe will fall to the ground and tremble when they see Jesus, the King of kings. But those who trusted in Jesus will not be afraid. We will gladly bow down, and we will join with the Father in the celebration, singing worship songs to Jesus.

Talk about It

> KIDS, ask your parents what is the greatest thing they ever gave up for another person.

(Parents, you can talk about giving blood so that others may live. Moms can talk about how they gave up months of their lives to carry a baby to term. Or you might have another story to tell.)

:: What is the greatest sacrifice that anyone gave up for another? *(The greatest sacrifice of all time is when Jesus gave up his life for us by dying on the cross for our sins.)*

:: What will happen on the final judgment day to the people who refused to believe and trust in Jesus? *(When the final judgment day comes, everyone will bow before Jesus and acknowledge him as the King of all.)*

Pray about It

Ask God to touch the hearts of every person in your family so that you gladly bow before Jesus now. Ask the Holy Spirit to change your heart so you want to love and trust in Jesus.

DAY FIVE _____

Discover It

Today is the day we look at a different Bible passage—from the book of Psalms or one of the prophets—to see what we can learn from it about Jesus or our salvation.

Read Psalm 103:8–18 from your Bible.

Think about It Some More

This psalm points forward to God's plan to rescue us through the sacrifice of Jesus on the cross. David said that God does not deal with us according to our sins or repay us according to our iniquities. That means that, even though we have sinned against God, he chose not to punish us for our sins. The only reason God can overlook our sins is that Jesus died in our place and took the punishment we deserved.

You might wonder how people like David were saved since they lived long before Jesus did. For those, like David, who lived before Jesus came to earth, God passed over their sins (Romans 3:25–26), knowing that Jesus would one day come to take their punishment as well. We are forgiven by looking back at God's saving plan. They were forgiven by looking forward to God's saving plan.

Talk about It

:: How far is the east from the west? *(Since east and west are opposites, they are as far away as they could ever be. God could not have removed our sins any farther.)*

:: What words did David use to describe God in this psalm? *(Parents, this psalm is rich with descriptions of God's character. If you have younger children and they can't remember, reread the psalm and have they raise their hands when they hear a word David used to describe God.)*

:: How long did David say God's love would last? *(In verse 17 David said God's love is from everlasting to everlasting—God's love will last forever.)*

 ## Pray about It

Thank God for his everlasting love, and thank him for putting our sins away as far as the east is from the west. Worship God by repeating the praises David wrote about him in this psalm.

Week 69

Keep Your Eyes on the Prize

Story 147 – *The Gospel Story Bible*

You will need a set of dominoes or blocks for this exercise. Once your family is gathered for Bible study, start stacking the blocks one on top of the other to build a tower. With each new block, congratulate yourself on your success. After you have a tower several blocks high, ask your children if they know what you are doing. Once they offer their guesses, tell them you are building a tower to heaven. Ask them if they think you will be successful. When they respond that your project is impossible, ask them to tell you why it is impossible to build a tower to heaven. Then share with them that, like building a tower to heaven is impossible, it is impossible to get to heaven by doing good works. Say, "This week we will learn how Paul considered all of his works as nothing when compared with Christ."

DAY ONE

Picture It

One of the greatest accomplishments in baseball is pitching a perfect game. In the history of professional Major League Baseball, fewer than two dozen pitchers have ever thrown perfect games. To pitch a perfect game a pitcher must get every single batter out at the plate, with no batters reaching even first base. That means no walks and no errors, and the pitcher can't hit a batter. Throwing a perfect game is so difficult that no pitcher has ever done it twice in his lifetime.

Following God's law is like pitching a perfect game, not just once but every day of your life. Just like one hit ruins a perfect game, so one sin ruins our standing before God. Getting to heaven by our works is like a pitcher throwing a perfect game every game for his whole career. All pitchers would agree: That is impossible.

 Read Philippians 3:1–6.

Think about It Some More

If ever there was a Jewish person who followed the law and could trust their works to get to heaven, it was Paul. You might say that, when it came to being a Jew, Paul pitched a perfect game. Even from his birth, Paul's parents followed God's law and had him circumcised as a baby. Paul said he was blameless according to the law. But Paul knew that even he was a sinner and that his only hope, his only confidence, was to trust in Jesus.

Even if we could be sinless on the outside, we are full of sin on the inside. We have bad attitudes and live for ourselves and not for God. Even when we do good things, we often do them so that people think well of us. None of us are good enough to go to heaven without Jesus.

Talk about It

:: What did Paul say he did to live a perfect life as a Jew? *(Parents, if your children can't remember or are not strong readers, reread the passage and have them raise their hands when they hear one of Paul's accomplishments.)*

:: What does Paul mean when he says that he puts no confidence in the flesh (v. 3)? *(When Paul says he puts no confidence in the flesh, he simply means that he isn't trusting in his own efforts to get to heaven. He is not placing his confidence in the things he has done.)*

:: What about us? What kind of good works do people think can get them to heaven? *(People think that if they never hurt anyone, if they go to church every Sunday, or if they obey their parents, God will let them into heaven. But the Bible tells us that even if we commit one sin we are guilty of breaking the whole law [James 2:10] and will not be allowed into heaven without God's forgiveness.)*

:: Can you think of a sin you committed just this week? *(Parents, help your children see that they are sinners and that even one sin breaks our perfect record of obedience and is rebellion against God.)*

Pray about It

Take turns confessing your sin to God and admit that without Jesus there is no way you can get to heaven.

DAY TWO

Remember It

What do you remember about yesterday's Bible passage? What do you think we will learn about today?

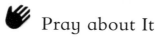 Read Philippians 3:7–8.

Think about It Some More

Yesterday we learned that even one sin is enough to keep us out of heaven. That is why Paul called all his good works rubbish. Picture a stinky, smelly trashcan with garbage rotting inside it on a hot day. That is what Paul said our good works are like in God's opinion. None of us can get to heaven based on our works. That is the bad news.

But today in our Bible passage, we learn about the good news. We can trade our sin for Jesus' perfect life. Jesus did what we could not do: He lived a perfect life without ever making a mistake or committing a sin. Remember the pitching illustration we used this week? Well, Jesus was like the pitcher who pitched a perfect game every game for his whole life. Jesus offers to trade our sinful record for his perfect record if we place our trust and hope in him. That is why Paul said his best good works were like garbage compared to knowing Jesus.

Talk about It

:: What is the bad news Paul spoke about? *(No one is good enough to get to heaven—not even the most righteous person in the world. Our best works are like garbage before God.)*

:: What is the good news? *(Even though our good works can't get us to heaven, Jesus lived a perfect life for us. If we trust in Jesus, we can trade our sins for his perfect record.)*

:: Why is it hard to think of our good works as rubbish or garbage? *(When we do something good, we like to pat ourselves on the back and think better of ourselves for it. But Paul knew that even our best works are like garbage compared to the work Jesus did on the cross on our behalf.)*

 Pray about It

Ask God to help you turn away from trusting in the good things that you do and turn to Jesus and trust in him instead.

DAY THREE _____

Connect It to the Gospel

Today is the day we connect this week's Bible story to the gospel. The gospel is the life, death, and resurrection of Jesus for our salvation. Can anyone guess how our story this week looks forward to or back at the gospel?

 Read Philippians 3:8–11.

Think about It Some More

Not only did Paul think all his good works were like garbage, he also knew that he could never be made righteous (good in God's sight) by obeying the law. One person might be better than another, but Paul knew that we all fall short of perfection. Obeying the law to get to God is like trying to jump across the Grand Canyon. The best long jumper in the world might get out as far as twenty-five feet, but would still fall far short of the five miles needed to reach the other side. In the same way, Paul knew that it was impossible for a person to obey the law. That is why Paul placed his hope in what Jesus did for him.

Jesus lived a perfect life for us, and then died to take away our sin. When we believe in Jesus, his perfect righteousness is added to our account. This is like jumping into a helicopter and trusting it to carry you over the Grand Canyon to the other side. We can't get to God on our own by obeying the law, but we can get to the other side by placing our faith and hope in Jesus.

Talk about It

:: Why can't anyone jump across the Grand Canyon? *(The Grand Canyon is about a mile wide at the narrowest part. No one could jump that far.)*

:: Why can't anyone get to heaven by obeying the law? *(In order to be with God in heaven, you must be perfectly righteous [perfectly good in God's eyes]. To be perfectly righteous, you would have to obey God's law perfectly and not sin even once. No person, however good, can make it through life without sinning. We can't even make it through one day without sinning.)*

:: If we can't become righteousness by obeying the law, how can we get the righteousness we need to go to heaven? *(We get our righteousness [our goodness before God] by trusting in Jesus' death on the cross. It was on the cross that Jesus took the punishment we deserved for our sins. Jesus is willing to trade his righteousness in exchange for the sins of anyone who will believe and put his faith in him. That is the best trade of all time.)*

 ## Pray about It

Confess that you are sinners who need to trust in Jesus. Then ask the Holy Spirit to help each person in your family believe in Jesus.

DAY FOUR _____

Remember It

What has God been teaching you this week through our Bible story?

 Read Philippians 3:12–17.

Think about It Some More

Paul compared trusting in Jesus to running a long-distance race. A runner in a marathon (a 26.2-mile race) could take the lead and be in first place for 15 miles. But if he stops after 15 miles, he won't win. He will get very tired, but he must press on and stay focused if he wants a chance at winning the race. That is the only way to win the race and get the prize. In a normal marathon, only one person wins the race, but in God's marathon, everyone who finishes the race gets the prize. Running the race consists of believing in Jesus until the day we die.

When Paul wrote the letter to the Philippians, he was still running. He had more years of his life to live for Jesus. He knew—and he wanted other believers to know—that running for Jesus our whole life is the only way to win the prize of heaven.

Talk about It

> KIDS, ask your parents how living their lives for Jesus has been like a long-distance race for them.

(Parents, help your children understand that you can't just say you are going to trust in Jesus and live for him for one day. You need to give Jesus your whole life. That means following him when things are going well, and continuing to run when things are difficult.)

:: Why do you think Paul compared the Christian life to a long race? *(A long race is not over quickly, so you've got to keep running to finish. That is what living the Christian life is like: You've got to keep living for Jesus.)*

:: How does remembering the prize and winning the prize help the runner keep running? *(The whole reason to run the race is to win the prize. If a runner is in the lead and he is getting tired, he might choose to give up. But if he remembers that he could win the prize if he keeps going, he won't give up.)*

:: For what prize are we running the race? *(The prize is living in heaven forever with Jesus.)*

 Pray about It

Ask God to help you keep your eyes on the prize of living in heaven forever with Jesus. Ask him to help you run the race to Jesus your whole life long.

DAY FIVE

Discover It

Today is the day we look at a different Bible passage—from the book of Psalms or one of the prophets—to see what we can learn from it about Jesus or our salvation.

 Read Psalm 34:1–8.

Think about It Some More

Psalm 34 is a wonderful prayer that David sang to God. When David said, "Oh, magnify the LORD with me" (v. 3), he was inviting us all to join in his song. David wanted everyone to trust in the Lord and join in praising him. Peter quoted verse 8 of this psalm and used it to describe our salvation in Jesus. He said, "Like newborn infants, long for the pure spiritual milk, that by it you may grow up to salvation—if indeed you have tasted that the Lord is good" (1 Peter 2:2–3). Both David and Peter knew that our only hope is to trust in the Lord's salvation. Today, looking back, we know that God brought us salvation through his Son, Jesus.

Talk about It

:: In this psalm, why is David praising the Lord? *(Parents, have your children reread the psalm or, if they are younger, reread it for them and have them lift their hands when they hear one of the reasons David is praising God. David praised God for answering his prayers and delivering him from his fears.)*

:: What does David ask all of us to do in verse 3? *(David invites us to join with him and praise the name of God together.)*

:: What does it mean to taste and see that the Lord is good? *(People like to taste a new food to see if they like it. David knew that if we gave trusting the Lord a try, we would see that trusting the Lord is much better than trusting in ourselves.)*

 Pray about It

Praise the Lord for all he has done for your family, and lift up your prayer requests to him.

Week 70

Character Counts

Story 148 – *The Gospel Story Bible*

For this exercise you will need three heavy plastic cups to juggle and three wine glasses set to the side. Tell the children you are learning to juggle and would like them to watch. Take the plastic cups and use them to juggle. (The object here is to drop cups, so don't be too good a juggler.) Ask your children if they think you are ready to juggle the wine glasses.

Since you have been dropping the plastic ones, they should say you are not ready to juggle the glasses. Then explain to them that people in the church are like the wine glasses, and that God won't let just anyone care for them. Then explain that this week they will learn about God's qualifications for pastors, and how they need to be able to live godly lives themselves before they are qualified to lead others.

DAY ONE

Picture It

When people go to the beach they like to look for shells. The best time to go searching for seashells is after a storm at low tide. Storms stir up the ocean and when the tide comes in and out the waves bring new shells onto the beach, but they also carry a lot of shell fragments. When you search for shells, you pass the broken ones up because you're look-ing for the beautifully shaped perfect ones. When you find a special shell, you put it into your bag and take it home.

In our story today, Paul wasn't searching for shells, but he was look-ing to train young men to help him with the work of ministry. There were plenty of men around, but Paul was looking for special men with godly character whom God had called to the work of the gospel. That is what he found in Timothy, and it is why Paul took Timothy with him to train him to help care for the churches that he started.

 Read Acts 16:1–5.

Think about It Some More

Timothy's mom was named Eunice. She and Timothy's grandmother, Lois, probably became Christians along with young Timothy during Paul's first missionary trip to Lystra, one of the cities in Galatia where Paul told people about Jesus. Since that first trip, Timothy had grown up, and now he stood out among the other Christian men. When Paul came through again, the people of the town all told him about young Timothy.

After meeting Timothy, Paul decided to take him along as a helper and train him to preach the gospel. So Paul took Timothy on his journey into Macedonia to preach the gospel in cities like Philippi, Thessalonica, Berea, and finally Athens, the capital of Greece. Timothy learned a lot from Paul. Later, when Paul wrote to the Philippians, he promised to send Timothy who, he said, would care for them better than anyone else he knew (Philippians 2:20).

Talk about It

:: How did Paul find out about Timothy? *(Parents, if your children are younger, reread the passage and have them raise their hands when they hear the correct answer: the brothers at Lystra and Iconium spoke well of Timothy to Paul.)*

:: Why do you think Paul wanted a young man like Timothy to join him? *(Paul needed help in caring for the churches.)*

:: If you were Paul, what qualities would you look for in a young person you could train to carry the gospel? *(Parents, you can have some fun with this one. Throw out some silly categories like throwing a football well or knowing how to play the piano. Then turn your children to consider the godly character that Paul most certainly spotted in Timothy.)*

:: How do you think God might want to use you someday in helping to spread the gospel? *(Parents, draw out your children here. Remind them that Timothy was a young man, maybe even a teen, when Paul first took him under his wing. Help them think of ways they can be serving in the church with you, and help them see*

*the importance of pursuing God with all their heart so that one day
they will be ready to be used of God in bigger ways.)*

 Pray about It

Ask God to help you grow closer to him so that he can use you to
serve him.

DAY TWO _____

Remember It

What do you remember about yesterday's Bible passage? What do you
think we will learn about today?

 Read 1 Timothy 3:1–7.

Think about It Some More

Yesterday we read how Paul invited Timothy to join him in his journey. Today, we read how Paul gave Timothy instructions on the kinds
of things to look for in other men who sense God's call to become
overseers. (*Overseer* is another name for pastor or elder.) When you
look at the list Paul gave Timothy, you'll see that almost all the items
are about a man's character and life. Only one, "able to teach," is
about how skilled he is. God calls pastors to lead the people by example. That is why it is really important that they honor and follow God
with their lives.

Talk about It

:: Why must a pastor have a godly character? *(All the people in
the church should follow the pastor's example. If he doesn't have a
godly character, he should not try to lead others in godliness.)*

:: Why does a pastor need to manage his own family well? *(If
he cannot lead his family, a small group of people, how can he lead
the church, a larger group of people? To use an analogy: If you find
it difficult to juggle three balls, you certainly won't be able to juggle
four balls.)*

:: Read 1 Samuel 16:7, which contains God's instructions to
Samuel who was sent to choose one of Jesse's sons to become
the new king. How is what God said to Samuel a lot like

what Paul wrote to Timothy? *(God told Samuel to look at a man's heart. The items on Paul's list would help Timothy to see whether a man's heart had been changed by God.)*

:: Why is this list a good one for all of us to follow? *(This is a great list to help us all know what is important to God and how we should all live.)*

 Pray about It

Take time to pray for your pastors. Pray that God would pour out grace on them and their families to live godly lives in service to Christ and the church.

DAY THREE _____

Connect It to the Gospel

Today is the day we connect this week's Bible story to the gospel. The gospel is the life, death, and resurrection of Jesus for our salvation. Can anyone guess how our story this week looks forward to or back at the gospel?

 Read 1 Timothy 3:8–13.

Think about It Some More

After giving a list of qualifications for pastors, Paul gave Timothy a similar list for deacons. Deacons are people whom God calls to help the pastors serve the people in the church. If a pastor has deacons at his side, he can spend more time praying, studying God's Word, and preaching the gospel. While teaching is not a part of the deacon's job, Paul did want them to understand the gospel. That is why he said they must hold the "mystery of faith," which is that Jesus Christ is God the Son who came to earth to die on the cross for our sins and rose again so that we could have everlasting life.

Talk about It

:: What is a deacon? *(Deacons are people whom God calls to serve the pastors of a church so that pastors have more time to pray, study, and teach the church.)*

:: How is the list Paul gave Timothy for deacons similar to the one Paul gave Timothy for pastors? *(Both list similar character qualities to show that God is more interested in someone's heart and life than in their outward performance.)*

:: Why is following by example a good way to learn? *(It is a lot easier to watch someone do something and then do it than it is to read about it in a book. Imagine reading in a book how to swing a baseball bat. It is much easier to watch someone hold a bat, and then copy him. In the same way, pastors and deacons show the other people in the church how to live by the example of their lives.)*

 Pray about It

Yesterday you prayed for the pastors of your church. Today, spend time praying for the other leaders and deacons.

DAY FOUR

Remember It

What has God been teaching you this week through our Bible story?

 Read 1 Timothy 3:14–16.

Think about It Some More

Large buildings need extra support to hold up the roof; the walls themselves are not strong enough to support the weight. Sometimes in large buildings, pillars go all the way up to the roof. A buttress is a pillar that stands as part of the wall. In old cathedrals, for example, buttresses line the walls. *(Parents: Search for "buttress picture" on the Internet to show the children.)*

Paul called the church the "pillar and buttress of the truth" (v. 15). When we live godly lives, people outside the church see us, and it helps them believe that God's Word is true. But if we live sinful lives, it gives a bad name to the church, and it makes people think that God's Word is not true. So by following Paul's instructions to live godly lives, we hold up the Word of God for all to see and believe.

Talk about It

> ● ● KIDS, ask your parents how many of the qualifi-
> ● ● cations for leaders apply to their lives.

:: Which of the qualifications on the list do you most struggle with? *(Parents, lead by confessing your weaknesses first, and then draw out your children.)*

:: Why did Paul call believers the church of the "living God"? *(Paul called believers the church of the "living God" because God's Spirit lives in the hearts and lives of every Christian. Our God is not a god of stone; he is a living God.)*

 ## Pray about It

Ask God to help you live out the character qualities Paul gave Timothy for pastors.

DAY FIVE

Discover It

Today is the day we look at a different Bible passage—from the book of Psalms or one of the prophets—to see what we can learn from it about Jesus or our salvation.

 Read Psalm 144.

Think about It Some More

Psalm 144 speaks about God's help in rescuing his people from danger. When David wrote this psalm, he was probably thinking of the many times God had saved him from his enemies. But when we read David's words, we think of Jesus. Jesus is the deliverer in whom we take refuge. So as we read this psalm, think of Jesus and the great victory he won for us when he died on the cross for our sins and rose again from the dead.

Talk about It

:: Why do you think David compared God to a fortress, a stronghold (a high tower), and a shield? *(A fortress, a stronghold, and a shield all protect people from danger. That is why David used them to describe God. God had protected David from his enemies.)*

:: From what do we need God to rescue us? *(We are all sinners who need God to rescue us from our sins.)*

:: What did David say he was going to do because God had protected him from his enemies (v. 9)? *(David said he was going to sing a new song to God. Actually, the words to this psalm may have been the new song David wrote and sang.)*

 Pray about It

Take time to sing a praise song as a family. If you know a song about God's rescue, sing that one.

Week 71

God Breathed the Scriptures

Story 149 – *The Gospel Story Bible*

You will need a magnifying lens with a small bifocal insert (a small, round spot that gives extra magnification). There is secret microprinting on newer United States currency that can only be read with a magnifying glass. Look at a few ten- and twenty-dollar bills and see if you can find the microprinting. Once you find one, bring that bill to Bible study along with the magnifying glass.

Tell your children that the magnifying lens can be compared with Scripture. Say, "To help us understand everything around us, we look through the lens of Scripture. It helps us look at our hearts and see the hidden sin, and it helps us see God." First, show them the line of microprinting without the magnifier and ask them what they see. Then teach them how to look using the magnifying lens to reveal the words hidden from sight. Say, "This week we will learn how the Scriptures are able to make us wise and show us God's truth about how to live a life that pleases the Lord."

DAY ONE

Picture It

If you don't wash your hands regularly, especially after using the bathroom or preparing food, you can pass germs from your hands to your body, and you or others can get very sick. You can become infected with salmonella food poisoning, hepatitis A, giardiasis, the flu, a cold, strep throat, typhoid, a staph infection, and more. Much of these sicknesses can easily be prevented by regularly washing your hands.

Our spiritual lives need to be cleaned up too. Sin works a lot like disease, and the Word of God does the job of the soap. That's why Paul wanted Timothy to know the list of sins that he would face in his ministry—because they could destroy him if he didn't apply God's Word to his life.

 Read 2 Timothy 3:1–9.

Think about It Some More

If you examine Paul's list of sins with the eyes of a detective, you can find clues that help identify the root sin. The biggest clue is found in the word *love*, which Paul keeps repeating—lovers of self, lovers of money, not loving good, and lovers of pleasure rather than lovers of God. Do you see the problem more clearly? Jesus said we can't love two masters. We will hate the one and love the other, for we can't love them both (Matthew 6:24). Paul's list of sins grows out of a love for the things of the world and not the things of God.

Talk about It

:: What three sinful loves did Paul list? *(Parents, if you have younger children who cannot read to find the answer, reread the passage and have them raise their hands when they hear that the people Paul described were lovers of self, money, and pleasure.)*

:: What kind of love do Christians trade away to love the world? *(We trade away our love for God to love the world.)*

:: Which of the sins on Paul's list have you been tempted by? *(Parents, this is a great opportunity to take the lead in confessing your sin in appropriate ways. Then help your children to share their own.)*

 Pray about It

Ask God to help you love him more than the things and the pleasures of the world.

DAY TWO

Remember It

What do you remember about yesterday's Bible passage? What do you think we will learn about today?

 Read 2 Timothy 3:10–15.

Think about It Some More

After giving Timothy a long list of the sins to watch out for, Paul reminded him of a secret weapon that would help him stay away from sin. That secret weapon was the Word of God. Paul said Timothy knew God's Word from childhood, and that the Word was able to make him wise and to point the way to God's salvation. Paul encouraged Timothy to remember all that he had been taught from God's Word and to follow Paul's example in living for Jesus. The great thing about Paul's advice to Timothy is that we can follow it too. We have the Word of God and the example of Paul preserved for us in the Bible. In fact, by reading this passage, we are already using the secret weapon of God's Word to fight the sin that wants to destroy us.

Talk about It

:: What is the secret weapon God gave us to fight against sin? *(the Word of God)*

:: How can the Word of God help us fight against sin? *(Parents, draw out your children here. The Word of God does two things: first, as we learned yesterday, it exposes sin; second, it points us to the truth that is able to make us wise in Christ Jesus.)*

:: How do we know that the Bible is not just for adults, but for children too? *(Paul said that Timothy learned God's Word from childhood.)*

 Pray about It

Ask God to help you grow in your love for God's Word so that you will want to read it every day. Ask God to use his Word to make you wise for salvation in Christ Jesus.

DAY THREE

Connect It to the Gospel

Today is the day we connect this week's Bible story to the gospel. The gospel is the life, death, and resurrection of Jesus for our salvation. Can anyone guess how our story this week looks forward to or back at the gospel?

 Read 2 Timothy 3:16.

Think about It Some More

Second Timothy 3:16 is one of the best Bible verses to memorize, and it is an easy one to remember because it has the same reference as John 3:16, another great memory verse. It tells us that, although the Bible was written with pen and ink, God breathed out the words that were written. God was behind the scenes, directing, by his Holy Spirit, those who wrote the Bible.

Since God directed the writing, we know that the Bible contains, not the words of men, but the words of God to us. That is why we can trust the Bible and know that the gospel is true. Because God is the author, we can be sure that Jesus lived a perfect life, died on the cross for our sins, and rose again from the dead. And that if we turn away from our sins and trust in Jesus, we can be forgiven and receive his free gift of righteousness (Jesus' perfect goodness).

Talk about It

:: What does Paul mean when he tells us that Scripture is "breathed out by God"? (*Parents, by using the analogy of a pen, you can explain that, although people wrote Scripture, God is the author. Write something with a pen and ask them if the pen wrote the lines. Of course, the pen did make the marks, but you used the pen as an instrument to write your words. Writers of the Bible were, in a manner of speaking, the "pens" of God.*)

:: What does Paul say we should use the Bible for? (*Parents, review the list in verse 16 and help your children think of practical ways to apply the list to their lives.*)

:: How has the Bible already helped you to grow? (*Parents, draw out your children on this one.*)

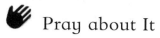 Pray about It

Thank God for giving us his Word.

DAY FOUR

Remember It

What has God been teaching you this week through our Bible story?

 Read 2 Timothy 4:1–5.

Think about It Some More

A *charge* is a very serious command that must be followed. An army soldier is charged with defending the country even at the cost of her life. A policeman is charged with upholding justice even if it means standing in harm's way to defend the good. In our Bible verse today, Paul charged Timothy to preach the Word of God at all times, in season and out of season.

Preaching the Word means telling people about Jesus and all he taught. To make it even more serious, Paul *charged* Timothy in front of God as a witness. That meant that God was watching the charge. Timothy would not be able to say, "But you never told me, Paul—I didn't know I was supposed to preach the gospel," for God was looking on as a witness.

Talk about It

> KIDS, ask your mom or dad if they have ever received a charge.

(Parents, the Bible gives us many serious commands even though it doesn't always use the word charge to describe them. Read Deuteronomy 30:16–20 to your children. This is a command to love God that was first given to Israel but was also passed on to all of us and repeated often in the Bible.)

:: Paul charged Timothy to preach the Word. What does preaching the Word mean? *(Preaching the Word means telling people about the message of the Bible, which we call the gospel—that*

God sent his only Son, Jesus, to die on the cross for our sins and rise again in victory over death so we could be forgiven and live forever in heaven as God's adopted children.)

:: What did Paul warn Timothy would happen to some of the people? *(Parents, if you have younger children, reread the passage and have them raise their hands when they hear the correct answer. You can even emphasize the words "turn away from listening to the truth" to give them a clue.)*

 Pray about It

Ask God to help you listen to the truth of God's Word so you don't turn or wander away from God.

DAY FIVE _____

Discover It

Today is the day we look at a different Bible passage—from the book of Psalms or one of the prophets—to see what we can learn from it about Jesus or our salvation.

 Read Isaiah 59:12–21.

Think about It Some More

Isaiah said that when God looked down at his people he saw that they were sinners who had turned their back on him to do evil, and that there was no one on earth who could save them. But then Isaiah said that God himself would bring salvation and uphold his people with his righteousness by sending them a Redeemer. Jesus is the Redeemer God sent. God told Isaiah that he was the one who gave him the words to speak. That is a lot like what Paul told Timothy when he said that the Word of God was "breathed out by God." Peter described the words the prophets spoke in much the same way. He said that the prophets didn't speak what they wanted to speak but they spoke God's words as they were "carried along by the Holy Spirit" (2 Peter 1:21).

Talk about It

:: How did God keep his promise to send a Redeemer? *(Jesus is the Redeemer God promised to send. Jesus paid the price for our sin by dying on the cross in our place.)*

:: How long did God tell Isaiah the words he gave to him would last? *(God said the words he gave Isaiah would last forever.)*

:: In verse 21 God said he was the one who put the words in Isaiah's mouth for him to speak. How is that a lot like what Paul taught Timothy when he said that all Scripture is "breathed out by God"? *(Both verses teach the same thing: that God is really the one who wrote the Bible. He just used writers as his instruments.)*

:: How is verse 17 like the armor of God Paul talked about? *(Two of the items listed are the same as Paul's armor listed in Ephesians 6: the helmet of salvation and the breastplate of righteousness.)*

 ## Pray about It

Thank God for keeping his promise to send a Redeemer to pay the penalty for our sins.

Week 72

The Heart's Desires

Story 150 – *The Gospel Story Bible*

Fill two glasses to the brim with water. Add red food coloring to the water in one glass and green to the other. Place each glass on a white paper towel on a table. (Protect the table with a plastic tablecloth or set the glasses on a plate or tray.) Tell your children that the red glass represents a person who is filled with love for the Lord in his heart. But the green one represents a greedy person who has love for money in her heart. Then bump each glass with your finger so that some of the colored liquid spills out. Explain that the bump represents somebody stealing something from the two people.

Point to the green glass and ask, "What comes out of the greedy person's heart when she is robbed?" The answer is greed and anger and other sins. Then point to the red glass and ask, "What comes out of the person's heart who loves the Lord when he is cheated?" The answer is love for God and forgiveness toward the person who robbed them. Say, "This week we will learn that our sinful reactions flow out of the sinful desires we have in our hearts."

DAY ONE _____

Picture It

What would you do if your bedroom ceiling started to drip water on a rainy day? A good first step is to place a large pot under the leak. The pot doesn't fix the problem, it only catches the water. You still need to find out where the water is coming from. Let's say you go into the attic above the ceiling and find water dripping from one of the rafters. You could move your large pot up into the attic. That would stop the water from dripping into your bedroom, but it still would not fix the real problem. More investigation is needed. You need to get out a flashlight and follow the dripping water to find the source of the leak, for example, a hole in the roof. You won't solve the problem until you find the *source* of the leak and patch the hole. In our Bible passage today, James helps us track where our sin begins and find its cause.

 Read James 4:1–2.

Think about It Some More

When people get angry at each other and say unkind things, they often blame the other person for making them angry. To solve the problem, they might leave the room or stop talking altogether. But that doesn't really fix anything. Inside their hearts the angry conversation usually continues.

Like searching out the cause of a leaky roof, you have to look for the cause of your anger. Although it was your mouth that spoke angry words, James tells us that we need to trace our sin back to the sinful desires in our hearts. We can't blame the other person for making us angry. We can't blame our mouth and say we didn't mean to say the angry things we did. We have to track the leak of our sin all the way back to the source: our sinful heart. Most often we get angry because we wanted something but didn't get what we wanted, so we got angry about it. We fall into sin when we trade loving and desiring Jesus and abiding (remaining) in him, for loving and desiring something in this world.

Talk about It

:: What did James say causes quarrels and fights? *(The simple answer is that we want or desire something, and, when we don't get what we want, we become angry and fight.)*

:: Can you remember a time when you argued or fought because you didn't get what you wanted? *(Parents, help your children remember here. You usually don't have to go back more than a few days to discover a time when sinful desires spilled out into a conflict.)*

:: What are some of the terrible things James said people do when they don't get what they want? *(James said people quarrel and fight and even kill one another when they don't get what they want.)*

:: What do you desire and not have that leads you to quarrel and fight? *(Parents, start by confessing your own sinful desires. Do you get angry if your children don't give you a clean room? Or what about your children keeping quiet after bedtime? Do you desire a quiet evening and get angry if you don't get one? After you share, help your children figure out the kinds of things that lead them to quarrel and fight.)*

 Pray about It

Ask God to help you love him more than the things of the world.

DAY TWO _____

Remember It

What do you remember about yesterday's Bible passage? What do you think we will learn about today?

 Read James 4:3–5.

Think about It Some More

Yesterday we learned that the sinful desires of our hearts lead to quarrels and fights. When we don't get what we want, we get angry. Today we learn that sometimes God doesn't give us what we want because we are friends with the world and not with him. That means we love the things of the world more than we love God. The Bible tells us that we are to love God with all of our heart, soul, mind, and strength (Mark 12:30).

God wants us to love him, not our things. That is why he doesn't give us everything we want. He knows that some things will steal the love away that we should have for him. A good way for a person to tell if he loves something more than God is by watching how he behaves when he doesn't get what he wants. If you get angry when you don't get what you want, that is a good sign that you love that thing more than you love God.

Talk about It

:: What kinds of things are people tempted to love more than God? *(The desire for just about anything, even a good thing, can become sinful if we love it more than we love God. Money is not evil; wanting money more than we want God is evil. Football or other sports are not evil, but loving them more than God is.)*

:: How do you know if you love something more than God? *(One way to tell if you love something more than God is watching what you do when you don't get it. If you get angry, then you probably love it more than God.)*

:: What kinds of things do you sometimes love more than God? *(Parents, this is another opportunity to lead in confessing your own weakness and sin. Then help your children do the same.)*

 Pray about It

Take time to confess where you have loved things more than you have loved God.

DAY THREE _____

Connect It to the Gospel

Today is the day we connect this week's Bible story to the gospel. The gospel is the life, death, and resurrection of Jesus for our salvation. Can anyone guess how our story this week looks forward to or back at the gospel?

 Read James 4:6–10.

Think about It Some More

Grace is a free gift, something you don't deserve or work for. The word *grace* in the Bible always points to the cross and the free gift of God's salvation. If it were not for Jesus dying on the cross, there would be no forgiveness, no salvation, and no help in fighting our sin. All of these are gifts—grace—to us. James tells us that the way to receive God's grace is to humble ourselves—to make ourselves low. We make ourselves low when we admit that we are weak sinners who need God's help. The proud don't receive God's grace because they don't think they need it. Isn't it amazing that all we need to do is turn away from our sin and call out to God for help to receive his grace? This is true both for our salvation and for living out the Christian life.

Talk about It

:: When we see the word *grace* in the Bible, what does it always point to? *(In the Bible, grace always points to Jesus and the free gift of salvation that he offers everyone who believes in him.)*

:: What does the word *grace* mean? *(Grace is something we received as a gift that we didn't deserve or work for.)*

:: To whom does James say God gives his grace? *(God gives his grace to the humble, to those who exalt God's desires over their own desires.)*

:: How does James say God responds to the proud? *(James tells us that God opposes, or is against, the proud.)*

 ## Pray about It

Ask God to help you to be humble by trusting in him instead of living a proud life, trusting in yourself.

DAY FOUR _____

Remember It

What has God been teaching you this week through our Bible story?

 Read James 4:11–17.

Think about It Some More

To remind us how weak we are, James said we don't even know what will happen tomorrow. The best we can do is guess about what will happen tomorrow. Even meteorologists who track storms moving across the country can't be certain where the storm will hit the next day. They can only guess. God, on the other hand, knows all the events of every day in the future for every person on earth! He can tell you exactly what will happen, for all things work according to his plan. We have to trust God for everything because we can't guarantee anything.

Remember, as believers, our real home is in heaven! The treasures of this life will all pass away. We shouldn't fix our gaze on the passing treasures of this world, but rather we should "run with endurance the race that is set before us, looking to Jesus, the founder and perfecter of our faith, who for the joy that was set before him endured the cross, despising the shame, and is seated at the right hand of the throne of God" (Hebrews 12:1–2).

Talk about It

> KIDS, ask your parents if their lives have turned out differently than they thought they would back when they were in high school.

(Parents, try to remember how you thought your life would turn out when you were still in high school. Is your occupation different or are you living in a different place? Help your children to see how little we know compared with God, who knows everything.)

:: Why does James compare our lives to a mist that soon disappears? *(James wants us to remember that our lives are short and that we are not as important as we sometimes think.)*

:: How does James describe sin? *(Parents, if you have younger children, reread verse 17 and have your children raise their hands when they hear the correct answer: sin is not doing the right thing.)*

 Pray about It

Ask God to help us stay humble as we remember that our lives are short and we don't even know what tomorrow will bring.

DAY FIVE

Discover It

Today is the day we look at a different Bible passage—from the book of Psalms or one of the prophets—to see what we can learn from it about Jesus or our salvation.

Read Psalm 22:7–8.

Think about It Some More

James reminded us, in our reading yesterday, that we are not like God. We don't even know what will happen tomorrow. But God is very different from us. He knows not only what will happen, he also controls all things. Psalm 22 is a great example of this. Long before Jesus died on the cross, God knew and planned his sacrifice down to the smallest detail. In Psalm 22, David said those who looked on Jesus would mock him. In Matthew 27:41 we read, "The chief priests, with the scribes and elders, mocked him." David said that those looking upon Jesus would wag their heads. In Matthew 27:39 we read, "Those who passed by derided him, wagging their heads."

David even prophesied that the people would say that the Lord should rescue Jesus from the cross. In Matthew 27:43 the people said, "He trusts in God; let God deliver him now." God knew all these things would happen hundreds of years before they did. Actually God always knew they would happen for he not only knows the future, he plans the future. Aren't you glad he planned for his Son to die on the cross, just the way he did, for us (Acts 2:23)?

Talk about It

:: Read Matthew 27:39–44 and compare it with Psalm 22:7–8. How are these two Bible passages the same? *(Both Psalm 22 and Matthew 27 describe the mocking that Jesus experienced during his crucifixion.)*

:: What do we learn about God from comparing these two passages? *(We learn that God knows the future long before it happens.)*

:: Why do you think God would have had David write down the details of Jesus dying on the cross hundreds of years before it happened? *(God wants us to know that he planned his Son's death down to the last detail.)*

 Pray about It

Thank God for giving up his Son even though he knew, long before Jesus was born, how terrible that would be.

Week 73

Born Again!

Story 151 – *The Gospel Story Bible*

Gather some silver polish and a rag, along with a piece of tarnished silver or silver-plated flatware or jewelry— even a quarter or dime will work. Tell your children that worldly treasures fade. Put a little polish on the rag and begin to polish the silver. Show your children the black tarnish coming off on the rag. Work the object thoroughly before showing them the shiny result. They will be amazed at just how much tarnish came off and the dramatic change in the object. Then explain to them that this week you will be learning how God is storing up for us in heaven an inheritance of treasure that will never fade or tarnish.

DAY ONE

Picture It

We call a meteorologist's prediction about tomorrow's weather a *forecast*. After studying the winds and looking at the clouds on satellite photos, future weather can be forecasted (predicted). Sometimes forecasts are correct, and sometimes not correct. Imagine what it would be like if there was a meteorologist who not only knew what future weather would be, but who could actually make weather forecasts come true. Those forecasts would be perfect.

This meteorologist wouldn't say, "You should probably take along an umbrella tomorrow because there is a good chance we will get some rain." Instead, the forecast would be: "If you are living on the north side of town, a thunderstorm will push through at 3:05 p.m. and last twenty-four minutes, dropping a half inch of rain." If forecasts like this came true every day, we would think the meteorologist was amazing because only God can forecast the future perfectly. And that is what we will learn in today's Bible story.

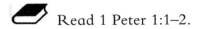 Read 1 Peter 1:1–2.

Think about It Some More

As we said, a weatherman's prediction of future weather is called a forecast. The word *forecast* means to predict events before they happen. A forecast, then, is a guess or prediction that may or may not come true. Peter used a similar but very different word, *foreknowledge,* to describe God's view of the future. While forecasting the future is a guess, God's foreknowledge is certain, and he is able to make all things work according to "the counsel of his will" (Ephesians 1:11), which means that he can make all things work according to his plan.

Peter told the exiles that, as God's elect or chosen believers, they were foreknown by God. That means they didn't become Christians by accident. They became Christians according to God's plan and purpose. What Peter meant was that God knew in advance they were going to become a part of his church.

Talk about It

:: How do we know Peter wrote First Peter? *(Many of the New Testament letters tell us who wrote them. In this case, Peter starts off his letter by giving us his name.)*

:: What is God's foreknowledge? *(God's foreknowledge is his knowing all things, including things in the future—things that have not happened yet.)*

:: How did Peter first learn that God's plan included the Gentiles (recall Acts 10)? *(Parents, feel free to give your children some clues. Peter first learned God was going to save the Gentiles when God gave him the vision of a large sheet coming down with both clean and unclean animals. Read through the account and focus on verses 34 and 35.)*

:: What does it mean to be sprinkled with the blood of Jesus? *(When Peter said that Christians were sprinkled with the blood of Jesus, he meant that Jesus' blood shed on the cross washed away their sins. Moses first sprinkled the blood of a sacrifice on the people of Israel to show they were under God's covenant. See Exodus 24:5–8.)*

✋ Pray about It

Thank God that he knows and keeps our future. Jesus said he would not lose anybody the Father gave him (John 6:37–39). Praise God that he can keep us safe for all time.

DAY TWO

Remember It

What do you remember about yesterday's Bible passage? What do you think we will learn about today?

 Read 1 Peter 1:3–5.

Think about It Some More

Yesterday we learned from God's Word that God knows and rules over the future and is able to make all things work according to his plan. God is able to bring every one of his children safely into heaven and keep them secure for all time. Jesus said he would not lose a single one the Father gave him (John 6:39). That is why Peter could tell the Christians he was writing to that one day they would go to heaven and that their inheritance (promised gift) would not perish (die) or fade, for it was being kept for them by God himself. When we have something valuable here on earth we put it into a safe, which is a thick steel box that can withstand fire and attack by burglars. When we believe in Jesus and become Christians, our future in heaven with Jesus is kept safe by God's promise, which is stronger than steel and lasts forever. Nothing or no one can take away God's promise of heaven.

Talk about It

:: Who is guarding our salvation in Jesus to make it safe so that our inheritance (our promised gift of heaven) will never be taken away? *(When God says that our inheritance, which is heaven, is kept safe for us and will never perish or fade, we can know it is true.)*

:: Can you remember a story in the Bible in which God said something would happen before it took place and then it happened just as he said? *(Parents, on the fifth day of each week we have studied the prophecies of the Bible. The most significant of these are the ones in which God predicted, way in advance, that Jesus would die for our sins. See if your children can remember one of those. Another great story is God telling Moses he will deliver his people out of Egypt before it happened.)*

:: What does it mean to be born again? *(When God saves us, he takes away our sin and gives us his righteousness. This is such a big change that the Bible compares it to being born all over again.)*

Pray about It

Thank God that he has the power to keep all his children safe and bring them all through life into heaven without losing even one.

DAY THREE _____

Connect It to the Gospel

Today is the day we connect this week's Bible story to the gospel. The gospel is the life, death, and resurrection of Jesus for our salvation. Can anyone guess how our story this week looks forward to or back at the gospel?

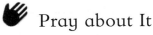 Read 1 Peter 1:6–9.

Think about It Some More

Peter said that God purifies our faith in Jesus like a goldsmith refines gold. When gold ore (rock) is mined, it is crushed into a powder so that the gold dust can be separated from the crushed rock. Then the gold is heated with fire until it melts. The molten gold separates, and the dross (anything that was *not* gold) floats to the top and is skimmed off and thrown away, leaving the pure gold behind. Peter said that the trials God brings to us refine us the same way that gold is made pure.

God sends trials to test and refine our faith (our belief and trust in the gospel), so that one day, when we get to heaven, our faith in God will shine like pure gold. When our lives are easy and free of trials, we tend to forget about God and trust in our own strength. But trials help us remember that we can't live without the Lord's help, and they point us back to trusting in Jesus and his sacrifice for us on the cross.

Talk about It

:: Peter said the believers were "grieved with various trials." What is a trial? (*A trial is any difficulty that we experience that forces us to trust in Jesus for help.*)

:: Why did Peter say God brings us trials? (*Peter said God brings us trials to test our faith. It is easy to forget about God when everything is going well. However, when difficulties that we cannot solve come, we are forced to turn to the Lord and trust him.*)

:: Can you think of a trial that you experienced that pushed you to trust God for help and have faith in him? *(Parents, most of our children don't have a lot of significant trials. Sickness is one they might relate to. Remind them of a time when they were sick and had to trust God to make them well.)*

 Pray about It

Even though we cannot see Jesus, we still praise him. Take time to praise the Lord for all he has done for your family over the past year.

DAY FOUR

Remember It

What has God been teaching you this week through our Bible story?

 Read 1 Peter 1:10–12.

Think about It Some More

In the Old Testament, God spoke to his people through prophets. It was the prophet's job to deliver God's messages to the people. That is how they knew in advance that God was going to send a Messiah one day to bring salvation to his people. They didn't know who it would be or when he would come. It was kind of like waiting for a baby to be born. A woman knows she is going to have a baby, but she doesn't know exactly when or what the child will look like. So while she and her husband wait, they try to figure out if it will be a boy or girl and when the baby will come.

Today, with ultrasound pictures, doctors can tell if an unborn baby is a boy or girl and give a better prediction as to when the baby will come. In a similar way, the prophets were so excited about the coming of the Messiah that they searched and asked each other questions to try and figure out when he was going to be born and who he would be. But God showed them that the prophecies they spoke about were not for their time. So all the Old Testament prophets died trusting in the Savior without even knowing his name.

Talk about It

> KIDS, ask your mom or dad what it was like for
> them trying to guess when you would be born
> or adopted and what you would be like. Also ask
> them how they picked your name.

(Parents, talk about the excitement and anticipation of the birth or adoption and what it was like to finally see them for the very first time.)

:: What didn't the prophets know about the Messiah God planned to send to deliver his people? *(The prophets didn't know when the Messiah would come or who he would be. They didn't know his name.)*

:: How was John the Baptist different from all the other prophets? *(John the Baptist was alive when the Messiah came. So he got to announce that God's Messiah had come. He was the only prophet to know the time of his coming and the name of God's Messiah.)*

 ## Pray about It

Thank God that we know who the Savior is. He is Jesus! Praise God that we know his name and that we know why he came—to die on the cross for our sins and rise again in victory!

DAY FIVE _____

Discover It

Today is the day we look at a different Bible passage—from the book of Psalms or one of the prophets—to see what we can learn from it about Jesus or our salvation.

Read Zechariah 13:7–9.

Think about It Some More

Zechariah was one of the prophets Peter spoke about. God told Zechariah that a Savior would come. God compared the Savior to a fountain that would cleanse God's people from their sin (Zechariah 13:1). In the verses we read today, God called the Messiah a shepherd who would be struck down. That is a hint pointing to the fact that Jesus would die on the cross. Jesus quoted Zechariah's prophecy to his disciples when he predicted they would all fall away from him (Matthew 26:31). If you remember, Peter objected, saying that he would never fall away. But in the end, he fled like the rest and denied Jesus three times.

We know from reading Peter's letter that Zechariah wondered about the meaning of the prophecy God gave him. Who was God's shepherd? When would he come? But God showed Zechariah, as he'd shown the other prophets, that it would not happen in his day. Reading Zechariah's prophecy today strengthens our faith as we see how God planned our salvation through Jesus a long time ago. Jesus didn't die by accident but according to God's loving, foreknown plan.

Talk about It

:: What did Zechariah know about Jesus? *(Parents, if your children don't get the answer, ask them a few leading questions like, Did Zechariah know about the name Jesus? Zechariah did not know Jesus' name or when he would come.)*

:: Peter said that God tests our faith like gold is refined (1 Peter 1:6–9). In what way is that similar to Zechariah 13:9? *(Zechariah's prophecy tells us that, in a future day, God would refine his people like silver and gold so that they would call out to him and worship the Lord. Peter knew Zechariah's prophecy and that it had come true.)*

:: The Old Testament prophets never got to see Jesus. But what do you think it was like for them when they got to heaven and saw the Lord? *(Parents, draw out your children here. The prophets must have been some of the most excited people to see the Son of God and hear about his plan. Along with the angels, they were watching from heaven when Jesus was born, lived, died on the cross, and rose again.)*

 Pray about It

Thank God for speaking through the prophets so we could see that Jesus' death was not by accident, but was planned by our loving Father in heaven to save us from our sins.

Week 74

God's Word Is Living

Story 152 – *The Gospel Story Bible*

Bring an apple, a cutting board, and a sharp knife to Bible study. Tell the children that God hid something special in the design of an apple and that you have a knife that is able to penetrate the core and reveal what is inside. Cut the apple in half through the middle, not up and down through the stem. Take a look at the slice and you will see that the design of the seeds is in the shape of a star! Ask your children if they knew there was a star hidden in the heart of an apple. Say, "This week we will learn how God's Word is able to divide our heart and reveal what is inside."

DAY ONE _____

Picture It

A two-edged sword is a very dangerous weapon because the blade is sharp on both sides. *(Parents: Hold up two steak knives back to back to give the children an idea of what the blade of a two-edged sword looks like.)* A two-edged sword is not curved or wide like a broad sword; it is straight and narrow to pierce through an opponent's armor. If you were in battle against someone who was wielding a two-edged sword, you would need to be aware of the blade swinging from the left, the right, or thrust straight at you. In our Scripture today, God compared his Word to a two-edged sword.

 Read Hebrews 4:12.

Think about It Some More

The Bible is different from every other book because it is alive. That doesn't mean that your Bible breathes or eats or can run away. The Bible is living because it is God's voice to us. Even though the words are written down, they were spoken by God and have not lost their power. So when we read Jesus' words, "Come to me, all who labor and are heavy laden, and I will give you rest" (Matthew 11:28), we know that Jesus wasn't just talking to the people back in his day. His Word still speaks to us today and offers us the very same rest.

God's Word speaks to us as we read it. It cuts deeply into our hearts to show us that we have sinned against God and need a Savior to rescue us from our sins. The Spirit of God uses the Word to cause us to believe and be born again. We can look good on the outside, and inside be filled with sin. The Word of God is able to expose our hearts and show us our sin. Once we see the sin hidden inside us, we have a reason to run to Jesus for forgiveness. That is when the Word of God can cut through our fears and encourage us as well.

Talk about It

:: What did the writer of Hebrews compare God's Word to? *(a two-edged sword)*

:: Why did the writer of Hebrews say that God's Word is living? *(The writer of Hebrews said that God's Word was living because it still speaks to us today. The Word of God is just as powerful today as it was the day it was spoken or first written down.)*

:: When the sword of God's Word cuts deeply into our lives, what does it show us? *(God's Word reveals the sins hidden deep in our heart.)*

:: Share a time when God's Word cut into your heart and convicted you of sin. *(Parents, while your children may never have been convicted by God's Word, this is an opportunity to share with them how the sword of God's Word has affected you.)*

 Pray about It

Thank God for giving us his living and active Word to show us our sin and his grace.

DAY TWO

Remember It

What do you remember about yesterday's Bible passage? What do you think we will learn about today?

 Read Hebrews 4:13.

Think about It Some More

Before you get on an airplane you must first go through a metal detector so the security agents can make sure you are not bringing something dangerous like a knife or a gun onto the plane. Your luggage is x-rayed to make sure you are not hiding something dangerous. That makes our planes safe because criminals and terrorists know they can't hide a gun and bring it on board. In our Bible passage today, we see that no one reading God's Word can hide sin from God. God's Word completely exposes sin.

The Word of God is like an x-ray machine for our heart. If you get caught trying to take a gun on an airplane, you will have to give account of that to the police. That means you will have to explain why you have it—and be judged. In the same way, God sees every part of us, so sin cannot hide. That is why the writer of Hebrews tells us that we are naked and exposed before God. We will have to give an account and be judged for every sin unless we trust in Jesus to forgive our sins.

Talk about It

:: How is God's Word like an airport x-ray machine of our heart? (*God's Word reveals our hidden sin just as an x-ray machine reveals a hidden gun inside a suitcase.*)

:: How can remembering that God sees all our sin help us live godly lives? (*When we realize that none of our sins can be hidden from God, we are more likely to fear the Lord and not sin. For example, motorists on the highway slow down when they see a police officer aiming a radar gun at traffic.*)

:: Instead of trying to hide our sin from God, what should we do? (*We should confess our sin and ask God to forgive us.*)

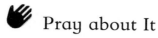 Pray about It

Ask God to help you remember that he can see everything. Ask him to help you confess your sin and not hide it.

DAY THREE

Connect It to the Gospel

Today is the day we connect this week's Bible story to the gospel. The gospel is the life, death, and resurrection of Jesus for our salvation. Can anyone guess how our story this week looks forward to or back at the gospel?

 Read Hebrews 4:14–15.

Think about It Some More

In the Old Testament, the high priest was the only priest who was allowed to enter the Most Holy Place, the deepest inner room of the Tabernacle, where God's presence lived. Once a year he would sprinkle himself with blood and bring the blood of an animal sacrifice into the Most Holy Place as payment for the sins of God's people. The high priest in the Old Testament was a picture of Jesus, who offered his blood as a sacrifice for our sins.

Today, Jesus is our high priest who stands before the presence of God the Father in heaven, the true Most Holy Place. There he stands with the nail marks still in his hands, forever showing God the Father that he paid the price for our sin. While he was on earth, Jesus was tempted like us, and even though he didn't sin, he knows how hard it is for us to fight temptation. That is why we can be sure he won't reject us when we call out to him for help in our prayers. If you were drowning and someone threw you a rope, you would grab it and hold on tightly so that you could be saved. In the same way we are told to hold on tight to our faith and trust in Jesus (that is what this passage calls our confession) so that we can be forgiven.

Talk about It

:: What does a high priest do? *(A high priest is the one who stands in the presence of God for his people to present a sacrifice as payment for their sins.)*

:: How is Jesus our high priest? *(Jesus became our high priest when he offered up his own life to God to atone for [cover] our sins. Jesus stands in heaven with the nail marks still in his hands as proof that our sins were paid for.)*

:: The writer of Hebrews says that we should hold fast to our confession. What is a confession, and why should we hold on tight to it? *(Parents, this is a tough one for children to answer. Asking them this question is more an opportunity to teach them what it means. Our confession is simply the words we spoke when we believed in Jesus and asked him to save us. We should hold fast to that confession because it is through believing in our heart and confessing with our mouth that we are saved. See Romans 10:9.)*

 Pray about It

Thank Jesus for becoming our high priest who knows how hard it is to fight temptation and for taking our sins upon himself when he died on the cross.

DAY FOUR _____

Remember It

What has God been teaching you this week through our Bible story?

 Read Hebrews 4:16.

Think about It Some More

Yesterday we learned that Jesus is our high priest who understands how difficult it is to fight off temptation and not sin. Today's verse tells us that we can bring our prayers to God with confidence. The sacrifice of Jesus and the wounds he bears on his body forever testify in the throne room of heaven to his sacrifice upon the cross as payment for our sins. Remember the temple curtain that tore in two? Because of the sacrifice of Jesus, the way into the presence of God is open. Those who place their trust in Jesus do not need to fear that God will punish them. But more than that, we can have confidence that, as children adopted into the family of God, he will give us mercy and grace in our time of need.

Talk about It

> KIDS, ask your parents to share a time when they went to God's throne of grace with confidence with an important prayer request.

(Parents, tell your children about a time when you prayed to God for help and mercy. That could be a time when you confessed your sin or brought a prayer request.)

:: What will we receive from God when we draw near his throne? *(Parents, if you have younger children who are not strong readers, reread the verse for today and have them raise their hands when they hear the correct answer to the question, which is that God gives us grace and mercy in our time of need.)*

:: What is the grace and mercy we get from God when we pray? *(Mercy is not getting the punishment we do deserve and grace is getting blessings we don't deserve, like forgiveness, healing, and help in our time of need.)*

 Pray about It

Take time to draw near the throne of grace by lifting up your prayers to God as a family.

DAY FIVE

Discover It

Today is the day we look at a different Bible passage—from the book of Psalms or one of the prophets—to see what we can learn from it about Jesus or our salvation.

Read Nahum 1.

Think about It Some More

Nahum was a prophet like Jonah to whom God gave a message to deliver to the city of Nineveh. Like Jonah, God said that he was going to bring his judgment against Nineveh's sins. But then in verse 15 there is a change. God gives Nahum a message for his people Judah. Instead of judgment, God promises to send a messenger to bring good news and peace.

Today, looking back on this prophecy, we know that Jesus was the messenger God promised to send to Judah. When he started his ministry, Jesus said, "The Spirit of the Lord is upon me, because he has anointed me to proclaim good news to the poor" (Luke 4:18). Jesus also said, "Peace I leave with you; my peace I give to you" (John 14:27). In verse 15, Nahum told God's people to remember their feasts, because those feasts, like the Passover feast, pointed to Jesus.

Talk about It

:: What is the good news that Jesus brought? (*The good news is that we can be forgiven for our sins if we trust in Jesus and in what he did when he died in our place on the cross, taking our punishment.*)

:: What kind of peace did Jesus bring? (*Jesus brought peace with God. Before Jesus came, we were God's enemies because of our sin. But after Jesus took our punishment, those who trust in Jesus go from being God's enemies to being his children, adopted into his family.*)

:: Nahum told God's people to remember their feasts. Do you remember how the feast of the Passover points to Jesus? (*Parents, give your children clues to help them remember what the Passover is all about. God told his people to kill a lamb and smear some of its blood on the doorframe of their house so that when the angel of death passed by, their firstborn sons would not be killed. God's judgment would pass over them. The lamb was killed as a substitute for their sin just as Jesus was killed as a substitute for us so that God's judgment would pass over us.*)

Pray about It

Thank Jesus for the good news of the gospel and thank him for bringing us peace with God.

Week 75

By Faith

Story 153 – *The Gospel Story Bible*

Bring an unopened bottle of seltzer to Bible study. (If you can find a bottle with a peel-off or clear see-through label, the effects will be easier to see.) Place the bottle on the table and tell your children that there is a gas hidden in the water. Ask them to look very closely to see if they can see it. They will not be able to see it. Then ask if they believe you are telling them the truth. They are likely to say yes. Explain to them that we use the word faith *to describe believing in something we cannot see.*

Say, "Faith is what we must have to believe in God, because we cannot see him. One day we will see him in heaven, but until then we must believe in Jesus by faith." Just after you say that, tell them to watch the bottle carefully, then crack open the top. Thousands of bubbles of gas will suddenly appear. Say, "This week we will learn that faith is what we need to please the Lord."

DAY ONE

Picture It

Gephyrophobia (ge-phy-ro-pho-bi-a) is the term for the fear of driving over bridges. A person who suffers from this condition is afraid to cross a bridge, especially a bridge over water. He doesn't have faith that the bridge will hold him up. Millions of people place their faith in bridges every day and drive over them. But some people don't have faith and fall into fear, thinking the bridge is going to collapse with them on it.

People find it hard to believe all kinds of things. Kids can have fears too. A lot of children have pupaphobia—a fear of puppets. No matter how much their teacher tells them that the puppets won't hurt them, they don't believe it. Other children have coulrophobia—a fear of clowns. No matter how much they are reassured, they don't believe that clowns are harmless, and they stiffen with fear anytime one comes near. Faith is the secret to conquering fear. If we had faith in what people tell us—that bridges and puppets and clowns are safe, for example—we would not need to be afraid. The faith most important to have is faith in God. Today we will see what the Bible teaches about faith.

 Read Hebrews 11:1–4.

Think about It Some More

Faith means believing in something you cannot see or touch. The writer of Hebrews gave the example of God creating the world out of nothing just by speaking. We can read the Bible story of God creating the world out of nothing, but no one saw God do it. The only way to believe it is by faith. From the very first verse of Scripture, we are called to believe things that we cannot see.

We also believe by faith that God is real. We can't see God or touch him. We can read about God in the Bible, but because we can't see him, we must have faith to believe that he is real. But believing in God is only the first step of faith. God wants us to place our faith in him to save us from our sins. To place our faith in Jesus is to trust him with our lives by believing in God's plan of salvation. That is the only way we can be saved and the only way we can please God. Hebrews 11 is filled with people whom God commended for their faith.

Talk about It

:: What is faith? (*Faith means believing and trusting in things that cannot be seen.*)

:: What example did the writer of Hebrews give of something that takes faith to believe? (*The writer of Hebrews used the example of God creating the world out of nothing simply by speaking.*)

:: Can you think of things you need to have faith in to believe? (*Parents, there are many things we need to have faith in to believe. For example, faith in the skill of the pilot flying the plane you're riding in; faith that the bridge you're crossing will hold you up; faith that your chair will support you; faith that the triple-washed spinach isn't contaminated.*)

:: What does it mean to have faith in God and trust him? *(Having faith in God means you believe that he is real even though you cannot see him. You believe in Jesus even though you were not born until long after he walked the earth.)*

 Pray about It

Ask God to give you faith to believe in him and not doubt.

DAY TWO

Remember It

What do you remember about yesterday's Bible passage? What do you think we will learn about today?

 Read Hebrews 11:4–12.

Think about It Some More

Yesterday we learned that faith means believing in something you cannot see. Hebrews 11 is God's faith hall of fame for people who trusted in God's plan to save them. The faith hall of fame starts with Abel, Enoch, Noah, Abraham, and Sarah. These men and women are mentioned here because faith is very important to God. In fact, verse 6 tells us that "without faith it is impossible to please" God. We can't trust in our own good works to please God because even the best of our good works are ruined by sin. But faith is different. Faith means believing and trusting in God's work and God's plan. Faith means trusting God for things we cannot see. Like when Noah believed God and built a big boat even though there was no water in sight.

Talk about It

:: What did the writer of Hebrews say was impossible to do without faith? *(Parents, if you have younger children, reread verse 6 and emphasize the words* please God.)

:: How did Abraham's life demonstrate faith in God? *(Abraham obeyed when God told him to move his family far from home. He obeyed not knowing where he was to go.)*

:: How did Sarah's life demonstrate faith in God? *(When God promised to give her a son, Sarah considered God faithful, which means she believed he was going to keep his promise.)*

 Pray about It

Ask God to help your faith grow so that you can live a life pleasing to him.

DAY THREE _____

Connect It to the Gospel

Today is the day we connect this week's Bible story to the gospel. The gospel is the life, death, and resurrection of Jesus for our salvation. Can anyone guess how our story this week looks forward to or back at the gospel?

 Read Hebrews 11:13–28.

Think about It Some More

Even though they didn't know who Jesus was, the men and women of the Old Testament were trusting in Jesus by believing in God and in his plan to rescue them. Just as we are saved by looking back to Jesus, they were saved by looking forward to God's saving plan.

For example, when Moses kept the Passover and trusted in the sprinkled blood as part of God's future saving plan, he was trusting in Jesus too. He may not have known it clearly at the time, but he knew the only way to go forward was to obey God, smear the blood of the lamb on his doorframe, and wait for God's salvation. God rescued Israel from the plague of death because the blood on the doorframe pointed ahead to the day when Jesus shed his blood on the cross so they/we could be forgiven.

Talk about It

:: How were the Old Testament heroes saved? *(They were saved by faith, trusting in God's future plan to deliver them. That future plan was Jesus. So when they trusted in God's future plan, they were trusting in Jesus, not their own works.)*

:: How did Abraham demonstrate faith by offering up his son Isaac? *(Abraham's faith enabled him to be willing to sacrifice his son. His faith in God's future promise was so strong that he didn't think killing his son would stop God. He believed that if Isaac were killed, God could raise his son from the dead. That is faith.)*

:: Whom did Moses choose over the wealth and treasures of Egypt? *(Parents, if your children are younger, reread verses 24–26 and ask them to raise their hands when they hear the correct answer. Then emphasize the word* Christ. *By rejecting Egypt and trusting in God's future plan, the writer of Hebrews said that Moses chose Christ and a heavenly reward over the passing wealth of earthly treasures.)*

:: The Old Testament heroes of the faith were saved by looking to God's future plan of salvation. How are we saved by faith? *(We are saved by faith when we look back at God's plan of salvation through Jesus who died on the cross for our sins.)*

 Pray about It

Praise God for the amazing way people, past or present, are saved by looking to the cross.

DAY FOUR

Remember It

What has God been teaching you this week through our Bible story?

 Read Hebrews 11:29–38.

Think about It Some More

The best news of Hebrews 11 is that the faith hall of fame is huge. There are too many names to be written there. Everyone who trusts in God's saving plan gets to be in God's faith hall of fame. Your name might not be listed there, but if you have faith in Jesus and his saving plan, then God is just as pleased with your faith as he was with that of Moses or Abraham. Remember, God's pleasure did not rest upon those men because of their good deeds. God's pleasure rested on them because they trusted in God's work and plan. So it is with us. When we trust in Jesus and believe in him to rescue us from our sins, we too become a part of God's faith hall of fame.

Talk about It

> KIDS, ask your parents which of the stories listed in the faith hall of fame (Hebrews 11) is their favorite, and why.

(Parents, even if you don't have a favorite, choose one of the stories to talk about and explain why you think it is an amazing display of faith.)

:: What is your favorite faith story, and why? *(Parents, now turn and ask your children the very same question.)*

:: If you were going to add men and women from the New Testament to God's faith hall of fame, whom would you add? *(Parents, try to help your children remember characters from the New Testament who trusted in God's saving plan. Some key ones are Mary trusting God to become pregnant with Jesus, Joseph trusting God enough to marry Mary, John the Baptist preaching about Jesus before he came, and the disciples leaving everything to follow Jesus.)*

:: Do you know anyone still living today who could be added to the faith hall of fame? *(Parents, remind your children that anyone who trusts Jesus for salvation is on that list.)*

Pray about It

Ask God to give the gift of faith to every person in your family, so that all your names will be added to the faith hall of fame.

DAY FIVE

Discover It

Today is the day we look at a different Bible passage—from the book of Psalms or one of the prophets—to see what we can learn from it about Jesus or our salvation.

Read Psalm 25.

Think about It Some More

David is mentioned in Hebrews 11:32 as a man in the faith hall of fame. In Psalm 25 we see why. David trusted in God's future plan to save him. David knew he was a sinner and could not save himself. Psalm 25 is a prayerful song that David wrote to ask God to forgive him and take away his sins. David didn't ask God to forgive his sin because of his own good works. David asked God to forgive his sin because of God's faithfulness and mercy.

Today, we can pray David's prayer for our own lives. Read the psalm again, only this time read it as a prayer to God. As you do, think of Jesus, who died on the cross to take away our sins. By trusting in God to take away his sins, David was trusting in Jesus. The last line, in which David asks God to redeem Israel, also points us to Jesus. The word *redeem* means to buy back. Jesus bought back God's people from death and judgment by redeeming us—buying us back with the price of his own life.

Talk about It

:: Why was David included in God's hall of fame of faith? *(Parents, your children can look for an answer in this psalm; for example, David prayed to God by faith to save him. Or they can think of a story that showed that David trusted in God's saving plan, like when he went up against Goliath.)*

:: Why is this a good psalm for us to pray for ourselves? *(Like David, we are sinners who need God's mercy to save us.)*

:: What did David say that pointed to Jesus? *(Parents, this is a tougher question. You can tell your children that the answer is in the last line. If you have younger children, read the last line and have them guess which word points to Jesus. David asked God to save Israel by redeeming them, which means buying them back. Jesus did that by dying on the cross for our sins.)*

 Pray about It

Take time to reread Psalm 25 as your prayer to God. *(Parents, give each of your children one verse to pray. If you have younger children, allow them to repeat after you, and so guide them through the prayer time.)*

Week 76

Loving One Another

Story 154 – *The Gospel Story Bible*

Ask your children what kind of gifts they like to receive from others. Now ask them what kind of gifts they like to give. Then ask them which they enjoy more: receiving gifts or giving gifts. Consider asking each of your children this week to think of something they own that they can give away to somebody else. Don't allow them to choose something that is worthless or broken. Encourage them to give away something of value. This week they will learn how giving is one important way we show our love to one another.

DAY ONE

Picture It

Before going on a long car trip, it is important to check to see if the car engine has enough oil, because oil is what enables the engine to run smoothly. Without oil, the car engine would get stuck and die (stop working). By looking at the dipstick, you can see how much oil is in the engine. If Christians were like cars, their dipstick would not measure oil, it would measure love inside their heart. Like oil for a car, love is so important that if a Christian doesn't have love, the Bible says that he is dead. That is what our Bible passage today is about.

 Read 1 John 3:11–15.

Think about It Some More

When you read the story of Cain and Abel, it is easy to compare yourself with Abel because you have never murdered anyone. You might think, "Wow, Cain was wicked. God even gave him a warning, but he killed his brother anyway. I would never do that." But we have all gotten angry and even hated people in our heart, and that is the same sin that Cain committed.

John says hating our brother is like murdering him in our heart. That was something that Jesus also taught (Matthew 5:22). When the Spirit of God comes to live inside us, he writes God's law upon our hearts and enables us to love God and one another. That is why John taught that loving our brothers is a sign that God has changed us and given us eternal life. The truth is that, if it were not for God's grace, we would all be like Cain.

Talk about It

:: What did John call a person who hates his brother? *(a murderer)*

:: Can you think of a time when you got angry and did not love someone? *(Parents, help your children out. Once they acknowledge their failure to love, explain that in the rest of this week's study we will learn how God can change us.)*

:: Why is it so difficult to love the people around us? *(Often, people around us stand in the way of our pleasures. If they take something we want or affect our peace or comfort, we can get angry with them. If we don't love Jesus more than the things of the world, when people stand in our way, we will get angry and not love them.)*

:: What kinds of things can we do to show our love toward one another? *(Parents, draw out your children here. See if they can come up with ways to love their enemies too.)*

 ## Pray about It

Confess the ways you have "murdered" your brothers and sisters and parents and friends with your anger, and ask God to change your heart so that you will love them instead.

DAY TWO

Remember It

What do you remember about yesterday's Bible passage? What do you think we will learn about today?

 Read 1 John 3:16–24.

Think about It Some More

We have a holiday called Valentine's Day on which we send notes to our friends telling them we love them. But just because people use the word *love* doesn't mean they really love one another. John tells us that true Christian love is more than words alone. True Christian love is all about actions, the things we do for one another. We can say we love, but if we do not help people in need, we are not really loving them.

Jesus gave us the best example when he laid down his life for us. The cross is the greatest demonstration of love. God didn't just say he loved us; he did something about it when he gave his only Son for us. Christians who are changed by the power of the Holy Spirit will follow Jesus' example. Paul says we can be sure God abides (lives) in us when we find ourselves loving the people around us in ways we didn't before we trusted the Lord.

Talk about It

:: What did God give that shows his great love for us? *(God gave his only Son, Jesus, to die on the cross for our sins.)*

:: Can you think of a way someone loved you by doing something for you? *(Parents, help your children remember a time when someone loved them by their actions, not just their words.)*

:: Name two things you could do today to show your love for those around you. *(Parents, help each of your children think of things they could do for one another, then follow up at the end of the day and talk about how it went.)*

 Pray about It

Ask God to help you love one another with deeds, not just words.

DAY THREE _____

Connect It to the Gospel

Today is the day we connect this week's Bible story to the gospel. The gospel is the life, death, and resurrection of Jesus for our salvation. Can anyone guess how our story this week looks forward to or back at the gospel?

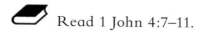 Read 1 John 4:7–11.

Think about It Some More

If a person asked you the question what is love, how would you answer? A lot of people would say that love is the wonderful feeling or emotion that you experience when you are attracted to someone. But in our Bible passage today, John describes love in a way that is more than feelings. He describes love as a sacrifice, something that you give. In this case, John uses the gospel to tell us what love means. God's description of love points to the cross. Although we didn't love God, he loved us and sent his Son to die in our place for our sins. That sacrifice, John tells us, is what love is all about. It is easy to show love to those who you know will love you back (Luke 6:32). But God loved us while we hated him (Romans 5:9–10). God loved us while we were his enemies. That is amazing love.

Talk about It

:: What did God do to show us his love? *(Parents, this question is best answered by quoting John 3:16, a verse you might consider memorizing as a family. Remind the children that the same man who wrote that gospel also wrote the letter we are reading this week.)*

:: In light of God's love to us, what does John say in 1 John 4:11 that we should do? *(Parents, if you have younger children who are not strong readers, reread verse 11 and have them raise their hands when they hear the answer: we should love one another.)*

:: What can we do to love one another? *(Parents, make sure your children move beyond saying kind things and giving kisses to doing things that require a measure of sacrifice, like doing their brother's chores or giving up their last piece of candy.)*

:: Who does God want us to love? *(We are to love both those who love us and those who don't, even our enemies. See Matthew 5:43–44.)*

 Pray about It

Ask God to fill you with his Holy Spirit and help you remember how he loved us while we were his enemies so that we can love others.

DAY FOUR

Remember It

What has God been teaching you this week through our Bible story?

 Read 1 John 4:12–21.

Think about It Some More

When we believe the gospel, that God loved us by giving up his only Son, God sends his Spirit to abide (or live) inside us. Once the Spirit of God lives in us, he begins to change us to be more like God so that we will want to love others more and more. The Holy Spirit does this for every Christian. That is why a person who consistently hates his brother can't also say he loves God.

That doesn't mean we are perfect and never say a mean thing toward others. But it does mean that we can't live a life full of anger and hate toward others and still say we believe and love Jesus. John was pretty strong on this point: "If anyone says, 'I love God,' and hates his brother, he is a liar; for he who does not love his brother whom he has seen cannot love God whom he has not seen" (1 John 4:20).

The point of John's argument wasn't to condemn but to encourage. The Christians he was writing to were not sure about their faith, and John wanted them to know what to look for to strengthen their confidence. He was basically saying, "Look, guys, there is no way you could believe and then love one another consistently unless God abides with you. The way you can be sure you are not an unbeliever is that unbelievers are all talk and no action."

Talk about It

> ● ● KIDS, ask your parents how the Holy Spirit has
> ● ● helped them love others.

(Parents, try to think of a time when God gave you grace to love someone who was your enemy. Perhaps remembering what Jesus did for you enabled you to show love toward that person.)

:: Can you think of a time when your mom or dad loved you even while you were disobeying them? *(Parents, it is okay to be a little self-serving here. Try to remind your children of times when you loved and forgave them. But don't give yourself the credit. Point back to Christ, who died on the cross for your sins while you were his enemy as your motivation.)*

:: What are some ways you have seen other family members show love toward one another? *(Parents, help your children share ways they see one another demonstrate love.)*

 Pray about It

Thank God for his example of love toward us, and ask him to give you the Holy Spirit so that you can love others as he does.

DAY FIVE

Discover It

Today is the day we look at a different Bible passage—from the book of Psalms or one of the prophets—to see what we can learn from it about Jesus or our salvation.

 Read Psalm 35.

Think about It Some More

Jesus taught his disciples that people would hate them just as they hated Jesus (John 15:20–25), and he said that Psalm 35:19 was a prophecy about him. Long before Jesus was born, David said he would be hated without cause (v. 19). People hated Jesus because he wasn't the kind of Messiah they wanted. They wanted an earthly king. The religious rulers hated Jesus for all kinds of reasons: They were jealous of his following, upset that he called them fakes (hypocrites), and furious when Jesus reached out to the Samaritans. People still hate Christians today. If someone says mean things about you because of your faith in Jesus, Psalm 35 is a good psalm to read and pray.

Talk about It

:: What did the people who hated Jesus do to him? *(The people who hated Jesus, arrested him, lied about him, and sentenced him to die on the cross.)*

:: Why did people hate Jesus? *(Because he told them they were sinners and could not save themselves.)*

:: How did Jesus treat those who hated him? *(Jesus loved his enemies. After all, he died for us while we were his enemies.)*

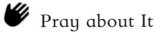 Pray about It

Use Psalm 35 as a prayer against your greatest enemies, Satan and the sin in your heart that would want to draw you away from God.

Week 77

Worthy Is the Lamb

Story 155 – *The Gospel Story Bible*

You will need a padlock and key for this exercise. Lock the padlock and pass it around to your children, asking them to try to open it. Explain how the shackle, the u-shaped piece that locks down, pops up when it is open. Have them try to pull it and open the lock. After a bit, ask why they are having trouble opening it. They will say they do not have the key. Agree and confirm that only the person with the key can open the lock. Then use the key to open the lock. Explain to them that, this week, they will be learning about a scroll locked with seven seals that could be opened only by the one who had the key. The person was Jesus, the Lamb, and the key was the gospel, his sacrifice on the cross, and the conquering of sin and death.

DAY ONE

Picture It

Imagine you go on trial for following Jesus and are found guilty and sent away to a remote island to live out the rest of your life alone. Then imagine that, one day as you are praying, a voice as loud as a trumpet shouts out from behind you commanding you to write down all that you see. Slowly and fearfully, you turn your head in the direction of the voice, and standing there is a man wearing a robe tied at the waist with a golden sash. His hair is white, his eyes are like flaming fire, and his face shines like the sun.

Sounds like a chapter from a science fiction book, doesn't it? But that is exactly what happened to the apostle John, who was imprisoned on the island of Patmos for preaching the gospel. The book of Revelation is a description of the amazing vision God gave him and commanded that he write down for us to read. Over the next two weeks, we are going to read a part of that vision from John's last book—the last book in the Bible.

 Read Revelation 5:1–5.

Think about It Some More

In the vision God gave to him, the apostle John saw God the Father sitting on the throne in heaven holding a scroll. The scroll, sealed with seven seals, represented the final plan of God to bring his judgment and rule to all the earth. But the seals could not be broken and the scroll could not be read by just anyone. They could be opened only by the person who had scored a victory over God's enemies. So a search was made to find anyone who could break the seals and announce God's victory. But no one was found who was worthy.

When no one was found to open the scroll, a great sadness swept over John. Then one of the elders of heaven spoke up, for he saw Jesus, the Lion of the tribe of Judah, coming forward toward the scroll. The elder knew that Jesus was worthy to break the seals and open the scroll, releasing the victory order of God. Jesus was worthy because he defeated Satan and canceled God's curse over man by giving his life in payment for sin to break the curse of sin so that God's plan of forgiveness and victory could be announced to all the heavens.

Talk about It

:: Why was John sad? *(No one was found worthy to open the scroll.)*

:: Read Genesis 49:9–10. How does this Old Testament passage fit with the passage we read today? *(When Jacob blessed his son Judah, Jesus' far-off great-grandfather, he called him a lion. Jesus is called a lion in our story today. Jacob said the scepter would not leave Judah, which meant Judah would have a king on the throne for all time. Jesus was the King whom Jacob spoke of.)*

:: What was written on the scroll? *(The final victory plan of God to restore his kingdom and destroy evil forever.)*

:: Why was Jesus worthy to open the scroll? *(Jesus was worthy because he died on the cross and took the punishment for the sins of all God's children. God planned to forgive, and Jesus' sacrifice on the cross made that plan possible.)*

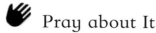 Pray about It

Praise Jesus that he is worthy to open the scroll for that tells us that his death on the cross worked to pay the price for our sin and remove the curse of sin forever. That is something worth celebrating.

DAY TWO

Remember It

What do you remember about yesterday's Bible passage? What do you think we will learn about today?

 Read Revelation 5:6–8.

Think about It Some More

Just when you think you've figured out what John wrote about in the book of Revelation, something that sounds crazy enters the vision: a lamb with seven horns and seven eyes. Most people try to picture in their mind a real lamb with seven real horns and seven real eyes. But John is not trying to describe a real creature—he is talking about Jesus. The horns and eyes are a creative way to say something important about our Lord. The horns represent his power, and the seven eyes show that he sees and knows everything, which tells us that he is God.

John's description also tells us that the lamb looked like it had been slain or killed. We know that, after Jesus rose from the dead, the nail marks remained in his hands. The scar of the sword that pierced his side was also there, showing that he had died but risen again. John's vision is telling us that Jesus, who died as a sacrifice but rose again to new life, walked up to the throne with all the power and authority of God and took the scroll from the hand of his Father, showing all of heaven that his death had paid the penalty for sin, and that victory over sin had been won. At that point, all the creatures of heaven fell down to worship, for the battle to destroy evil was won by the Son of God.

Talk about It

:: What do the seven horns of the Lamb represent? *(The seven horns represent the Lamb's power.)*

:: What do the seven eyes of the Lamb represent? *(The seven eyes tell us that the Lamb sees and knows everything.)*

:: Why did the creatures and people in heaven fall down before Jesus when he took the scroll? *(They fell down and worshiped him.)*

 Pray about It

Praise Jesus for his power, his knowledge, and his sacrifice upon the cross.

DAY THREE _____

Connect It to the Gospel

Today is the day we connect this week's Bible story to the gospel. The gospel is the life, death, and resurrection of Jesus for our salvation. Can anyone guess how our story this week looks forward to or back at the gospel?

 Read Revelation 5:9–14.

Think about It Some More

Did you know that when we go to church on Sunday and sing songs to Jesus, we are joining the multitude of angels and saints in heaven singing praises to Jesus for his gospel victory over sin? After Jesus took the scroll, a great celebration of praise burst out in all of heaven. The words of their song celebrated the victory of Jesus on the cross. The creatures and elders around the throne, together with all the angels of heaven were singing. They were all singing the same song: "Worthy is the Lamb." Anytime we sing any song of praise, we are joining all of heaven in shouting praises to Jesus.

Talk about It

:: What does verse 9 say that Jesus accomplished by shedding his blood? *(Parents, if you have younger children, reread that verse and emphasize the phrase "by your blood you ransomed people for God." That means that Jesus paid the price [his very life] to conquer our sin.)*

:: Where do you see the promise God first gave to Abraham in our Scripture today? *(Parents, if your children don't remember God's promise to Abraham, read Genesis 12:3 to them. God kept his promise to bless all the nations of the earth through Jesus, the far-off great-grandson of Abraham.)*

:: Why is everyone in heaven celebrating? *(Everyone is celebrating because Jesus took the scroll. If he was able to take the scroll from the hand of God the Father, then he was able to open it too.)*

 Pray about It

There are a few worship songs that include the words "worthy is the Lamb." If you know one of them, sing it as a family to celebrate Jesus. If not, pray aloud together the praise recorded in verses 9–10.

DAY FOUR

Remember It

What has God been teaching you this week through our Bible story?

 Read Revelation 6.

Think about It Some More

Not only was Jesus worthy to take the scroll, but he was also able to break the seals and begin the final judgment of God. As each of the seals was broken open, another judgment of God swept across the earth. One day in the future, when God brings his final judgment, those who trust in Jesus won't have to fear. For all who trust in Jesus are forgiven. Just as the judgment of God passed over the homes that had the blood of the lamb painted on the doorframes, so God's final judgment will pass over all believers. But those who do not believe will be swept away, along with all evil and the enemies of God. They will try to hide, but no one will be able to escape the judgment of God.

Talk about It

> KIDS, ask your parents if they were ever afraid of God's judgment.

(Most everyone has thought about God's judgment for sin and been afraid of what would happen if they died without believing. Share about a time when you were afraid—and about the peace you now have because you believe in Jesus.)

:: What is going to happen to all evil when Jesus returns to conquer it? *(Jesus will judge all evil and punish everyone whose sins are not forgiven: those who did not trust in Jesus.)*

:: When Jesus returns to judge the earth, what will those who refused to believe try to do (vv. 15–16)? *(Parents, if you have younger children who are not strong readers, reread the verses and have them raise their hands when they hear the correct answer, which is that they tried to hide. Remind your children that this is the same thing Adam and Eve did in the garden when they sinned. But no one can hide from God.)*

 ## Pray about It

Ask Jesus to bring his salvation to every person in your family, putting his Spirit into your hearts so you will believe and trust in him and be saved on the day of God's judgment.

DAY FIVE

Discover It

Today is the day we look at a different Bible passage—from the book of Psalms or one of the prophets—to see what we can learn from it about Jesus or our salvation.

Read Psalm 89:1–29.

Think about It Some More

Psalm 89 was written about King David but was fulfilled by King Jesus. Jesus is the "Holy One of Israel" (v. 18)—the King who reigns upon David's throne for all generations. It is through Jesus that God was able to save the offspring of David and keep his covenant promise forever. God kept his promise by sending Jesus to die on the cross for the sins of his people. That is the only way King David—or any of us—could be rescued. Jesus' victory over sin is the main celebration of Revelation. John opened the book of Revelation by saying, "To him who loves us and has freed us from our sins by his blood and made us a kingdom, priests to his God and Father, to him be glory and dominion forever and ever. Amen" (Revelation 1:5–6).

Talk about It

:: What clues tell us that this psalm about David is really about Jesus too? *(Parents, by this time your children should be able to look for clues that point to Jesus. Words like* salvation *and for-ever point to him. Also, Jesus is the Holy One of Israel mentioned in verse 18.)*

:: Why is God's promise to David a promise to us too? *(Parents, tell your children that there is a clue in verses 1 and 4. The answer is that we are one of the generations that came after David whom God will save. God makes known his faithfulness through the gospel story of Jesus.)*

:: In verses 27–29, how did God keep his promise to David? *(Parents, reread those verses to your children. God kept those promises by sending his Son, Jesus, to die for David's sins. That is the only way David, his offspring, or any of us, could be saved.)*

 ## Pray about It

Recite Psalm 89:13–18 together as a family as a prayer of praise to God.

Week 78

At the Throne Worshiping

Story 156 – *The Gospel Story Bible*

In heaven, there will be people of every language at the throne worshiping. Just to give your children a sense of some of the languages, here are a number of ways to say hello *in different tongues.*

:: *Swahili*—Jambo
:: *Russian*—Pre-vyet
:: *Japanese*—Ohayou gozaimasu
:: *German*—Hallo
:: *French*—Salut
:: *Congo*—Mambo
:: *Burmese*—Mingalarbar
:: *Hebrew*—Shalom
:: *Spanish*—Hola
:: *Tamil*—Vanakkam
:: *Mandarin Chinese*—Nee-how

Say, *"This week we will be learning about the different peoples of the earth who will be gathered around the throne worshiping the Lamb with one voice and singing one song of praise."*

DAY ONE

Picture It

If you take one pinch of sand between your fingers and spill it onto a white piece of paper, you will see that there are hundreds of tiny grains, so many that it is very difficult to count them all. Now imagine what it would be like if you had to count all the sand on the seashore. Even one bucket of sand would be impossible for a person to count. All the way back in Genesis, God told Abraham that he was going to give him so many children and grandchildren and great-grandchildren that they would outnumber the sand on the seashore and be impossible to count (Genesis 22:17–18). Imagine what it will be like to see all those people in heaven one day. In the book of Revelation, God gave John a vision of heaven, and he saw all those people gathered around the throne of God. That is the story we are reading today.

 Read Revelation 7:1–10.

Think about It Some More

Did you ever take a sneak peek at the last chapter of a book to see what was going to happen in the end? When we read the book of Revelation, we get a sneak peek of what the end of God's story is all about. And when we read chapter 7, we see that, in the end of God's story, God keeps his promise to Abraham. Remember from way back at the beginning how God told Abraham he was going to give him more children than anyone could count and make him into a great nation?

God also said that all the nations of the earth would be blessed through him (Genesis 22:18). Here in chapter 7 of John's vision, we get a sneak peek into heaven to see that God keeps his promise to Abraham. Through Jesus, people from every nation, more than can be counted, will one day all sing the same song: "Salvation belongs to our God who sits on the throne, and to the Lamb!" In the vision they all wear white robes to show that their sins have been washed away.

Talk about It

:: What was God's promise to Abraham? (*God promised to give Abraham more children than anyone could count, and he promised that all the nations of the earth would be blessed by through Abraham's offspring.*)

:: How many people were there in heaven? (*There were more people in heaven than you could count.*)

:: By reading Revelation 7, how can you tell God kept his promise to Abraham? (*There are more people in heaven than anyone can count, and there are people there from every tribe of Israel and every nation.*)

Pray about It

Praise God for his faithfulness and for keeping his promises to Abraham.

DAY TWO _____

Remember It

What do you remember about yesterday's Bible passage? What do you think we will learn about today?

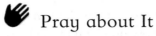 Read Revelation 7:11–12.

Think about It Some More

Imagine what it will be like one day when there is no more sin and when all the Christians from every tribe and language and all the angels join together to praise Jesus and worship God. It will be the greatest celebration of all time!

But when we read about this celebration, we should ask ourselves, "Will *we* be there with the others worshiping?" There is only one way you can be a part of that great crowd of people worshiping God in heaven: You have to believe in his Son, Jesus—in his death and resurrection—and first bow your knee in worship to God on earth. The only way to become a part of the people of God in heaven is to trust in Jesus here while you are on earth, so that you can have your sins washed away.

Talk about It

:: What were all the people and angels in heaven doing? *(They were worshiping God.)*

:: How does a person get to heaven to be a part of the crowd of people who are worshiping there? *(There is only one way to get to heaven: to trust in Jesus to take your sins away. Everyone who trusts in Jesus and what he did when he died on the cross will go to heaven.)*

:: How is our worship on Sunday a lot like the worship John saw in heaven? *(Our worship on Sunday is a lot like the worship in heaven because we are all worshiping God for sending Jesus to deliver us from our sins.)*

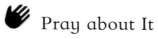 Pray about It

Sing a favorite worship song as a family. Pretend you are in heaven celebrating God's victory over sin.

DAY THREE _____

Connect It to the Gospel

Today is the day we connect this week's Bible story to the gospel. The gospel is the life, death, and resurrection of Jesus for our salvation. Can anyone guess how our story this week looks forward to or back at the gospel?

 Read Revelation 7:13–17.

Think about It Some More

When your clothes are dirty, you put them in a washing machine and add detergent to get them clean again. But when you want to wash your sin away, detergent won't work. The only thing that will take the stain of your sin away is washing it in the blood of the Lamb. But that doesn't mean you pour lamb's blood on your clothes. What washing in the blood of the Lamb means is that you believe that Jesus died on the cross and shed his blood for you to take away your sins, and that he rose again from the dead in victory. When you trust in Jesus, the Lamb of God, he washes away your sins. There won't be any sadness in heaven, only joy as we worship the Lord forever and ever.

Talk about It

:: What color were the robes of the saints in heaven? *(They wore white robes.)*

:: Why are all the people in heaven wearing white robes? *(The white robes show that their sins have been washed away by the blood of the lamb.)*

:: What is heaven going to be like? *(Parents, if you have younger children, reread the passage and ask them to raise their hands when they hear you describe something about heaven. Jesus is going to be our shepherd in heaven and wipe every tear from our eyes. We won't be thirsty or hungry, which means we will have all that we need and we will be completely satisfied.)*

 Pray about It

Ask God to help you believe in Jesus, the Lamb of God, so that the stain of your sin can be washed away.

DAY FOUR _____

Remember It

What has God been teaching you this week through our Bible story?

 Read Revelation 21:1–8.

Think about It Some More

Yesterday we caught a peek at what heaven is going to be like, and we learned that God is going to take all our sadness away. In today's Bible passage, we jump to the end of Revelation to learn more about heaven. At the end of the world, God is going to destroy all sin and make the earth new again. Instead of us going up to live forever in heaven, God is going to make us a great city on earth where he will live with us. We think of heaven as a place above the earth, but heaven is less about a location and more about whom we are with. Heaven is any place where we get to live with God—both before and after he re-creates the earth.

In that new earth, no one will ever get sick or die. There won't be any sadness at all. All evil and sin will be cast into the lake of fire, which we call hell, and be locked up forever. (See also Revelation 20:10–15.) All of God's children who believe in Jesus and his death on the cross will live forever. That means we will get to see all our great-grandparents, aunts and uncles, and all our relatives and friends who trusted in Jesus but died before we did. We will also get to meet all the heroes of the faith, like Abraham, Moses, Peter, and Paul, plus King David and all the prophets. Heaven will be a great celebration that never ends. Day after day for all eternity we will celebrate all that Jesus did for us.

Talk about It

> ● ●   KIDS, ask your mom or dad what they are most
> ● ●   looking forward to in heaven.

(Parents, you can share about meeting Jesus, seeing loved ones who have died, or even being free from some affliction or sin.)

:: Apart from Jesus, which hero of the faith would you first like to talk to when you get to heaven? *(Parents, draw your children out here.)*

:: What is going to happen to the people who refused to believe in Jesus? *(They will be cast into the lake of fire.)*

:: How can we be sure that we will go to heaven? *(Jesus died for the sins of anyone who will believe and trust in him. If a person trusts in the Lord, he or she will go to heaven to live with Jesus forever.)*

 ## Pray about It

Ask God to help the unbelievers you know turn away from their sins and trust in Jesus and his death and resurrection so they can live forever in heaven with him.

DAY FIVE

Discover It

Today is the day we look at a different Bible passage—from the book of Psalms or one of the prophets—to see what we can learn from it about Jesus or our salvation.

 Read Psalm 96.

Think about It Some More

When a person is guilty of a crime, he is arrested and put into prison to await trial before a judge. When the trial is over, he stands before the judge to hear the judge's decision. If he is found guilty, the judge describes his punishment and sends him back to prison. But if the judge finds him not guilty, he is immediately set free, never to be tried again for that crime.

Did you know we will all be judged before God? For those who trusted in Jesus, God the Father, the great Judge, will declare them "not guilty." That is why Psalm 96 tells us to celebrate God's judgment. The only way celebrating God's judgments make sense is if we remember that Jesus took the penalty we deserved upon himself so that we are declared innocent and welcomed into heaven. Psalm 96 is an invitation to start our not-guilty celebration early here on earth and tell everyone about God's wonderful salvation—so they can believe and be set free from the judgment of God for their sin too.

Talk about It

:: God's judgment sounds pretty scary. What kind of people would want to celebrate God's judgment, those who are guilty or those who are not guilty? *(The only people who would ever celebrate God's judgment are those who are not guilty and will be set free by his judgment.)*

:: How is it that we can we be set free on God's judgment day when we have sinned against God all our lives? *(Jesus paid the penalty we deserved for our sin so that on judgment day we will be found not guilty if we have trusted in Jesus and his work on the cross.)*

:: What kinds of things does this psalm say we should do to celebrate our salvation? *(Sing and praise God and tell everyone about our salvation.)*

:: What is the greatest of God's marvelous works? *(The greatest of God's marvelous works was when he sent his only Son, Jesus, to earth to die as our substitute, so that we could be forgiven.)*

 Pray about It

Pick out your favorite worship song and sing as a family. Shout for joy and dance around, for one day we will be set free from all sin and spend eternity with Jesus our King.